STO

This is the back of the book.
You wouldn't want to spoil a great ending!

This book is printed "manga-style," in the authentic Japanese right-to-left format. Since none of the artwork has been flipped or altered, readers get to experience the story just as the creator intended. You've been asking for it, so TOKYOPOP® delivered: authentic, hot-off-the-press, and far more fun!

DIRECTIONS

1
2
3
4
5
6
7
8
9
10

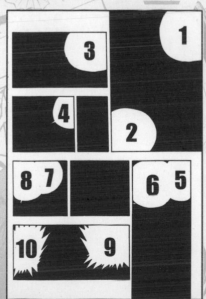

If this is your first time reading manga-style, here's a quick guide to help you understand how it works.

It's easy... just start in the top right panel and follow the numbers. Have fun, and look for more 100% authentic manga from TOKYOPOP®!

THE MANGA REVOLUTION · LEADING
漫画革命

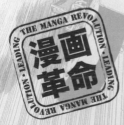

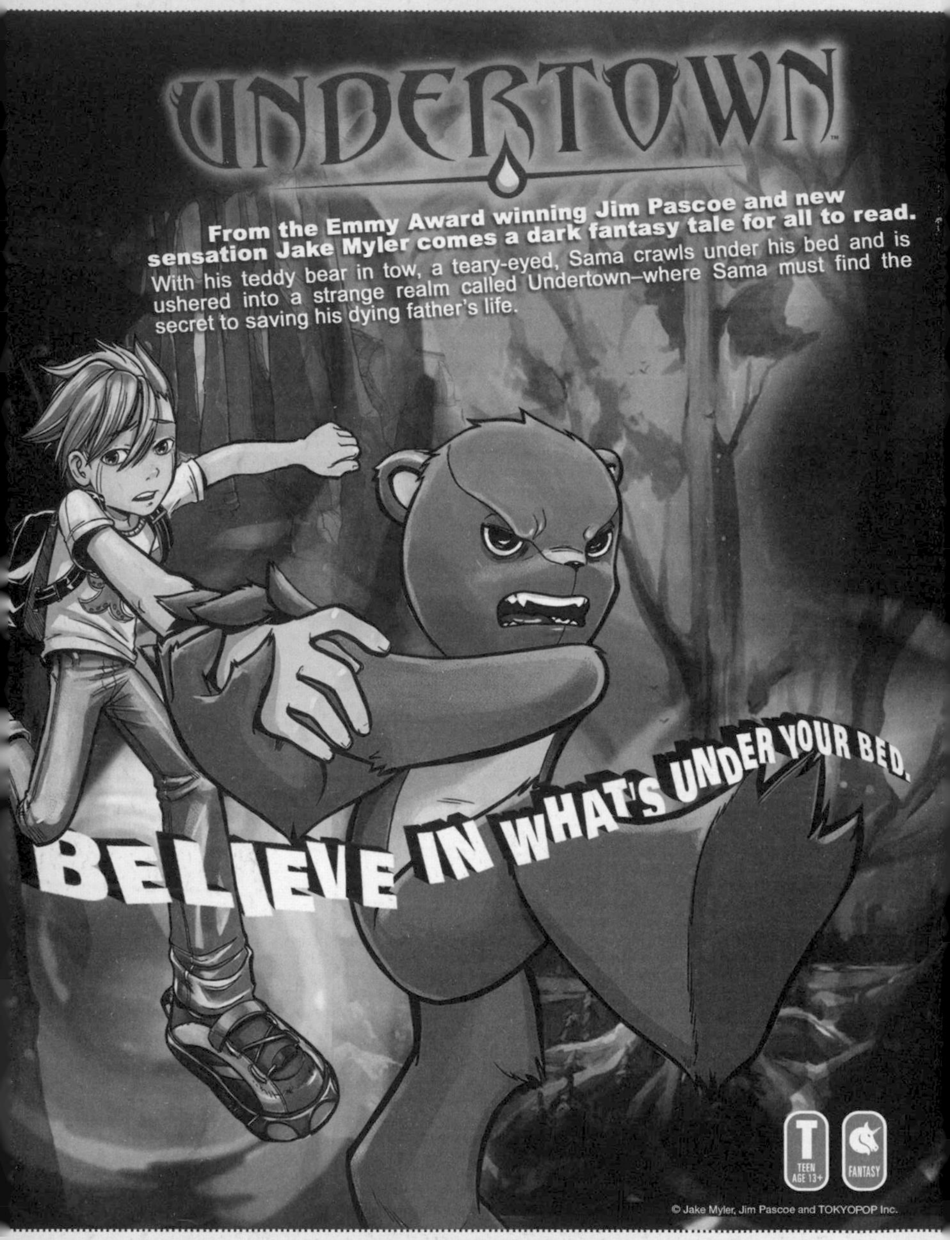
UNDERTOWN™
From the Emmy Award winning Jim Pascoe and new sensation Jake Myler comes a dark fantasy tale for all to read.
With his teddy bear in tow, a teary-eyed, Sama crawls under his bed and is ushered into a strange realm called Undertown–where Sama must find the secret to saving his dying father's life.
BELIEVE IN WHAT'S UNDER YOUR BED.
T TEEN AGE 13+
FANTASY
© Jake Myler, Jim Pascoe and TOKYOPOP Inc.

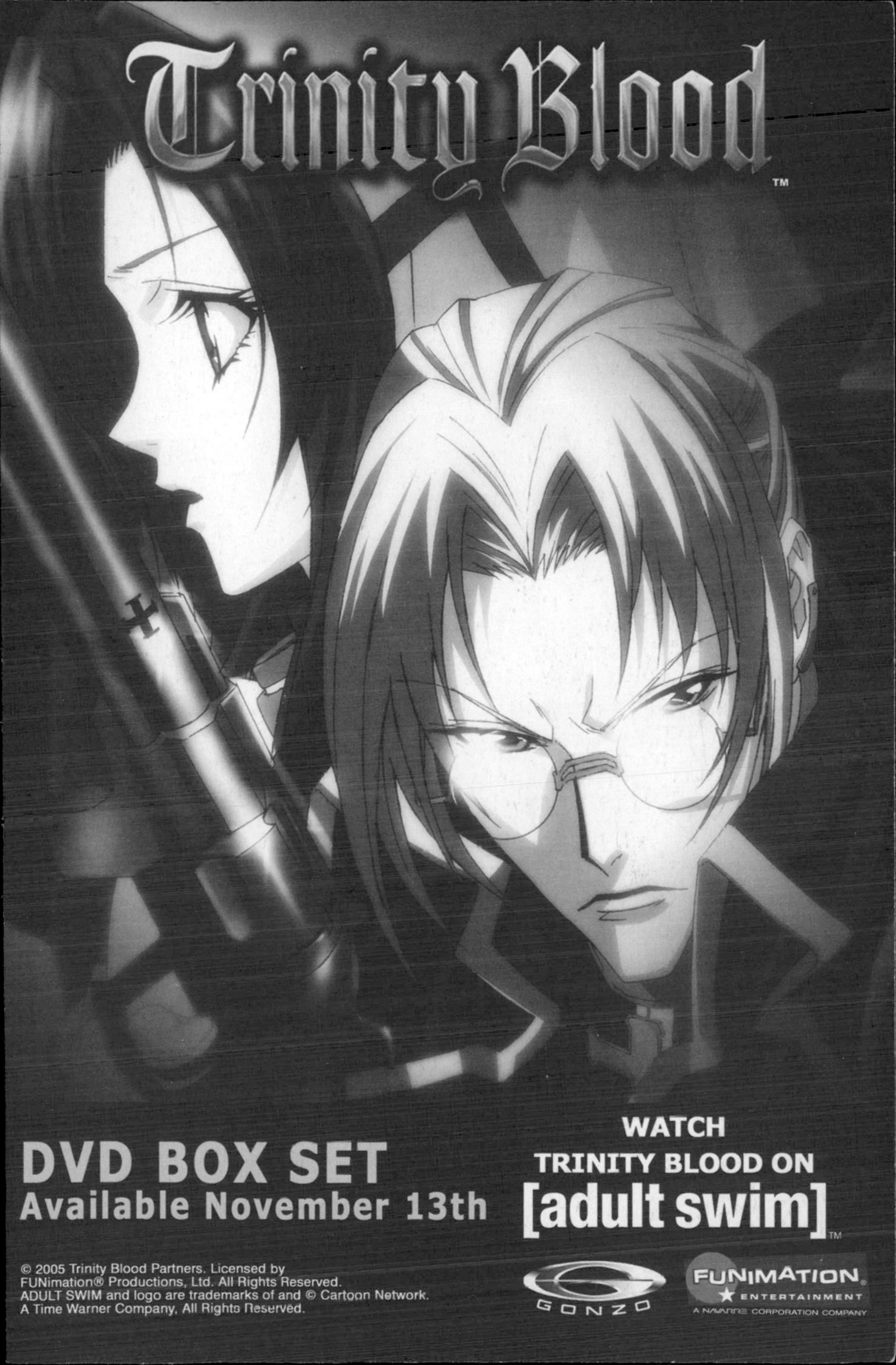

Trinity Blood™
DVD BOX SET
Available November 13th
WATCH
TRINITY BLOOD ON
[adult swim]™
© 2005 Trinity Blood Partners. Licensed by
FUNimation® Productions, Ltd. All Rights Reserved.
ADULT SWIM and logo are trademarks of and © Cartoon Network.
A Time Warner Company, All Rights Reserved.
GONZO
FUNIMATION.
ENTERTAINMENT
A NAVARRE CORPORATION COMPANY

Chapter 40: The Road We Wander
In this chapter, the bear bag springs into action. If you look inside, you might even find a hospital or two. Complete with an incredible doctor...

Chapter 41: "I Like You"
This chapter's title page doesn't show what it looks like it might (show what?). A lot of people said it was "erotic!" I'm glad. I'll keep working hard. I'm going to keep on believing that it was a complement. But saying, "I like you" with this drawing...? Hmmm...

Chapter 42: The Silent Compass Speaks Not
When it was printed in the magazine, this chapter's title page was a full spread color illustration of Alzeid~this book's page count was limited, though, so I had to cut it out. When my assistant saw it, her first words were, "Is he so full of love?" Of course he is. He's just a little twisted, that's all.
In any case, how can the heroine carry the hero on her back? It's not possible. With a height difference of 30 cm (one foot) and weight difference of 24 kg (53 lbs), it's just not possible.

Chapter 43: The Name Rules
My assistant (different from the one above) gave names to the couple that appears in the beginning of the chapter--David and Kaede-san. She had a complete character sketch and storyline that she explained with great enthusiasm. But I must tell you, that these characters are mine. Mine. Oh well, it's official, official. This is Endoh's first and last boy's love. It's extremely valuable.

Chapter 44: Counting on Fingers
Rayborn. From figuring out the dialogue to drawing the pictures, this episode was not easy to work on. Since I've had this part of the story planned out for years, you'd think I would have considered him dead from the moment he appeared, but... When the character leaves the confines of your own head and appears on public display, perhaps he takes on a life of his own independent of what you had planned for him.

Chapter 45: The Color of Silence
To add a little explanation, the method for making the serum described here is a little outdated. These days a much cooler looking serum machine makes serums that are free of allergens. Centrifuges...I want one.

Chapter 46: I Don't Have Words to Fill the Gap
It was uncomfortable drawing Alzeid gasping for air in front of a little girl. Like a pervert. (A misunderstanding.) Like it's shown in the flashback, Kiara's hair is actually black. He's dyeing it, the delinquent.

assistant works

kaori komori
Alice Tsukada
mika Ozaki

editor

Yousuke Sugino

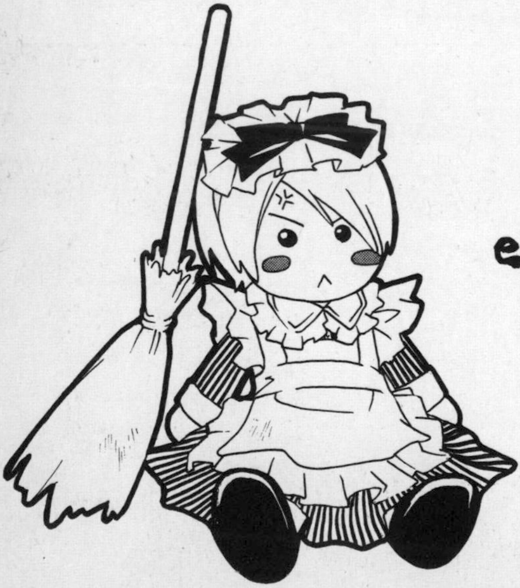

Thank you.

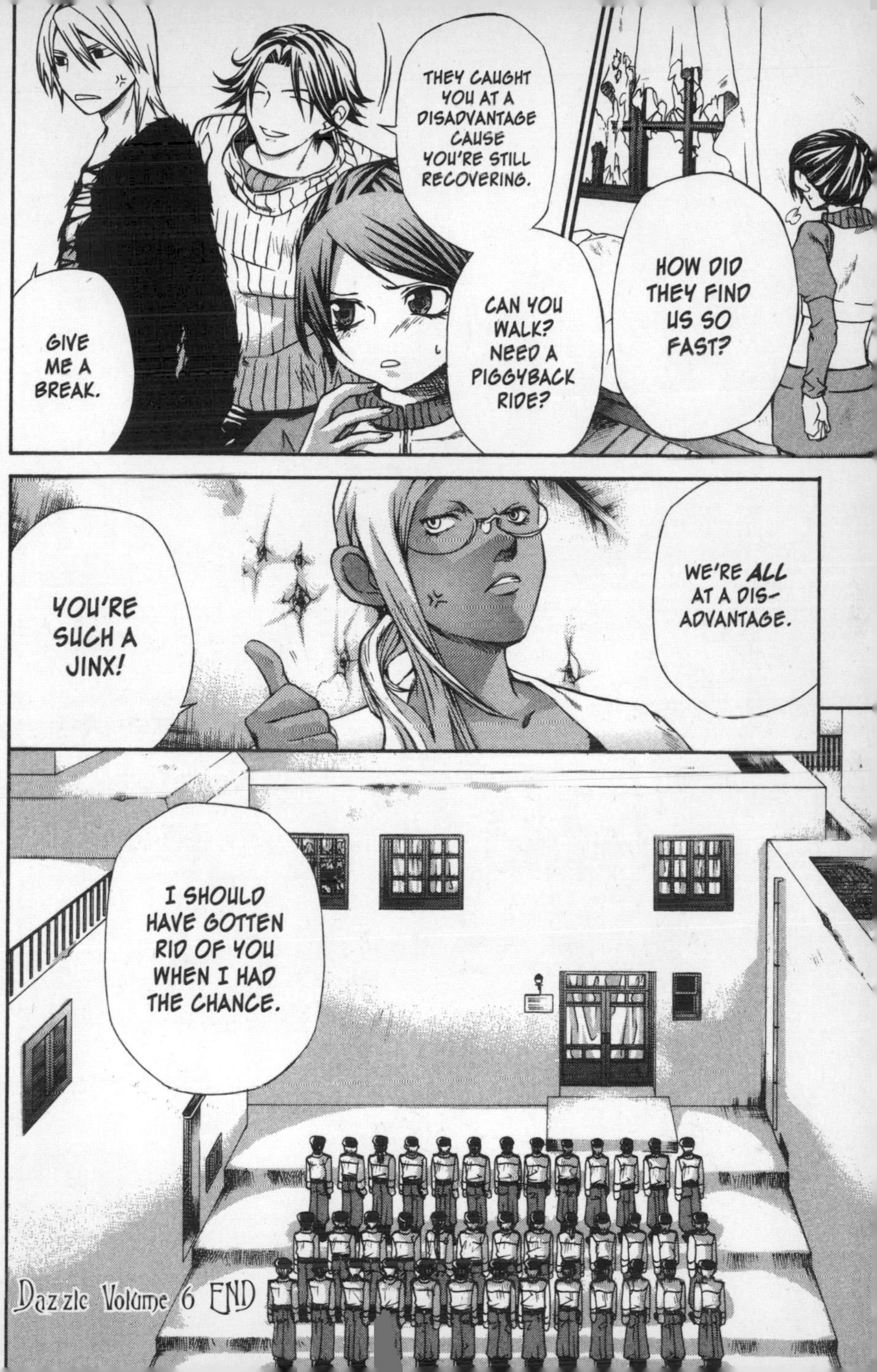
HOW DID THEY FIND US SO FAST?
THEY CAUGHT YOU AT A DISADVANTAGE CAUSE YOU'RE STILL RECOVERING.
CAN YOU WALK? NEED A PIGGYBACK RIDE?
GIVE ME A BREAK.
WE'RE **ALL** AT A DIS-ADVANTAGE.
YOU'RE SUCH A JINX!
I SHOULD HAVE GOTTEN RID OF YOU WHEN I HAD THE CHANCE.
Dazzle Volume 6 END

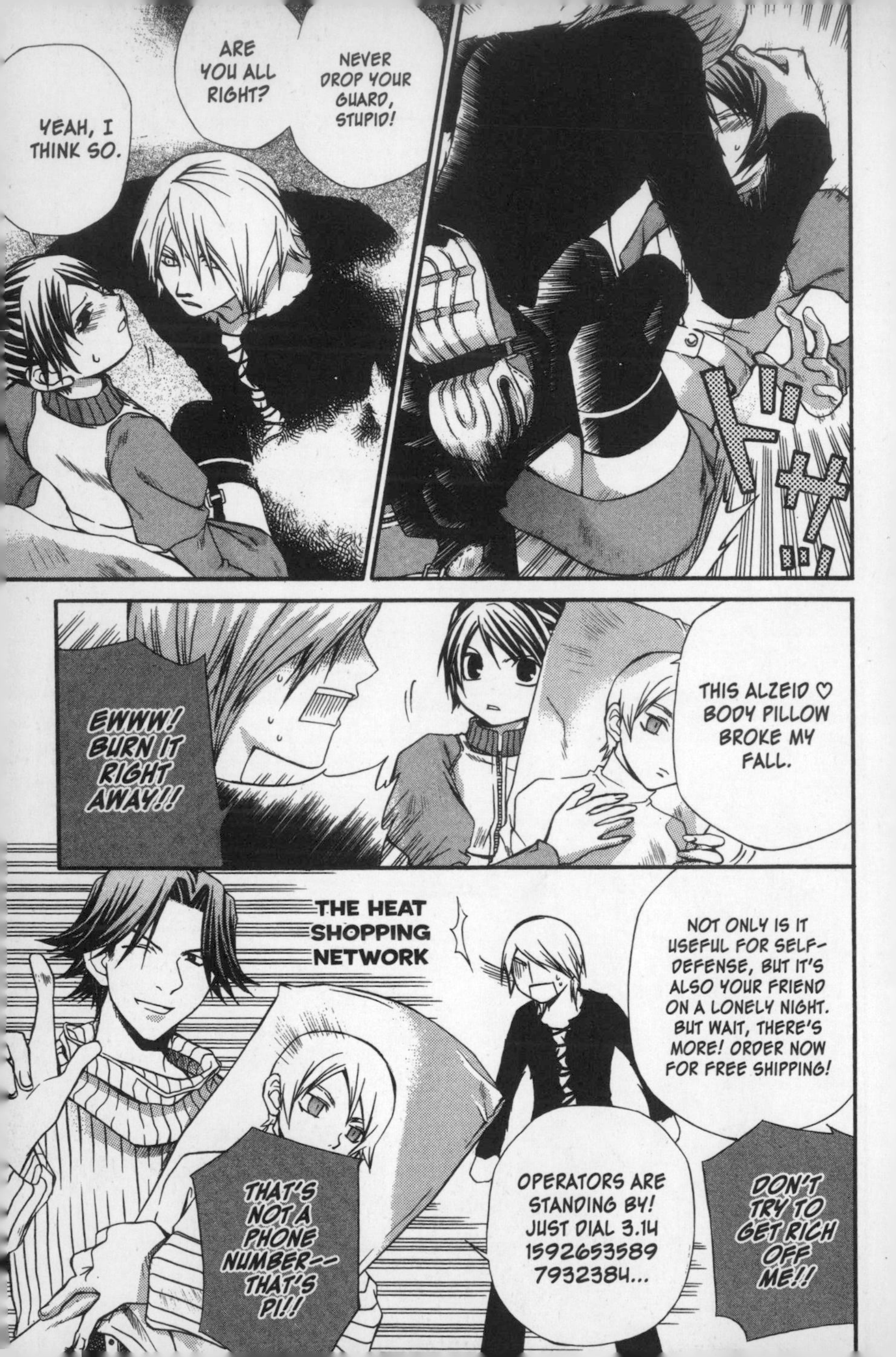
NEVER DROP YOUR GUARD, STUPID!
ARE YOU ALL RIGHT?
YEAH, I THINK SO.
THIS ALZEID ♡ BODY PILLOW BROKE MY FALL.
EWWW! BURN IT RIGHT AWAY!!
THE HEAT SHOPPING NETWORK
NOT ONLY IS IT USEFUL FOR SELF-DEFENSE, BUT IT'S ALSO YOUR FRIEND ON A LONELY NIGHT. BUT WAIT, THERE'S MORE! ORDER NOW FOR FREE SHIPPING!
OPERATORS ARE STANDING BY! JUST DIAL 3.14 1592653589 7932384...
DON'T TRY TO GET RICH OFF ME!!
THAT'S NOT A PHONE NUMBER-- THAT'S PI!!

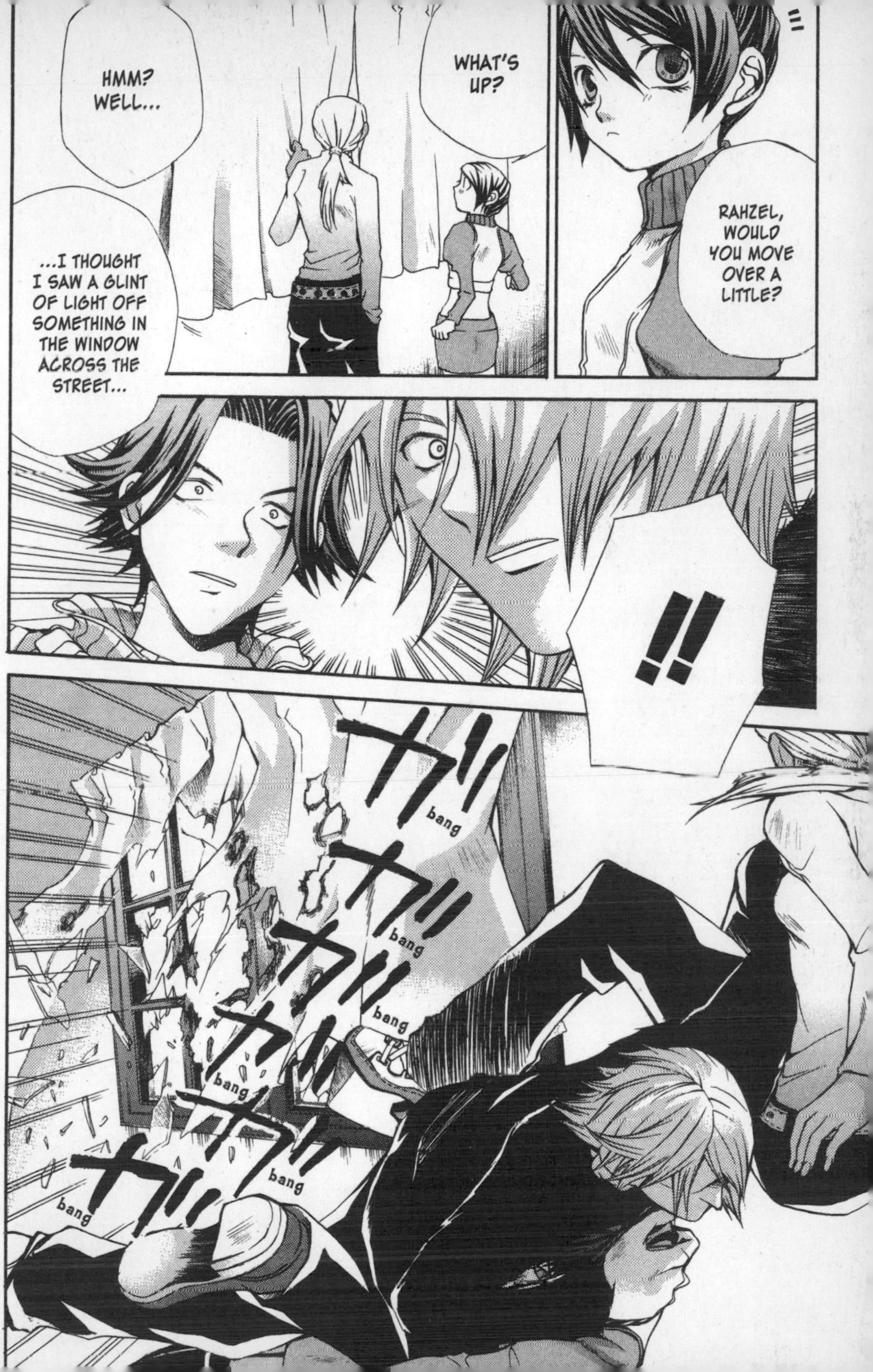

RAHZEL, WOULD YOU MOVE OVER A LITTLE?
WHAT'S UP?
HMM? WELL...
...I THOUGHT I SAW A GLINT OF LIGHT OFF SOMETHING IN THE WINDOW ACROSS THE STREET...
!!
bang
bang
bang
bang
bang
bang

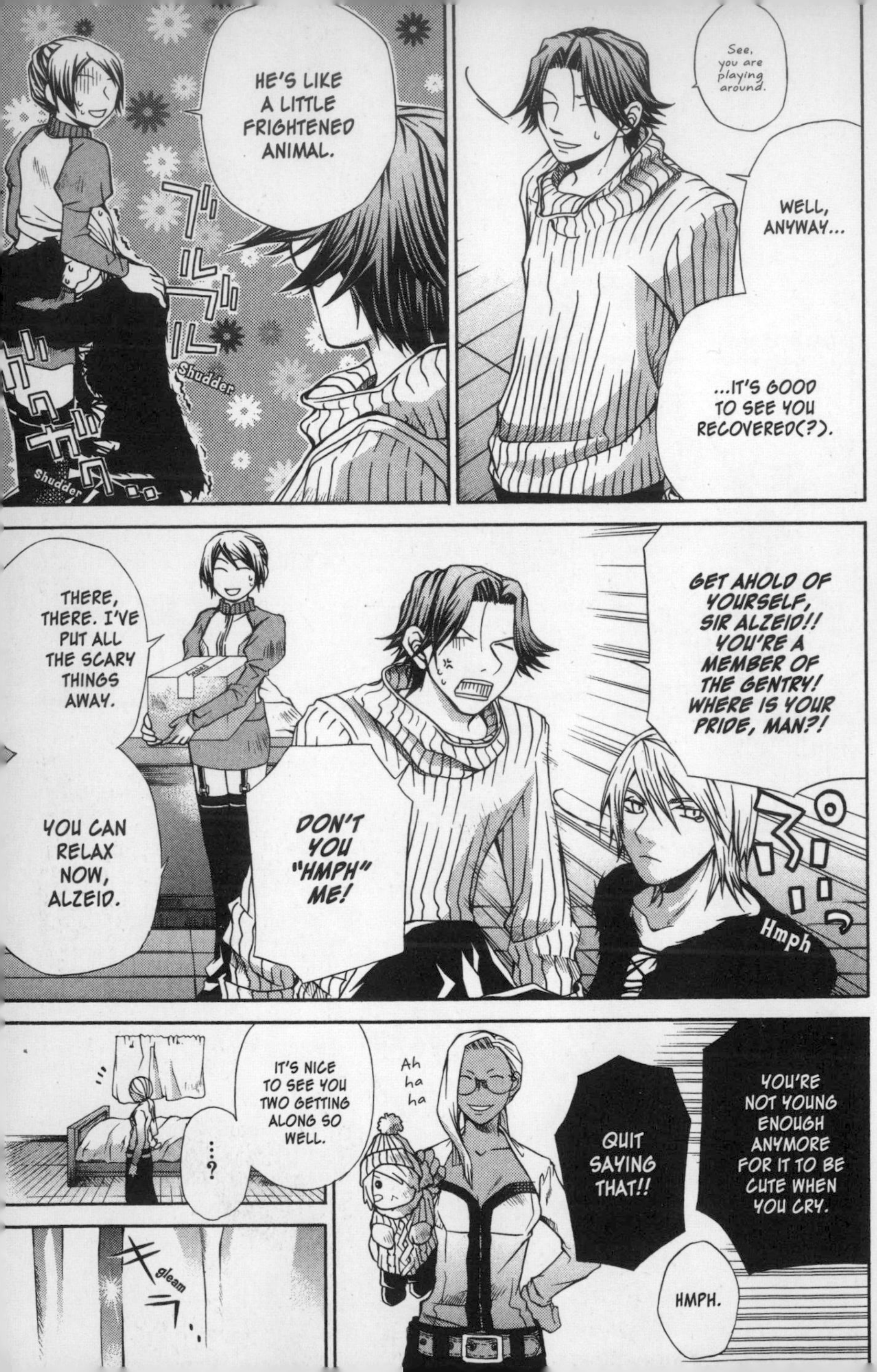
See, you are playing around.
WELL, ANYWAY...
...IT'S GOOD TO SEE YOU RECOVERED(?).
HE'S LIKE A LITTLE FRIGHTENED ANIMAL.
Shudder
Shudder
GET AHOLD OF YOURSELF, SIR ALZEID!! YOU'RE A MEMBER OF THE GENTRY! WHERE IS YOUR PRIDE, MAN?!
Hmph
DON'T YOU "HMPH" ME!
THERE, THERE. I'VE PUT ALL THE SCARY THINGS AWAY.
YOU CAN RELAX NOW, ALZEID.
YOU'RE NOT YOUNG ENOUGH ANYMORE FOR IT TO BE CUTE WHEN YOU CRY.
QUIT SAYING THAT!!
HMPH.
Ah ha ha
IT'S NICE TO SEE YOU TWO GETTING ALONG SO WELL.
...?
gleam

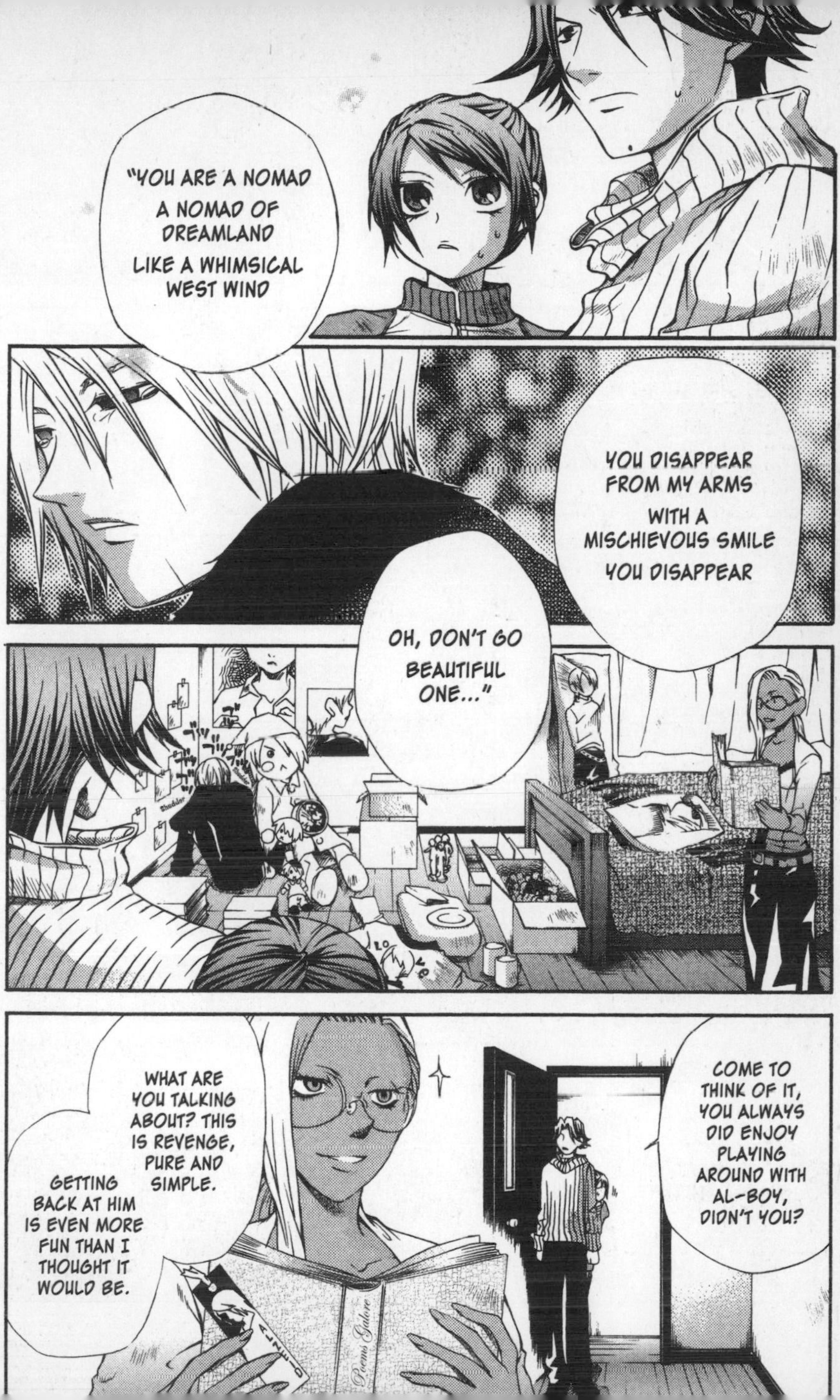
"YOU ARE A NOMAD
A NOMAD OF DREAMLAND
LIKE A WHIMSICAL WEST WIND
YOU DISAPPEAR FROM MY ARMS
WITH A MISCHIEVOUS SMILE
YOU DISAPPEAR
OH, DON'T GO BEAUTIFUL ONE..."
COME TO THINK OF IT, YOU ALWAYS DID ENJOY PLAYING AROUND WITH AL-BOY, DIDN'T YOU?
WHAT ARE YOU TALKING ABOUT? THIS IS REVENGE, PURE AND SIMPLE.
GETTING BACK AT HIM IS EVEN MORE FUN THAN I THOUGHT IT WOULD BE.
Poems Galore

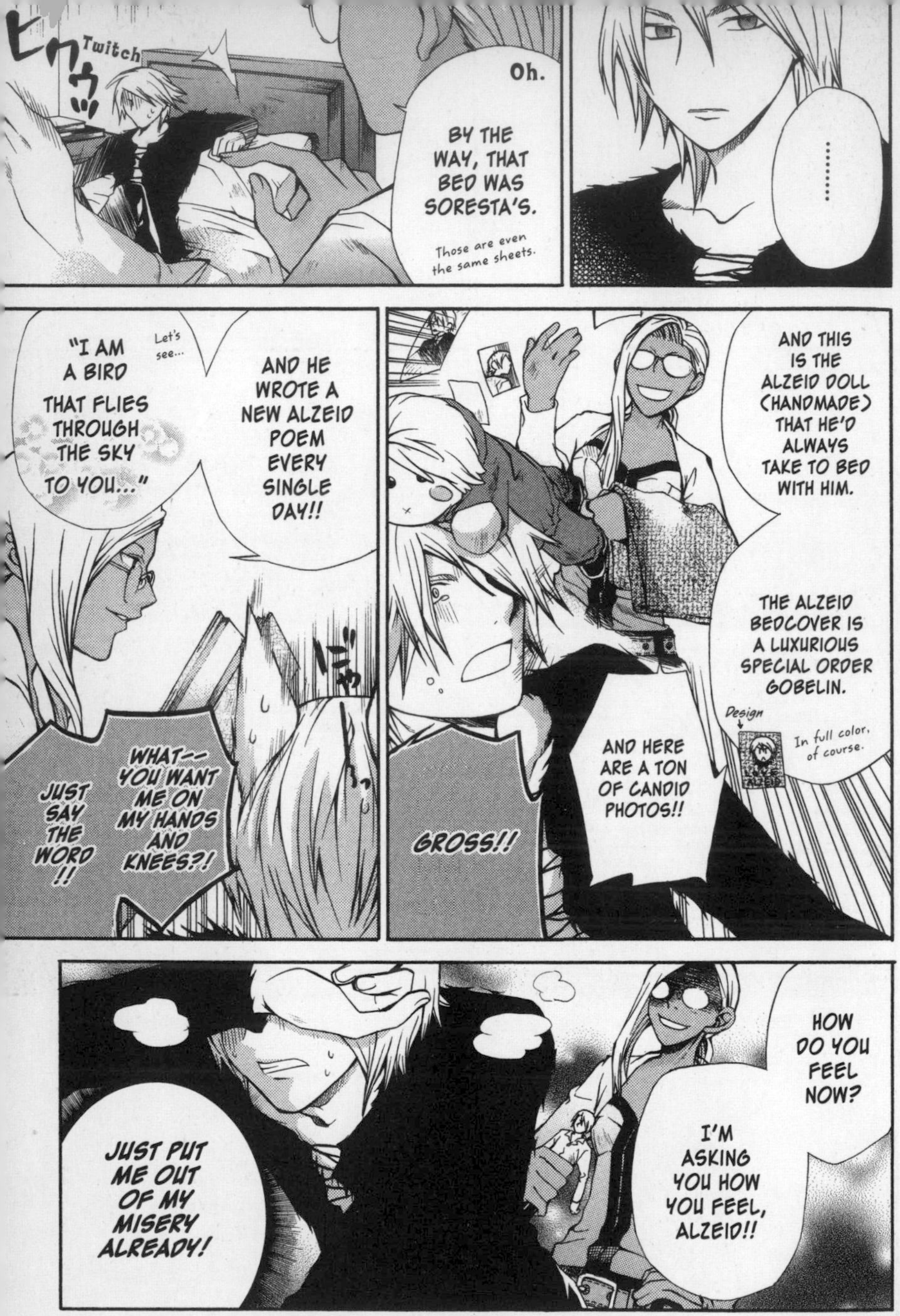
......
Oh.
BY THE WAY, THAT BED WAS SORESTA'S.
Those are even the same sheets.
Twitch
AND THIS IS THE ALZEID DOLL (HANDMADE) THAT HE'D ALWAYS TAKE TO BED WITH HIM.
THE ALZEID BEDCOVER IS A LUXURIOUS SPECIAL ORDER GOBELIN.
Design
In full color, of course.
AND HERE ARE A TON OF CANDID PHOTOS!!
GROSS!!
AND HE WROTE A NEW ALZEID POEM EVERY SINGLE DAY!!
Let's see...
"I AM A BIRD THAT FLIES THROUGH THE SKY TO YOU..."
WHAT-- YOU WANT ME ON MY HANDS AND KNEES?!
JUST SAY THE WORD!!
HOW DO YOU FEEL NOW?
I'M ASKING YOU HOW YOU FEEL, ALZEID!!
JUST PUT ME OUT OF MY MISERY ALREADY!

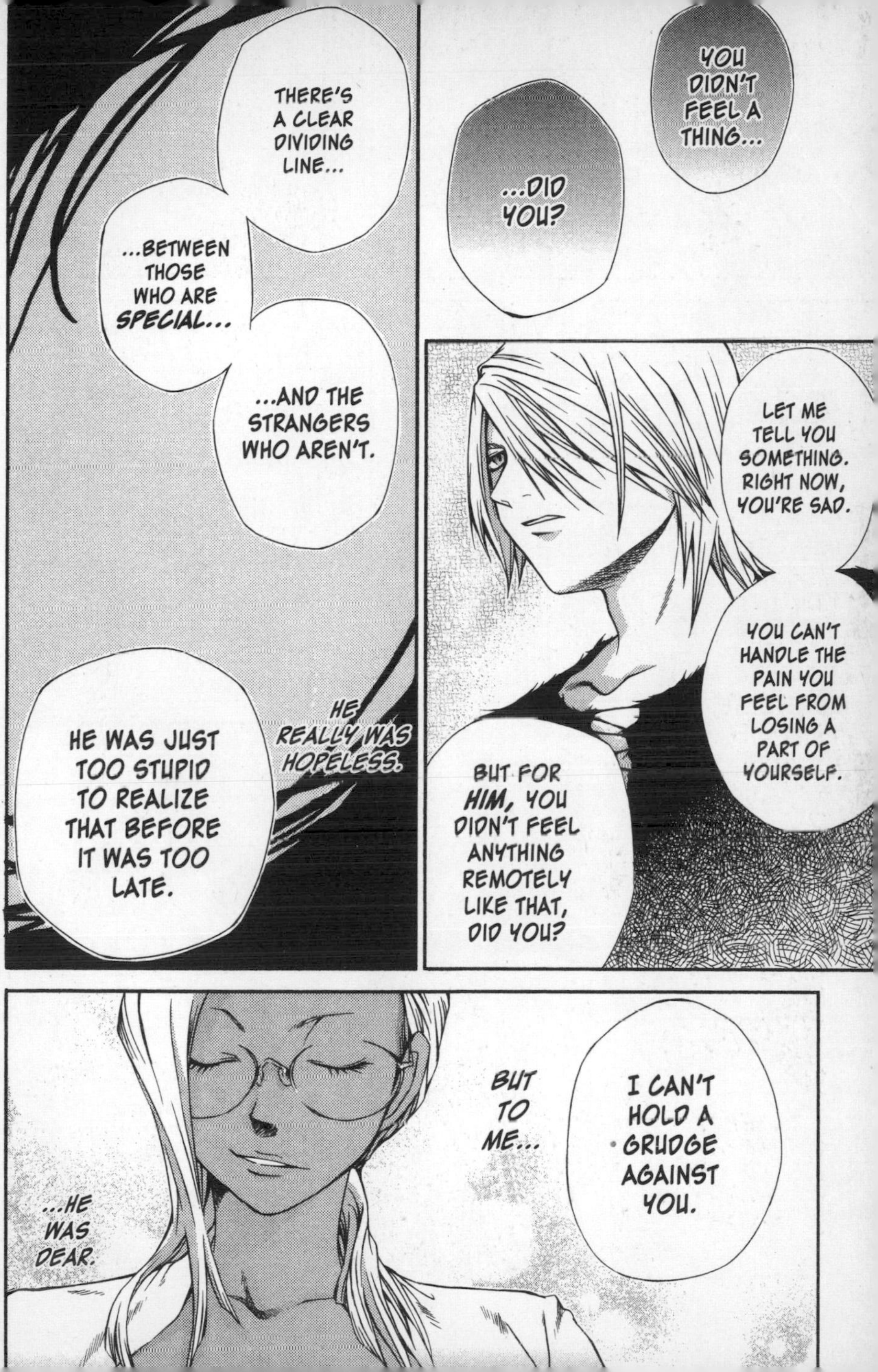
YOU DIDN'T FEEL A THING...
...DID YOU?
LET ME TELL YOU SOMETHING. RIGHT NOW, YOU'RE SAD.
YOU CAN'T HANDLE THE PAIN YOU FEEL FROM LOSING A PART OF YOURSELF.
BUT FOR *HIM*, YOU DIDN'T FEEL ANYTHING REMOTELY LIKE THAT, DID YOU?
THERE'S A CLEAR DIVIDING LINE...
...BETWEEN THOSE WHO ARE *SPECIAL*...
...AND THE STRANGERS WHO AREN'T.
HE REALLY WAS HOPELESS.
HE WAS JUST TOO STUPID TO REALIZE THAT BEFORE IT WAS TOO LATE.
I CAN'T HOLD A GRUDGE AGAINST YOU.
BUT TO ME...
...HE WAS DEAR.

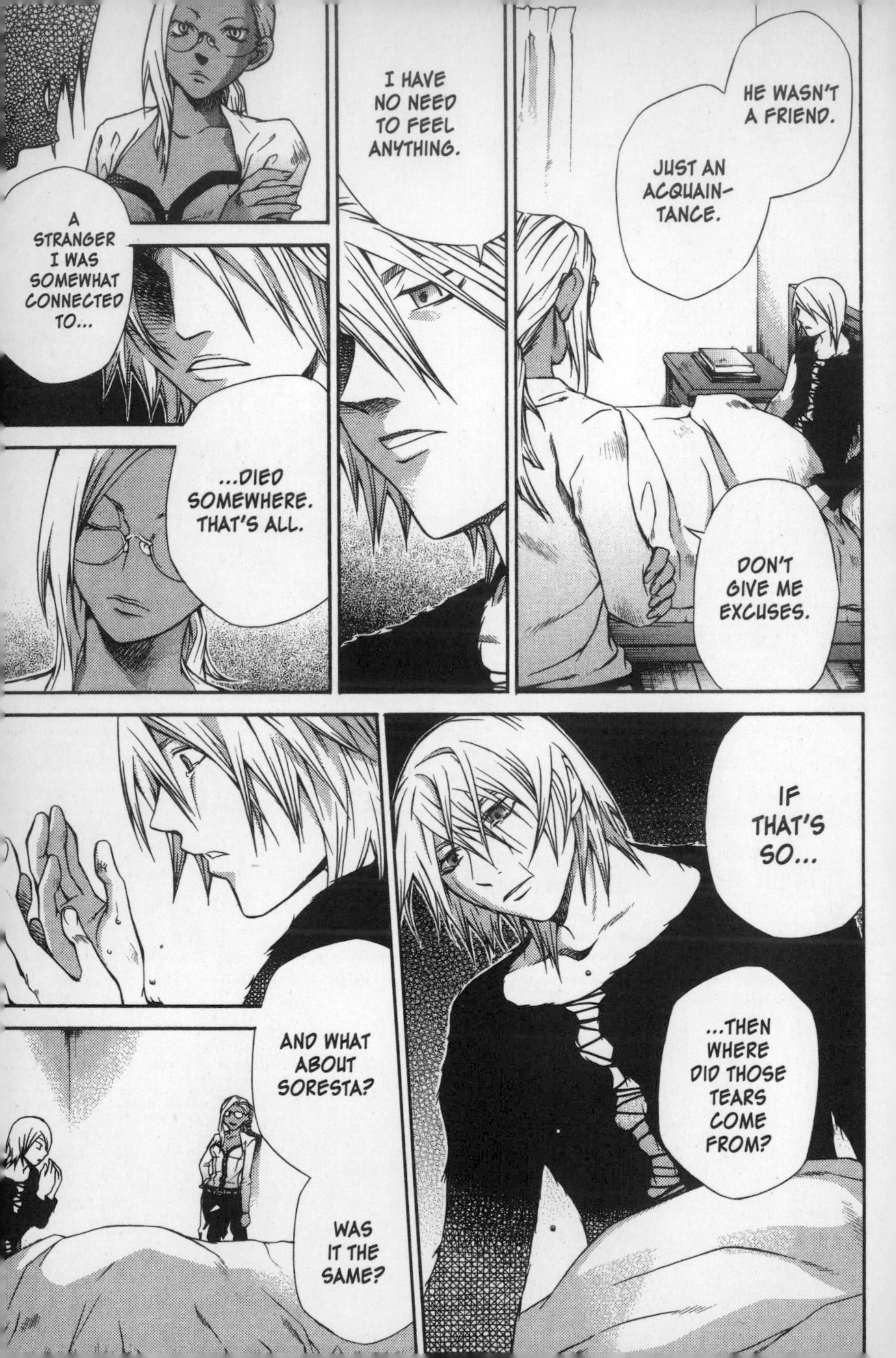
HE WASN'T A FRIEND.
JUST AN ACQUAIN-TANCE.
DON'T GIVE ME EXCUSES.
I HAVE NO NEED TO FEEL ANYTHING.
A STRANGER I WAS SOMEWHAT CONNECTED TO...
...DIED SOMEWHERE. THAT'S ALL.
IF THAT'S SO...
...THEN WHERE DID THOSE TEARS COME FROM?
AND WHAT ABOUT SORESTA?
WAS IT THE SAME?

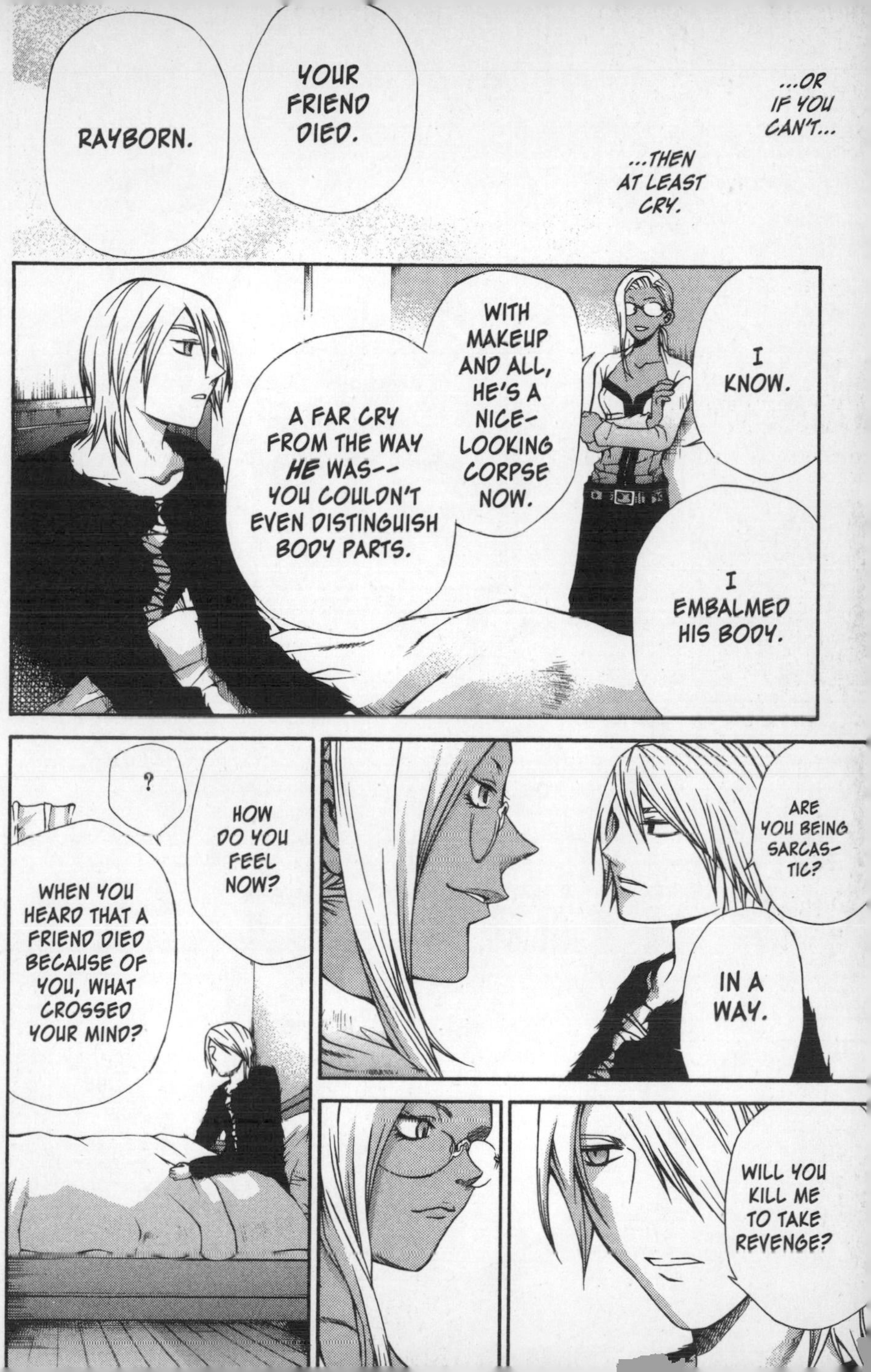
...OR IF YOU CAN'T...
...THEN AT LEAST CRY.
YOUR FRIEND DIED.
RAYBORN.
I KNOW.
I EMBALMED HIS BODY.
WITH MAKEUP AND ALL, HE'S A NICE-LOOKING CORPSE NOW.
A FAR CRY FROM THE WAY *HE* WAS-- YOU COULDN'T EVEN DISTINGUISH BODY PARTS.
ARE YOU BEING SARCASTIC?
IN A WAY.
WILL YOU KILL ME TO TAKE REVENGE?
HOW DO YOU FEEL NOW?
?
WHEN YOU HEARD THAT A FRIEND DIED BECAUSE OF YOU, WHAT CROSSED YOUR MIND?

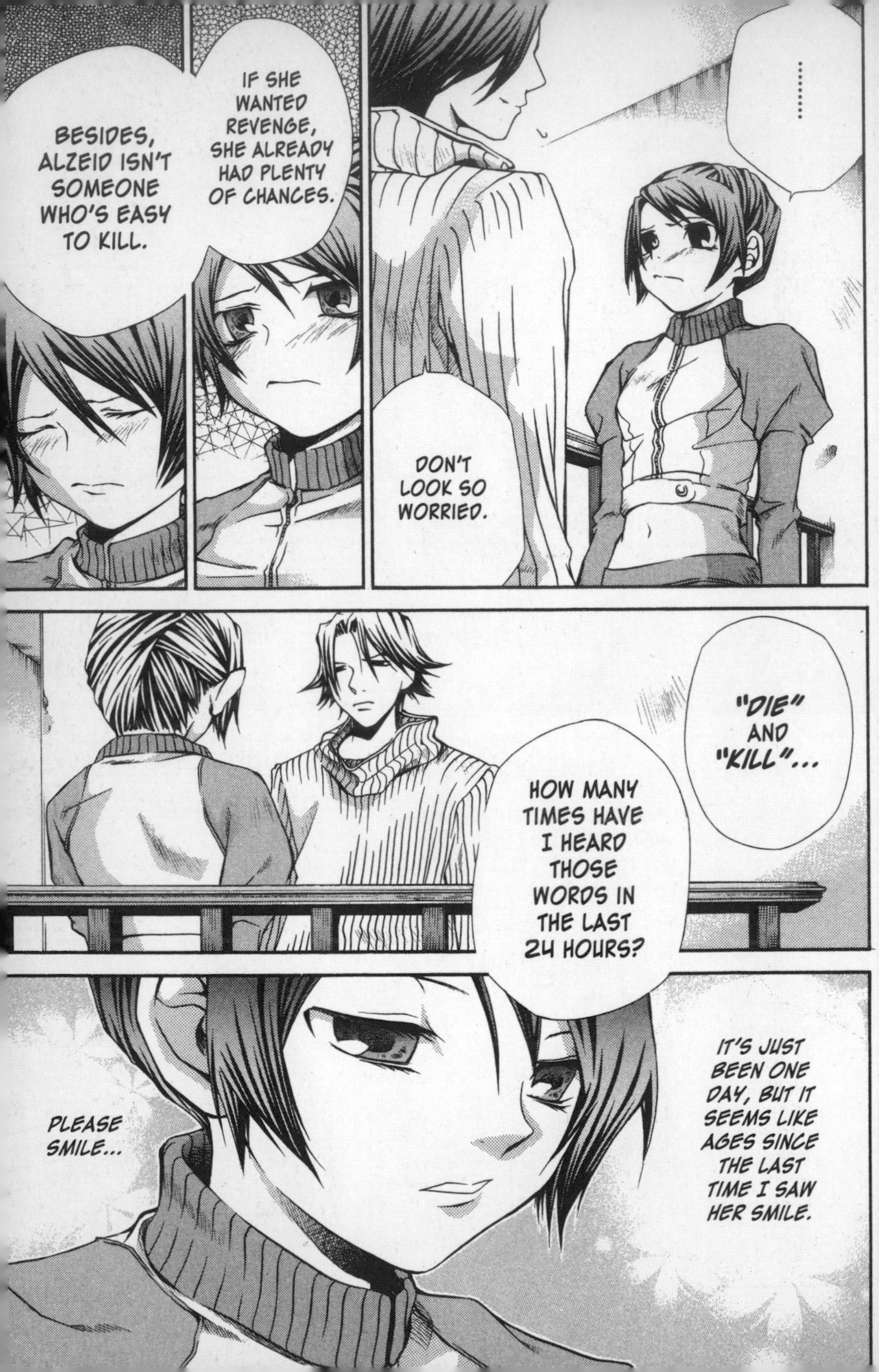
......
DON'T LOOK SO WORRIED.
IF SHE WANTED REVENGE, SHE ALREADY HAD PLENTY OF CHANCES.
BESIDES, ALZEID ISN'T SOMEONE WHO'S EASY TO KILL.
"DIE" AND "KILL"...
HOW MANY TIMES HAVE I HEARD THOSE WORDS IN THE LAST 24 HOURS?
IT'S JUST BEEN ONE DAY, BUT IT SEEMS LIKE AGES SINCE THE LAST TIME I SAW HER SMILE.
PLEASE SMILE...

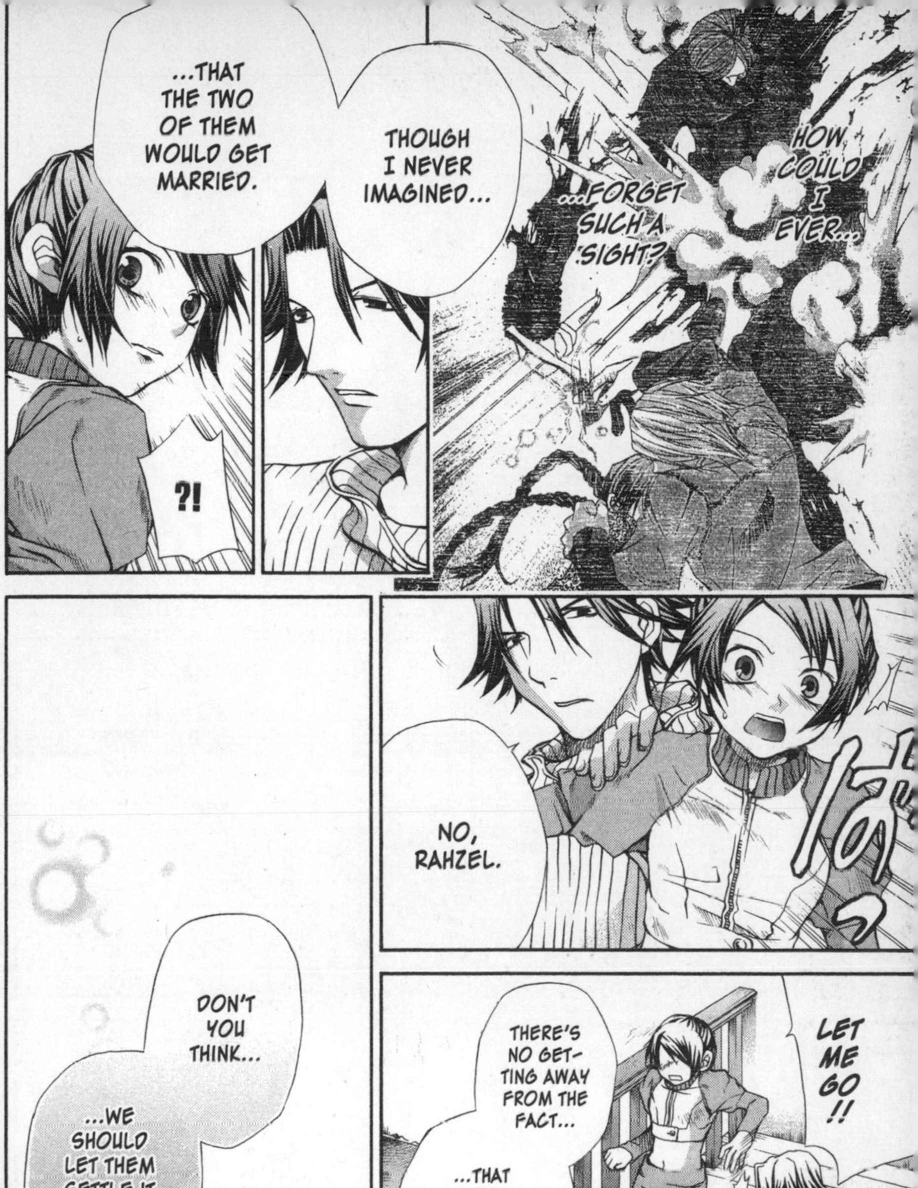
HOW COULD I EVER...
...FORGET SUCH A SIGHT?
THOUGH I NEVER IMAGINED...
...THAT THE TWO OF THEM WOULD GET MARRIED.
?!
NO, RAHZEL.
LET ME GO!!
THERE'S NO GET-TING AWAY FROM THE FACT...
...THAT ALZEID KILLED TAYLOR'S HUSBAND, NO MATTER WHAT THE REASON WAS...
DON'T YOU THINK...
...WE SHOULD LET THEM SETTLE IT BETWEEN THE TWO OF THEM?

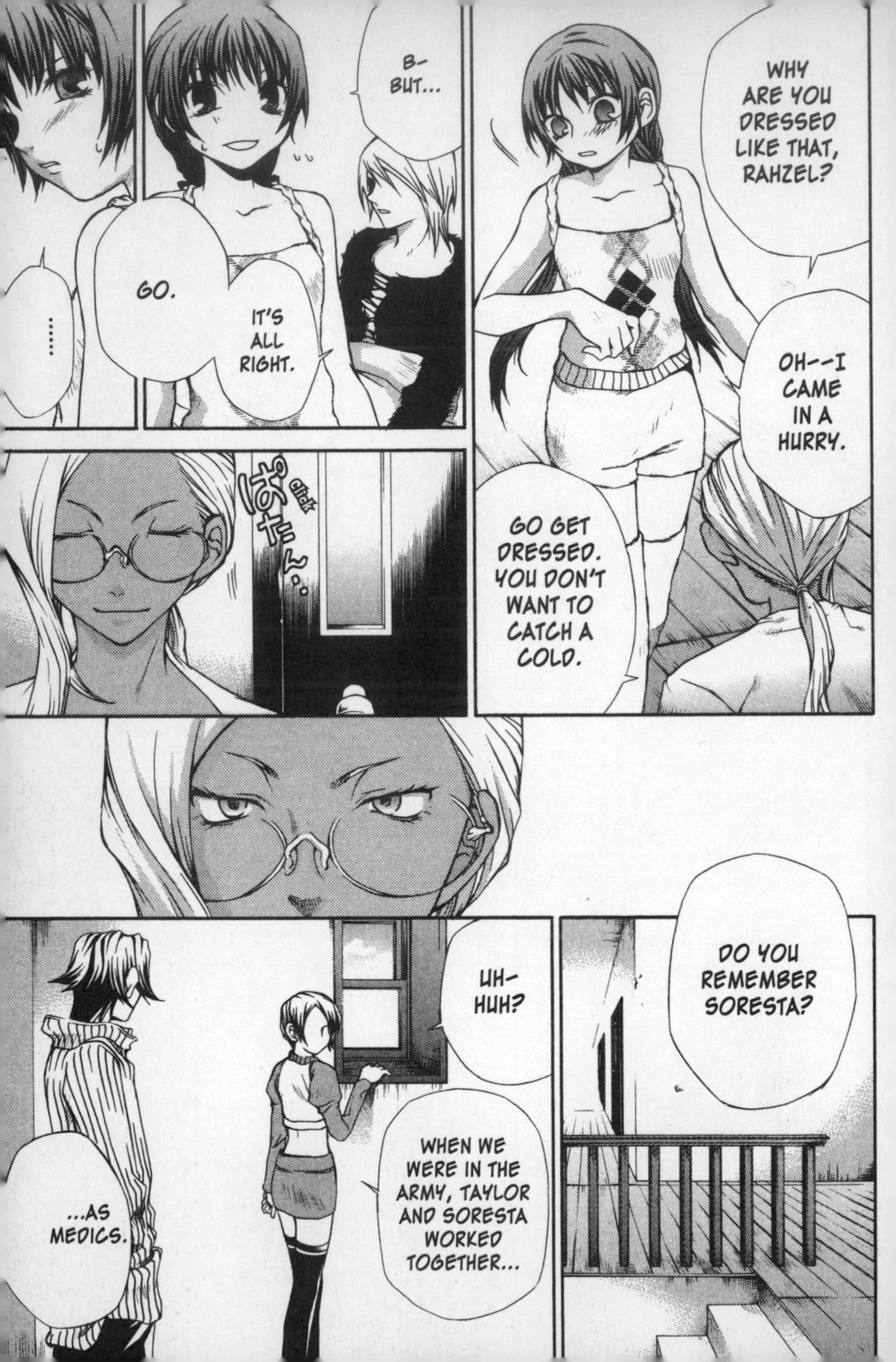
WHY ARE YOU DRESSED LIKE THAT, RAHZEL?
OH--I CAME IN A HURRY.
GO GET DRESSED. YOU DON'T WANT TO CATCH A COLD.
B-BUT...
IT'S ALL RIGHT.
GO.
......
click
ぱたん。
DO YOU REMEMBER SORESTA?
UH-HUH?
WHEN WE WERE IN THE ARMY, TAYLOR AND SORESTA WORKED TOGETHER...
...AS MEDICS.

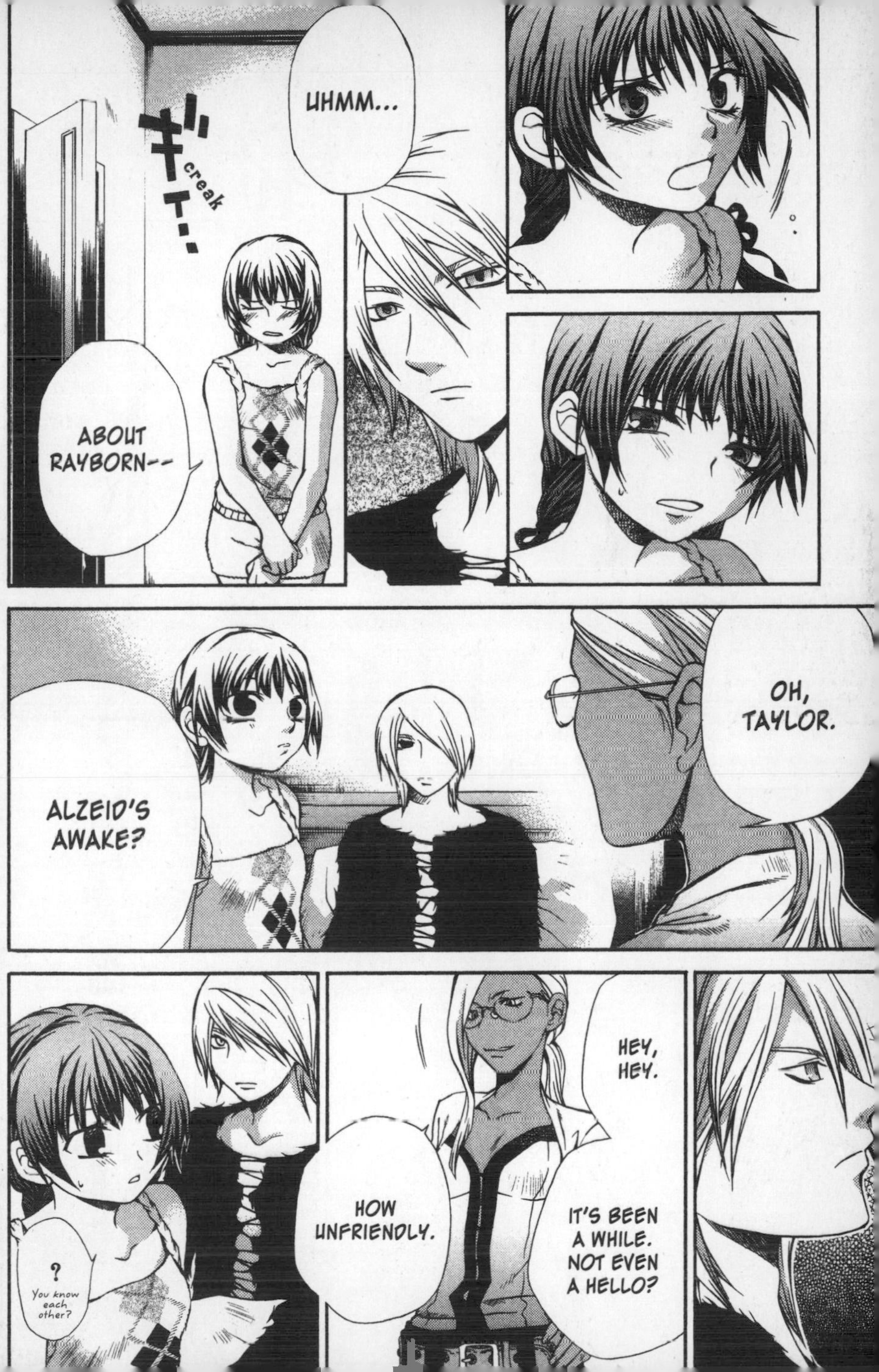
UHMM...
creak
ABOUT RAYBORN--
OH, TAYLOR.
ALZEID'S AWAKE?
HEY, HEY.
IT'S BEEN A WHILE. NOT EVEN A HELLO?
HOW UNFRIENDLY.
?
You know each other?

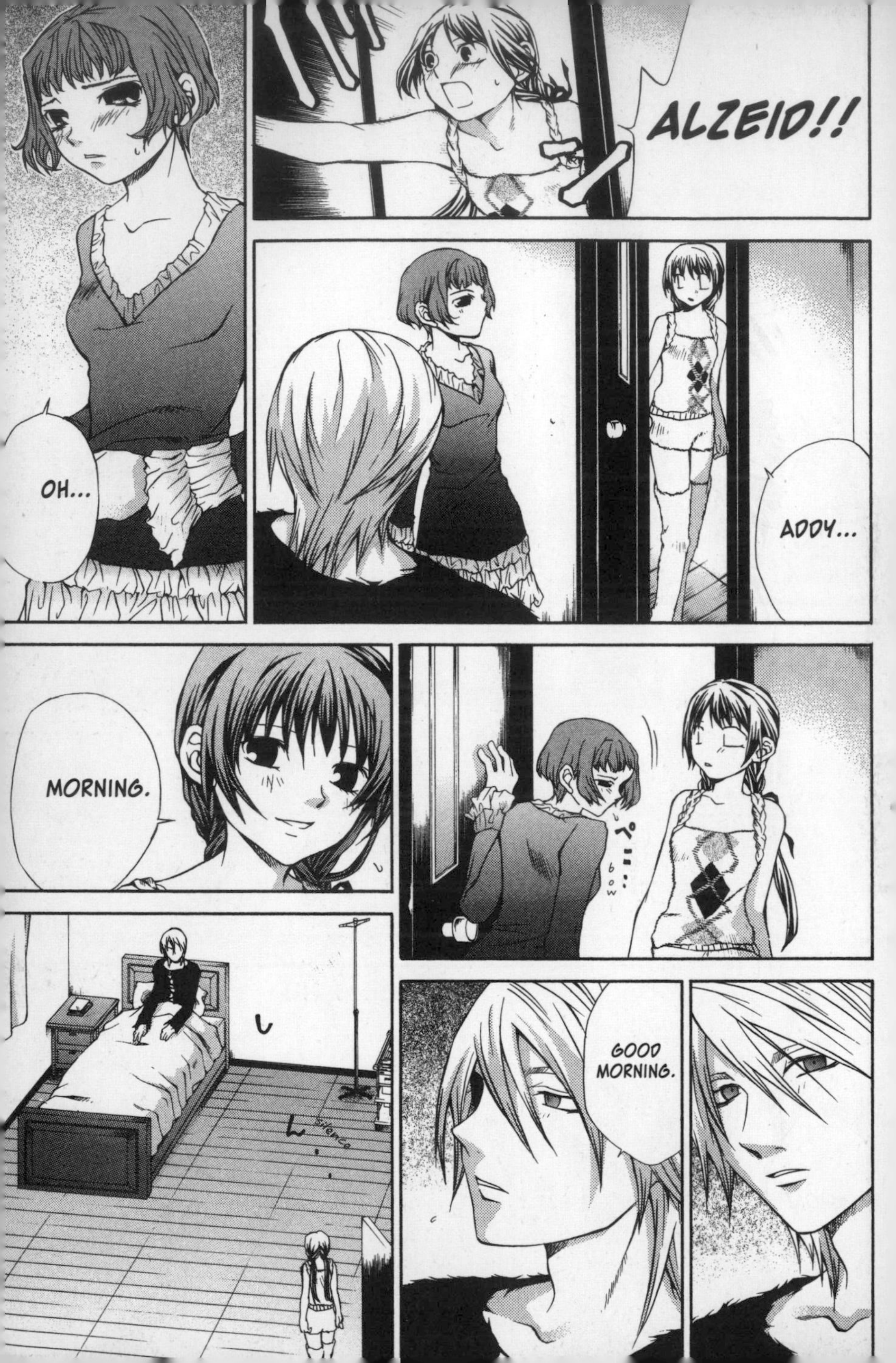
ALZEID!!
ADDY...
OH...
ペこ..
bow
MORNING.
GOOD MORNING.
し
ん
silence

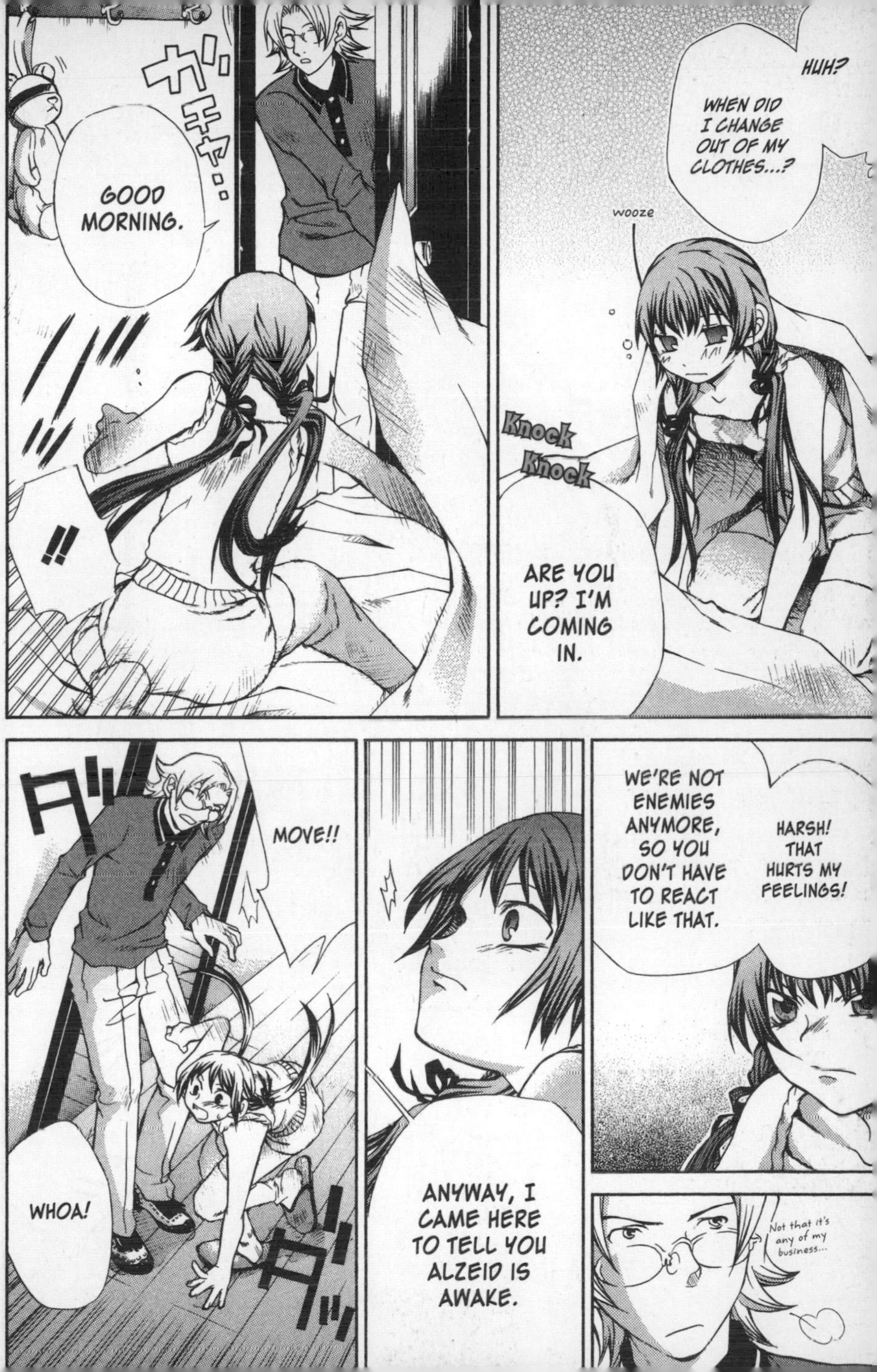
HUH?
WHEN DID I CHANGE OUT OF MY CLOTHES...?
wooze
Knock Knock
ARE YOU UP? I'M COMING IN.
カチャ
GOOD MORNING.
!!
WE'RE NOT ENEMIES ANYMORE, SO YOU DON'T HAVE TO REACT LIKE THAT.
HARSH! THAT HURTS MY FEELINGS!
Not that it's any of my business...
ANYWAY, I CAME HERE TO TELL YOU ALZEID IS AWAKE.
MOVE!!
WHOA!

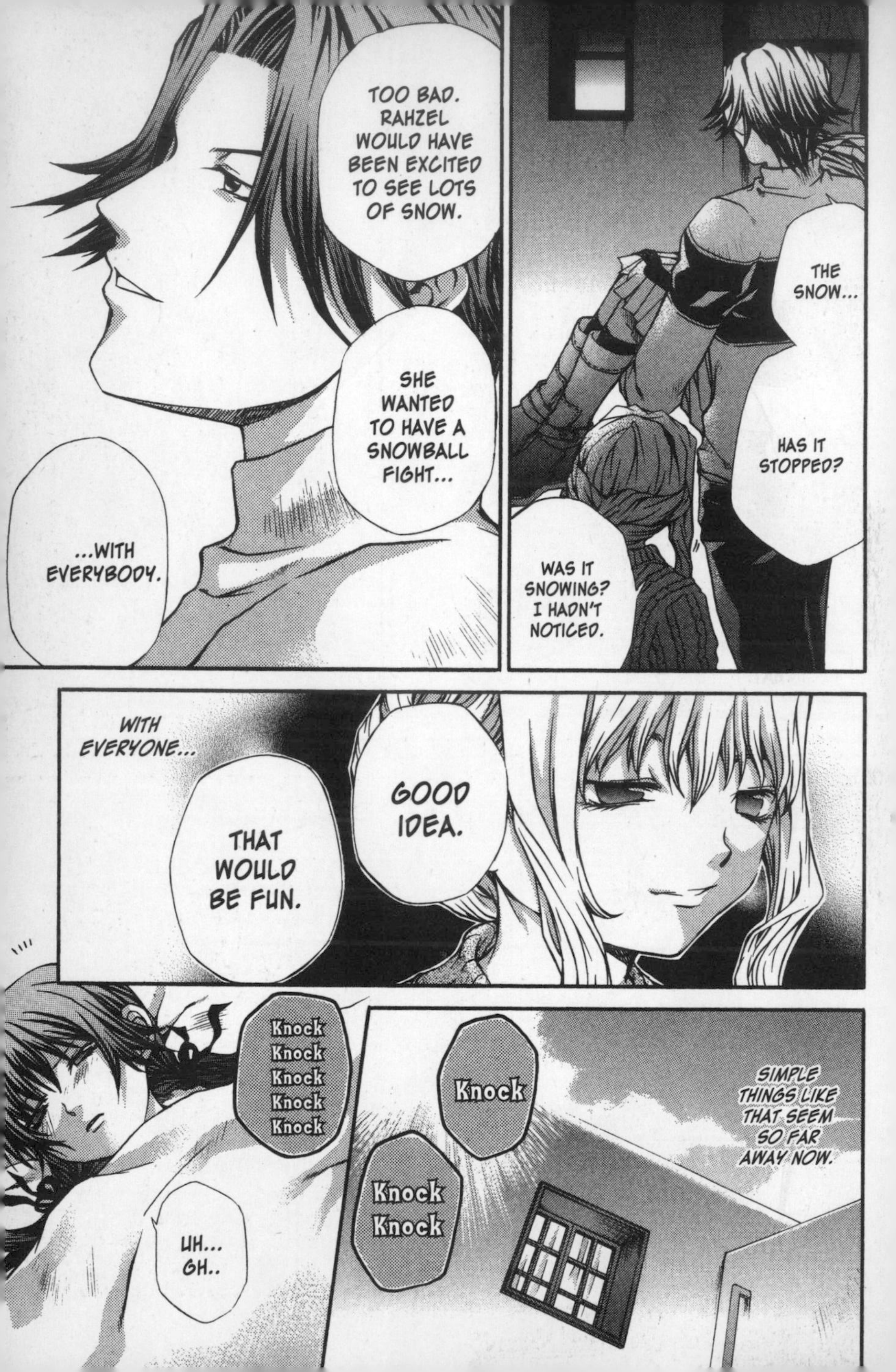
THE SNOW...
HAS IT STOPPED?
WAS IT SNOWING? I HADN'T NOTICED.
TOO BAD. RAHZEL WOULD HAVE BEEN EXCITED TO SEE LOTS OF SNOW.
SHE WANTED TO HAVE A SNOWBALL FIGHT...
...WITH EVERYBODY.
GOOD IDEA.
WITH EVERYONE...
THAT WOULD BE FUN.
SIMPLE THINGS LIKE THAT SEEM SO FAR AWAY NOW.
Knock
Knock Knock
Knock Knock Knock Knock Knock
UH... GH..

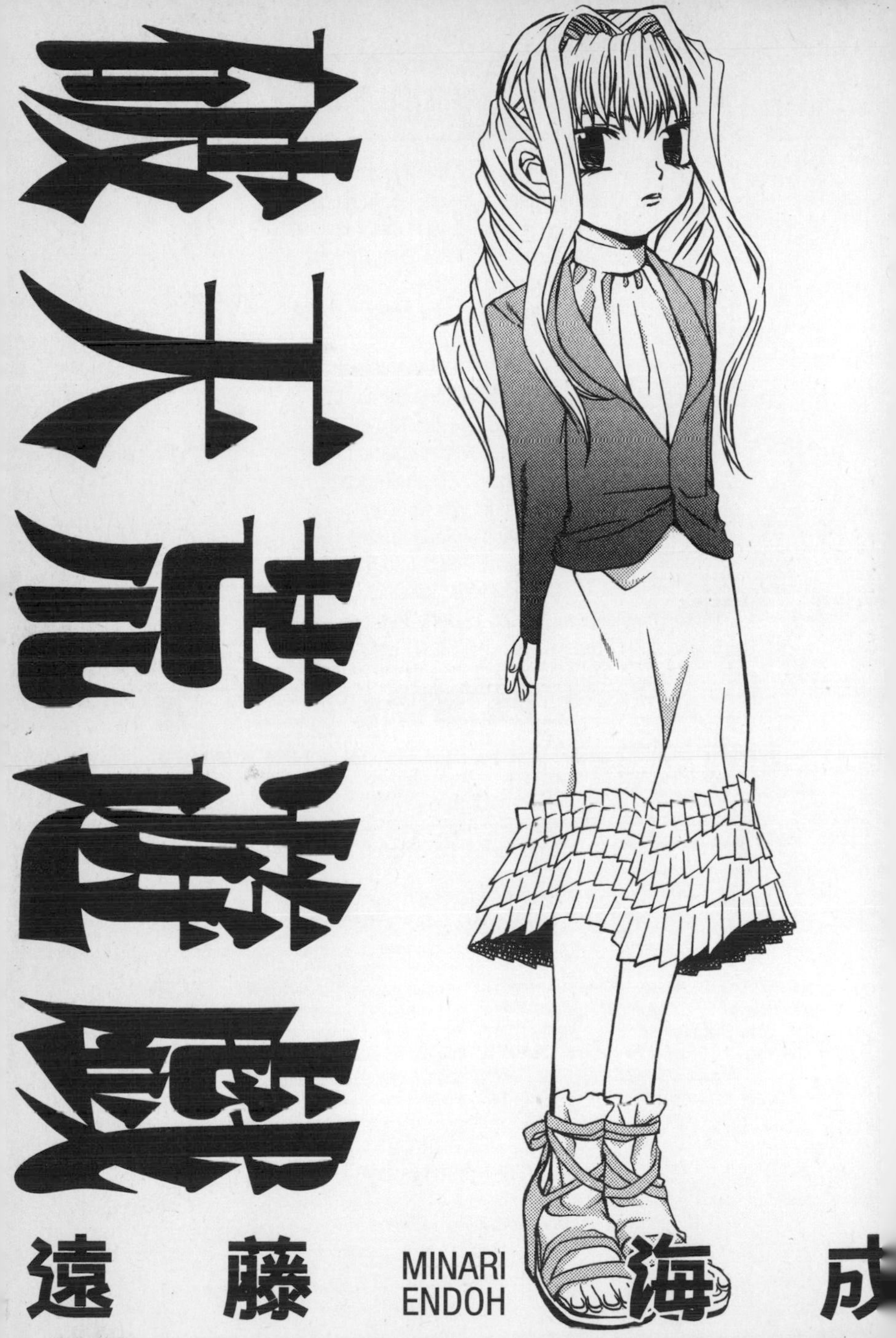

遠藤 海成

MINARI ENDOH

Dazzle Volume 6
Created by Minari Endoh

Translation - Yuko Fukami
English Adaptation - Karen S. Ahlstrom
Copy Editor - Stephanie Duchin
Retouch and Lettering - Star Print Brokers
Production Artist - Mike Estacio
Graphic Designer - Jose Macasocol, Jr.

Editor - Peter Ahlstrom
Digital Imaging Manager - Chris Buford
Pre-Production Supervisor - Erika Terriquez
Art Director - Anne Marie Horne
Production Manager - Elisabeth Brizzi
Managing Editor - Vy Nguyen
VP of Production - Ron Klamert
Editor-in-Chief - Rob Tokar
Publisher - Mike Kiley
President and C.O.O. - John Parker
C.E.O. and Chief Creative Officer - Stuart Levy

A ⊙ **TOKYOPOP** Manga

TOKYOPOP and ⊙ are trademarks or registered trademarks of TOKYOPOP Inc.

TOKYOPOP Inc.
5900 Wilshire Blvd. Suite 2000
Los Angeles, CA 90036

E-mail: info@TOKYOPOP.com
Come visit us online at www.TOKYOPOP.com

ISBN: 978-1-59816-097-0

First TOKYOPOP printing: September 2007
10 9 8 7 6 5 4 3 2 1
Printed in the USA

DAZZLE™

Vol. 6

Minari Endoh

HAMBURG // LONDON // LOS ANGELES // TOKYO

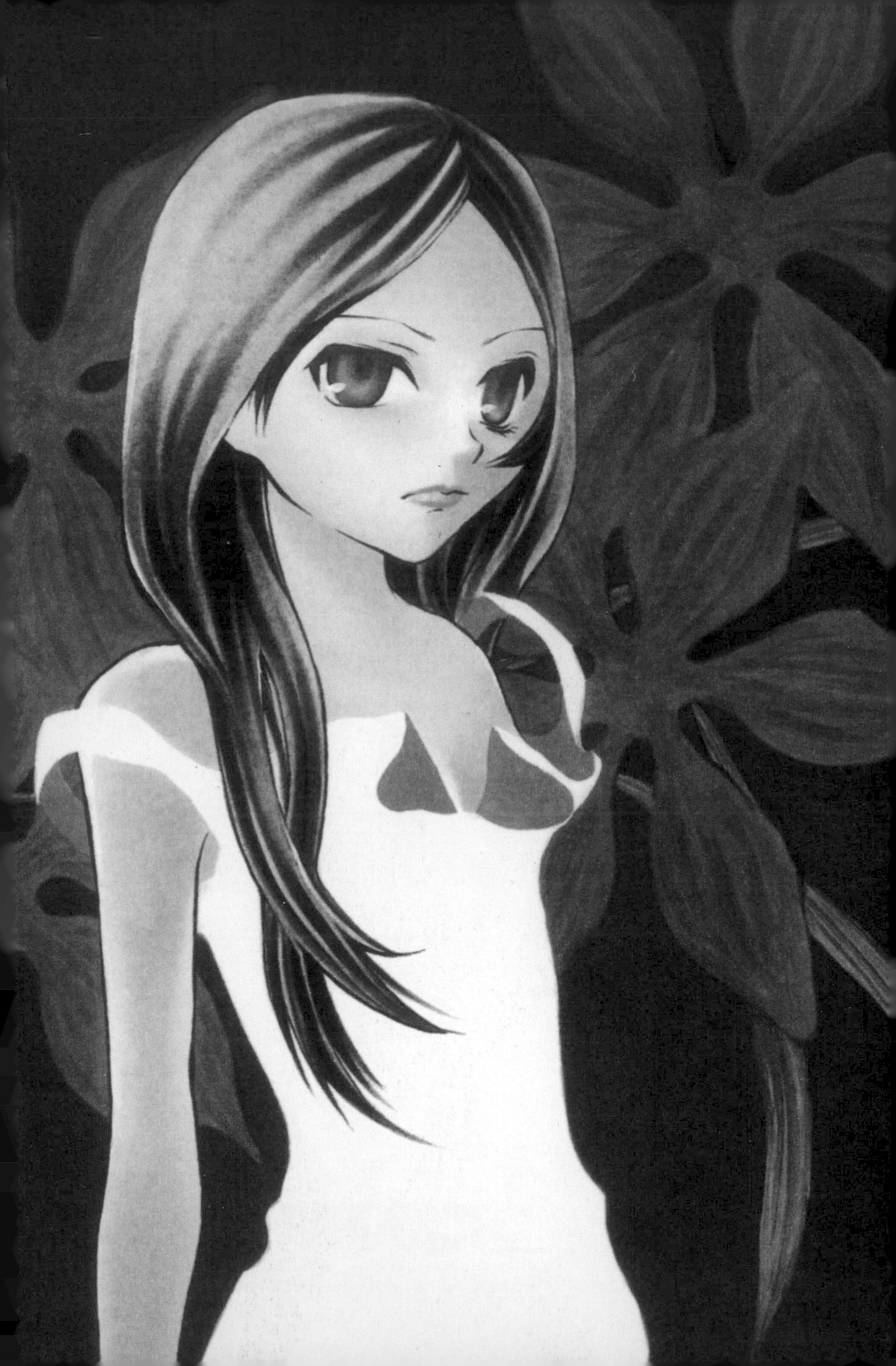

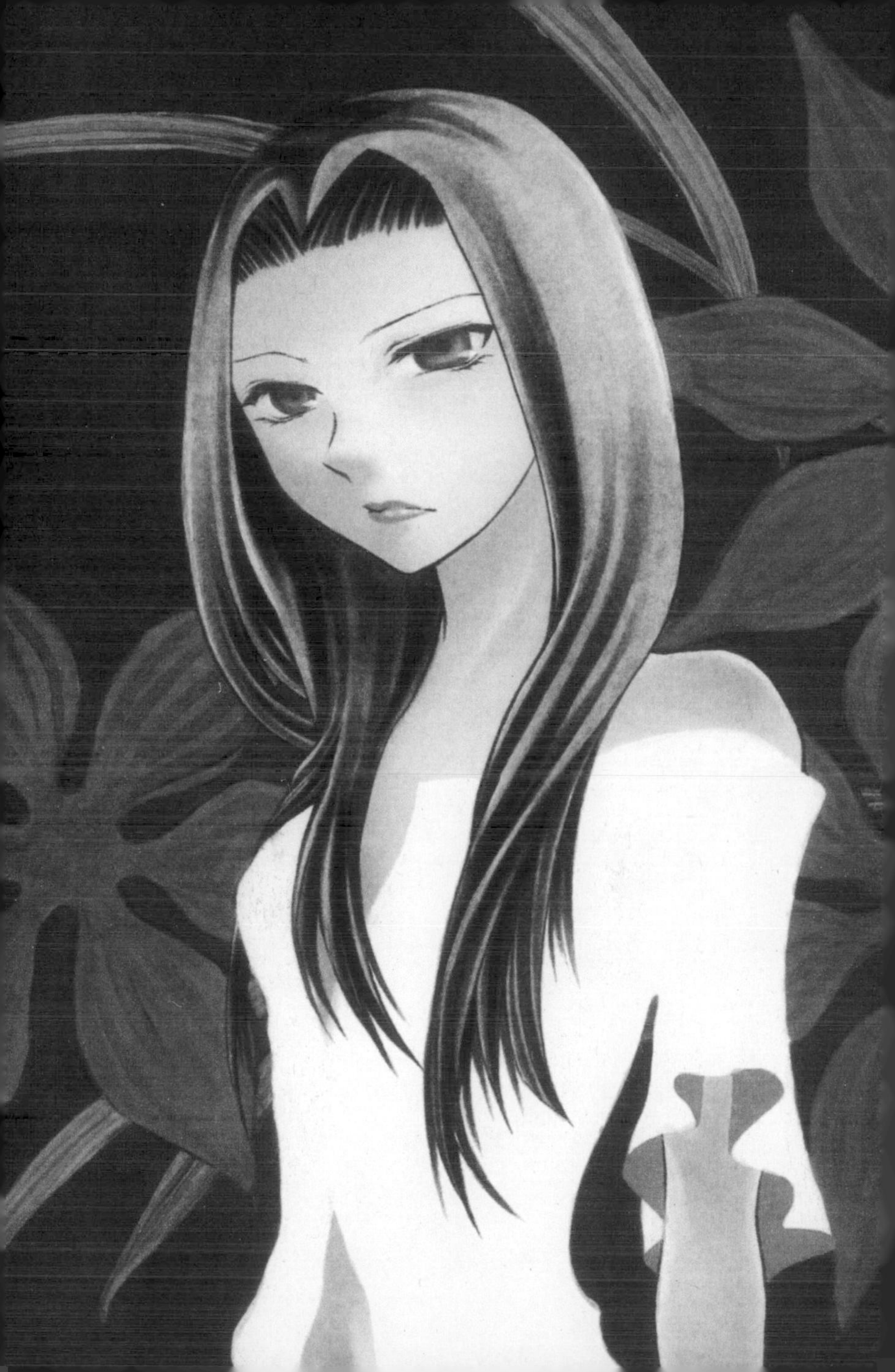

When Rahzel's father suddenly kicked her out of the house to go on a training journey and hone her magical abilities, he didn't expect her to immediately fall in with Alzeid, an albino magic user in search of the woman who killed his father. They were soon joined in their travels by Baroqueheat, Alzeid's associate from his army days, who has taken quite a liking to Rahzel--much to her dismay. Yet somehow, through multiple trials and adventures, this mismatched trio has formed a bond as strong as a family's ties.

But one of Baroqueheat's older brothers, Kiara, has been observing their journey and pulling the strings behind the scenes, leading to an incident where Rahzel got kidnapped and dosed with a drug called Angel Text. Yet the kidnapper apparently went too far when he tried to mindwipe Rahzel and take over her body, because Kiara killed him for it. Additionally, Baroqueheat and Kiara's older sister Natsume matches the description of the woman Alzeid says killed his father--but as far as her brothers or her sister Branowen know, she's a murder victim herself.

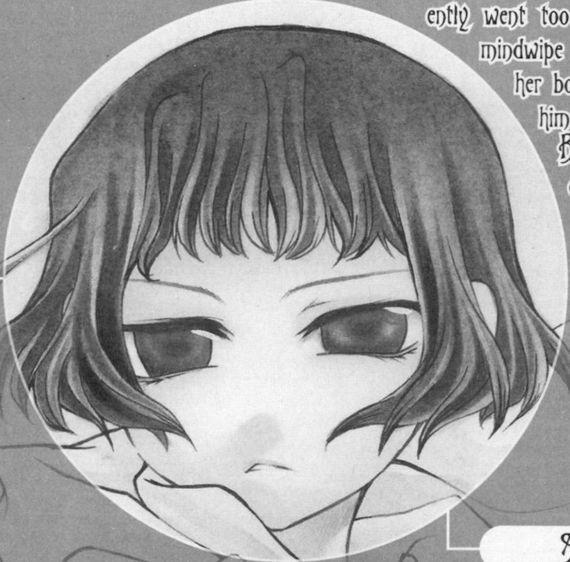

Story So Far...

Now Rahzel and company have traveled by ship to the port town of Acanea, accompanied by Rayborn, a teen whose life Rahzel saved and who she has promised to say "I like you" to 100 million times. On the ship Rahzel is met by a mysterious longhaired albino boy claiming Rahzel has promised to give him a name, who warns her of danger ahead before teleporting away--back to Kiara. And in Acanea, a pair of assassins suddenly attack Alzeid as soon as they learn his name--because that is the known alias of the white-haired, red-eyed boy who has been terrorizing the town. Rahzel tricks them into temporary defeat, but Alzeid has been poisoned by the assassins' weapons...

Contents

Delinquent

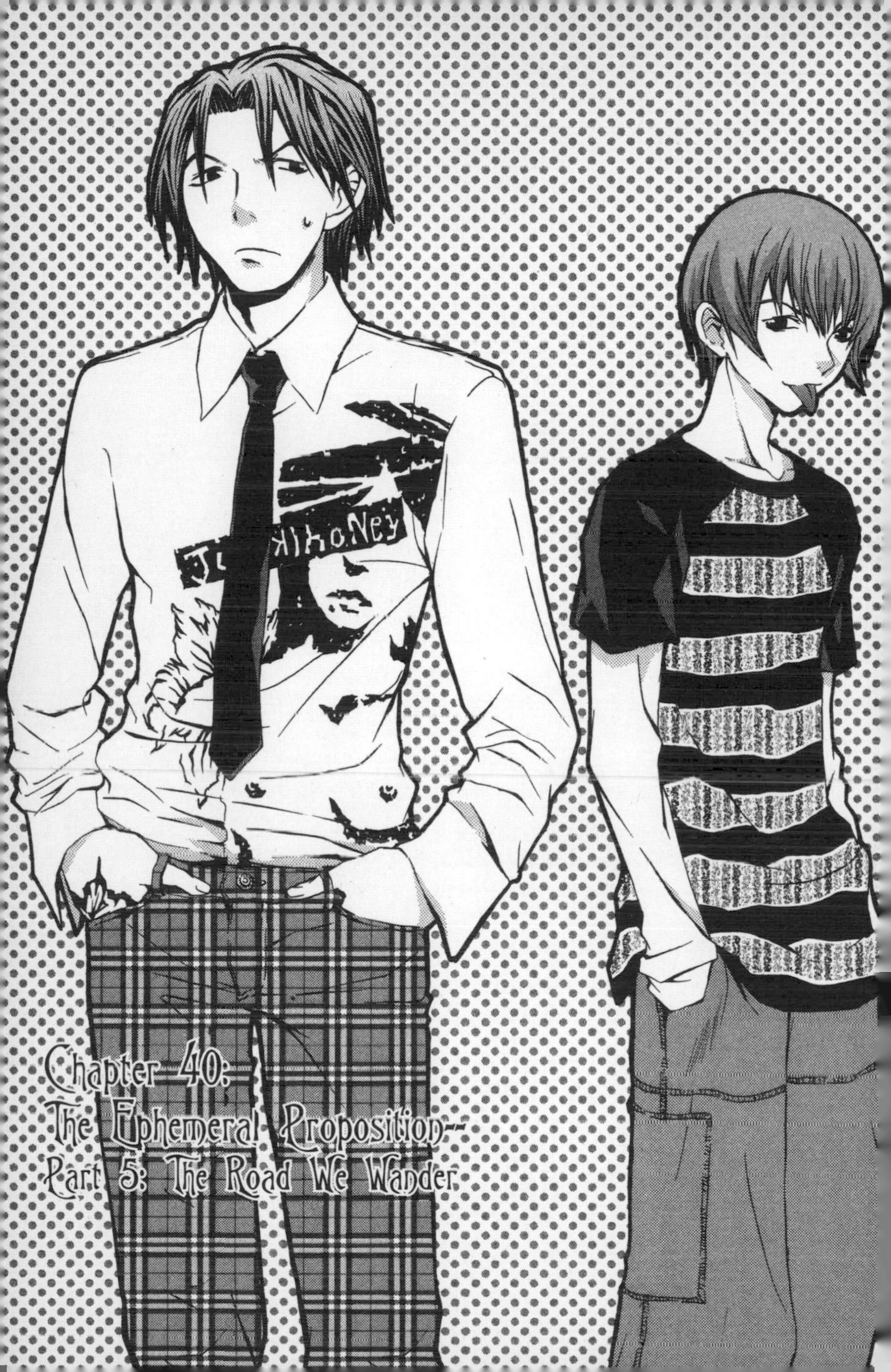

Chapter 40: The Ephemeral Proposition--Part 5: The Road We Wander

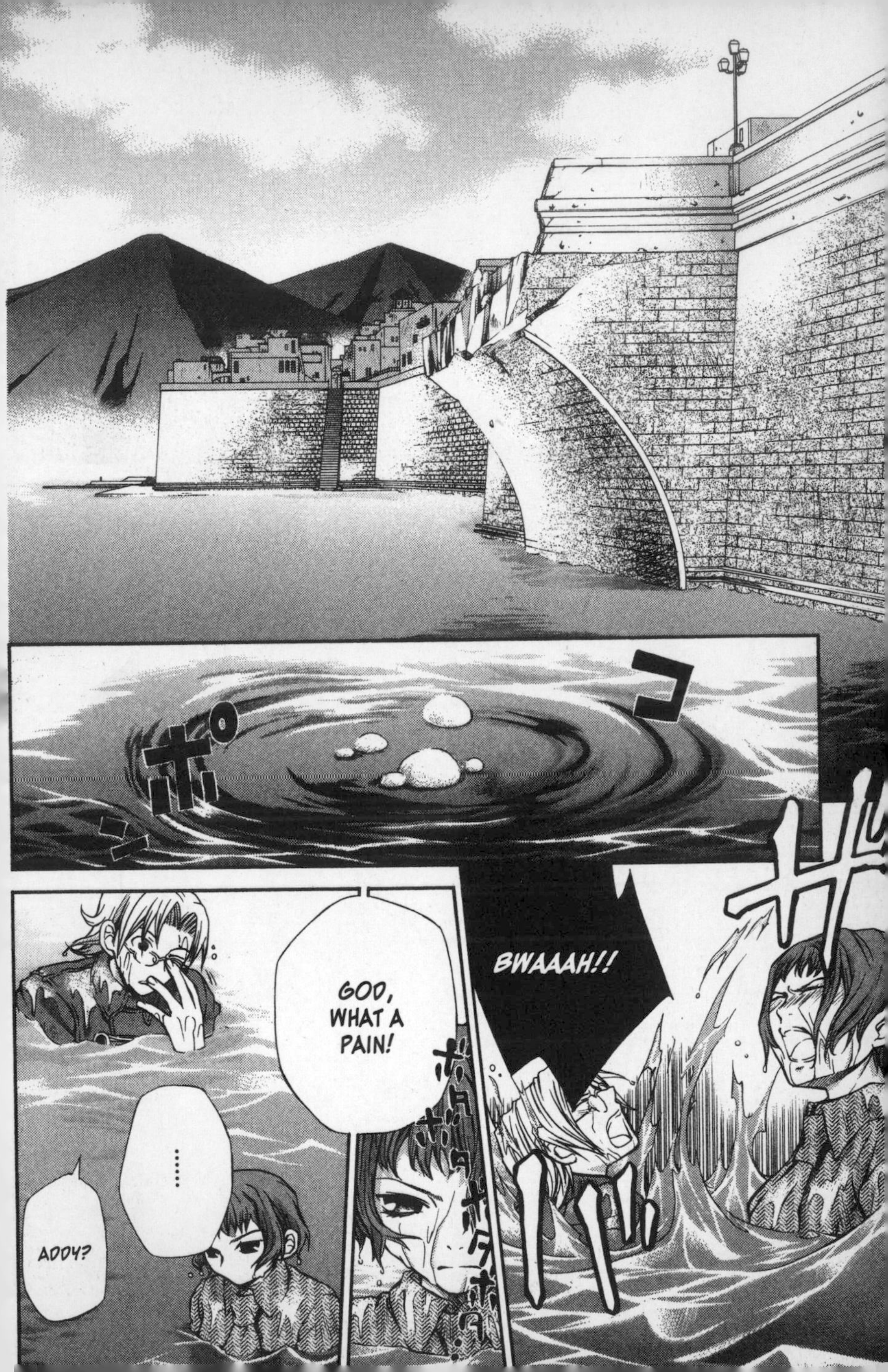
BWAAAH!!
GOD, WHAT A PAIN!
......
ADDY?

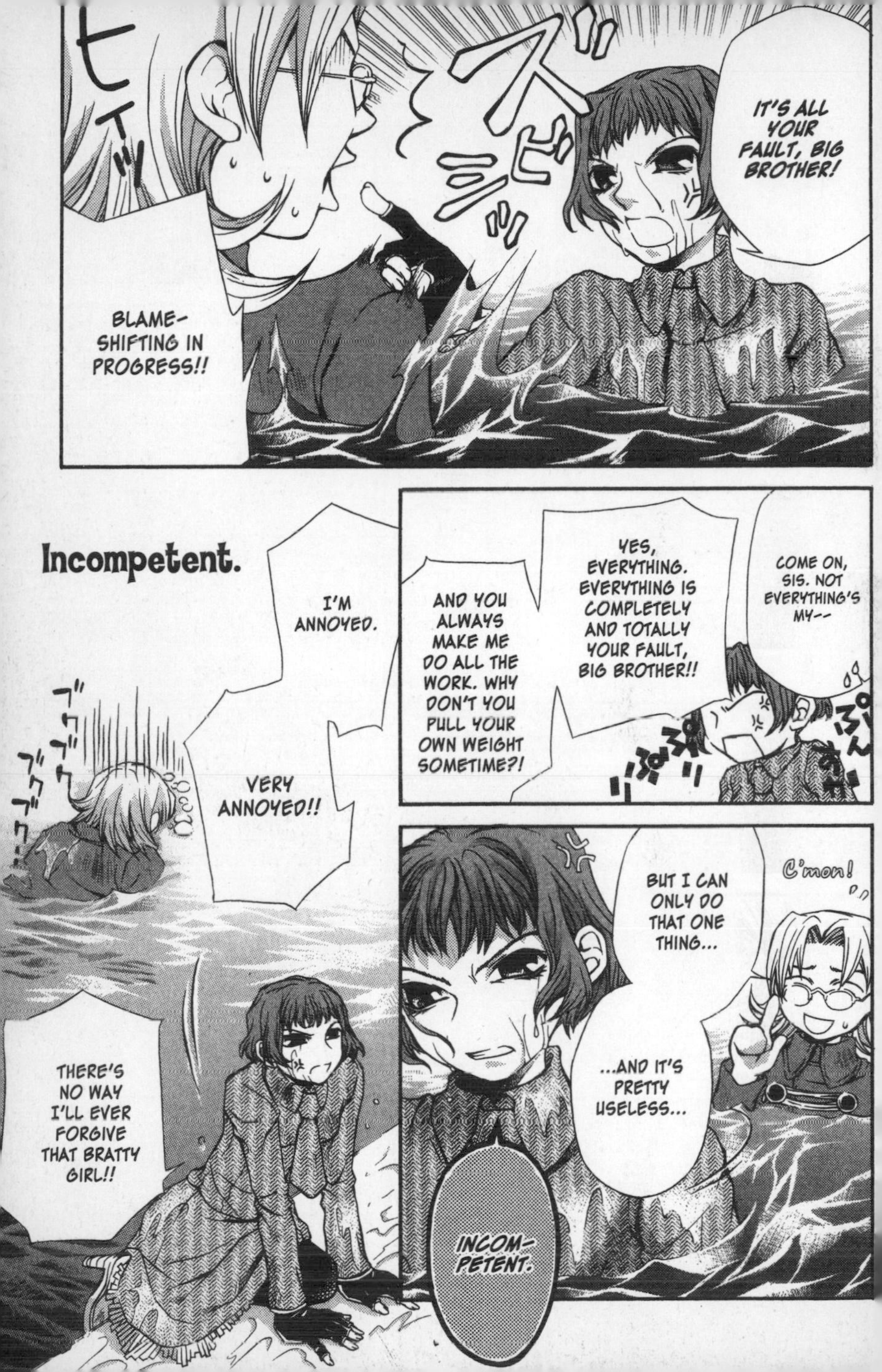
IT'S ALL YOUR FAULT, BIG BROTHER!
BLAME-SHIFTING IN PROGRESS!!
COME ON, SIS. NOT EVERYTHING'S MY--
YES, EVERYTHING. EVERYTHING IS COMPLETELY AND TOTALLY YOUR FAULT, BIG BROTHER!!
AND YOU ALWAYS MAKE ME DO ALL THE WORK. WHY DON'T YOU PULL YOUR OWN WEIGHT SOMETIME?!
C'mon!
BUT I CAN ONLY DO THAT ONE THING...
...AND IT'S PRETTY USELESS...
INCOMPETENT.
Incompetent.
I'M ANNOYED.
VERY ANNOYED!!
THERE'S NO WAY I'LL EVER FORGIVE THAT BRATTY GIRL!!

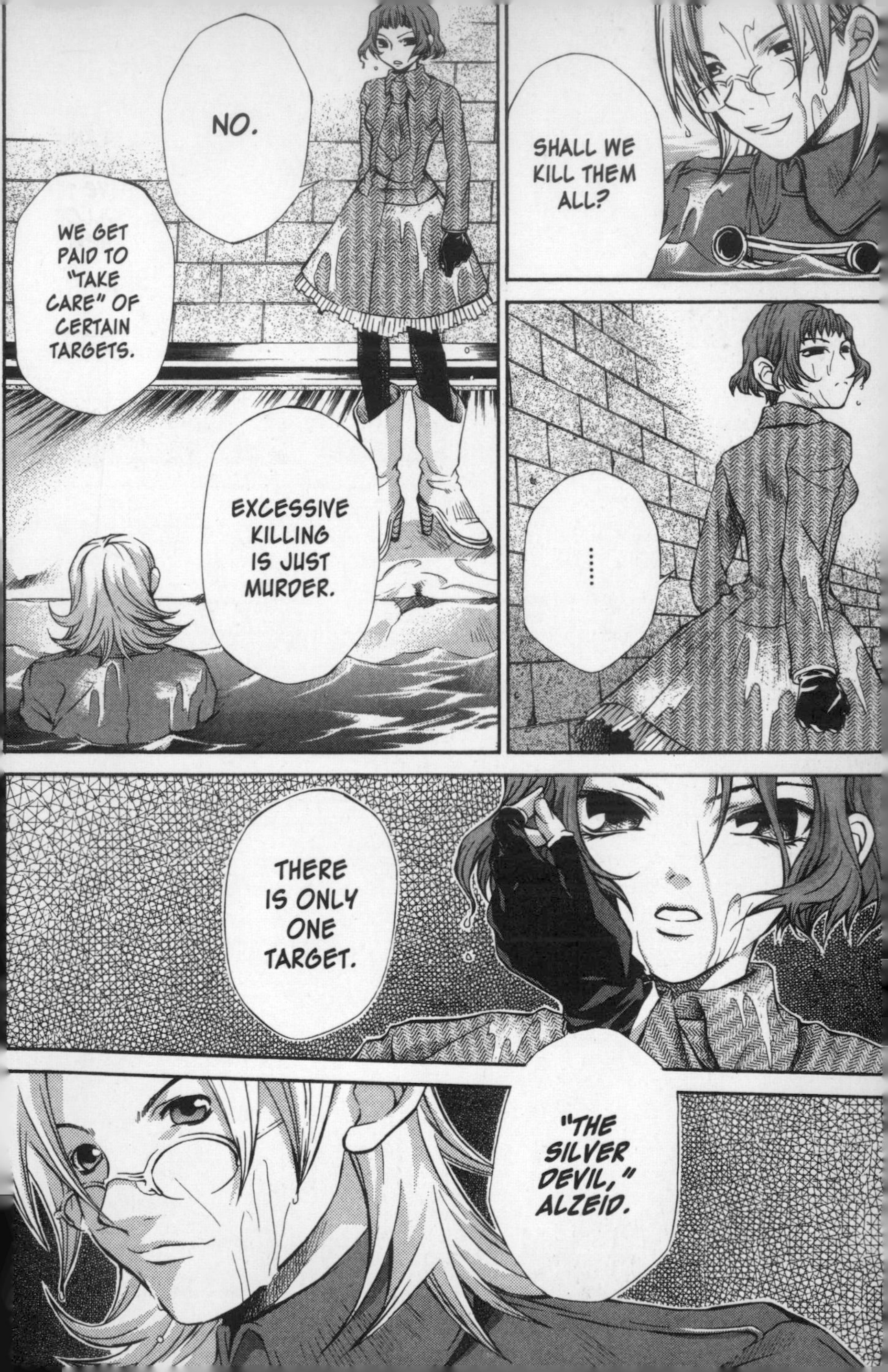
SHALL WE KILL THEM ALL?
......
NO.
WE GET PAID TO "TAKE CARE" OF CERTAIN TARGETS.
EXCESSIVE KILLING IS JUST MURDER.
THERE IS ONLY ONE TARGET.
"THE SILVER DEVIL," ALZEID.

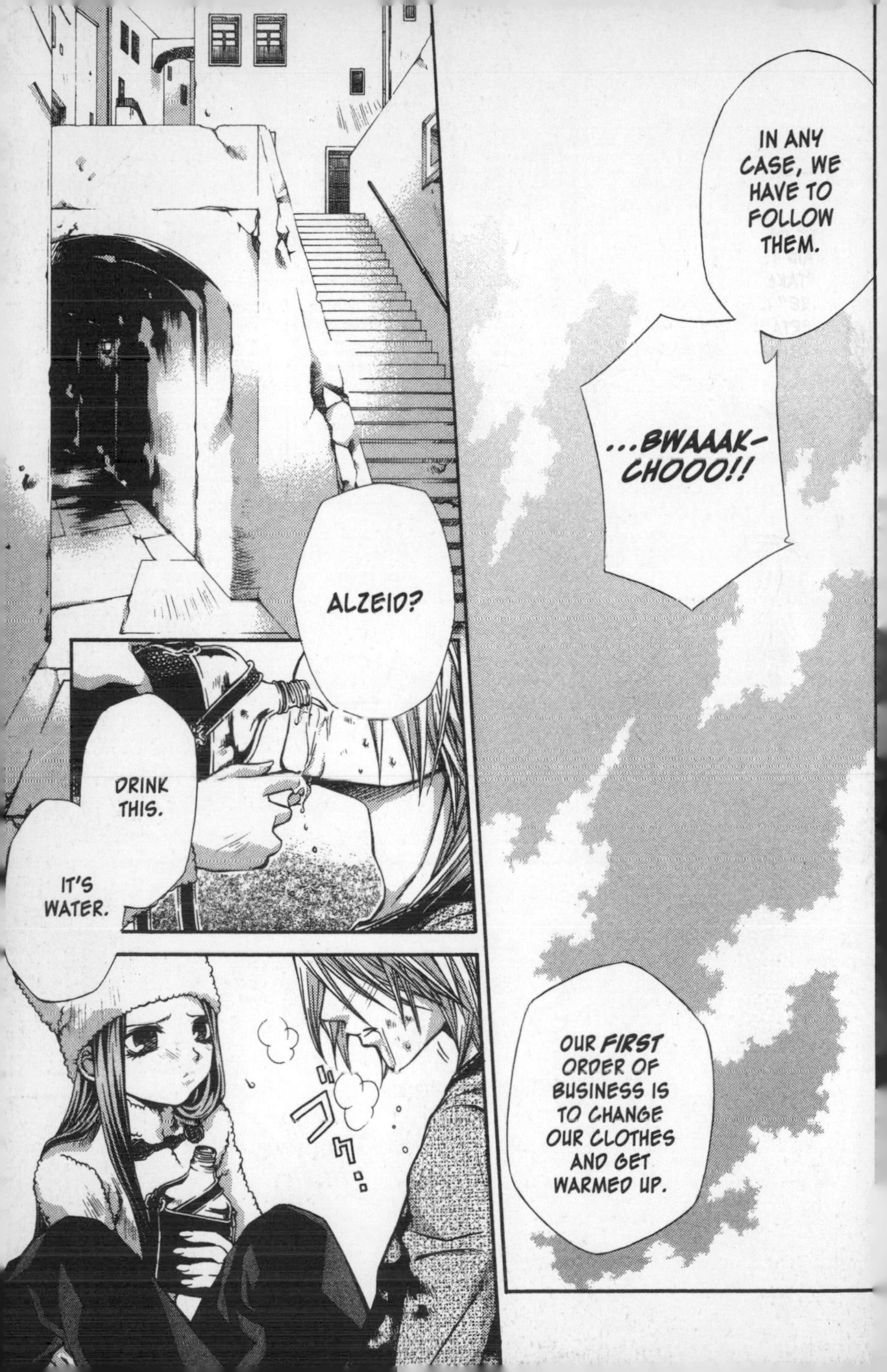
IN ANY CASE, WE HAVE TO FOLLOW THEM.
...BWAAAK-CHOOO!!
OUR *FIRST* ORDER OF BUSINESS IS TO CHANGE OUR CLOTHES AND GET WARMED UP.
ALZEID?
DRINK THIS.
IT'S WATER.

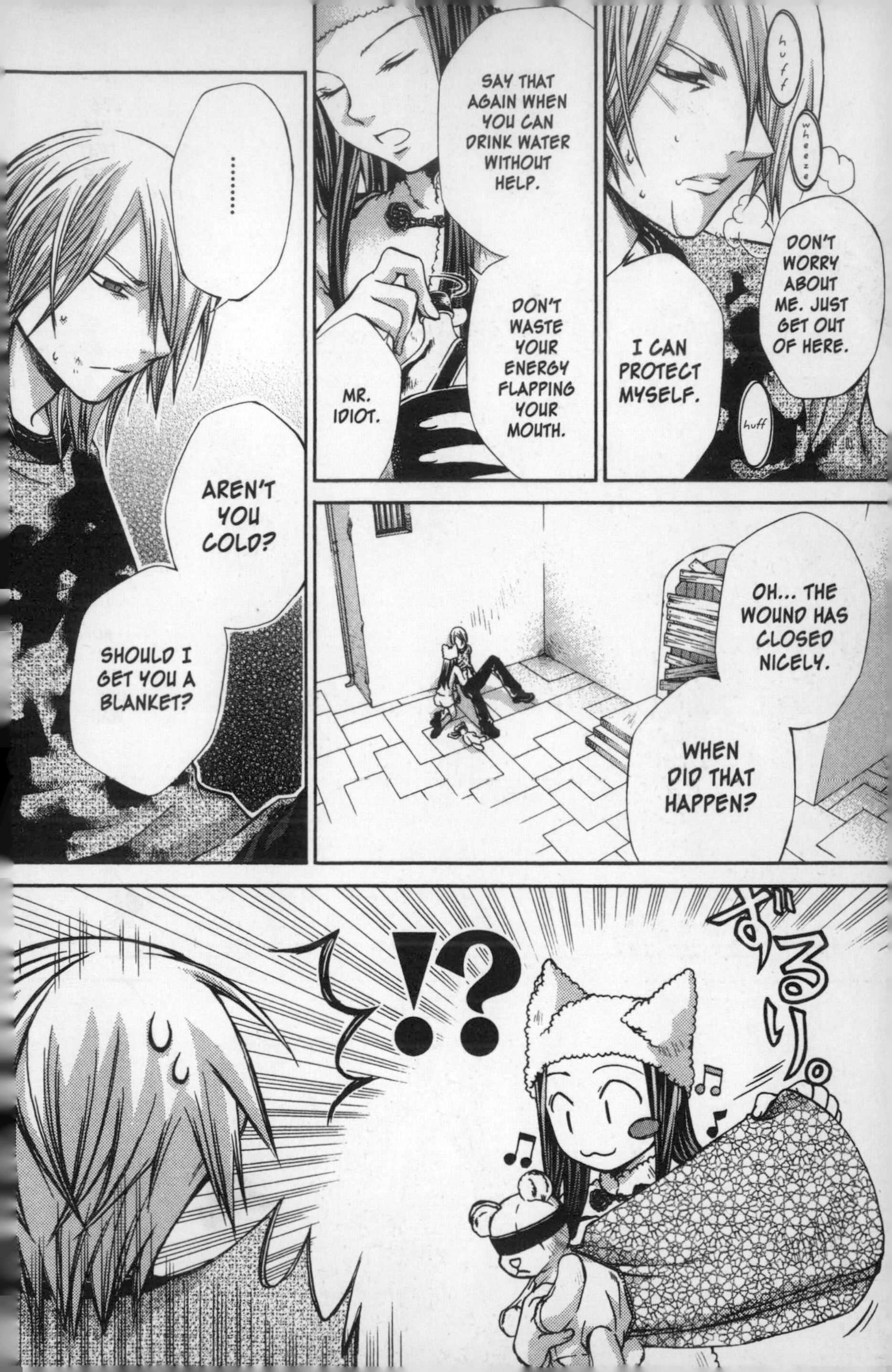
huff
wheeze
DON'T WORRY ABOUT ME. JUST GET OUT OF HERE.
huff
I CAN PROTECT MYSELF.
SAY THAT AGAIN WHEN YOU CAN DRINK WATER WITHOUT HELP.
DON'T WASTE YOUR ENERGY FLAPPING YOUR MOUTH.
MR. IDIOT.
OH... THE WOUND HAS CLOSED NICELY.
WHEN DID THAT HAPPEN?
......
AREN'T YOU COLD?
SHOULD I GET YOU A BLANKET?
!?

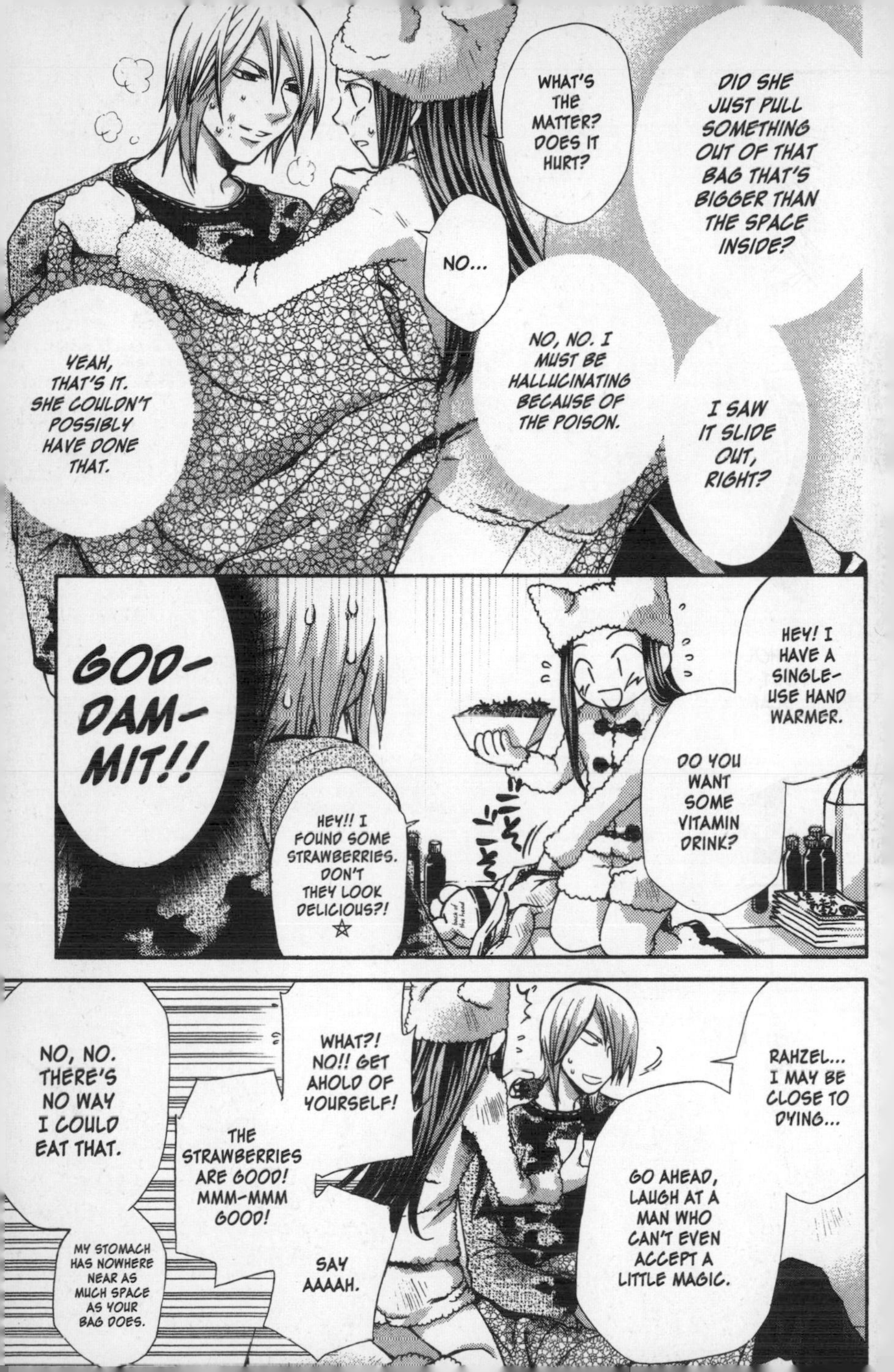
DID SHE JUST PULL SOMETHING OUT OF THAT BAG THAT'S BIGGER THAN THE SPACE INSIDE?
WHAT'S THE MATTER? DOES IT HURT?
NO...
I SAW IT SLIDE OUT, RIGHT?
NO, NO. I MUST BE HALLUCINATING BECAUSE OF THE POISON.
YEAH, THAT'S IT. SHE COULDN'T POSSIBLY HAVE DONE THAT.
HEY! I HAVE A SINGLE-USE HAND WARMER.
DO YOU WANT SOME VITAMIN DRINK?
HEY!! I FOUND SOME STRAWBERRIES. DON'T THEY LOOK DELICIOUS?! ☆
GOD-DAM-MIT!!
RAHZEL... I MAY BE CLOSE TO DYING...
GO AHEAD, LAUGH AT A MAN WHO CAN'T EVEN ACCEPT A LITTLE MAGIC.
WHAT?! NO!! GET AHOLD OF YOURSELF!
THE STRAWBERRIES ARE GOOD! MMM-MMM GOOD!
SAY AAAAH.
NO, NO. THERE'S NO WAY I COULD EAT THAT.
MY STOMACH HAS NOWHERE NEAR AS MUCH SPACE AS YOUR BAG DOES.

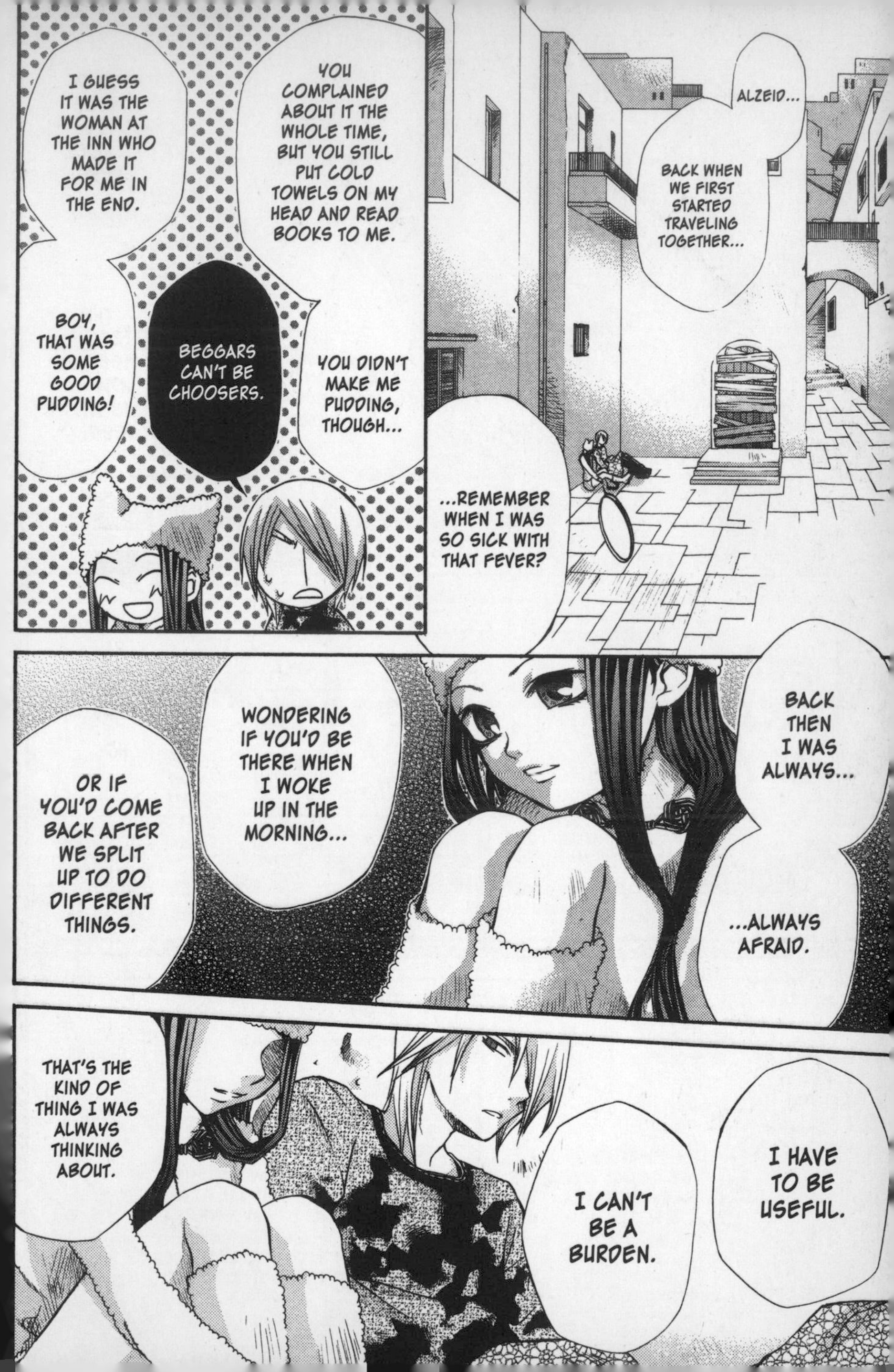
ALZEID...
BACK WHEN WE FIRST STARTED TRAVELING TOGETHER...
...REMEMBER WHEN I WAS SO SICK WITH THAT FEVER?
YOU COMPLAINED ABOUT IT THE WHOLE TIME, BUT YOU STILL PUT COLD TOWELS ON MY HEAD AND READ BOOKS TO ME.
I GUESS IT WAS THE WOMAN AT THE INN WHO MADE IT FOR ME IN THE END.
YOU DIDN'T MAKE ME PUDDING, THOUGH...
BEGGARS CAN'T BE CHOOSERS.
BOY, THAT WAS SOME GOOD PUDDING!
BACK THEN I WAS ALWAYS...
...ALWAYS AFRAID.
WONDERING IF YOU'D BE THERE WHEN I WOKE UP IN THE MORNING...
OR IF YOU'D COME BACK AFTER WE SPLIT UP TO DO DIFFERENT THINGS.
I HAVE TO BE USEFUL.
I CAN'T BE A BURDEN.
THAT'S THE KIND OF THING I WAS ALWAYS THINKING ABOUT.

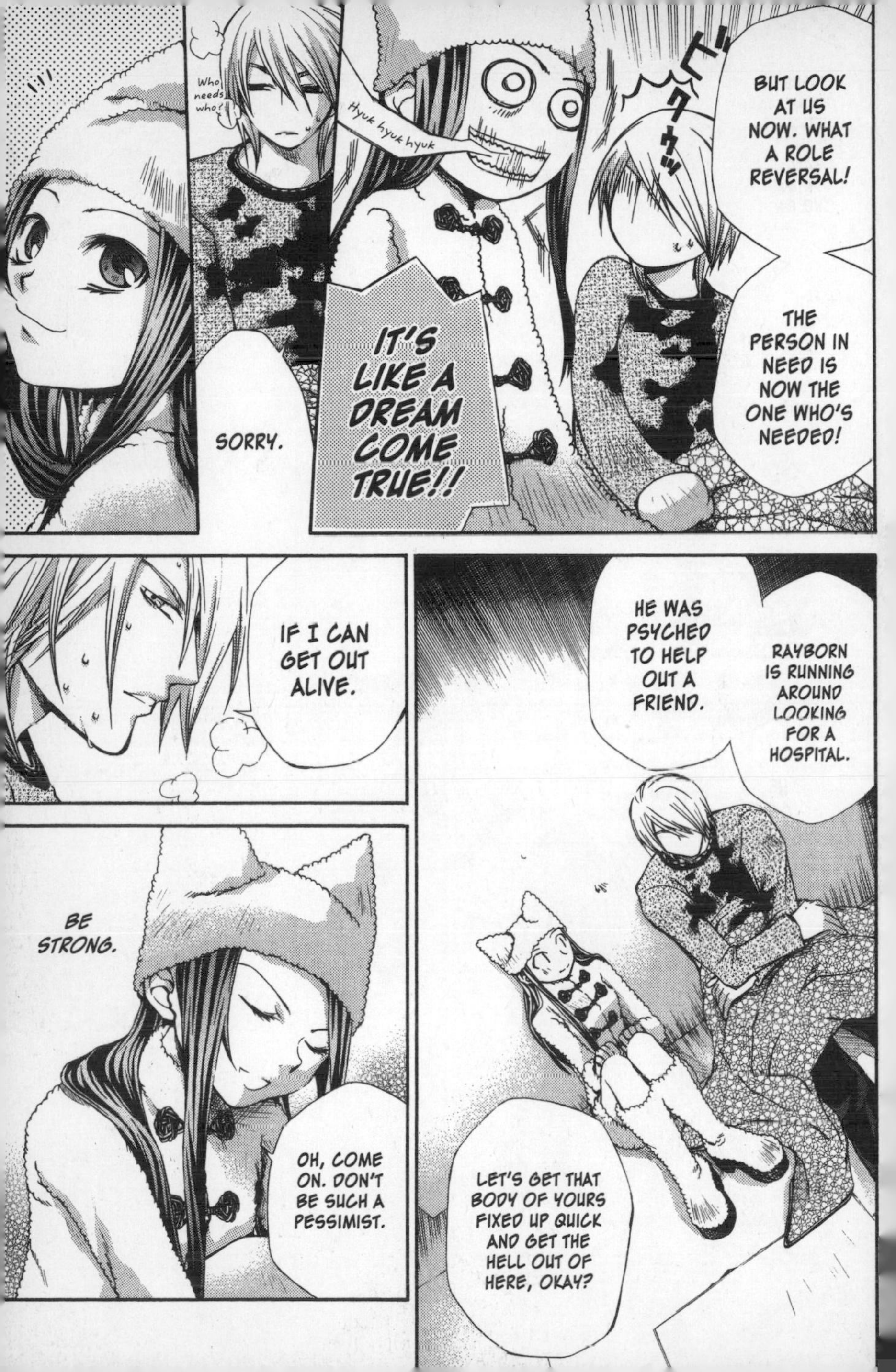
BUT LOOK AT US NOW. WHAT A ROLE REVERSAL!
THE PERSON IN NEED IS NOW THE ONE WHO'S NEEDED!
Hyuk hyuk hyuk
IT'S LIKE A DREAM COME TRUE!!
Who needs who?
SORRY.
RAYBORN IS RUNNING AROUND LOOKING FOR A HOSPITAL.
HE WAS PSYCHED TO HELP OUT A FRIEND.
LET'S GET THAT BODY OF YOURS FIXED UP QUICK AND GET THE HELL OUT OF HERE, OKAY?
IF I CAN GET OUT ALIVE.
OH, COME ON. DON'T BE SUCH A PESSIMIST.
BE STRONG.

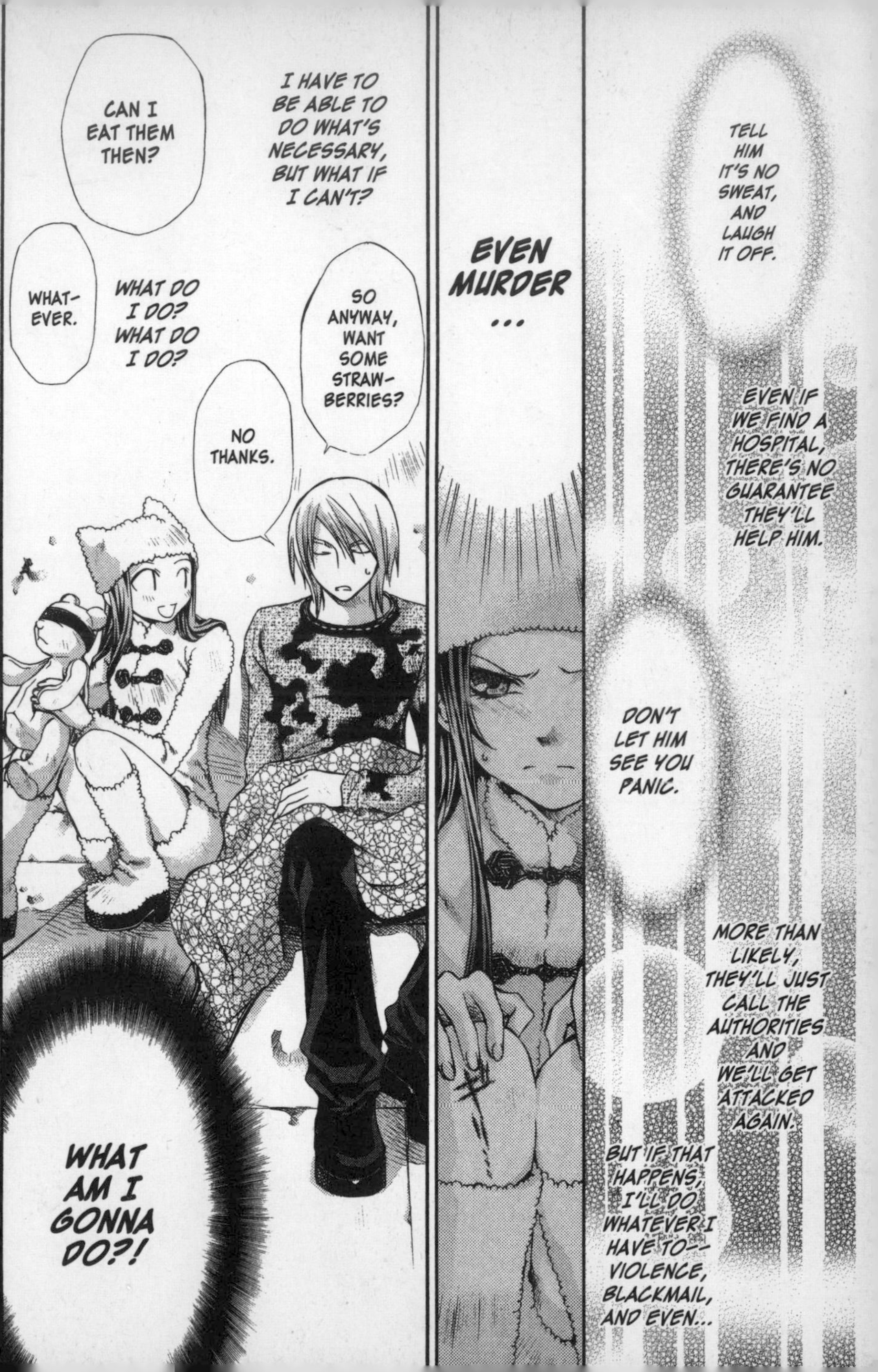
TELL HIM IT'S NO SWEAT, AND LAUGH IT OFF.
EVEN IF WE FIND A HOSPITAL, THERE'S NO GUARANTEE THEY'LL HELP HIM.
DON'T LET HIM SEE YOU PANIC.
MORE THAN LIKELY, THEY'LL JUST CALL THE AUTHORITIES AND WE'LL GET ATTACKED AGAIN.
BUT IF THAT HAPPENS, I'LL DO WHATEVER I HAVE TO-- VIOLENCE, BLACKMAIL, AND EVEN...
EVEN MURDER...
I HAVE TO BE ABLE TO DO WHAT'S NECESSARY, BUT WHAT IF I CAN'T?
SO ANYWAY, WANT SOME STRAWBERRIES?
NO THANKS.
CAN I EAT THEM THEN?
WHAT-EVER.
WHAT DO I DO? WHAT DO I DO?
WHAT AM I GONNA DO?!

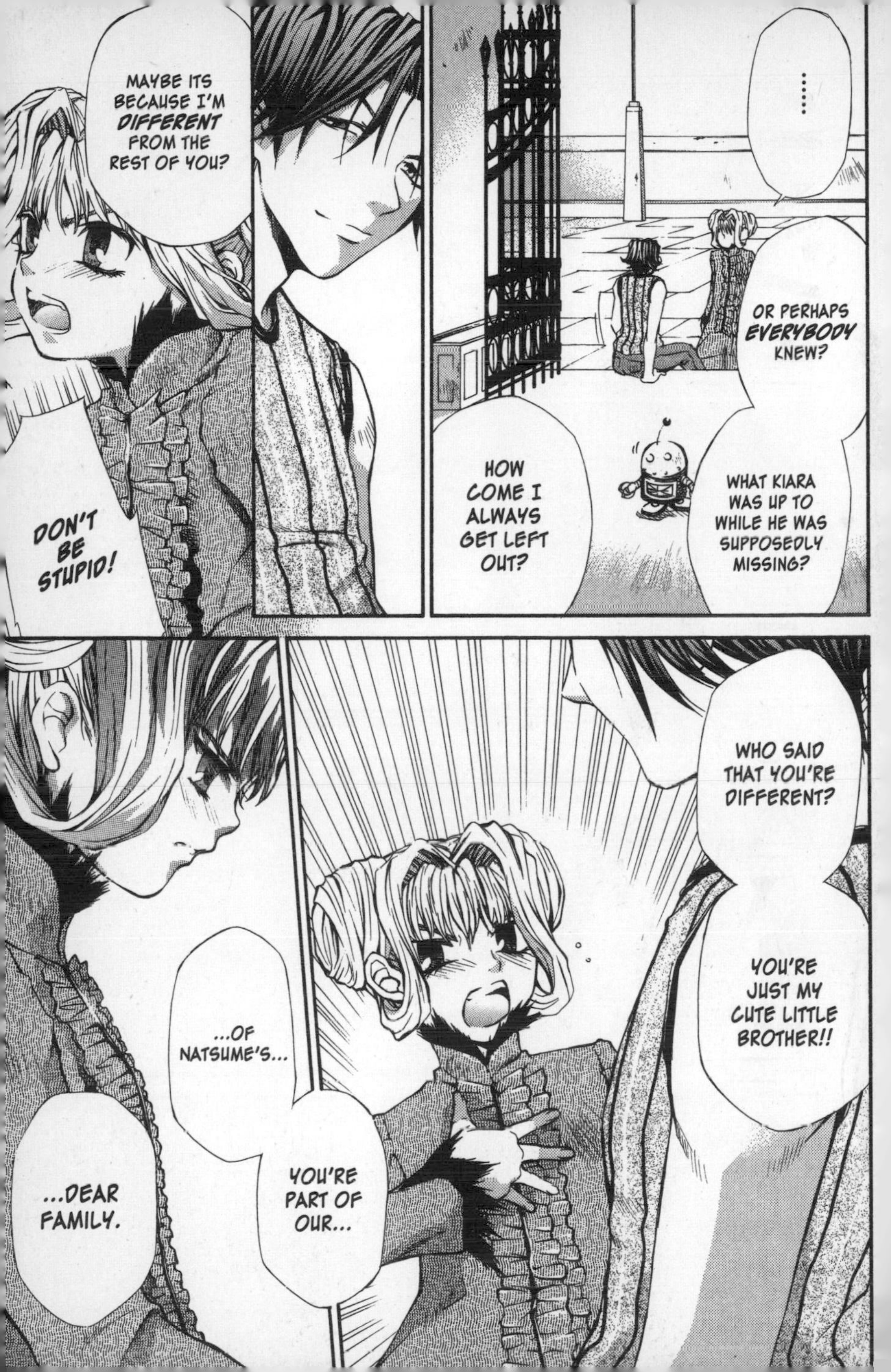
......
OR PERHAPS EVERYBODY KNEW?
WHAT KIARA WAS UP TO WHILE HE WAS SUPPOSEDLY MISSING?
HOW COME I ALWAYS GET LEFT OUT?
MAYBE ITS BECAUSE I'M DIFFERENT FROM THE REST OF YOU?
DON'T BE STUPID!
WHO SAID THAT YOU'RE DIFFERENT?
YOU'RE JUST MY CUTE LITTLE BROTHER!!
YOU'RE PART OF OUR...
...OF NATSUME'S...
...DEAR FAMILY.

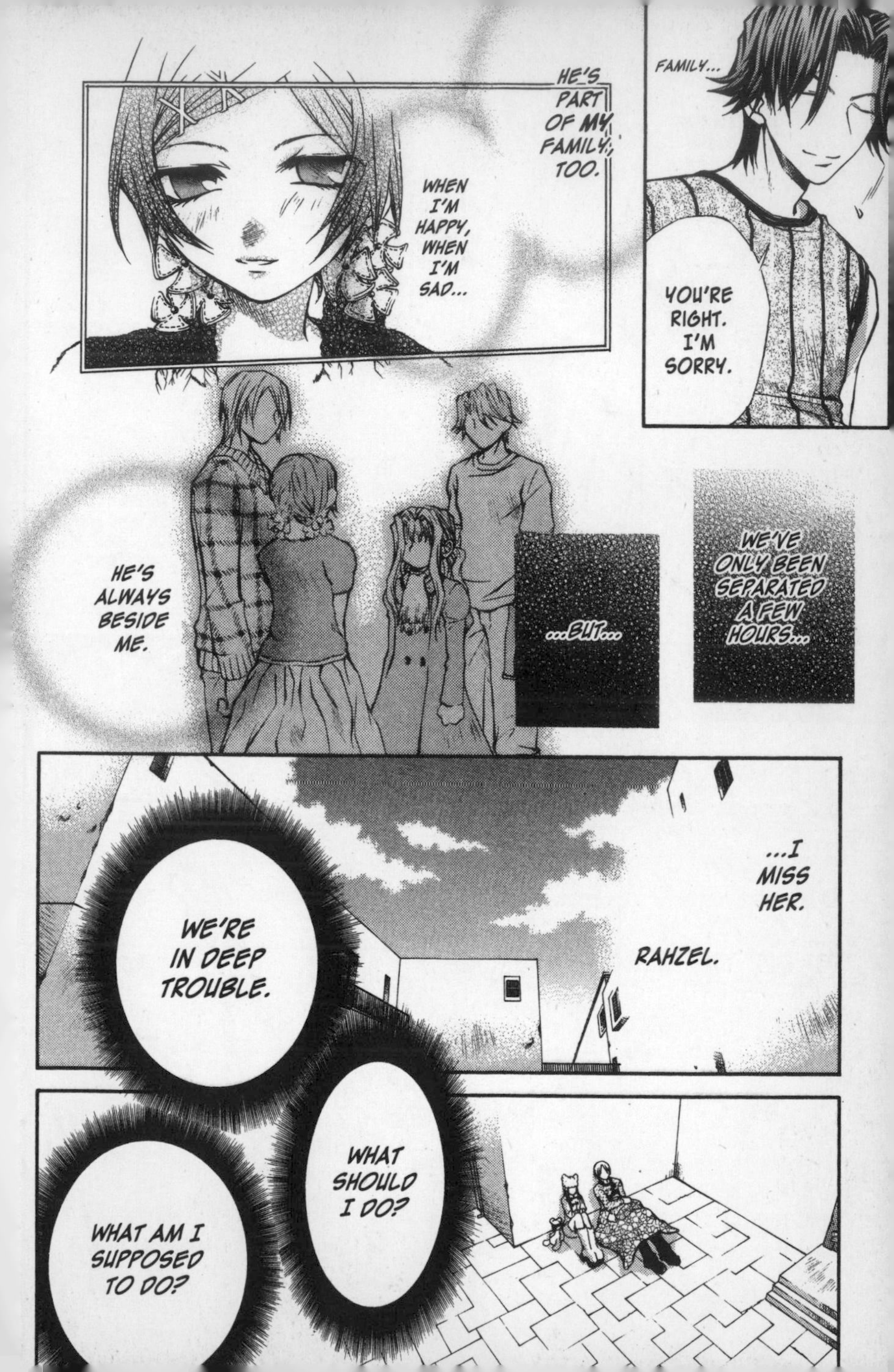
FAMILY...
YOU'RE RIGHT. I'M SORRY.
HE'S PART OF MY FAMILY, TOO.
WHEN I'M HAPPY, WHEN I'M SAD...
WE'VE ONLY BEEN SEPARATED A FEW HOURS...
...BUT...
HE'S ALWAYS BESIDE ME.
...I MISS HER.
RAHZEL.
WE'RE IN DEEP TROUBLE.
WHAT SHOULD I DO?
WHAT AM I SUPPOSED TO DO?

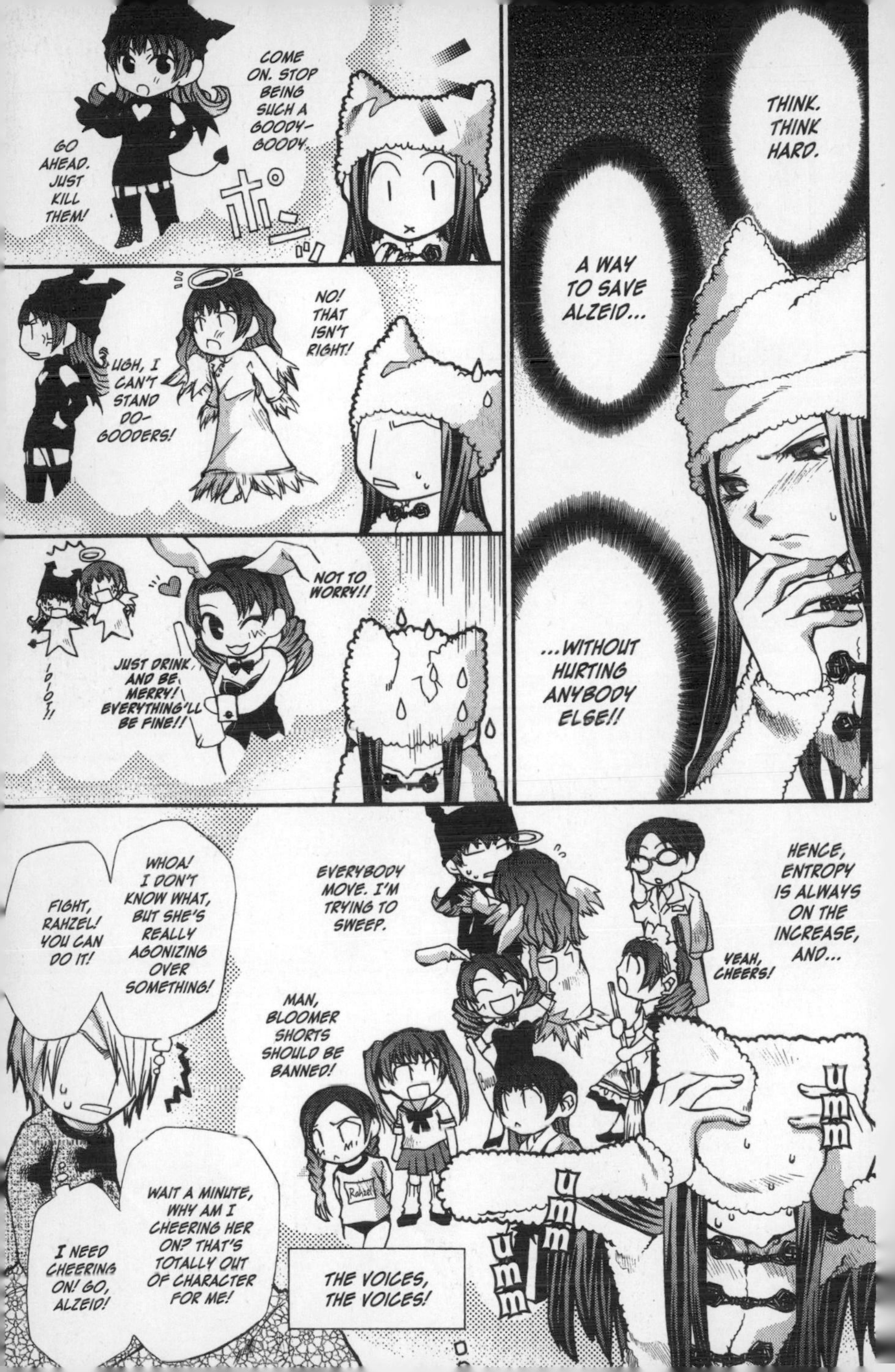
THINK. THINK HARD.
A WAY TO SAVE ALZEID...
...WITHOUT HURTING ANYBODY ELSE!!
COME ON. STOP BEING SUCH A GOODY-GOODY.
GO AHEAD. JUST KILL THEM!
ポー
NO! THAT ISN'T RIGHT!
UGH, I CAN'T STAND DO-GOODERS!
NOT TO WORRY!!
JUST DRINK AND BE MERRY! EVERYTHING'LL BE FINE!!
IDIOT!!
HENCE, ENTROPY IS ALWAYS ON THE INCREASE, AND...
YEAH, CHEERS!
EVERYBODY MOVE. I'M TRYING TO SWEEP.
MAN, BLOOMER SHORTS SHOULD BE BANNED!
WHOA! I DON'T KNOW WHAT, BUT SHE'S REALLY AGONIZING OVER SOMETHING!
FIGHT, RAHZEL! YOU CAN DO IT!
WAIT A MINUTE, WHY AM I CHEERING HER ON? THAT'S TOTALLY OUT OF CHARACTER FOR ME!
I NEED CHEERING ON! GO, ALZEID!
THE VOICES, THE VOICES!
UMM
UMM
UMM
Rahzel

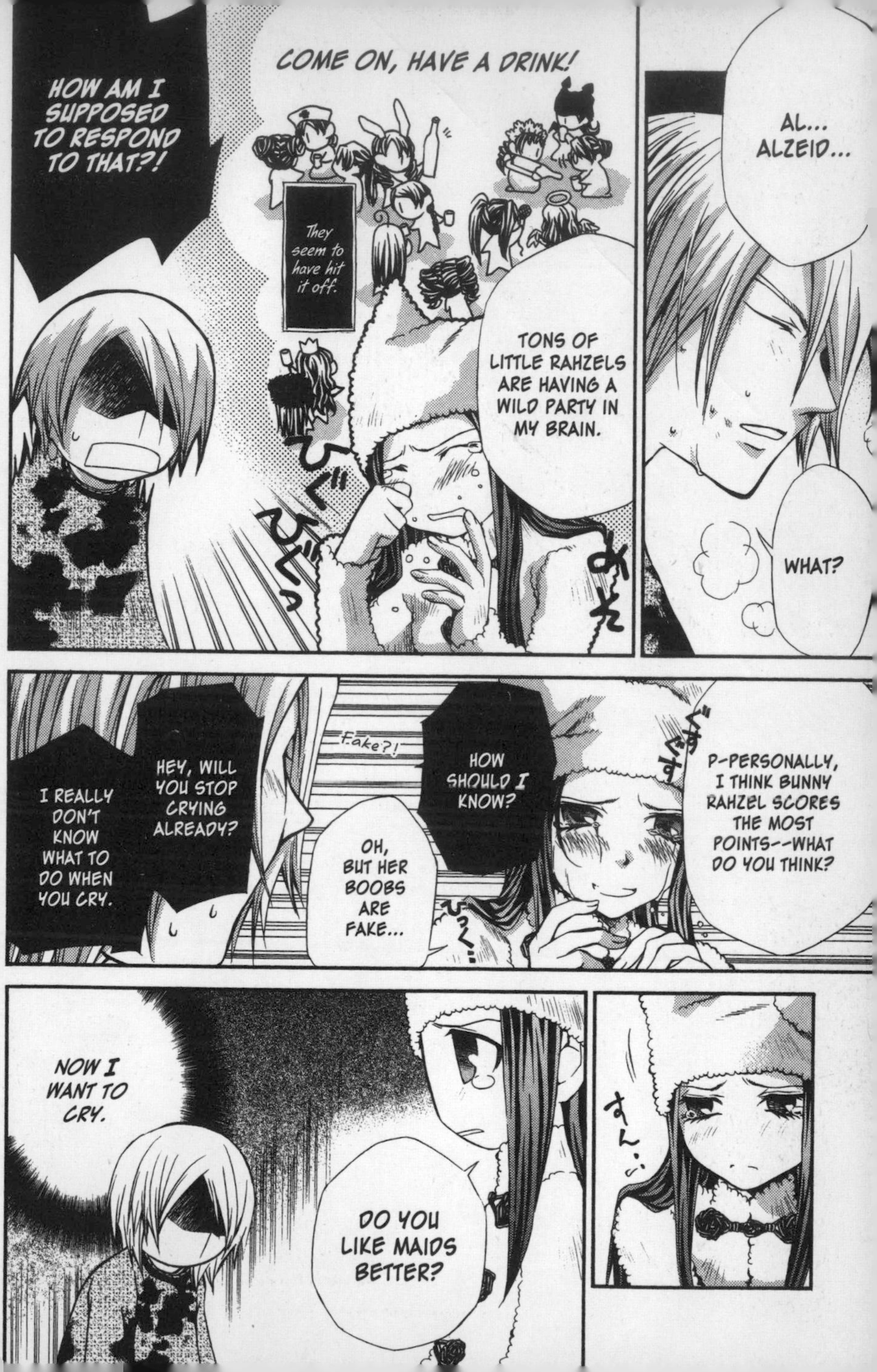
AL... ALZEID...
WHAT?
TONS OF LITTLE RAHZELS ARE HAVING A WILD PARTY IN MY BRAIN.
COME ON, HAVE A DRINK!
They seem to have hit it off.
HOW AM I SUPPOSED TO RESPOND TO THAT?!
P-PERSONALLY, I THINK BUNNY RAHZEL SCORES THE MOST POINTS--WHAT DO YOU THINK?
ぐすぐす
HOW SHOULD I KNOW?
OH, BUT HER BOOBS ARE FAKE...
Fake?!
HEY, WILL YOU STOP CRYING ALREADY?
I REALLY DON'T KNOW WHAT TO DO WHEN YOU CRY.
すん…
DO YOU LIKE MAIDS BETTER?
NOW I WANT TO CRY.

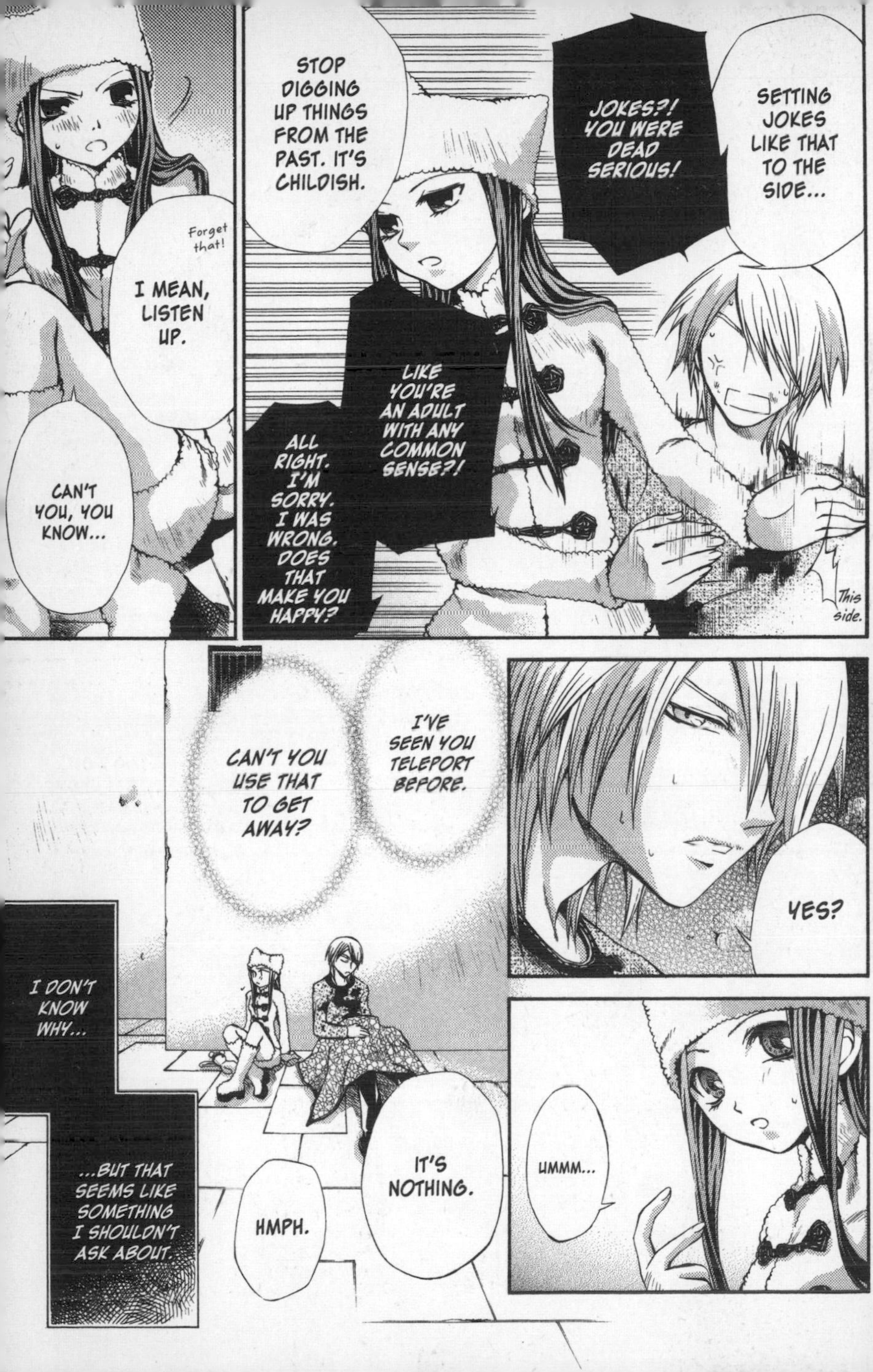
SETTING JOKES LIKE THAT TO THE SIDE...
JOKES?! YOU WERE DEAD SERIOUS!
STOP DIGGING UP THINGS FROM THE PAST. IT'S CHILDISH.
LIKE YOU'RE AN ADULT WITH ANY COMMON SENSE?!
ALL RIGHT. I'M SORRY. I WAS WRONG. DOES THAT MAKE YOU HAPPY?
This side.
Forget that!
I MEAN, LISTEN UP.
CAN'T YOU, YOU KNOW...
YES?
UMMM...
I'VE SEEN YOU TELEPORT BEFORE.
CAN'T YOU USE THAT TO GET AWAY?
IT'S NOTHING.
HMPH.
I DON'T KNOW WHY...
...BUT THAT SEEMS LIKE SOMETHING I SHOULDN'T ASK ABOUT.

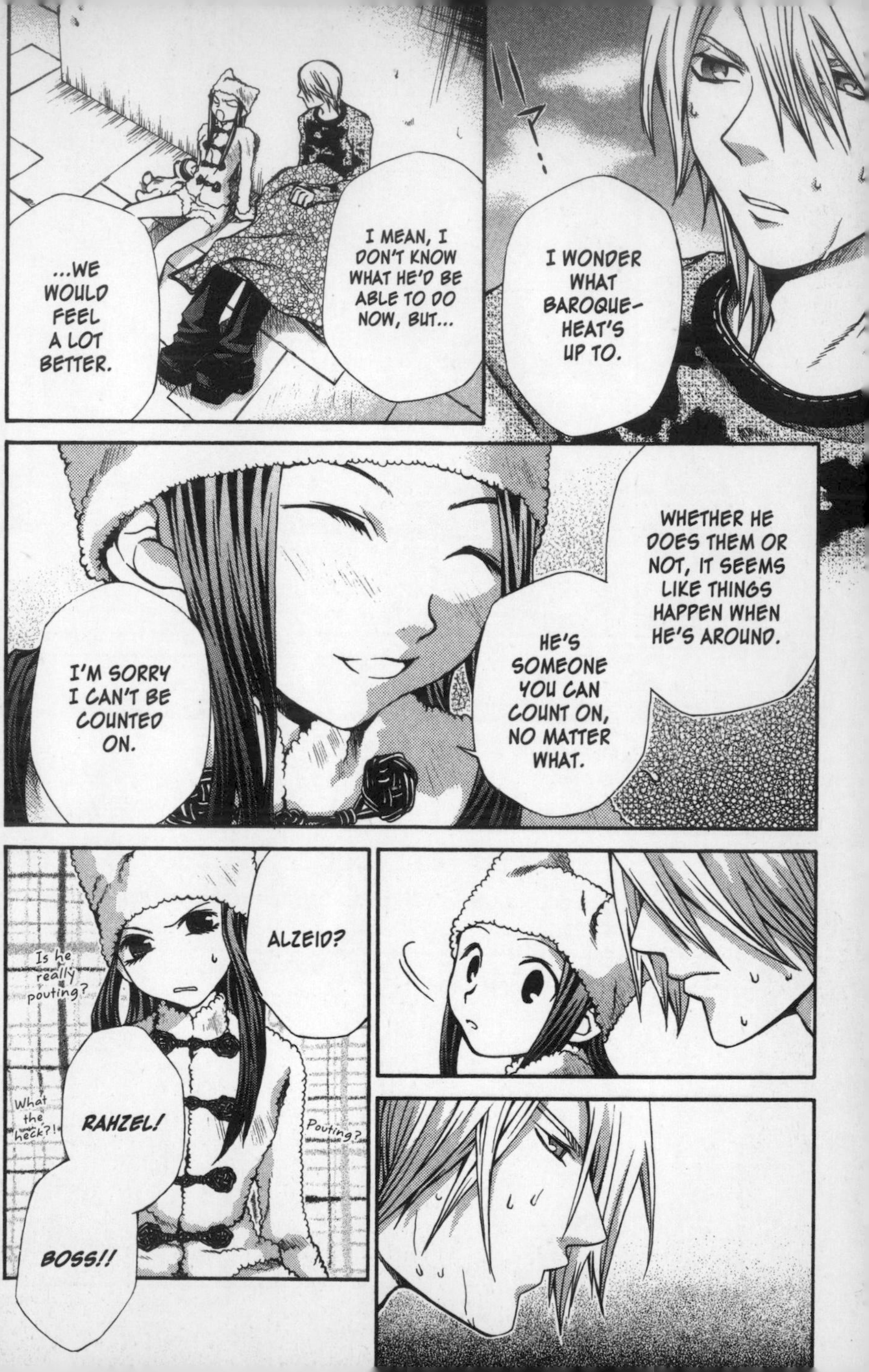
I WONDER WHAT BAROQUE-HEAT'S UP TO.
I MEAN, I DON'T KNOW WHAT HE'D BE ABLE TO DO NOW, BUT...
...WE WOULD FEEL A LOT BETTER.
WHETHER HE DOES THEM OR NOT, IT SEEMS LIKE THINGS HAPPEN WHEN HE'S AROUND.
HE'S SOMEONE YOU CAN COUNT ON, NO MATTER WHAT.
I'M SORRY I CAN'T BE COUNTED ON.
ALZEID?
Is he really pouting?
Pouting?
RAHZEL!
What the heck?!
BOSS!!

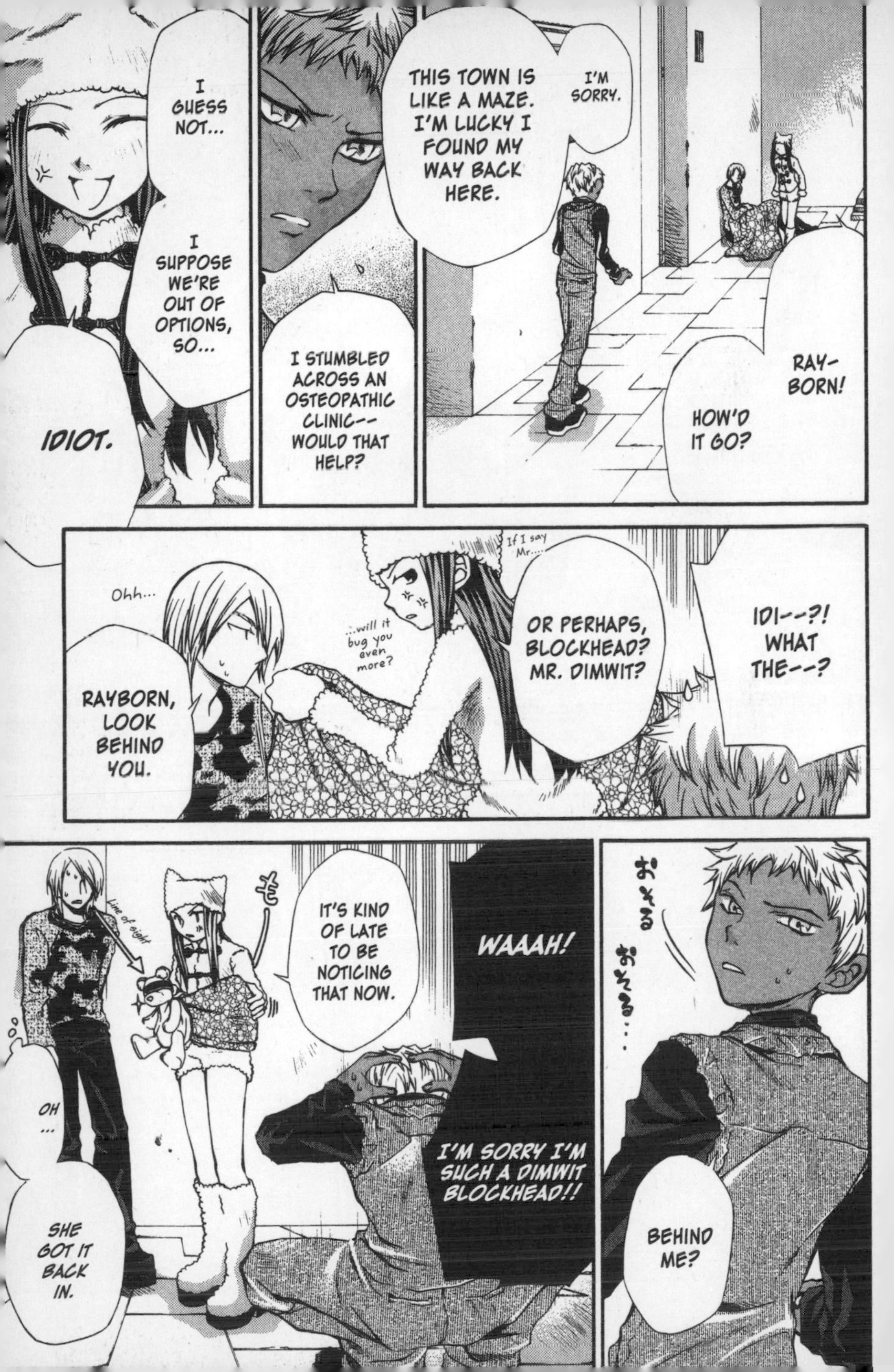

RAY-BORN!
HOW'D IT GO?
I'M SORRY.
THIS TOWN IS LIKE A MAZE. I'M LUCKY I FOUND MY WAY BACK HERE.
I STUMBLED ACROSS AN OSTEOPATHIC CLINIC--WOULD THAT HELP?
I GUESS NOT...
I SUPPOSE WE'RE OUT OF OPTIONS, SO...
IDIOT.
IDI--?! WHAT THE--?
If I say Mr....
...will it bug you even more?
OR PERHAPS, BLOCKHEAD? MR. DIMWIT?
Ohh...
RAYBORN, LOOK BEHIND YOU.
おそる おそる...
BEHIND ME?
WAAAH!
I'M SORRY I'M SUCH A DIMWIT BLOCKHEAD!!
IT'S KIND OF LATE TO BE NOTICING THAT NOW.
も
Line of sight
OH ...
SHE GOT IT BACK IN.

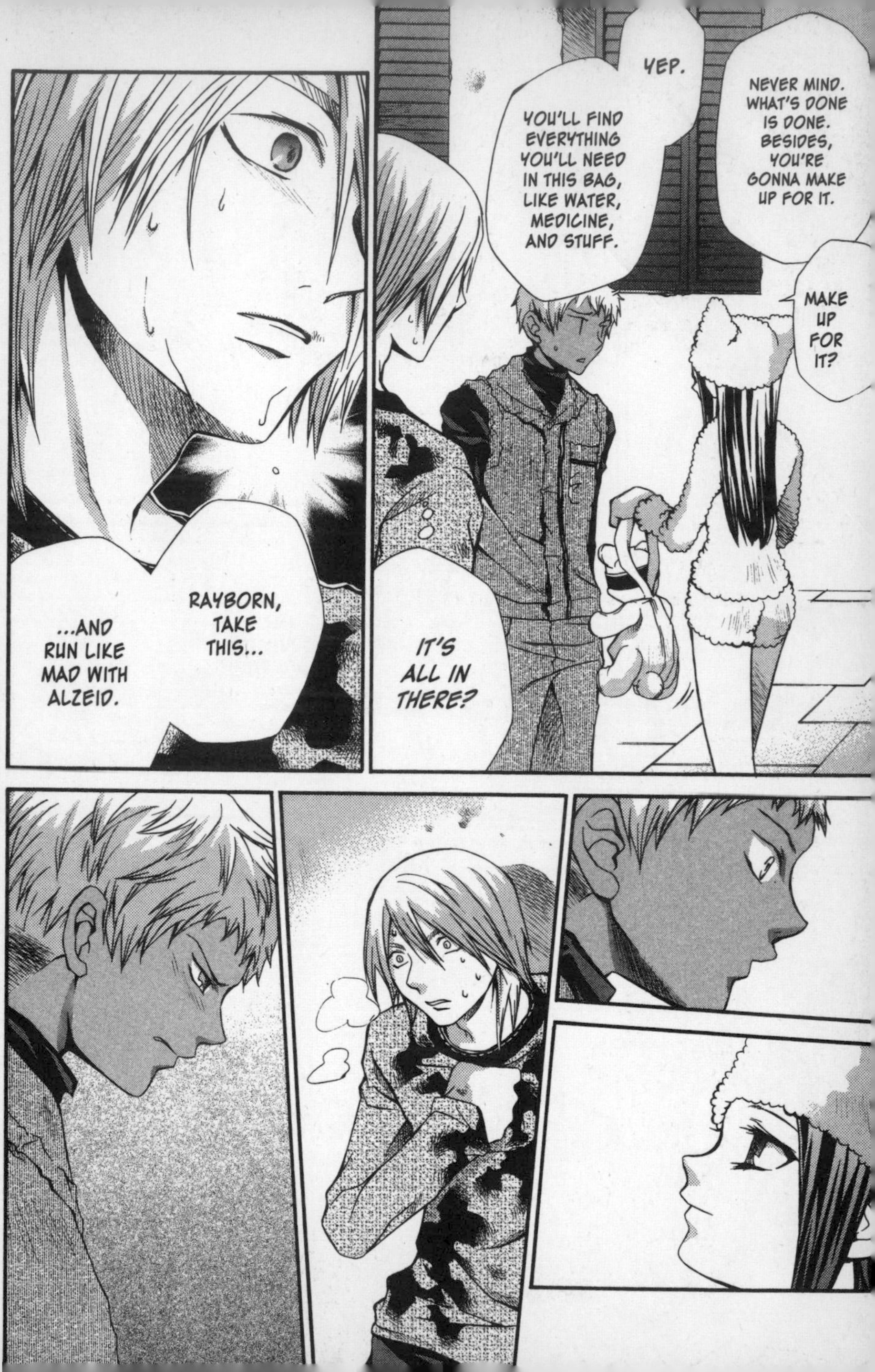
NEVER MIND. WHAT'S DONE IS DONE. BESIDES, YOU'RE GONNA MAKE UP FOR IT.
YEP.
YOU'LL FIND EVERYTHING YOU'LL NEED IN THIS BAG, LIKE WATER, MEDICINE, AND STUFF.
MAKE UP FOR IT?
IT'S ALL IN THERE?
RAYBORN, TAKE THIS...
...AND RUN LIKE MAD WITH ALZEID.

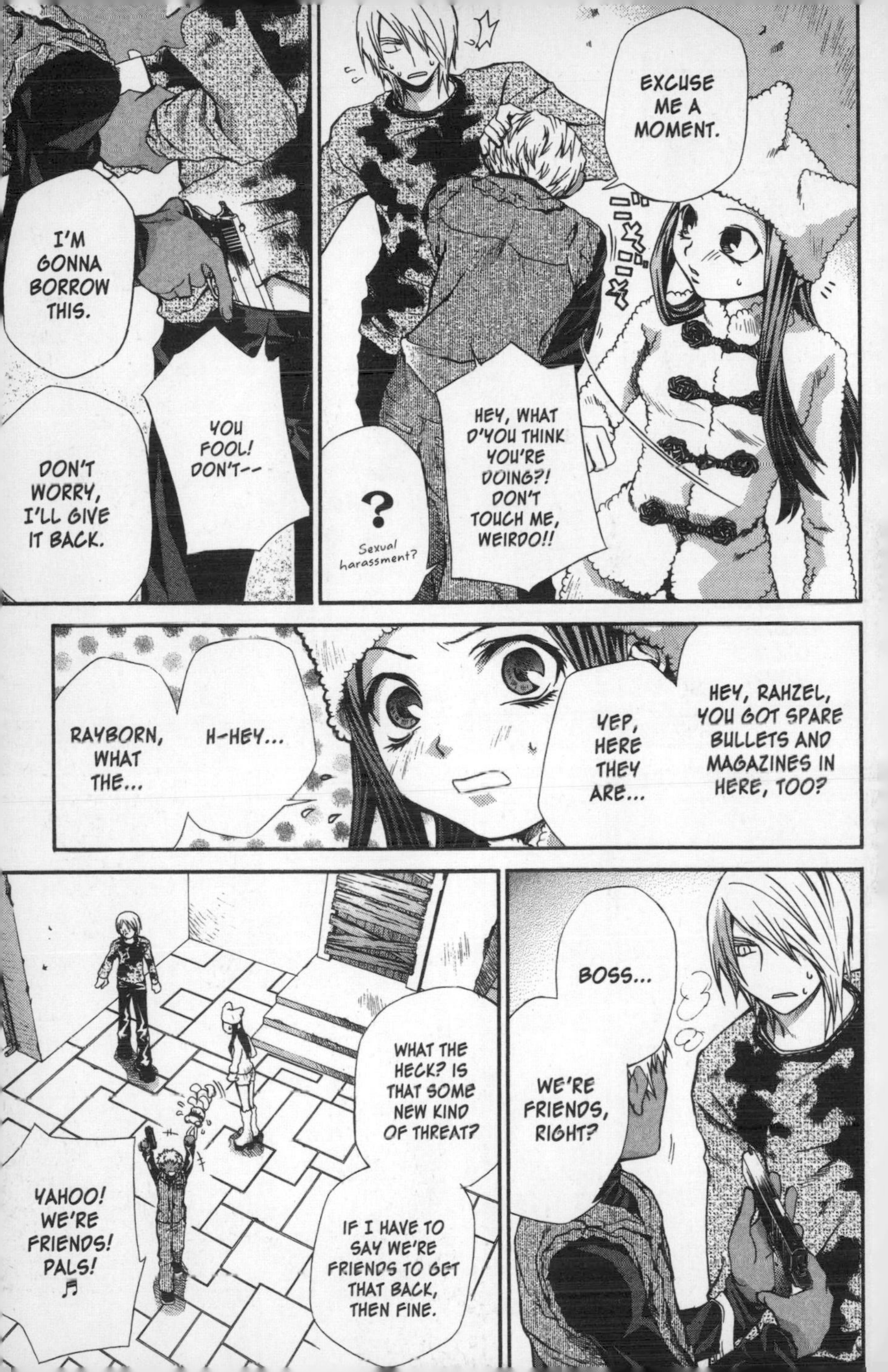
EXCUSE ME A MOMENT.
HEY, WHAT D'YOU THINK YOU'RE DOING?! DON'T TOUCH ME, WEIRDO!!
?
Sexual harassment?
I'M GONNA BORROW THIS.
YOU FOOL! DON'T--
DON'T WORRY, I'LL GIVE IT BACK.
HEY, RAHZEL, YOU GOT SPARE BULLETS AND MAGAZINES IN HERE, TOO?
YEP, HERE THEY ARE...
H-HEY...
RAYBORN, WHAT THE...
BOSS...
WE'RE FRIENDS, RIGHT?
WHAT THE HECK? IS THAT SOME NEW KIND OF THREAT?
IF I HAVE TO SAY WE'RE FRIENDS TO GET THAT BACK, THEN FINE.
YAHOO! WE'RE FRIENDS! PALS! ♬

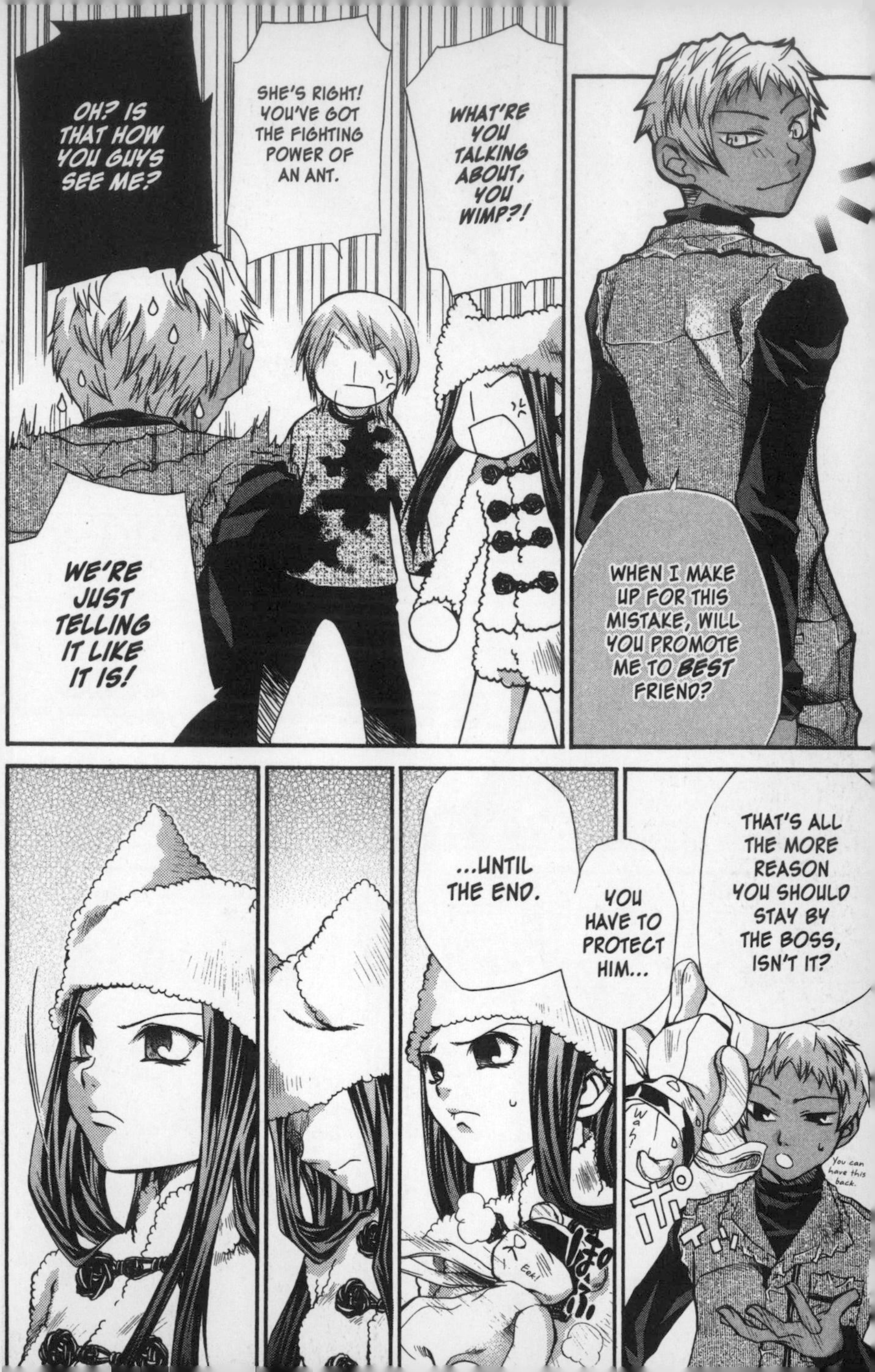
WHEN I MAKE UP FOR THIS MISTAKE, WILL YOU PROMOTE ME TO BEST FRIEND?
WHAT'RE YOU TALKING ABOUT, YOU WIMP?!
SHE'S RIGHT! YOU'VE GOT THE FIGHTING POWER OF AN ANT.
OH? IS THAT HOW YOU GUYS SEE ME?
WE'RE JUST TELLING IT LIKE IT IS!
THAT'S ALL THE MORE REASON YOU SHOULD STAY BY THE BOSS, ISN'T IT?
You can have this back.
Wa?!
YOU HAVE TO PROTECT HIM...
...UNTIL THE END.
Eek!

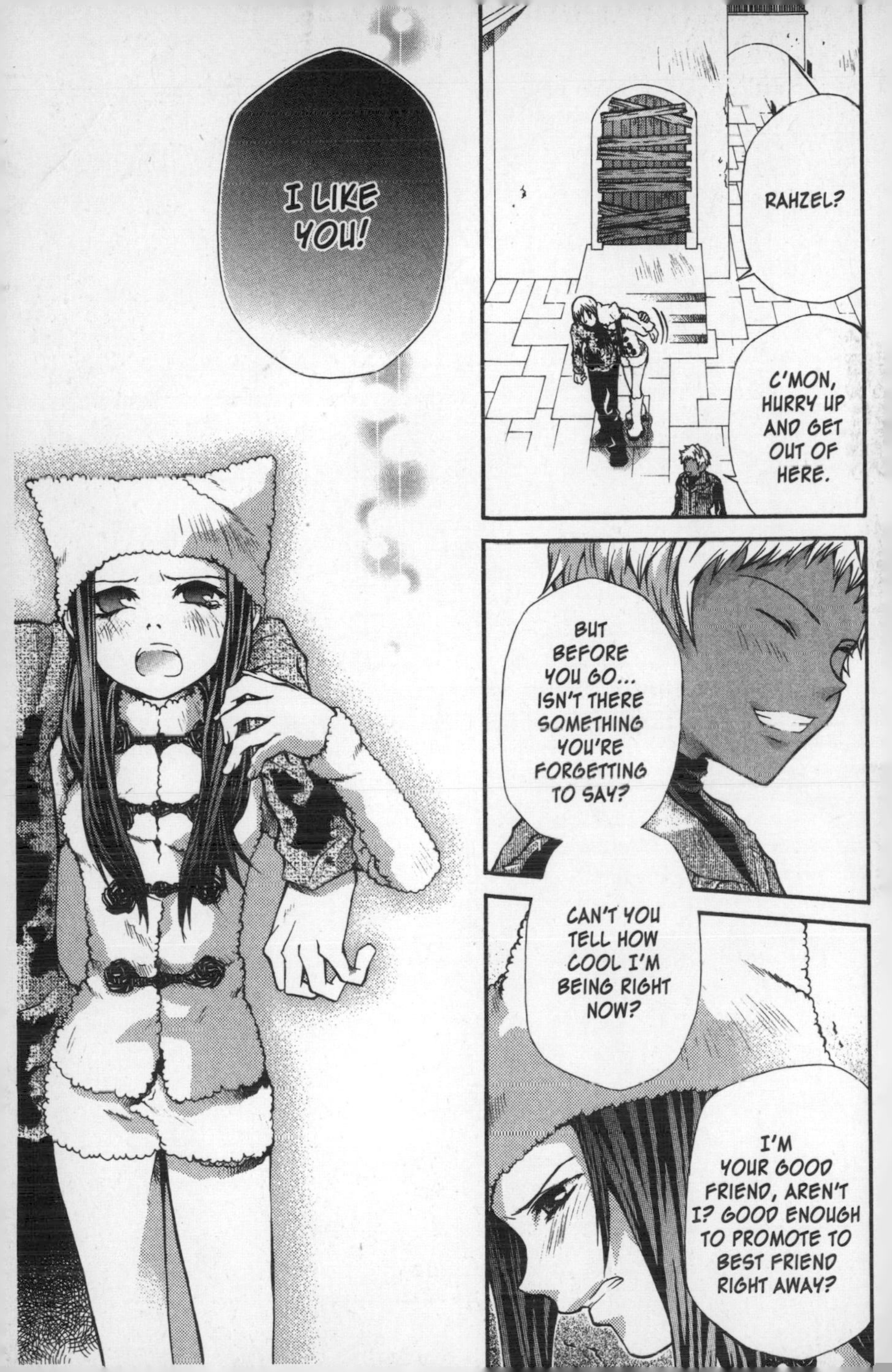
RAHZEL?
C'MON, HURRY UP AND GET OUT OF HERE.
BUT BEFORE YOU GO... ISN'T THERE SOMETHING YOU'RE FORGETTING TO SAY?
CAN'T YOU TELL HOW COOL I'M BEING RIGHT NOW?
I'M YOUR GOOD FRIEND, AREN'T I? GOOD ENOUGH TO PROMOTE TO BEST FRIEND RIGHT AWAY?
I LIKE YOU!

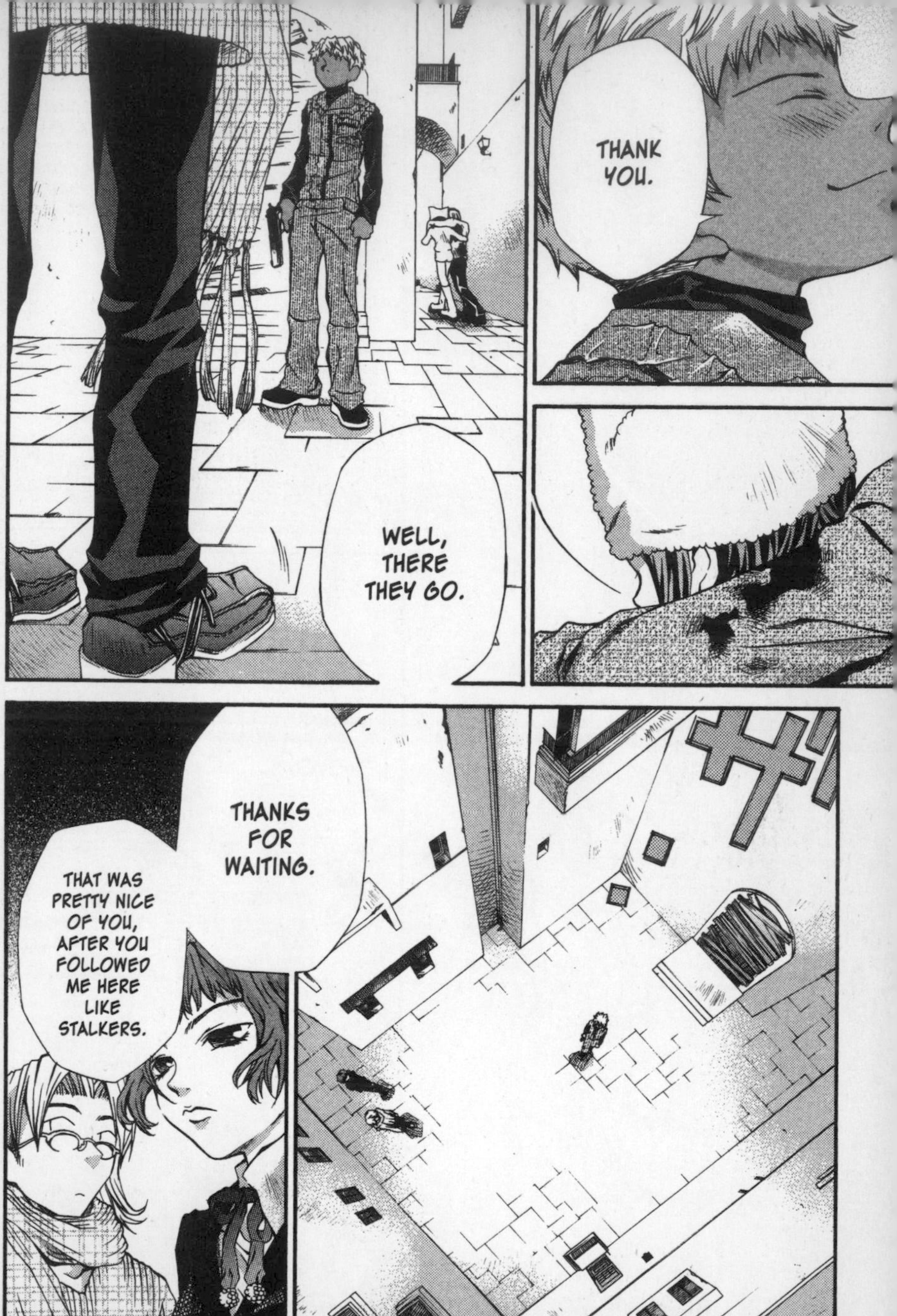
THANK YOU.
WELL, THERE THEY GO.
THANKS FOR WAITING.
THAT WAS PRETTY NICE OF YOU, AFTER YOU FOLLOWED ME HERE LIKE STALKERS.

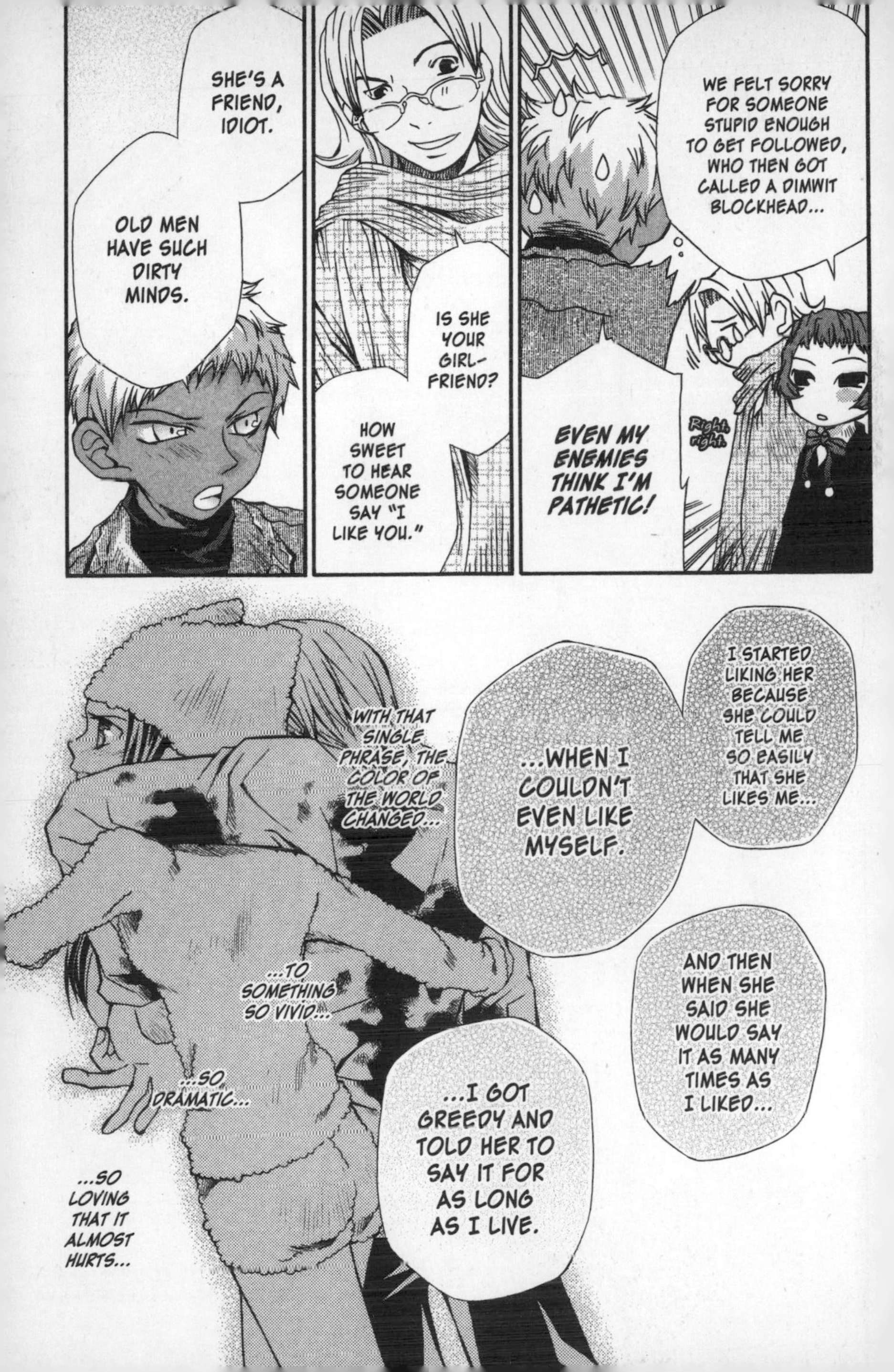
WE FELT SORRY FOR SOMEONE STUPID ENOUGH TO GET FOLLOWED, WHO THEN GOT CALLED A DIMWIT BLOCKHEAD...
Right, right.
EVEN MY ENEMIES THINK I'M PATHETIC!
IS SHE YOUR GIRL-FRIEND?
HOW SWEET TO HEAR SOMEONE SAY "I LIKE YOU."
SHE'S A FRIEND, IDIOT.
OLD MEN HAVE SUCH DIRTY MINDS.
I STARTED LIKING HER BECAUSE SHE COULD TELL ME SO EASILY THAT SHE LIKES ME...
...WHEN I COULDN'T EVEN LIKE MYSELF.
WITH THAT SINGLE PHRASE, THE COLOR OF THE WORLD CHANGED...
AND THEN WHEN SHE SAID SHE WOULD SAY IT AS MANY TIMES AS I LIKED...
...I GOT GREEDY AND TOLD HER TO SAY IT FOR AS LONG AS I LIVE.
...TO SOMETHING SO VIVID...
...SO DRAMATIC...
...SO LOVING THAT IT ALMOST HURTS...

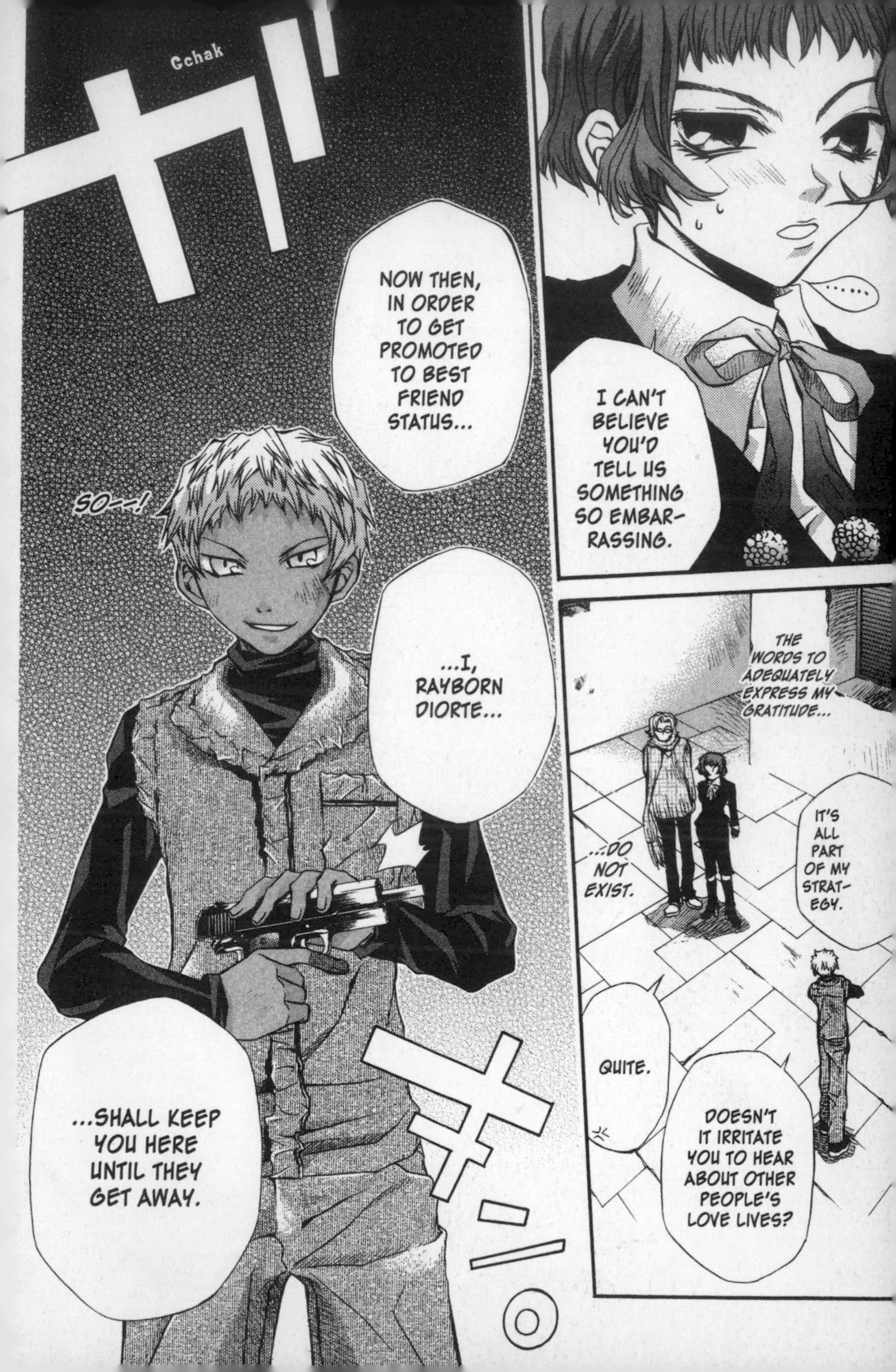
......
I CAN'T BELIEVE YOU'D TELL US SOMETHING SO EMBARRASSING.
THE WORDS TO ADEQUATELY EXPRESS MY GRATITUDE...
IT'S ALL PART OF MY STRATEGY.
...DO NOT EXIST.
DOESN'T IT IRRITATE YOU TO HEAR ABOUT OTHER PEOPLE'S LOVE LIVES?
QUITE.
Gchak
NOW THEN, IN ORDER TO GET PROMOTED TO BEST FRIEND STATUS...
SO--!
...I, RAYBORN DIORTE...
...SHALL KEEP YOU HERE UNTIL THEY GET AWAY.

Chapter 42: The Ephemeral Proposition--

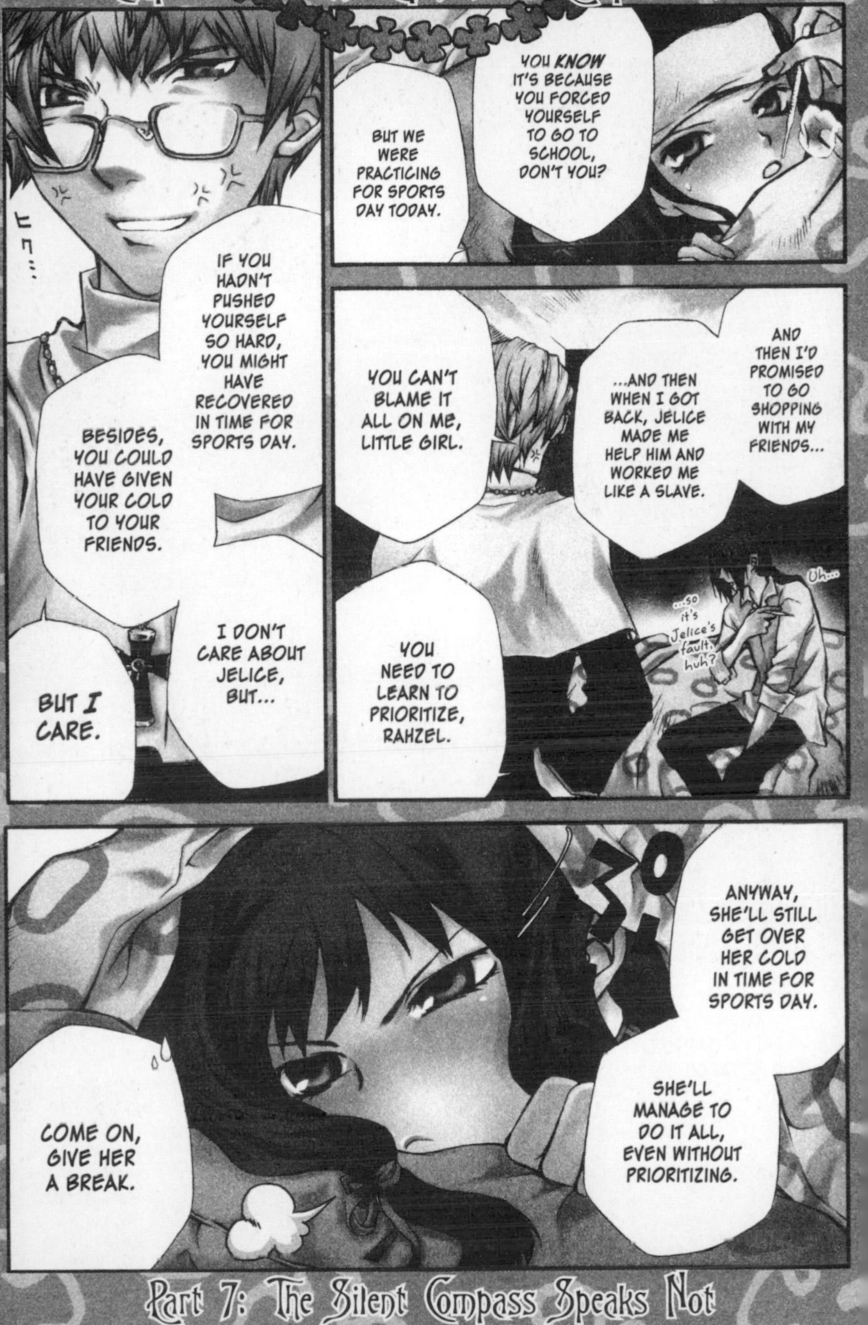
YOU *KNOW* IT'S BECAUSE YOU FORCED YOURSELF TO GO TO SCHOOL, DON'T YOU?
BUT WE WERE PRACTICING FOR SPORTS DAY TODAY.
AND THEN I'D PROMISED TO GO SHOPPING WITH MY FRIENDS...
...AND THEN WHEN I GOT BACK, JELICE MADE ME HELP HIM AND WORKED ME LIKE A SLAVE.
YOU CAN'T BLAME IT ALL ON ME, LITTLE GIRL.
Uh...
...so it's Jelice's fault, huh?
YOU NEED TO LEARN TO PRIORITIZE, RAHZEL.
ヒク…
IF YOU HADN'T PUSHED YOURSELF SO HARD, YOU MIGHT HAVE RECOVERED IN TIME FOR SPORTS DAY.
BESIDES, YOU COULD HAVE GIVEN YOUR COLD TO YOUR FRIENDS.
I DON'T CARE ABOUT JELICE, BUT...
BUT *I* CARE.
ANYWAY, SHE'LL STILL GET OVER HER COLD IN TIME FOR SPORTS DAY.
SHE'LL MANAGE TO DO IT ALL, EVEN WITHOUT PRIORITIZING.
COME ON, GIVE HER A BREAK.

Part 7: The Silent Compass Speaks Not

Dazzle Q&A

Q: How come you never see Rahzel's undies, even when she's wearing a miniskirt?

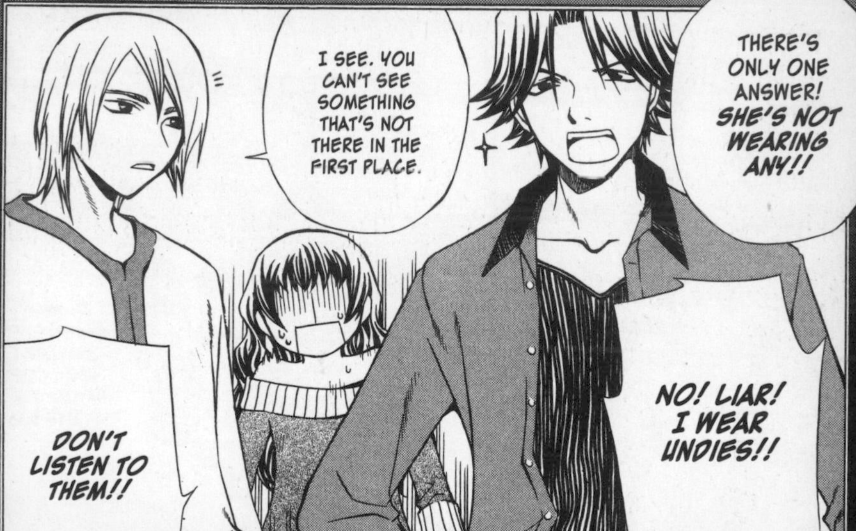
THERE'S ONLY ONE ANSWER! SHE'S NOT WEARING ANY!!
I SEE. YOU CAN'T SEE SOMETHING THAT'S NOT THERE IN THE FIRST PLACE.
NO! LIAR! I WEAR UNDIES!!
DON'T LISTEN TO THEM!!

I look forward to your questions.

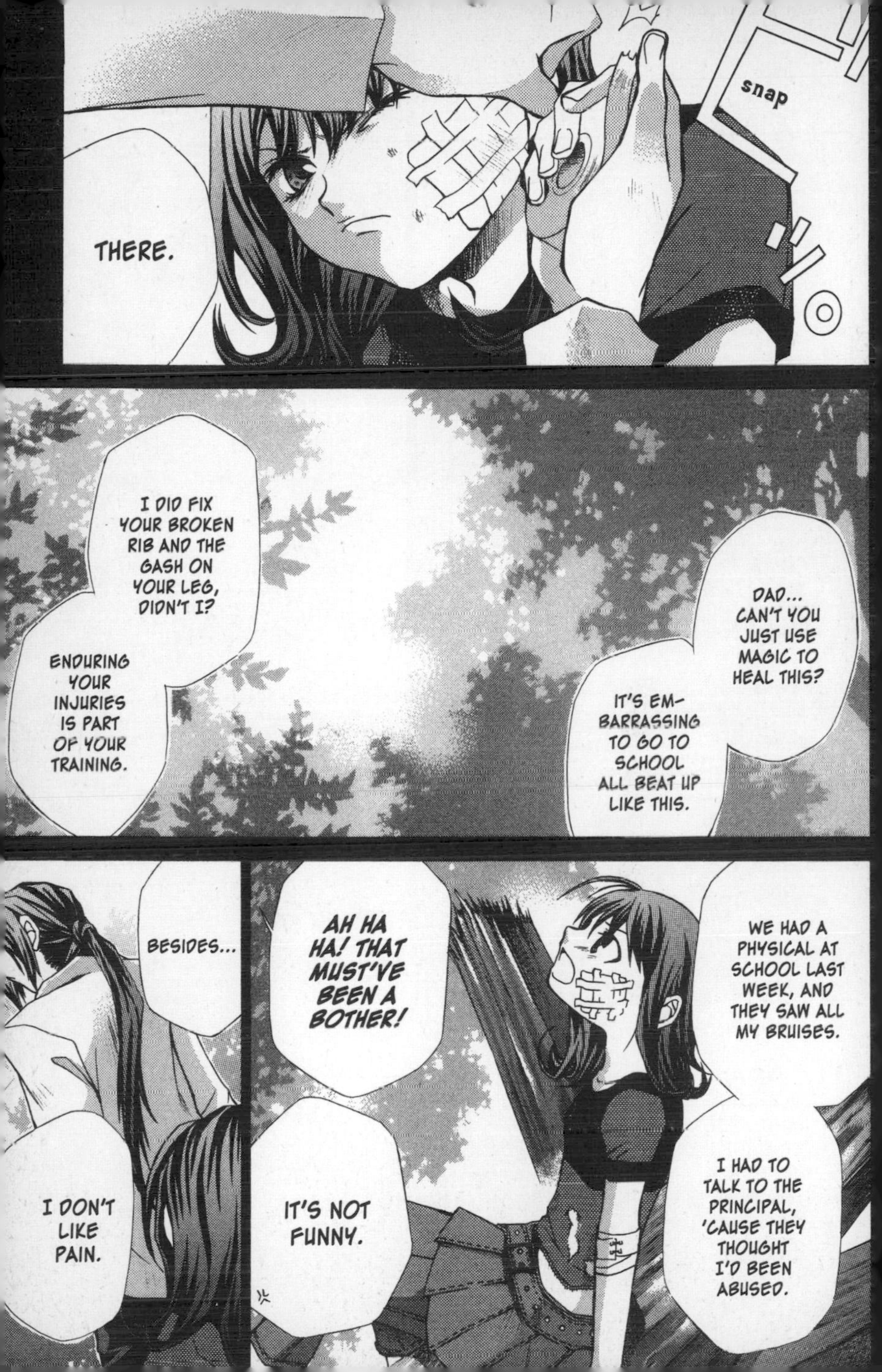
snap
THERE.
DAD... CAN'T YOU JUST USE MAGIC TO HEAL THIS?
IT'S EM-BARRASSING TO GO TO SCHOOL ALL BEAT UP LIKE THIS.
I DID FIX YOUR BROKEN RIB AND THE GASH ON YOUR LEG, DIDN'T I?
ENDURING YOUR INJURIES IS PART OF YOUR TRAINING.
WE HAD A PHYSICAL AT SCHOOL LAST WEEK, AND THEY SAW ALL MY BRUISES.
I HAD TO TALK TO THE PRINCIPAL, 'CAUSE THEY THOUGHT I'D BEEN ABUSED.
AH HA HA! THAT MUST'VE BEEN A BOTHER!
IT'S NOT FUNNY.
BESIDES...
I DON'T LIKE PAIN.

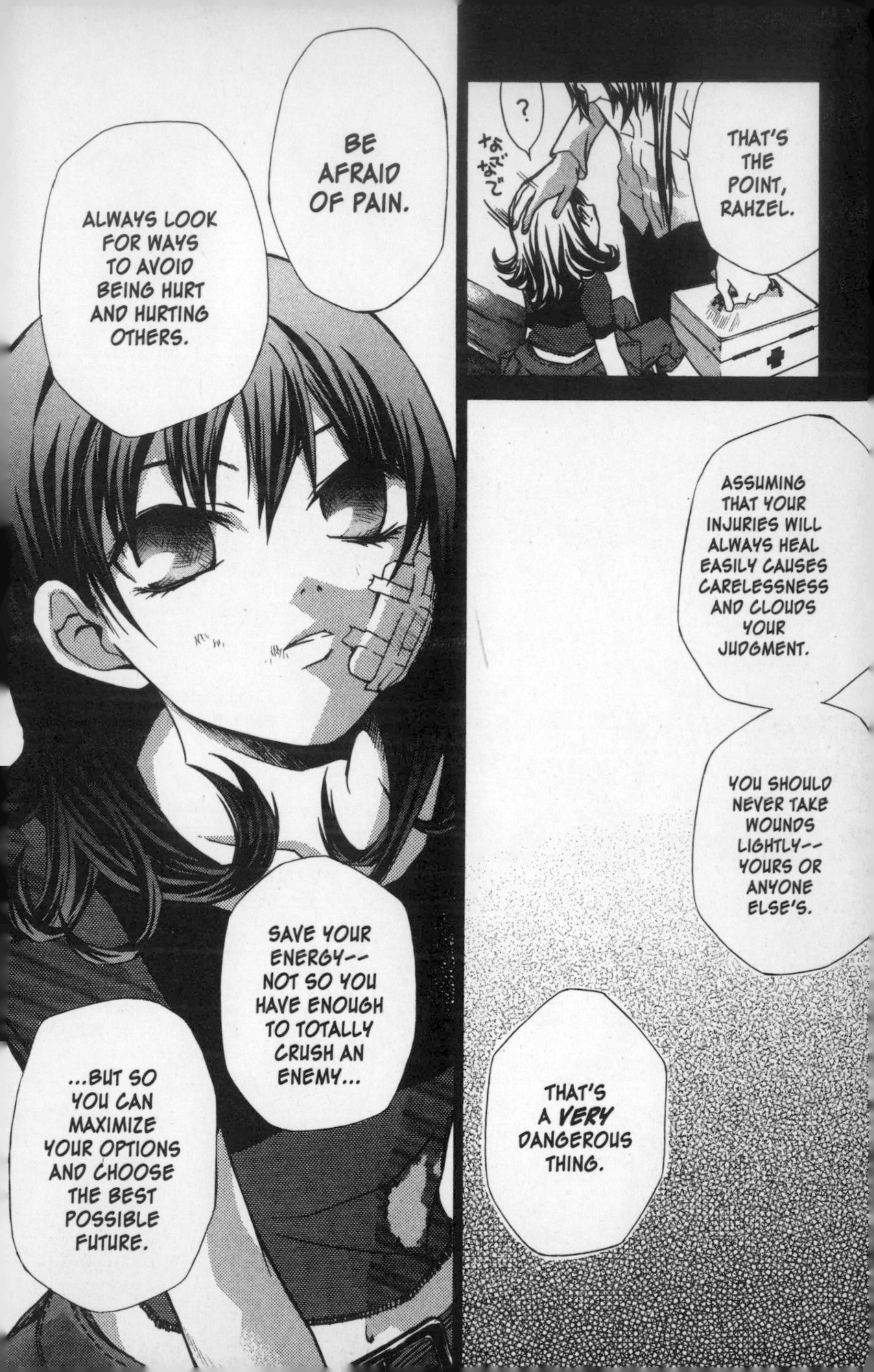
THAT'S THE POINT, RAHZEL.
?
なでなで
ASSUMING THAT YOUR INJURIES WILL ALWAYS HEAL EASILY CAUSES CARELESSNESS AND CLOUDS YOUR JUDGMENT.
YOU SHOULD NEVER TAKE WOUNDS LIGHTLY--YOURS OR ANYONE ELSE'S.
THAT'S A *VERY* DANGEROUS THING.
BE AFRAID OF PAIN.
ALWAYS LOOK FOR WAYS TO AVOID BEING HURT AND HURTING OTHERS.
SAVE YOUR ENERGY--NOT SO YOU HAVE ENOUGH TO TOTALLY CRUSH AN ENEMY...
...BUT SO YOU CAN MAXIMIZE YOUR OPTIONS AND CHOOSE THE BEST POSSIBLE FUTURE.

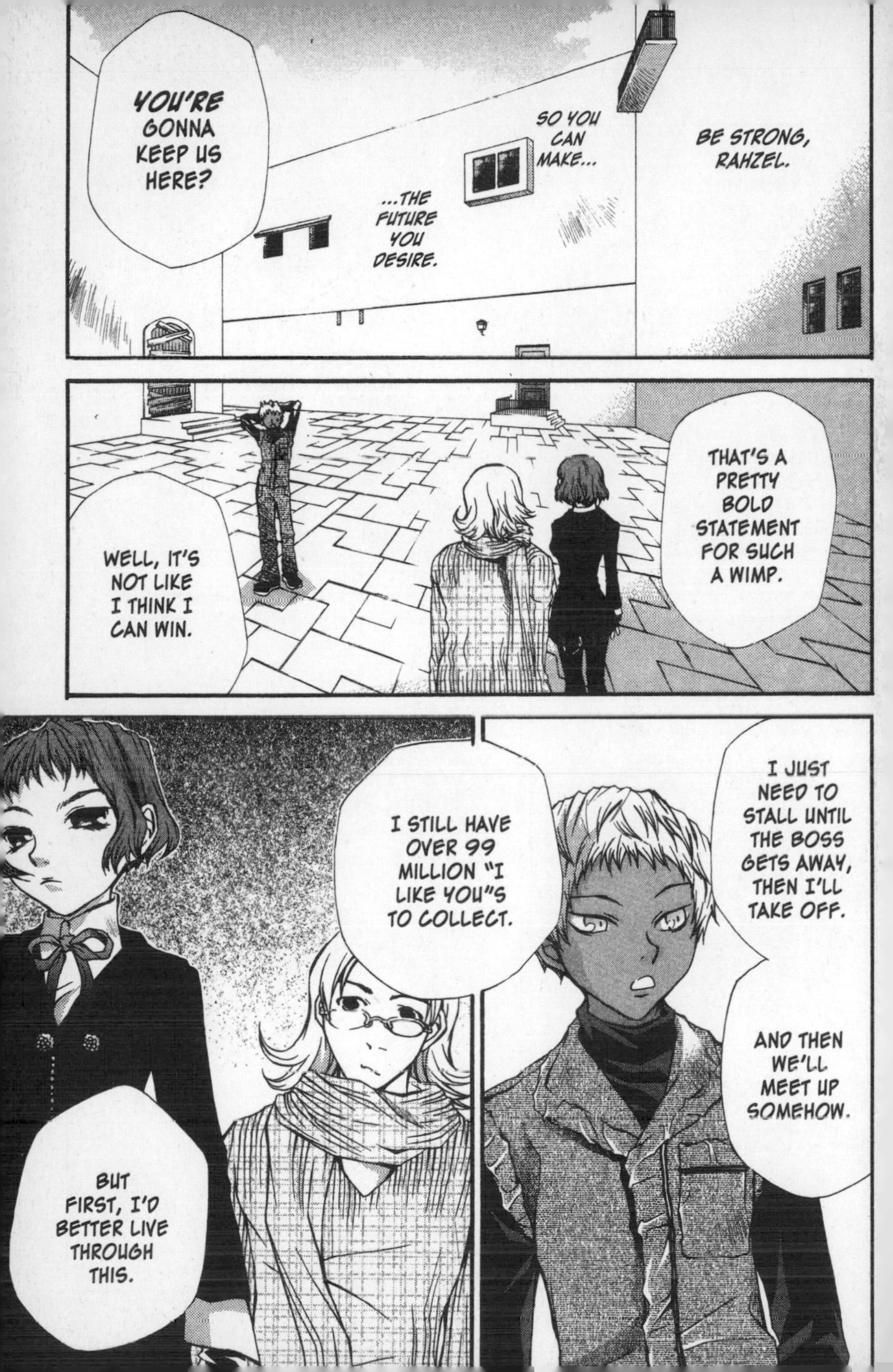
BE STRONG, RAHZEL.
SO YOU CAN MAKE...
...THE FUTURE YOU DESIRE.
YOU'RE GONNA KEEP US HERE?
THAT'S A PRETTY BOLD STATEMENT FOR SUCH A WIMP.
WELL, IT'S NOT LIKE I THINK I CAN WIN.
I JUST NEED TO STALL UNTIL THE BOSS GETS AWAY, THEN I'LL TAKE OFF.
AND THEN WE'LL MEET UP SOMEHOW.
I STILL HAVE OVER 99 MILLION "I LIKE YOU"S TO COLLECT.
BUT FIRST, I'D BETTER LIVE THROUGH THIS.

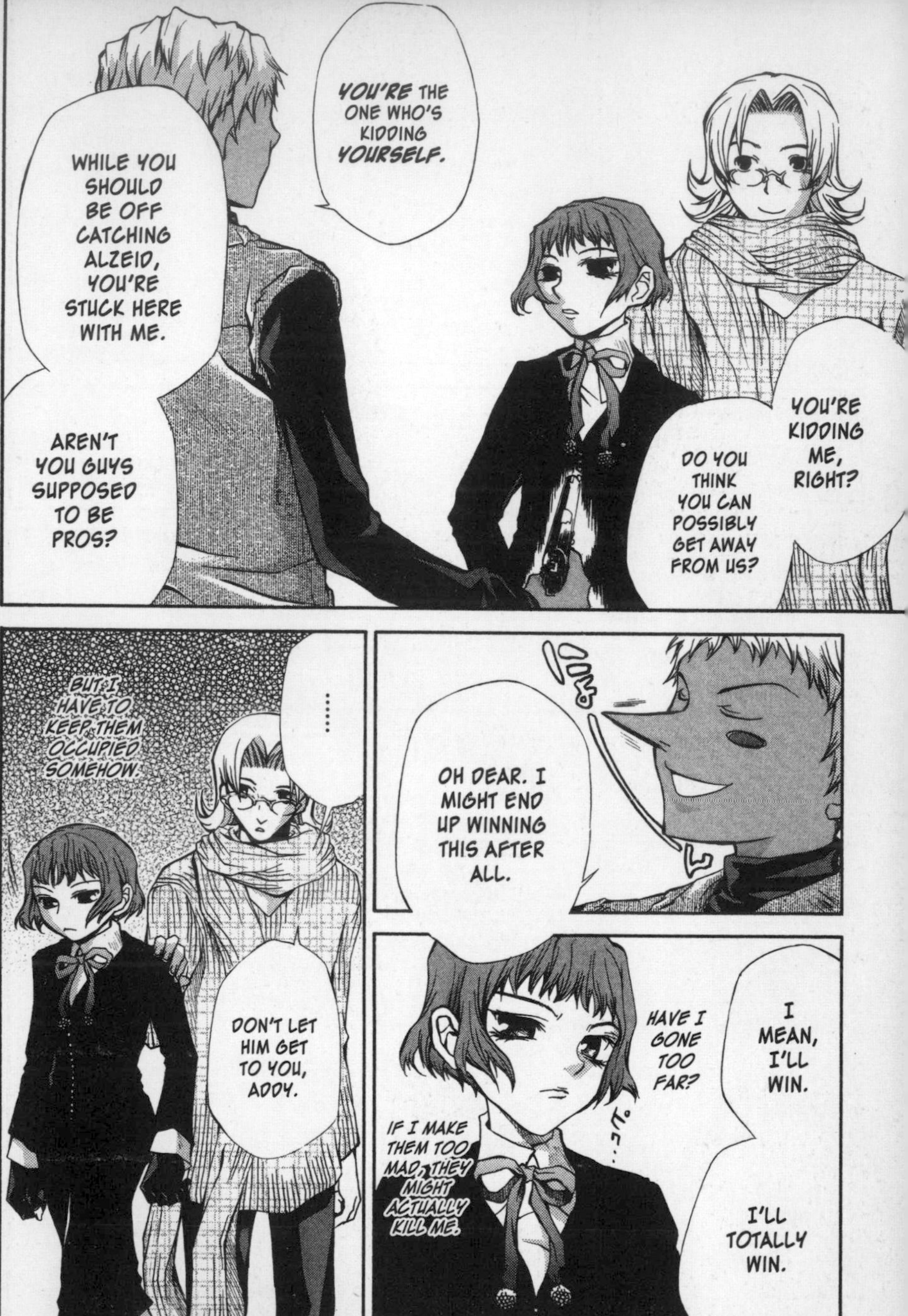
YOU'RE KIDDING ME, RIGHT?
DO YOU THINK YOU CAN POSSIBLY GET AWAY FROM US?
YOU'RE THE ONE WHO'S KIDDING YOURSELF.
WHILE YOU SHOULD BE OFF CATCHING ALZEID, YOU'RE STUCK HERE WITH ME.
AREN'T YOU GUYS SUPPOSED TO BE PROS?
OH DEAR. I MIGHT END UP WINNING THIS AFTER ALL.
I MEAN, I'LL WIN.
HAVE I GONE TOO FAR?
I'LL TOTALLY WIN.
IF I MAKE THEM TOO MAD, THEY MIGHT ACTUALLY KILL ME.
......
BUT I HAVE TO KEEP THEM OCCUPIED SOMEHOW.
DON'T LET HIM GET TO YOU, ADDY.

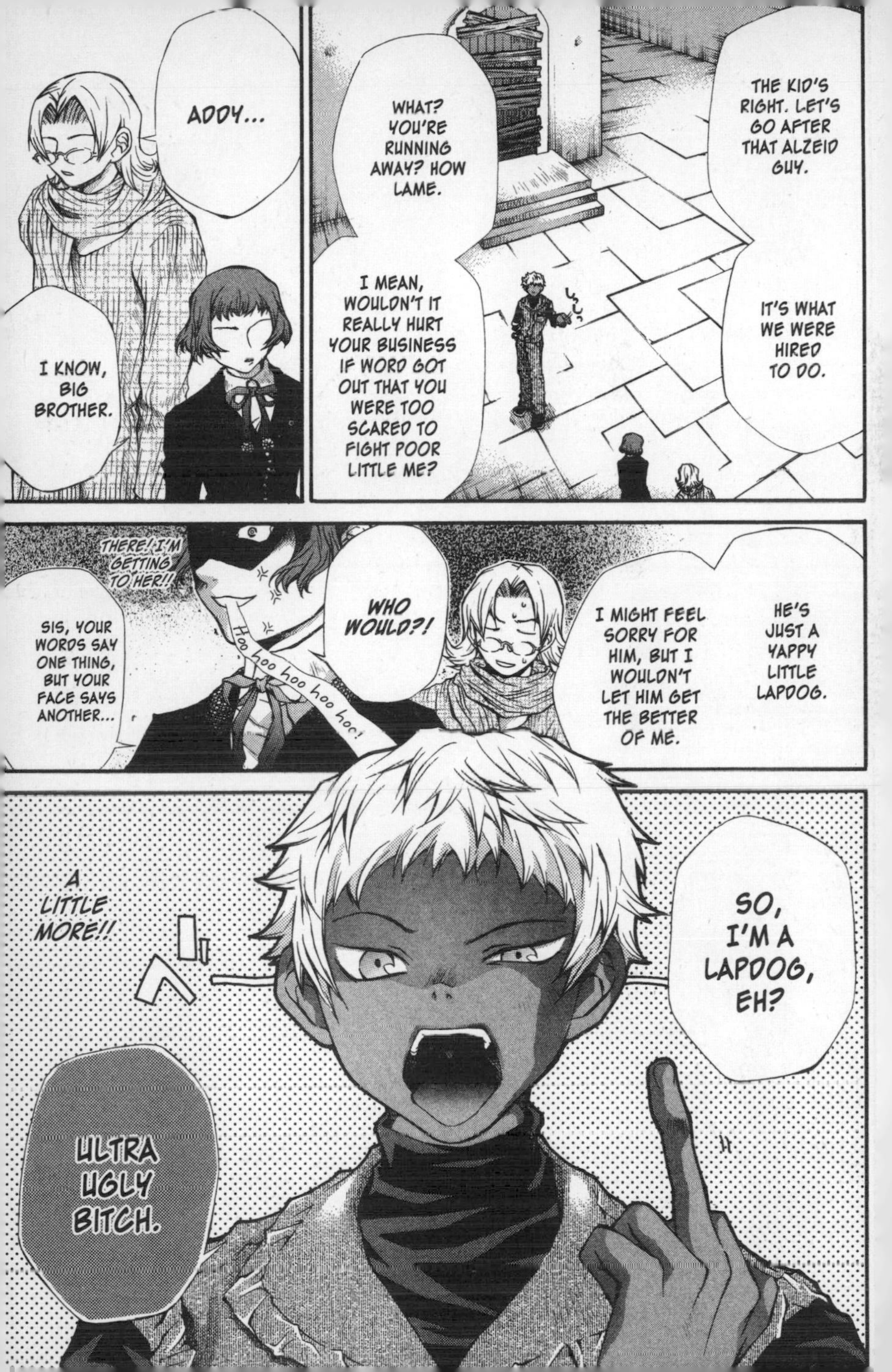
WHAT? YOU'RE RUNNING AWAY? HOW LAME.
I MEAN, WOULDN'T IT REALLY HURT YOUR BUSINESS IF WORD GOT OUT THAT YOU WERE TOO SCARED TO FIGHT POOR LITTLE ME?
THE KID'S RIGHT. LET'S GO AFTER THAT ALZEID GUY.
IT'S WHAT WE WERE HIRED TO DO.
ADDY...
I KNOW, BIG BROTHER.
HE'S JUST A YAPPY LITTLE LAPDOG.
I MIGHT FEEL SORRY FOR HIM, BUT I WOULDN'T LET HIM GET THE BETTER OF ME.
WHO WOULD?!
Hoo hoo hoo hoo hoo!
THERE! I'M GETTING TO HER!!
SIS, YOUR WORDS SAY ONE THING, BUT YOUR FACE SAYS ANOTHER...
SO, I'M A LAPDOG, EH?
A LITTLE MORE!!
ULTRA UGLY BITCH.

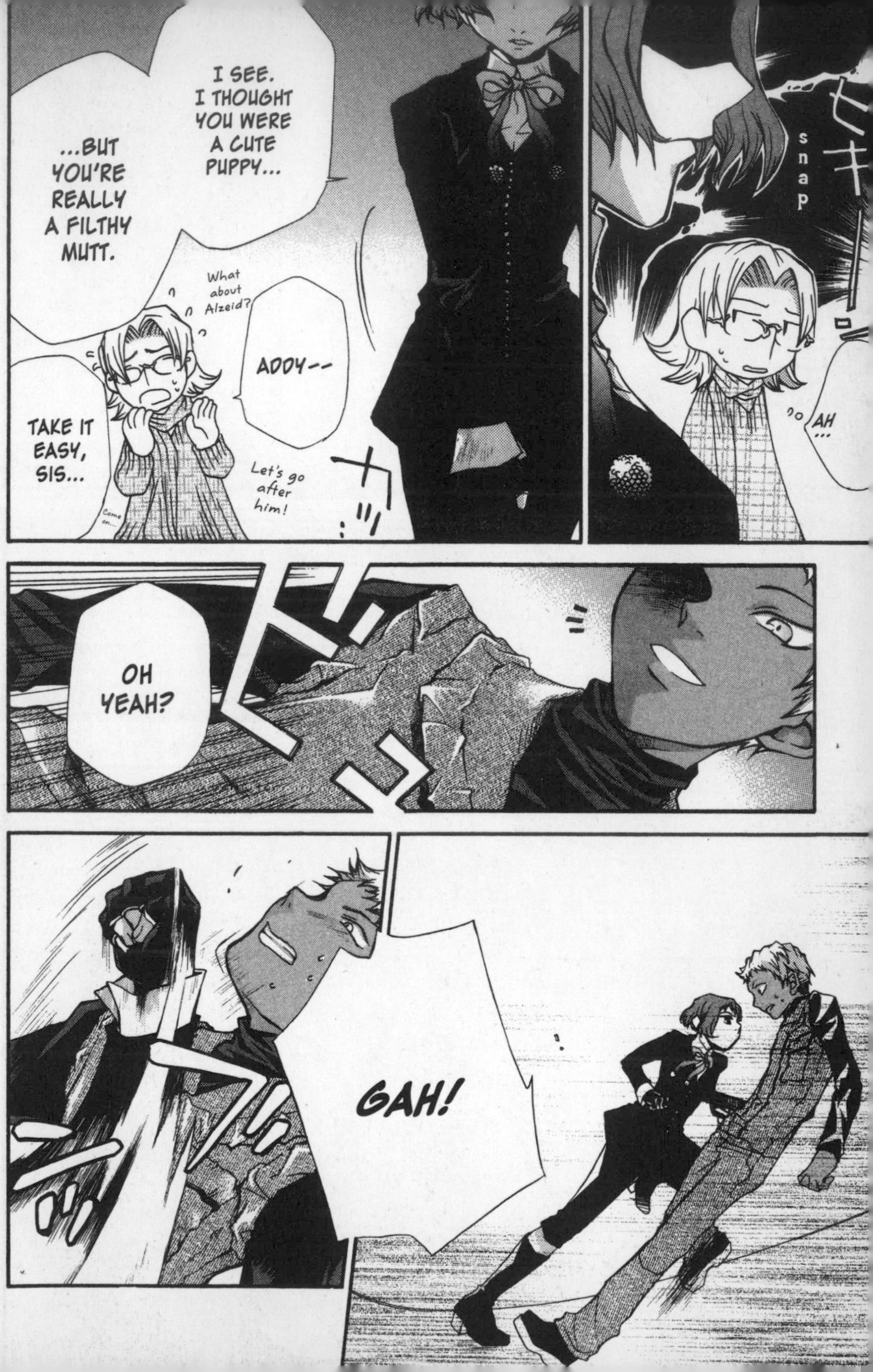
snap
AH ...
I SEE. I THOUGHT YOU WERE A CUTE PUPPY...
...BUT YOU'RE REALLY A FILTHY MUTT.
What about Alzeid?
ADDY--
Let's go after him!
TAKE IT EASY, SIS...
Come on...
OH YEAH?
GAH!

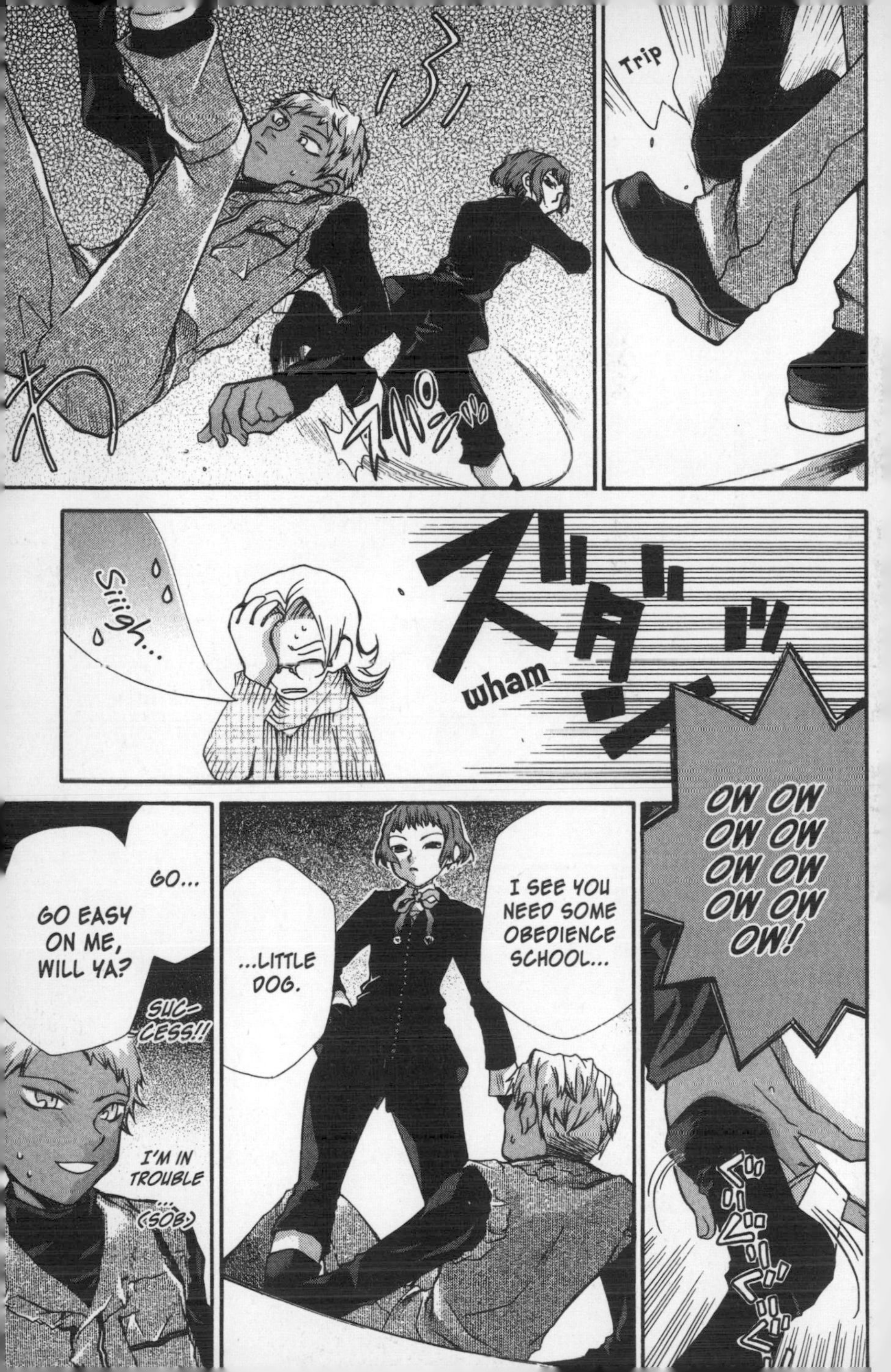
Trip
wham
Siiigh...
OW OW OW OW OW OW OW OW OW!
I SEE YOU NEED SOME OBEDIENCE SCHOOL...
...LITTLE DOG.
GO...
GO EASY ON ME, WILL YA?
SUC-CESS!!
I'M IN TROUBLE... (SOB)

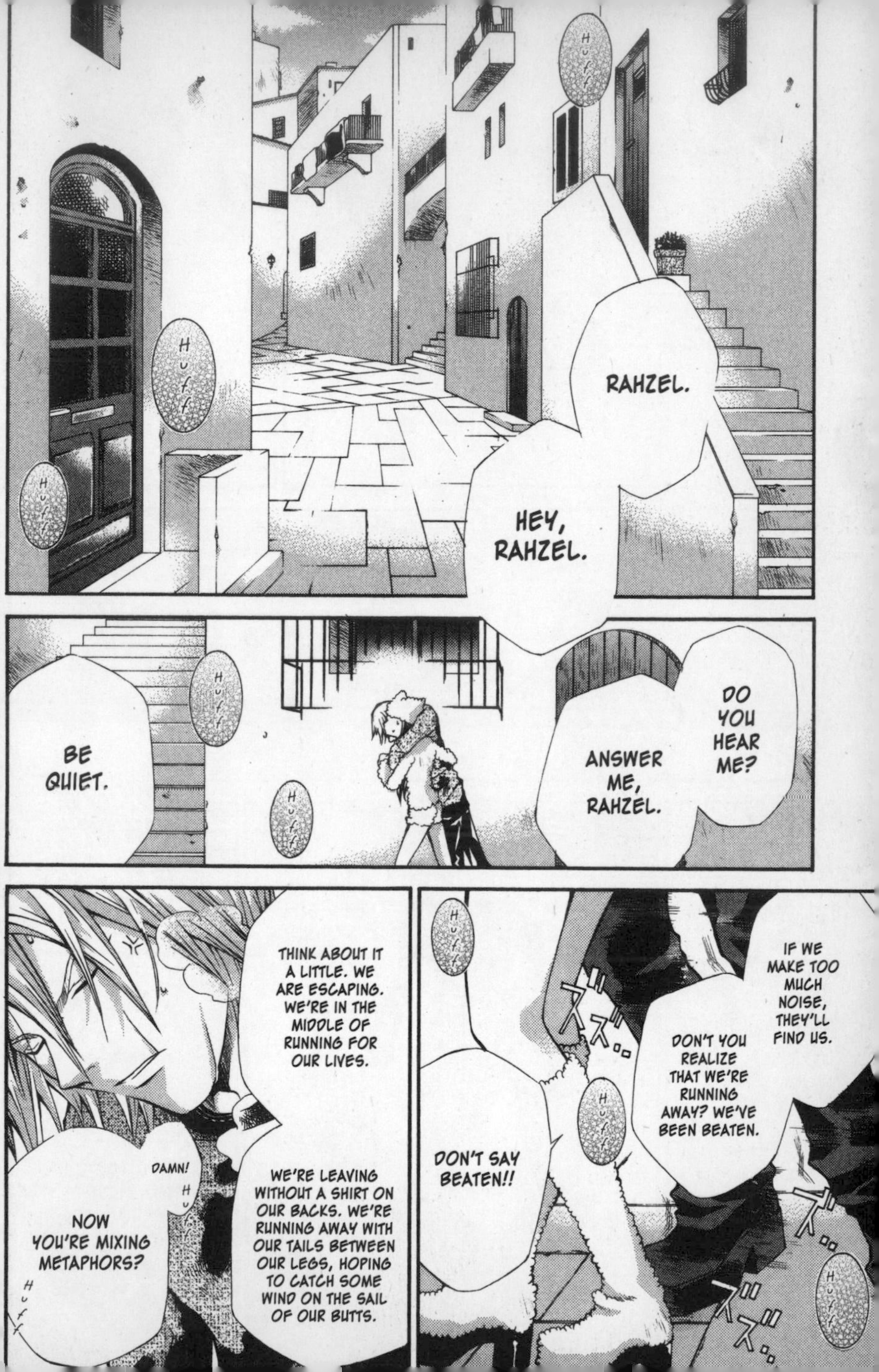
Huff
RAHZEL.
HEY, RAHZEL.
Huff
Huff
DO YOU HEAR ME?
ANSWER ME, RAHZEL.
Huff
BE QUIET.
Huff
IF WE MAKE TOO MUCH NOISE, THEY'LL FIND US.
DON'T YOU REALIZE THAT WE'RE RUNNING AWAY? WE'VE BEEN BEATEN.
Huff
DON'T SAY BEATEN!!
Huff
Huff
THINK ABOUT IT A LITTLE. WE ARE ESCAPING. WE'RE IN THE MIDDLE OF RUNNING FOR OUR LIVES.
WE'RE LEAVING WITHOUT A SHIRT ON OUR BACKS. WE'RE RUNNING AWAY WITH OUR TAILS BETWEEN OUR LEGS, HOPING TO CATCH SOME WIND ON THE SAIL OF OUR BUTTS.
DAMN!
Huff
NOW YOU'RE MIXING METAPHORS?
Huff

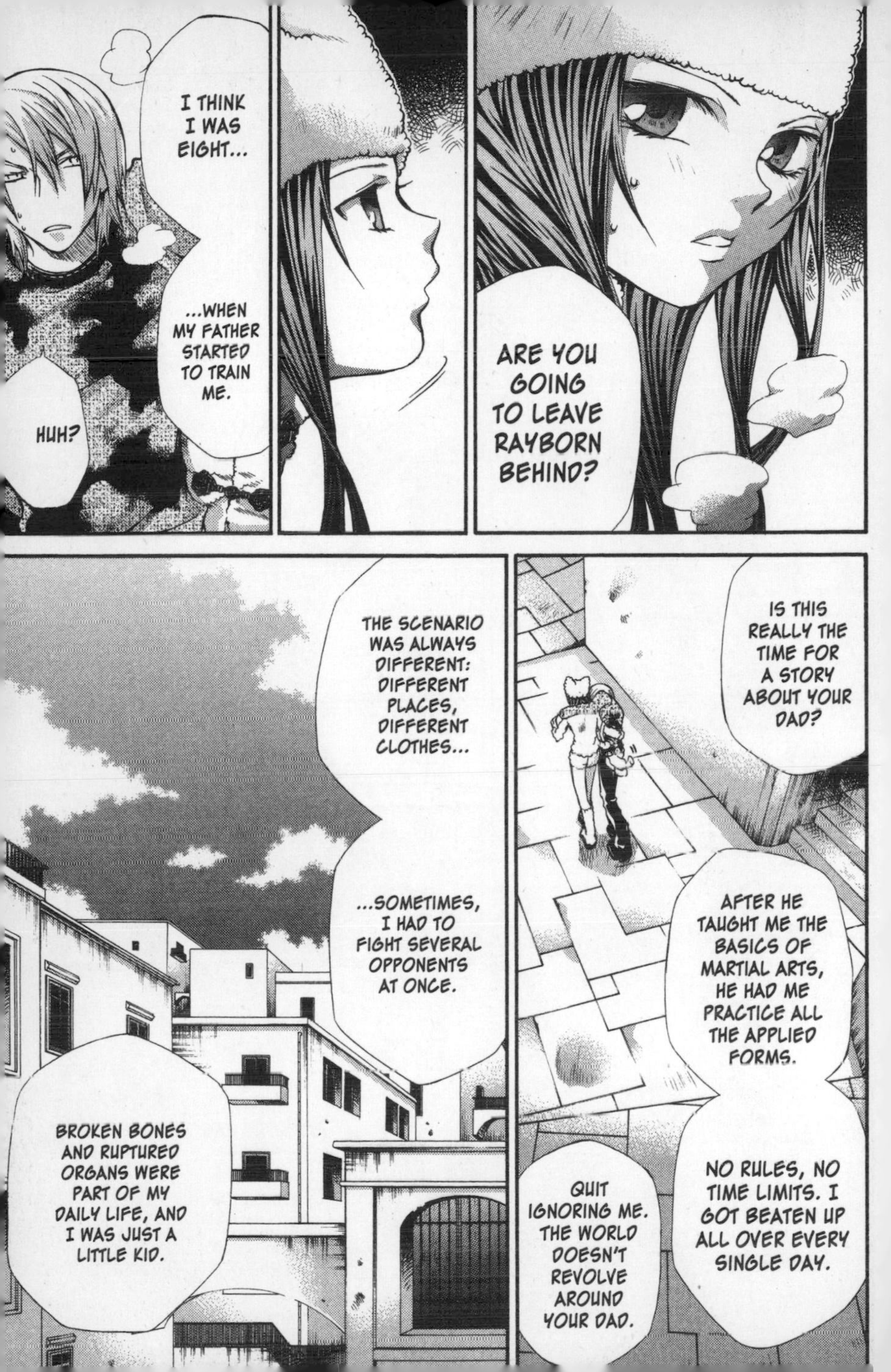
ARE YOU GOING TO LEAVE RAYBORN BEHIND?
I THINK I WAS EIGHT...
...WHEN MY FATHER STARTED TO TRAIN ME.
HUH?
IS THIS REALLY THE TIME FOR A STORY ABOUT YOUR DAD?
AFTER HE TAUGHT ME THE BASICS OF MARTIAL ARTS, HE HAD ME PRACTICE ALL THE APPLIED FORMS.
NO RULES, NO TIME LIMITS. I GOT BEATEN UP ALL OVER EVERY SINGLE DAY.
QUIT IGNORING ME. THE WORLD DOESN'T REVOLVE AROUND YOUR DAD.
THE SCENARIO WAS ALWAYS DIFFERENT: DIFFERENT PLACES, DIFFERENT CLOTHES...
...SOMETIMES, I HAD TO FIGHT SEVERAL OPPONENTS AT ONCE.
BROKEN BONES AND RUPTURED ORGANS WERE PART OF MY DAILY LIFE, AND I WAS JUST A LITTLE KID.

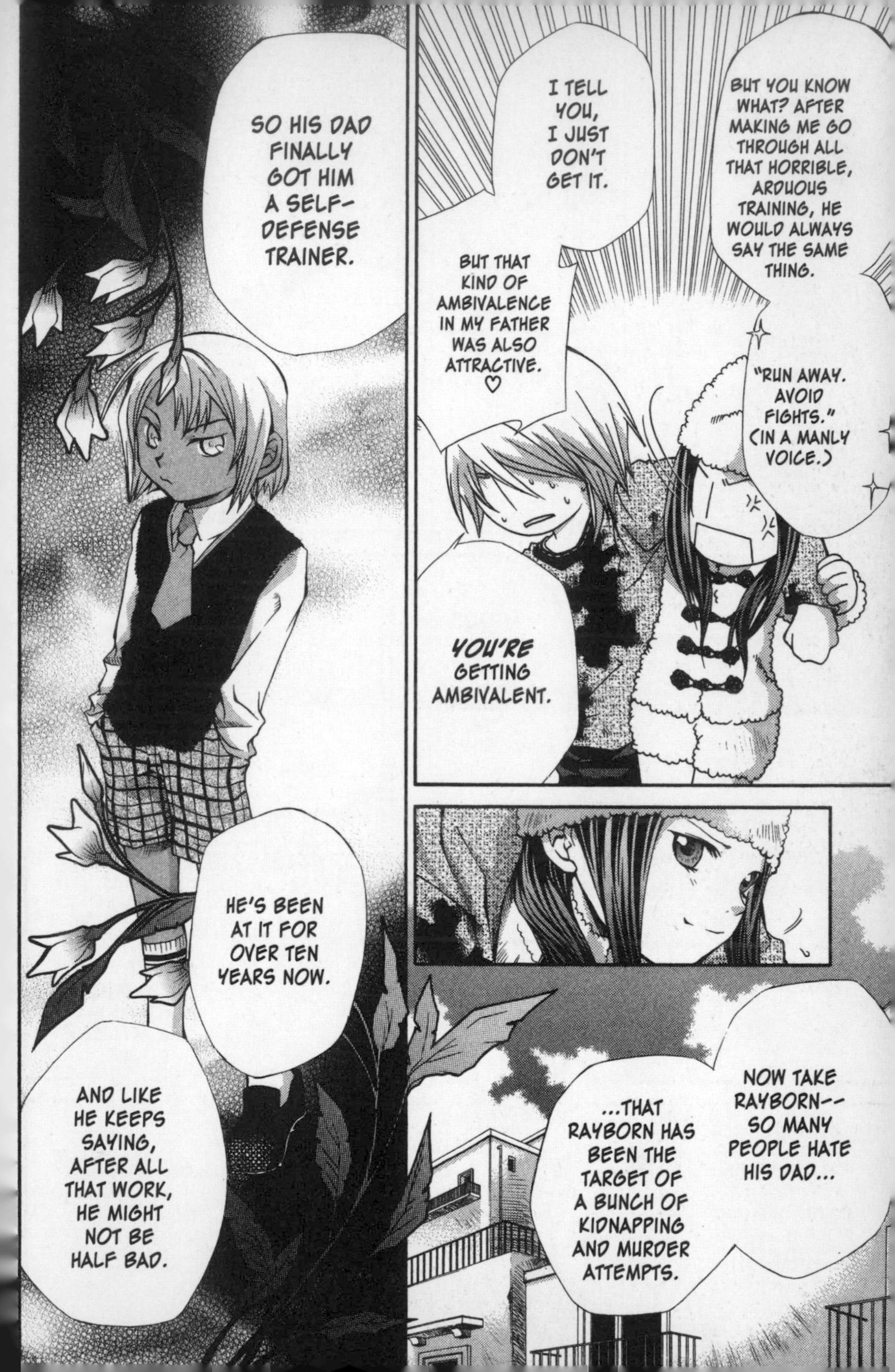
BUT YOU KNOW WHAT? AFTER MAKING ME GO THROUGH ALL THAT HORRIBLE, ARDUOUS TRAINING, HE WOULD ALWAYS SAY THE SAME THING.
I TELL YOU, I JUST DON'T GET IT.
"RUN AWAY. AVOID FIGHTS." (IN A MANLY VOICE.)
BUT THAT KIND OF AMBIVALENCE IN MY FATHER WAS ALSO ATTRACTIVE. ♡
YOU'RE GETTING AMBIVALENT.
NOW TAKE RAYBORN-- SO MANY PEOPLE HATE HIS DAD...
...THAT RAYBORN HAS BEEN THE TARGET OF A BUNCH OF KIDNAPPING AND MURDER ATTEMPTS.
SO HIS DAD FINALLY GOT HIM A SELF-DEFENSE TRAINER.
HE'S BEEN AT IT FOR OVER TEN YEARS NOW.
AND LIKE HE KEEPS SAYING, AFTER ALL THAT WORK, HE MIGHT NOT BE HALF BAD.

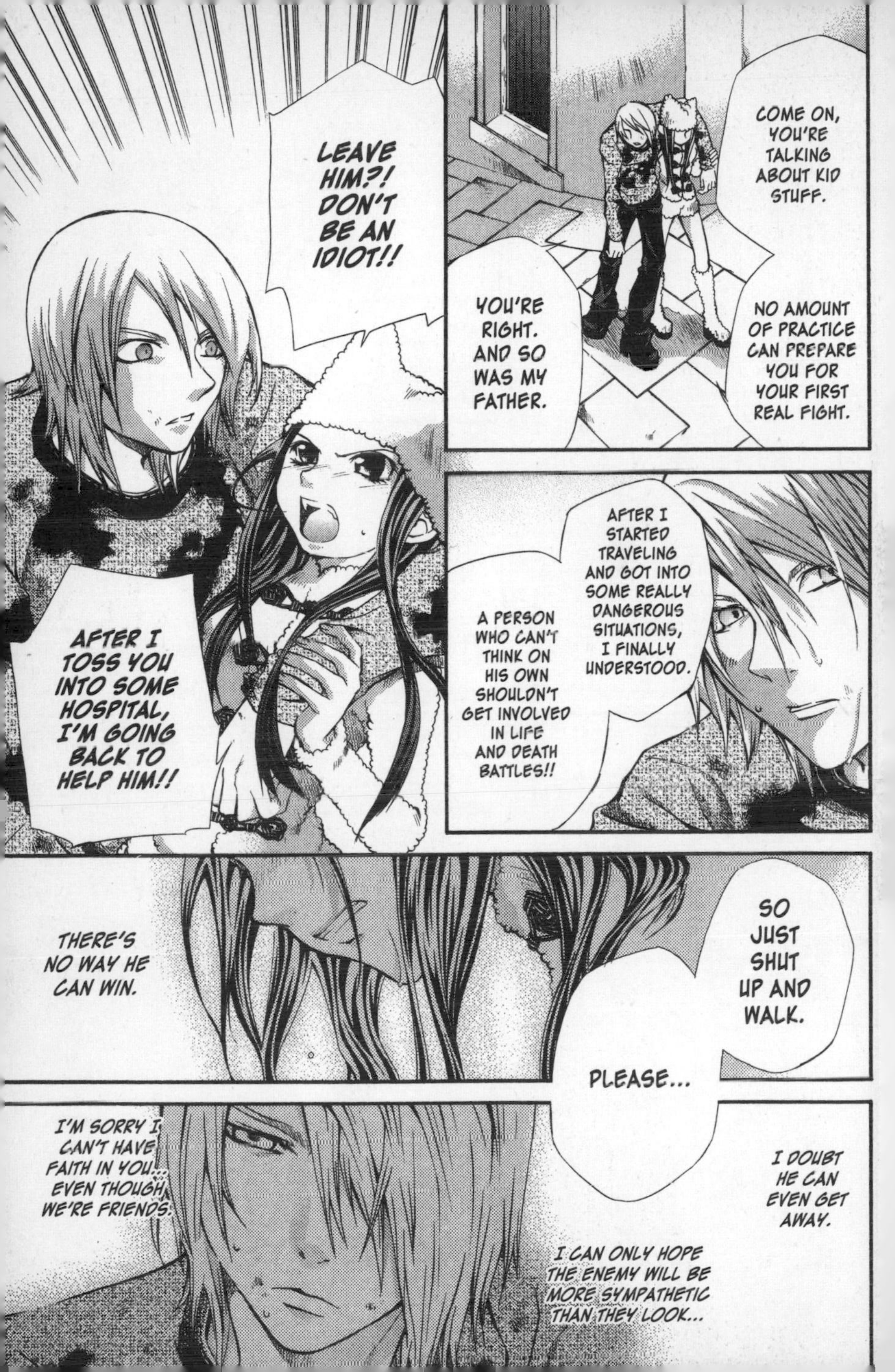
COME ON, YOU'RE TALKING ABOUT KID STUFF.
NO AMOUNT OF PRACTICE CAN PREPARE YOU FOR YOUR FIRST REAL FIGHT.
YOU'RE RIGHT. AND SO WAS MY FATHER.
AFTER I STARTED TRAVELING AND GOT INTO SOME REALLY DANGEROUS SITUATIONS, I FINALLY UNDERSTOOD.
A PERSON WHO CAN'T THINK ON HIS OWN SHOULDN'T GET INVOLVED IN LIFE AND DEATH BATTLES!!
LEAVE HIM?! DON'T BE AN IDIOT!!
AFTER I TOSS YOU INTO SOME HOSPITAL, I'M GOING BACK TO HELP HIM!!
SO JUST SHUT UP AND WALK.
THERE'S NO WAY HE CAN WIN.
PLEASE...
I DOUBT HE CAN EVEN GET AWAY.
I CAN ONLY HOPE THE ENEMY WILL BE MORE SYMPATHETIC THAN THEY LOOK...
I'M SORRY I CAN'T HAVE FAITH IN YOU... EVEN THOUGH WE'RE FRIENDS.

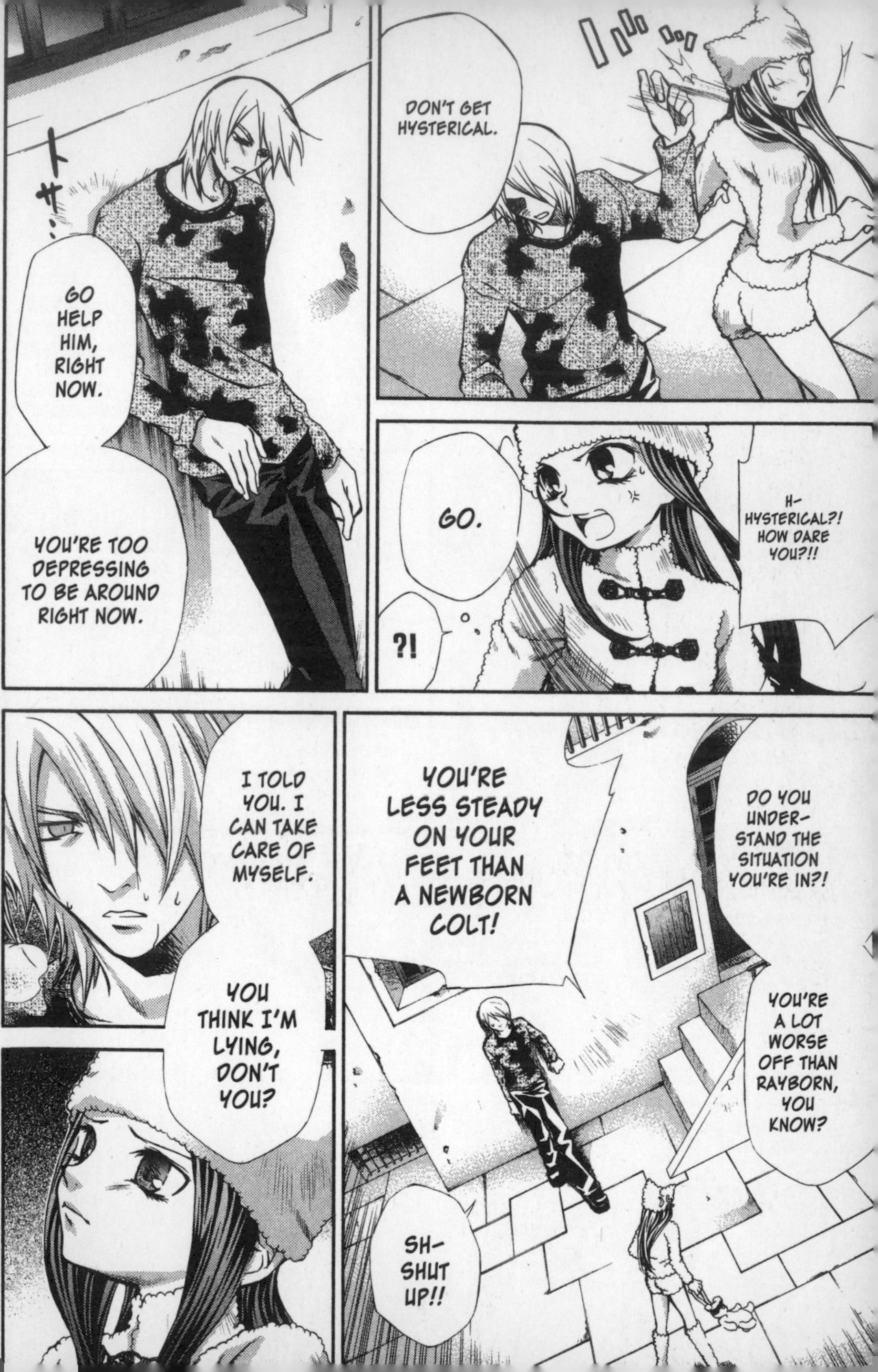
DON'T GET HYSTERICAL.
H-HYSTERICAL?! HOW DARE YOU?!!
GO.
?!
トサ…
GO HELP HIM, RIGHT NOW.
YOU'RE TOO DEPRESSING TO BE AROUND RIGHT NOW.
DO YOU UNDER-STAND THE SITUATION YOU'RE IN?!
YOU'RE LESS STEADY ON YOUR FEET THAN A NEWBORN COLT!
YOU'RE A LOT WORSE OFF THAN RAYBORN, YOU KNOW?
SH-SHUT UP!!
I TOLD YOU. I CAN TAKE CARE OF MYSELF.
YOU THINK I'M LYING, DON'T YOU?

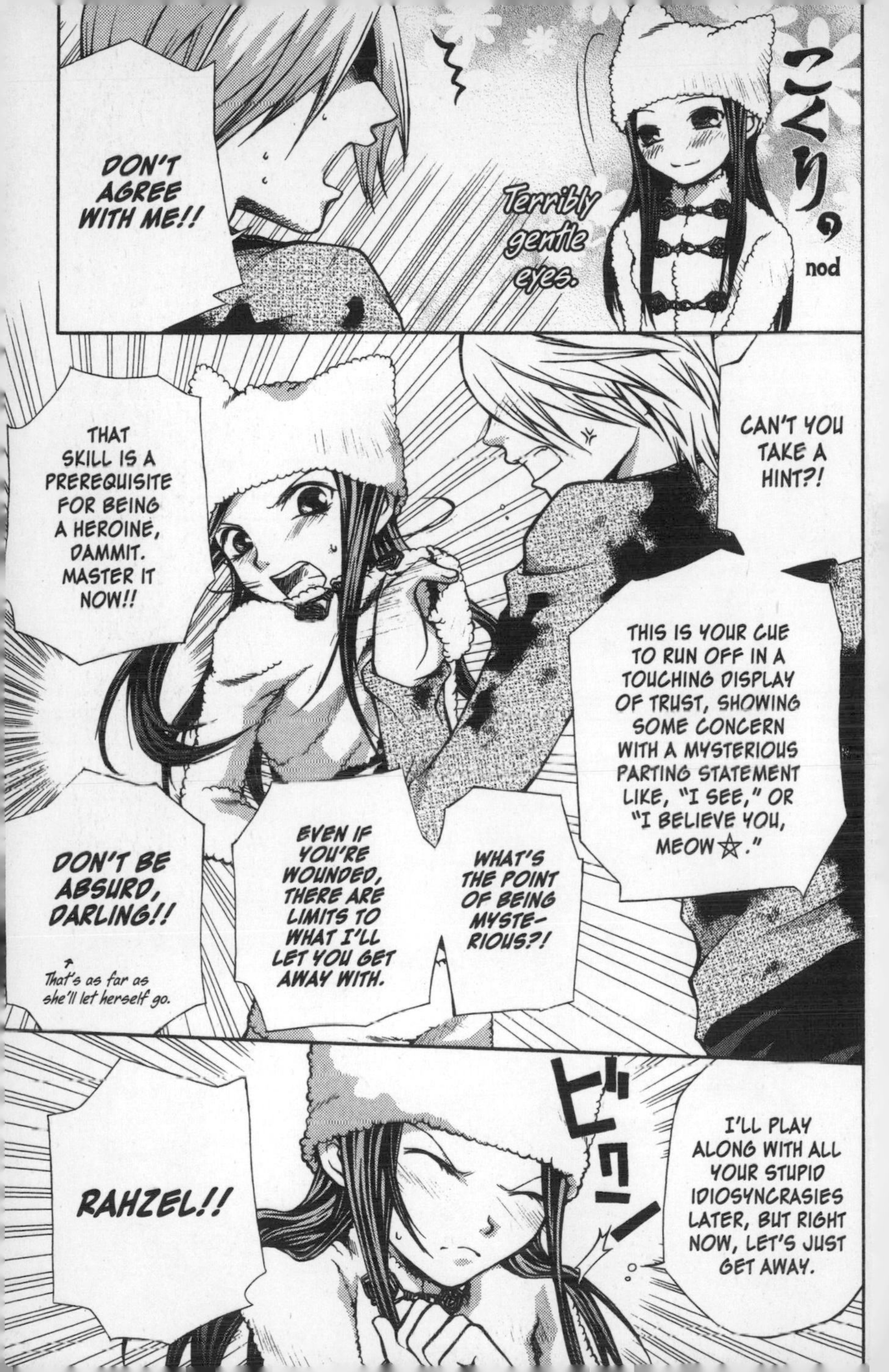
こくり
nod
Terribly gentle eyes.
DON'T AGREE WITH ME!!
CAN'T YOU TAKE A HINT?!
THAT SKILL IS A PREREQUISITE FOR BEING A HEROINE, DAMMIT. MASTER IT NOW!!
THIS IS YOUR CUE TO RUN OFF IN A TOUCHING DISPLAY OF TRUST, SHOWING SOME CONCERN WITH A MYSTERIOUS PARTING STATEMENT LIKE, "I SEE," OR "I BELIEVE YOU, MEOW☆."
WHAT'S THE POINT OF BEING MYSTE-RIOUS?!
EVEN IF YOU'RE WOUNDED, THERE ARE LIMITS TO WHAT I'LL LET YOU GET AWAY WITH.
DON'T BE ABSURD, DARLING!!
That's as far as she'll let herself go.
I'LL PLAY ALONG WITH ALL YOUR STUPID IDIOSYNCRASIES LATER, BUT RIGHT NOW, LET'S JUST GET AWAY.
ビクッ!
RAHZEL!!

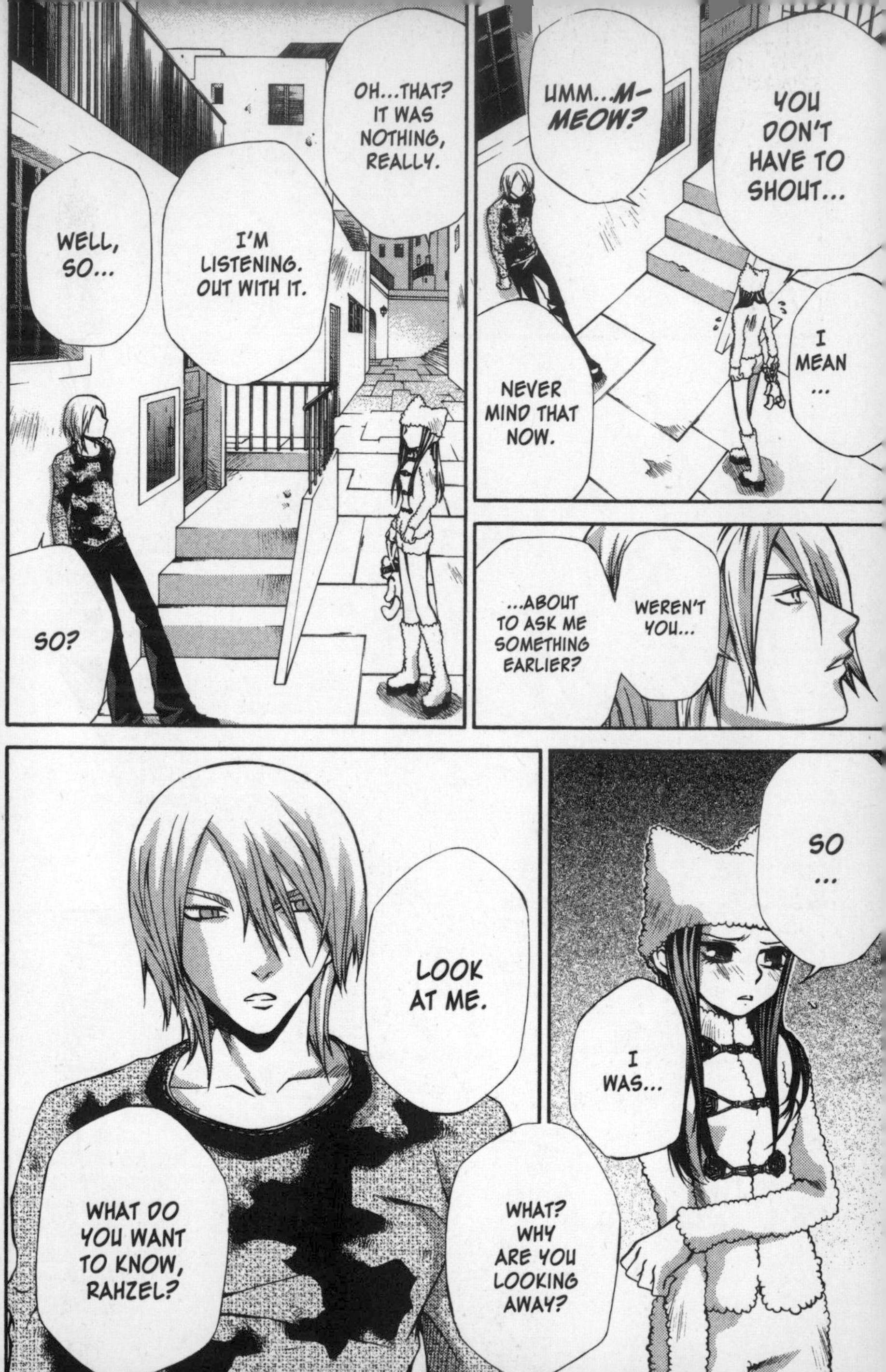
YOU DON'T HAVE TO SHOUT...
UMMM...*M-MEOW?*
I MEAN...
NEVER MIND THAT NOW.
WEREN'T YOU...
...ABOUT TO ASK ME SOMETHING EARLIER?
OH...THAT? IT WAS NOTHING, REALLY.
I'M LISTENING. OUT WITH IT.
WELL, SO...
SO?
SO...
I WAS...
LOOK AT ME.
WHAT? WHY ARE YOU LOOKING AWAY?
WHAT DO YOU WANT TO KNOW, RAHZEL?

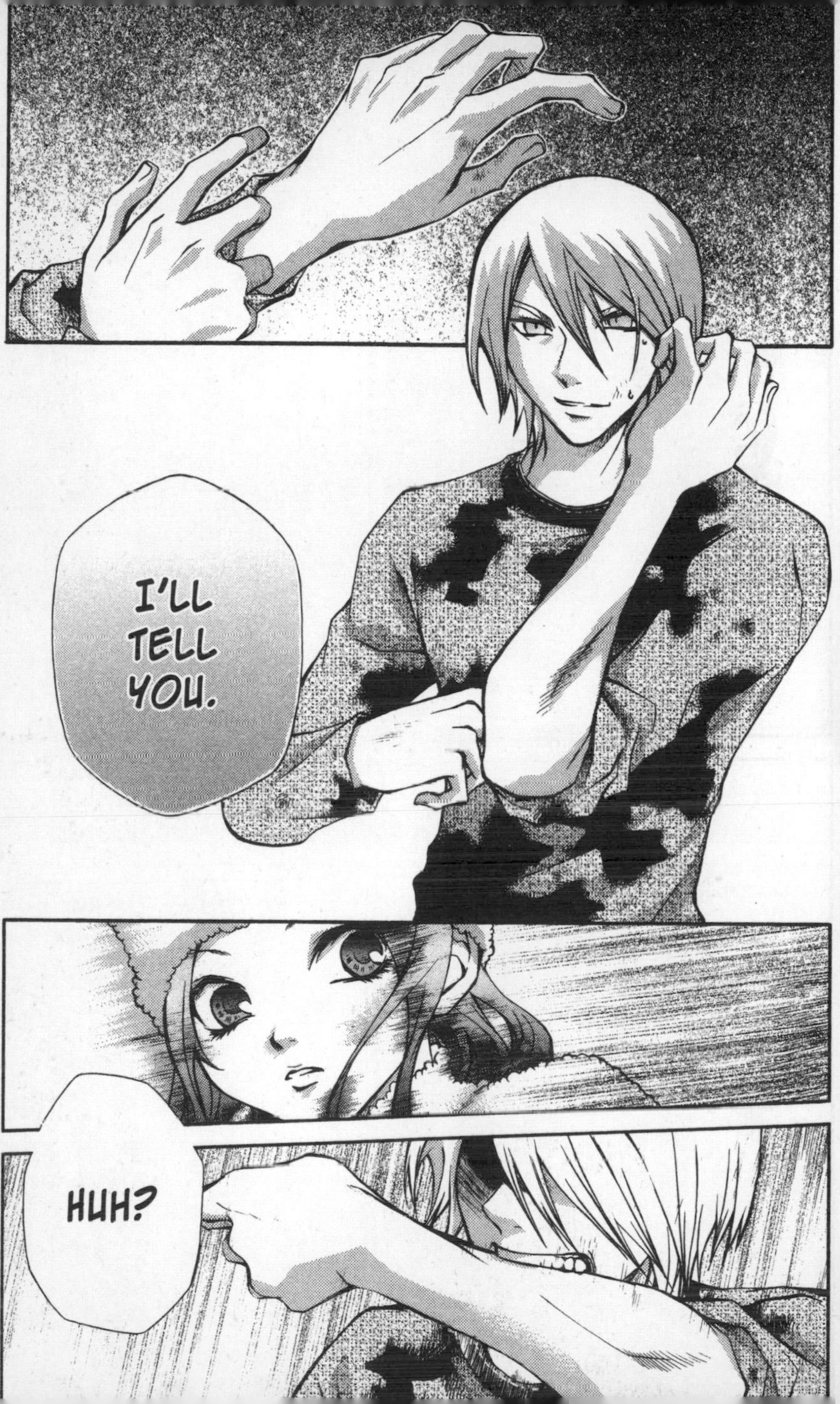
I'LL TELL YOU.
HUH?

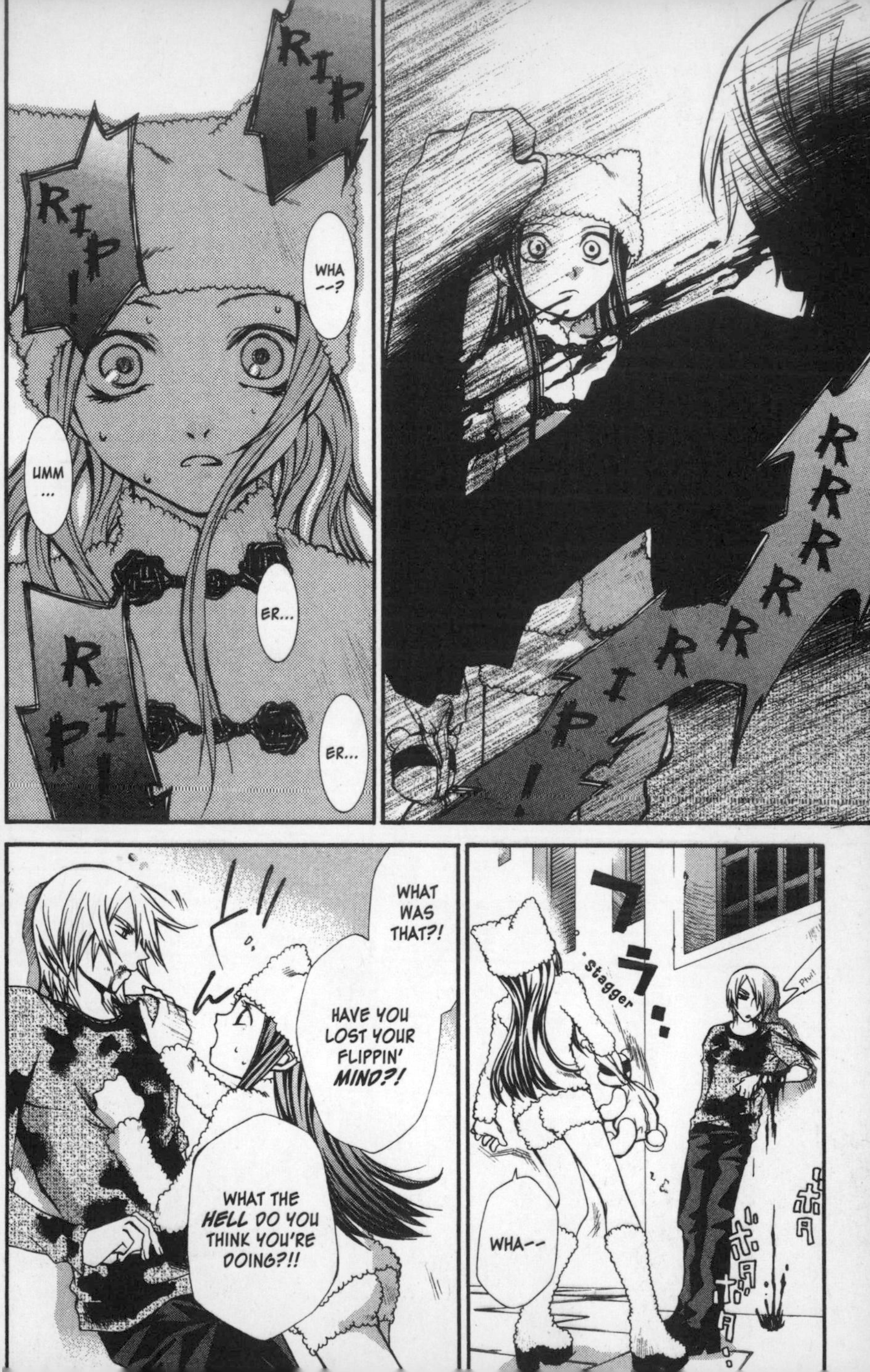
RRRRRRIP!
RIP!
RIP!
WHA--?
UMM...
ER...
ER...
RIP!
stagger
Ptui!
WHA--
WHAT WAS THAT?!
HAVE YOU LOST YOUR FLIPPIN' MIND?!
WHAT THE HELL DO YOU THINK YOU'RE DOING?!!

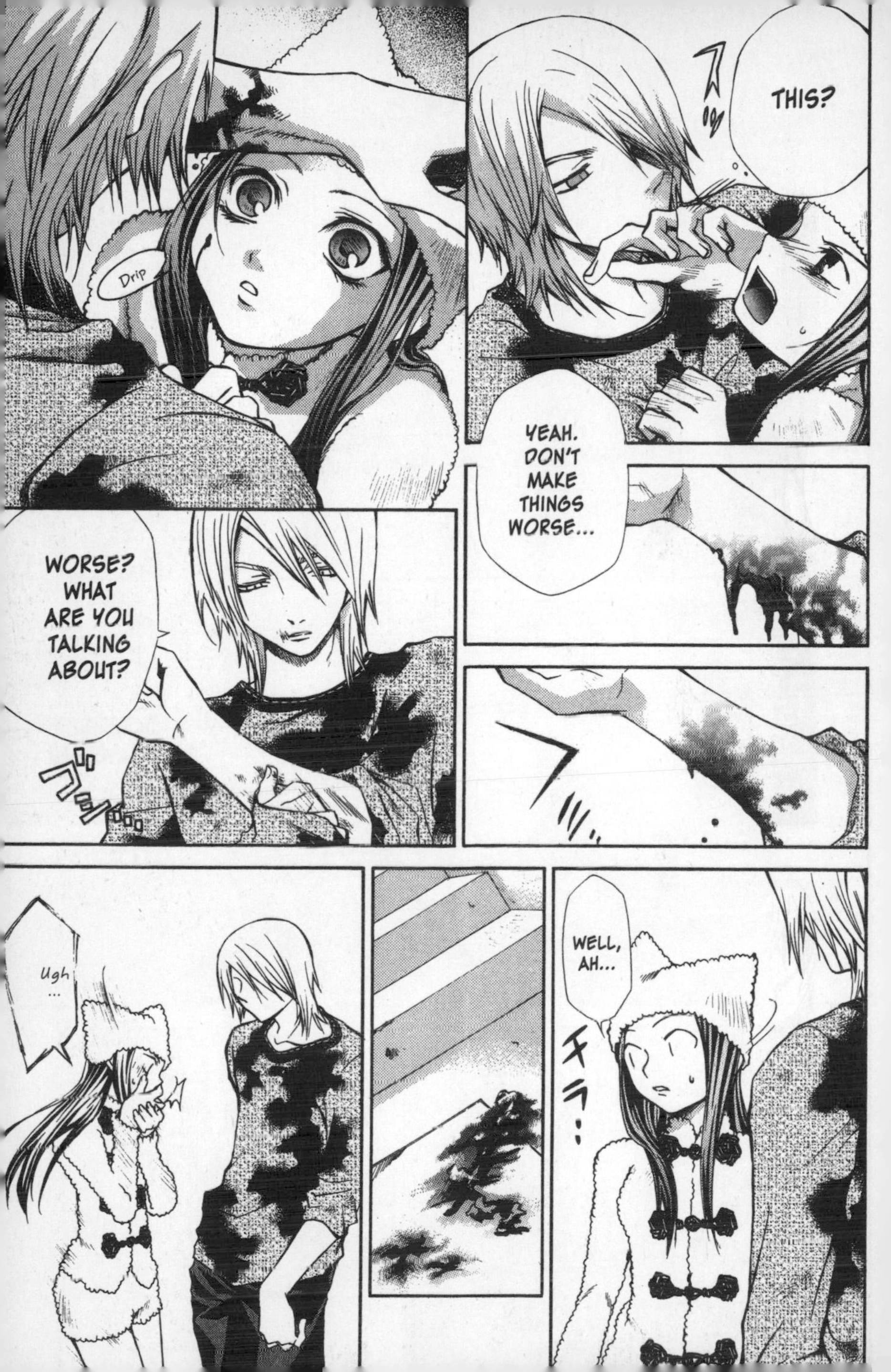
THIS?
Drip
YEAH. DON'T MAKE THINGS WORSE...
WORSE? WHAT ARE YOU TALKING ABOUT?
WELL, AH...
チラ
Ugh ...

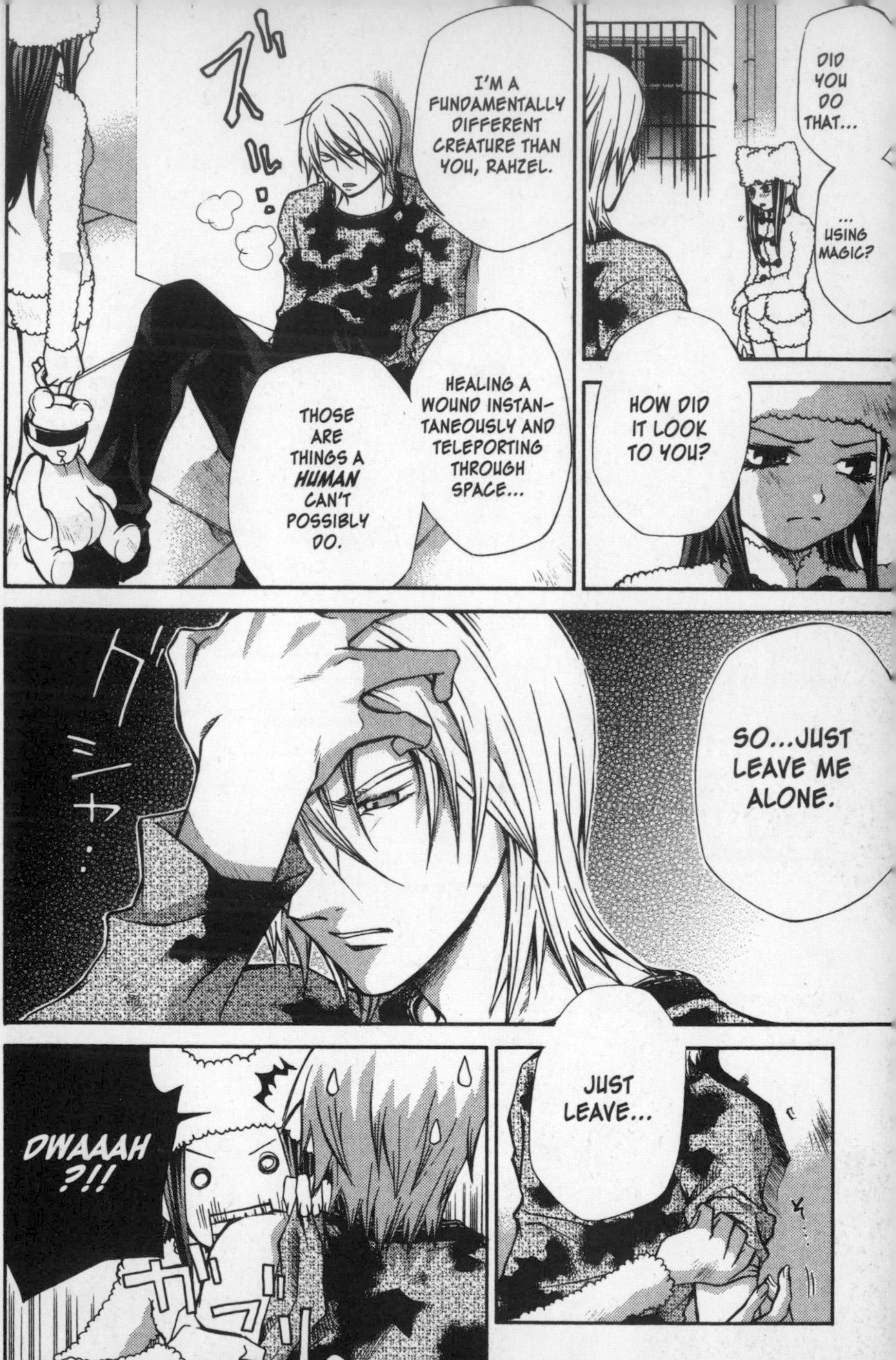
DID YOU DO THAT...
...USING MAGIC?
HOW DID IT LOOK TO YOU?
I'M A FUNDAMENTALLY DIFFERENT CREATURE THAN YOU, RAHZEL.
HEALING A WOUND INSTANTANEOUSLY AND TELEPORTING THROUGH SPACE...
THOSE ARE THINGS A *HUMAN* CAN'T POSSIBLY DO.
SO...JUST LEAVE ME ALONE.
JUST LEAVE...
DWAAAH ?!!

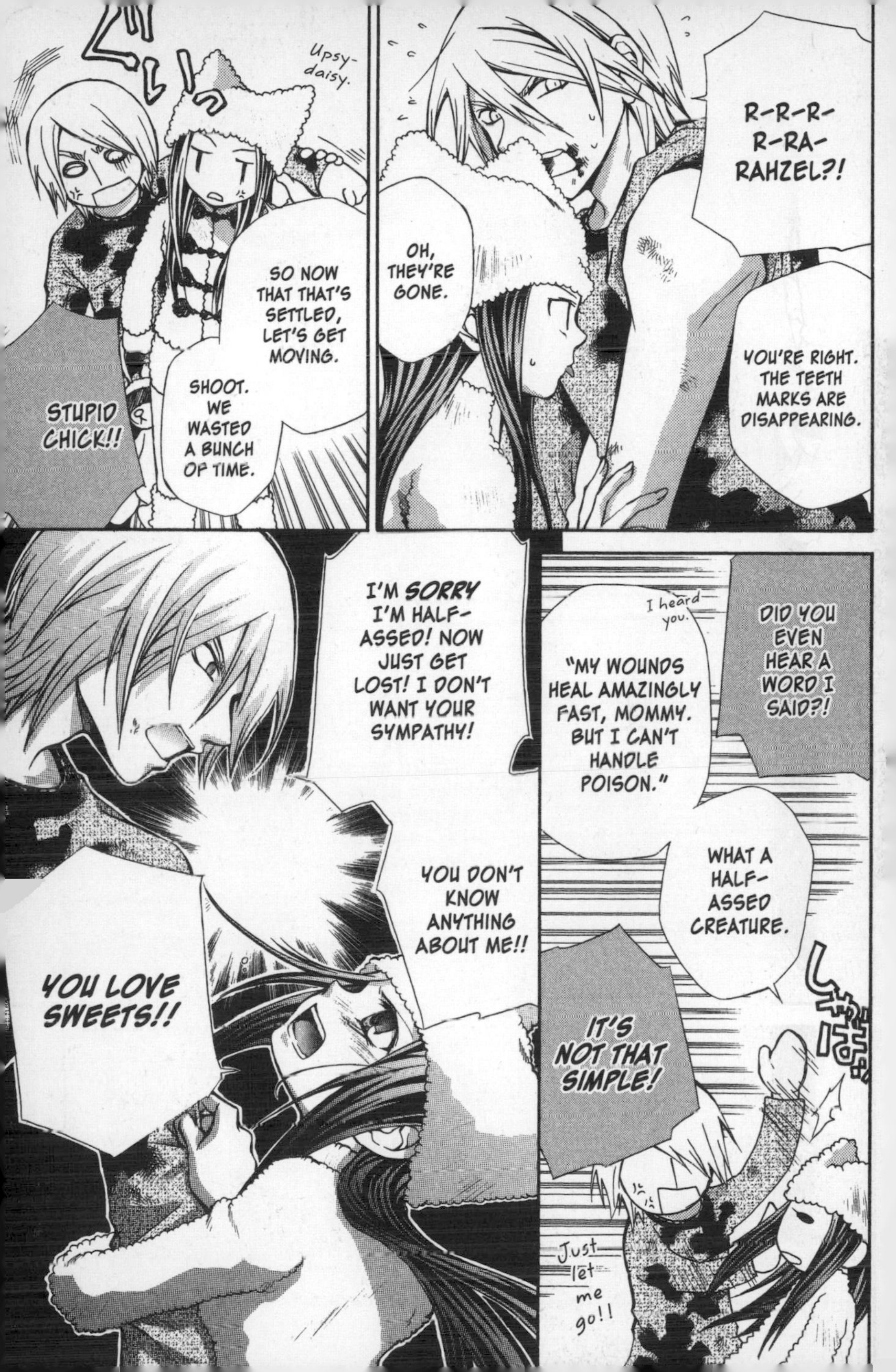
R-R-R-R-RA-RAHZEL?!
YOU'RE RIGHT. THE TEETH MARKS ARE DISAPPEARING.
OH, THEY'RE GONE.
Upsy-daisy.
SO NOW THAT THAT'S SETTLED, LET'S GET MOVING.
SHOOT. WE WASTED A BUNCH OF TIME.
STUPID CHICK!!
DID YOU EVEN HEAR A WORD I SAID?!
I heard you.
"MY WOUNDS HEAL AMAZINGLY FAST, MOMMY. BUT I CAN'T HANDLE POISON."
WHAT A HALF-ASSED CREATURE.
IT'S NOT THAT SIMPLE!
Just let me go!!
I'M SORRY I'M HALF-ASSED! NOW JUST GET LOST! I DON'T WANT YOUR SYMPATHY!
YOU DON'T KNOW ANYTHING ABOUT ME!!
YOU LOVE SWEETS!!

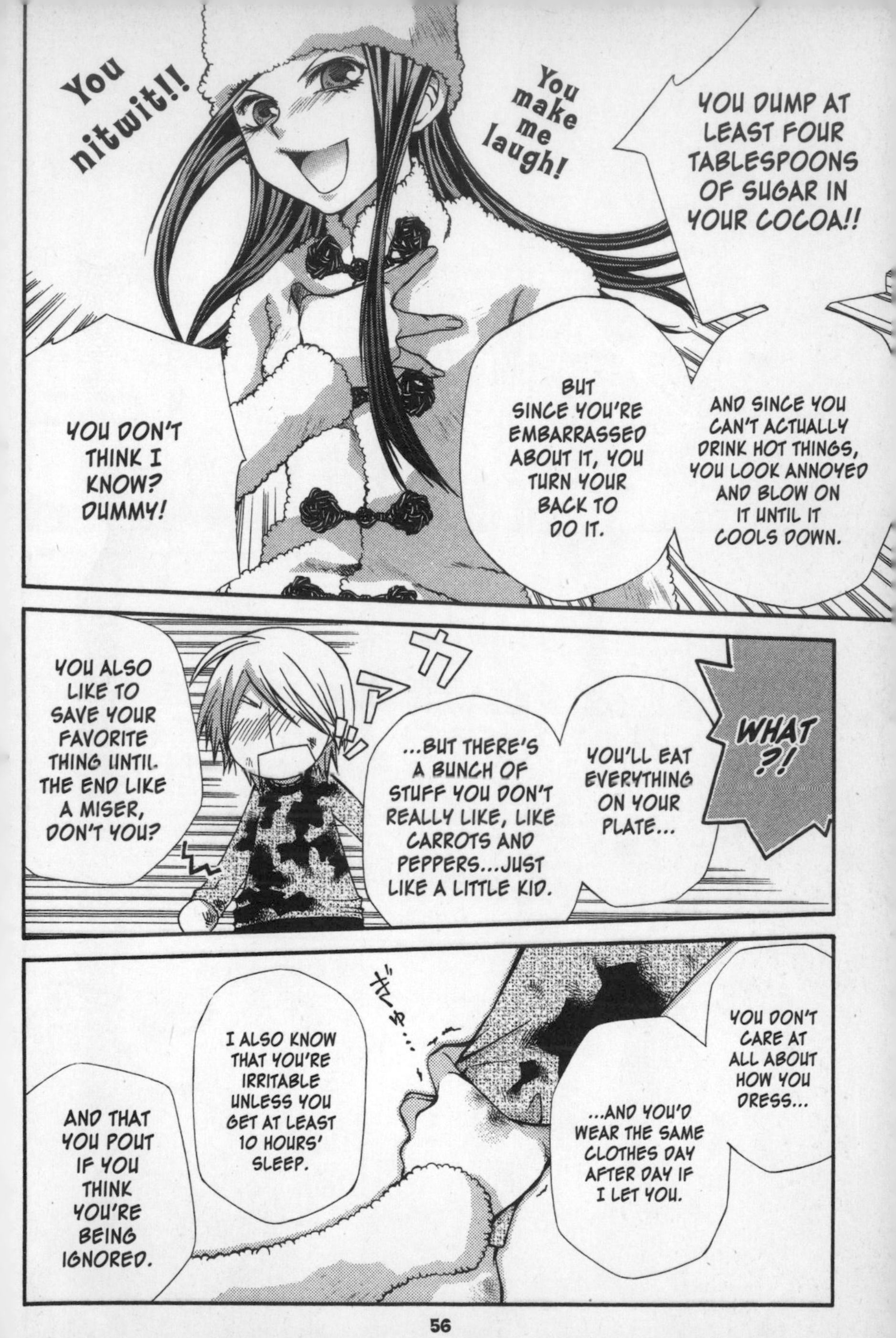

YOU DUMP AT LEAST FOUR TABLESPOONS OF SUGAR IN YOUR COCOA!!
You make me laugh!
You nitwit!!
AND SINCE YOU CAN'T ACTUALLY DRINK HOT THINGS, YOU LOOK ANNOYED AND BLOW ON IT UNTIL IT COOLS DOWN.
BUT SINCE YOU'RE EMBARRASSED ABOUT IT, YOU TURN YOUR BACK TO DO IT.
YOU DON'T THINK I KNOW? DUMMY!
WHAT?!
YOU'LL EAT EVERYTHING ON YOUR PLATE...
...BUT THERE'S A BUNCH OF STUFF YOU DON'T REALLY LIKE, LIKE CARROTS AND PEPPERS...JUST LIKE A LITTLE KID.
YOU ALSO LIKE TO SAVE YOUR FAVORITE THING UNTIL THE END LIKE A MISER, DON'T YOU?
YOU DON'T CARE AT ALL ABOUT HOW YOU DRESS...
...AND YOU'D WEAR THE SAME CLOTHES DAY AFTER DAY IF I LET YOU.
I ALSO KNOW THAT YOU'RE IRRITABLE UNLESS YOU GET AT LEAST 10 HOURS' SLEEP.
AND THAT YOU POUT IF YOU THINK YOU'RE BEING IGNORED.

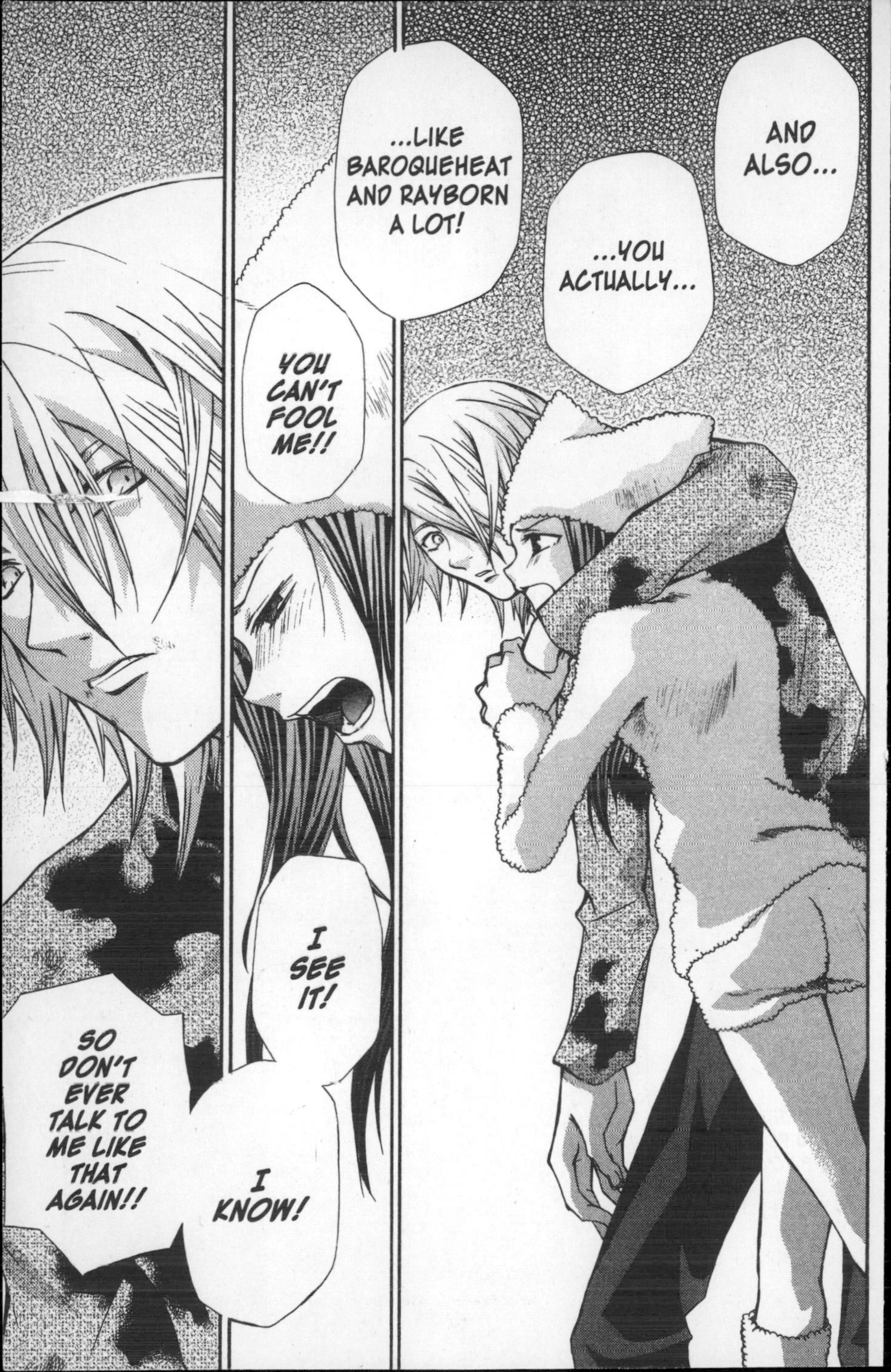
AND ALSO...
...YOU ACTUALLY...
...LIKE BAROQUEHEAT AND RAYBORN A LOT!
YOU CAN'T FOOL ME!!
I SEE IT!
I KNOW!
SO DON'T EVER TALK TO ME LIKE THAT AGAIN!!

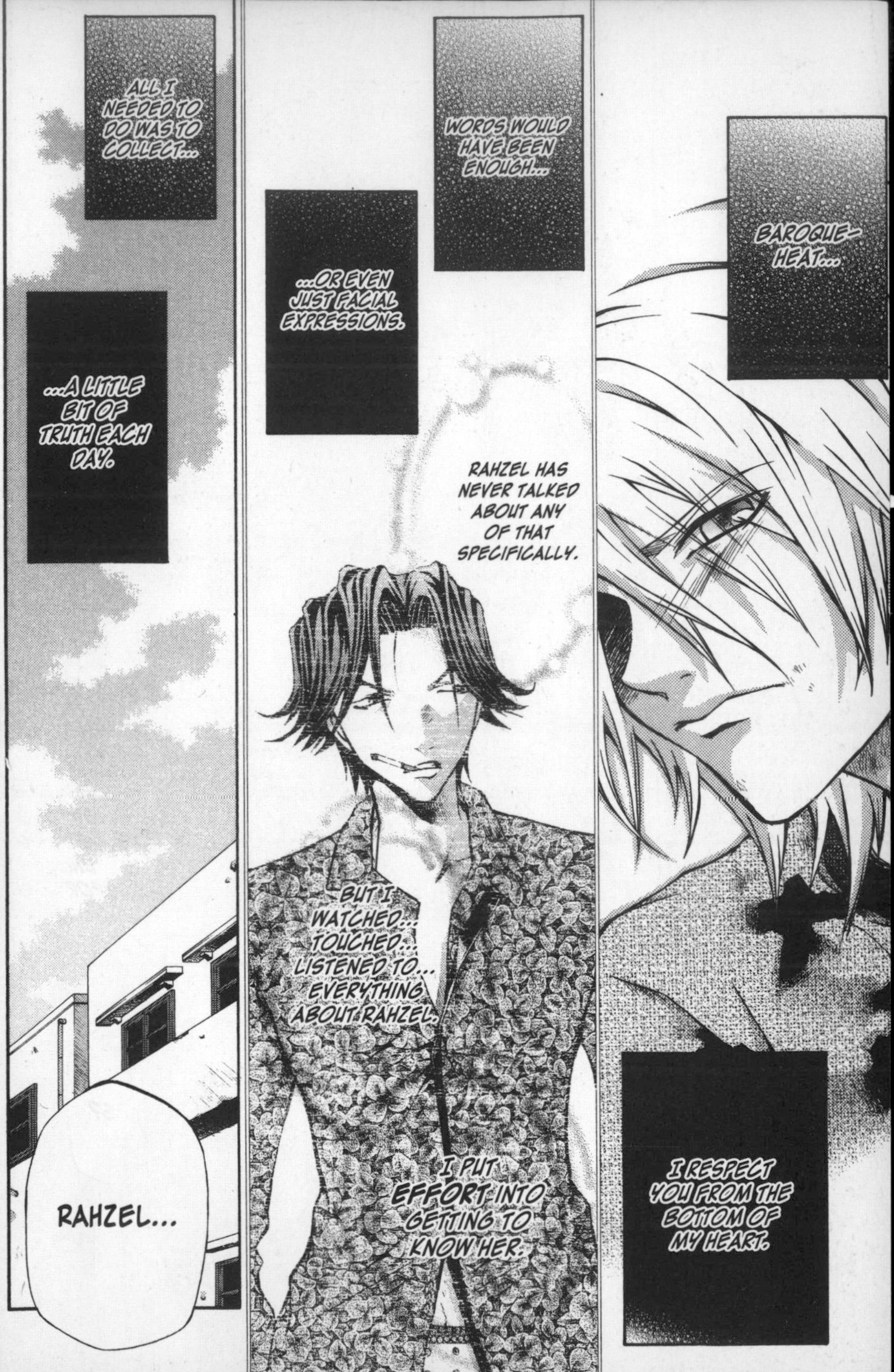
BAROQUE-HEAT...
I RESPECT YOU FROM THE BOTTOM OF MY HEART.
WORDS WOULD HAVE BEEN ENOUGH...
...OR EVEN JUST FACIAL EXPRESSIONS.
RAHZEL HAS NEVER TALKED ABOUT ANY OF THAT SPECIFICALLY.
BUT I WATCHED... TOUCHED... LISTENED TO... EVERYTHING ABOUT RAHZEL.
I PUT EFFORT INTO GETTING TO KNOW HER.
ALL I NEEDED TO DO WAS TO COLLECT...
...A LITTLE BIT OF TRUTH EACH DAY.
RAHZEL...

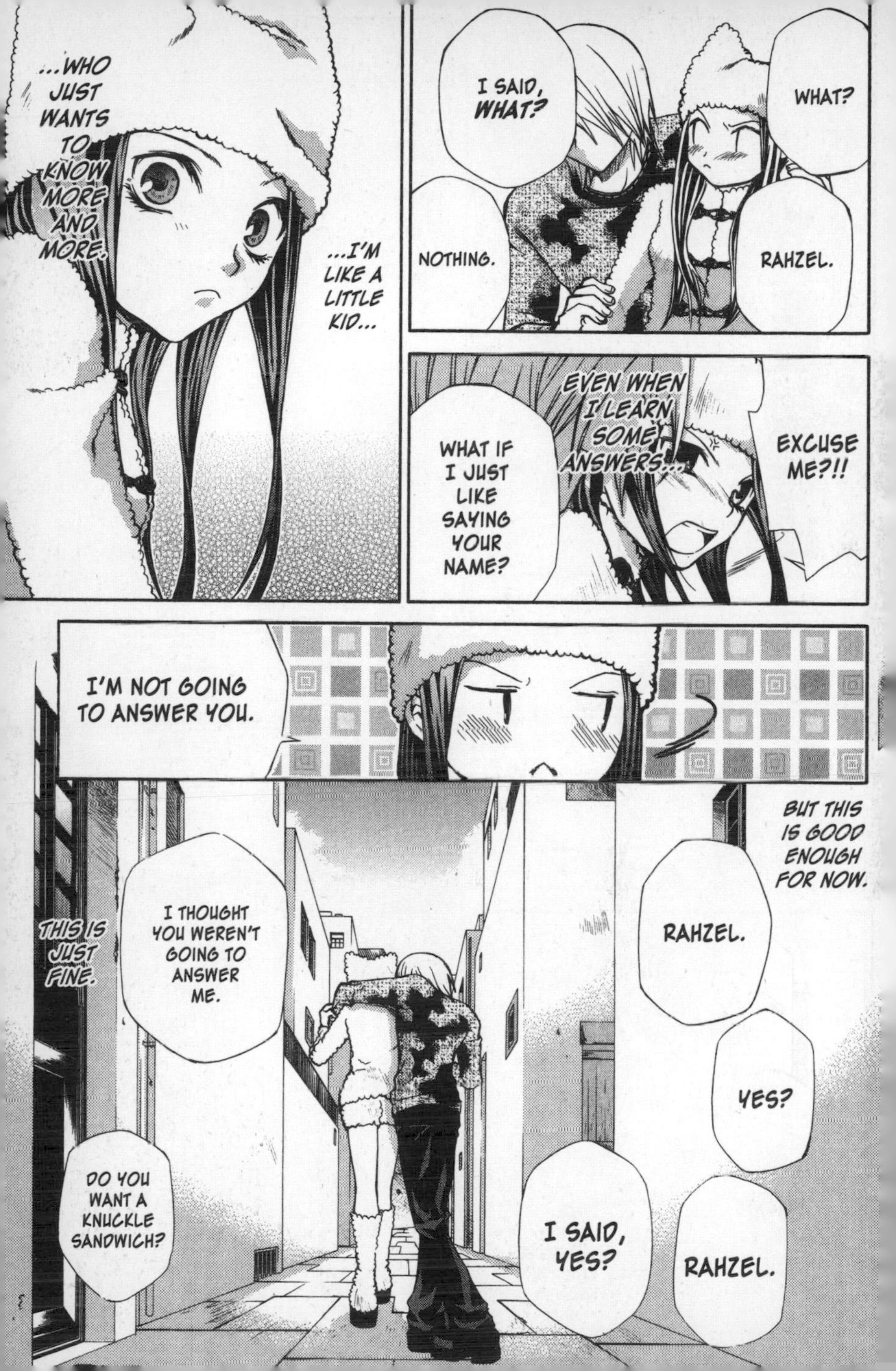
WHAT?
I SAID, WHAT?
RAHZEL.
NOTHING.
EXCUSE ME?!!
EVEN WHEN I LEARN SOME ANSWERS...
WHAT IF I JUST LIKE SAYING YOUR NAME?
...I'M LIKE A LITTLE KID...
...WHO JUST WANTS TO KNOW MORE AND MORE.
I'M NOT GOING TO ANSWER YOU.
BUT THIS IS GOOD ENOUGH FOR NOW.
RAHZEL.
YES?
RAHZEL.
I SAID, YES?
I THOUGHT YOU WEREN'T GOING TO ANSWER ME.
THIS IS JUST FINE.
DO YOU WANT A KNUCKLE SANDWICH?

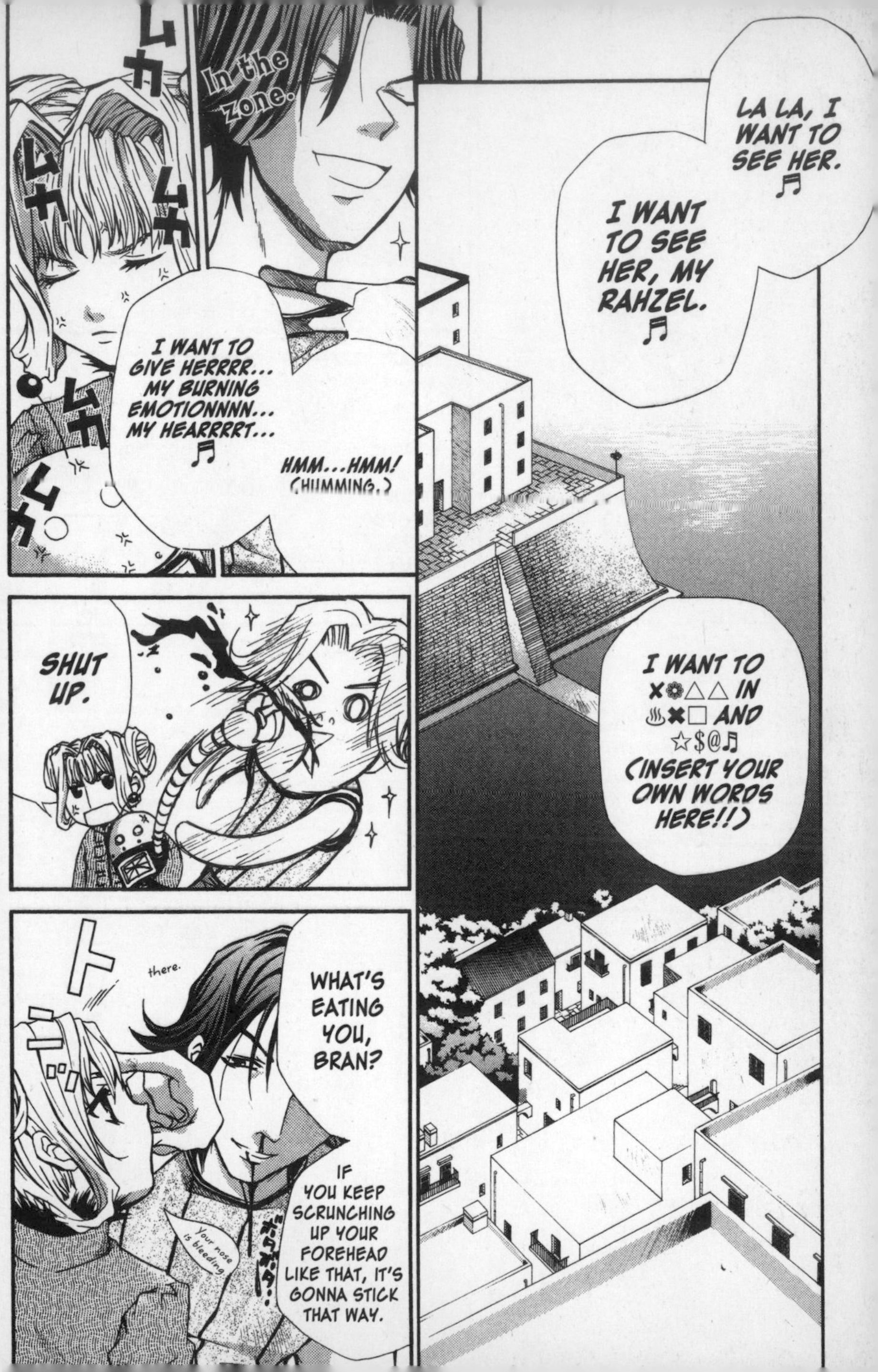
LA LA, I WANT TO SEE HER. ♬
I WANT TO SEE HER, MY RAHZEL. ♬
I WANT TO ×✿△△ IN ♨✖□ AND ☆$@♬ (INSERT YOUR OWN WORDS HERE!!)
In the zone.
ムカ
ムカ
ムカ
ムカ
ムカ
I WANT TO GIVE HERRRR... MY BURNING EMOTIONNNN... MY HEARRRRT... ♬
HMM...HMM! (HUMMING.)
SHUT UP.
WHAT'S EATING YOU, BRAN?
ト
there.
IF YOU KEEP SCRUNCHING UP YOUR FOREHEAD LIKE THAT, IT'S GONNA STICK THAT WAY.
ボタボタ
Your nose is bleeding.

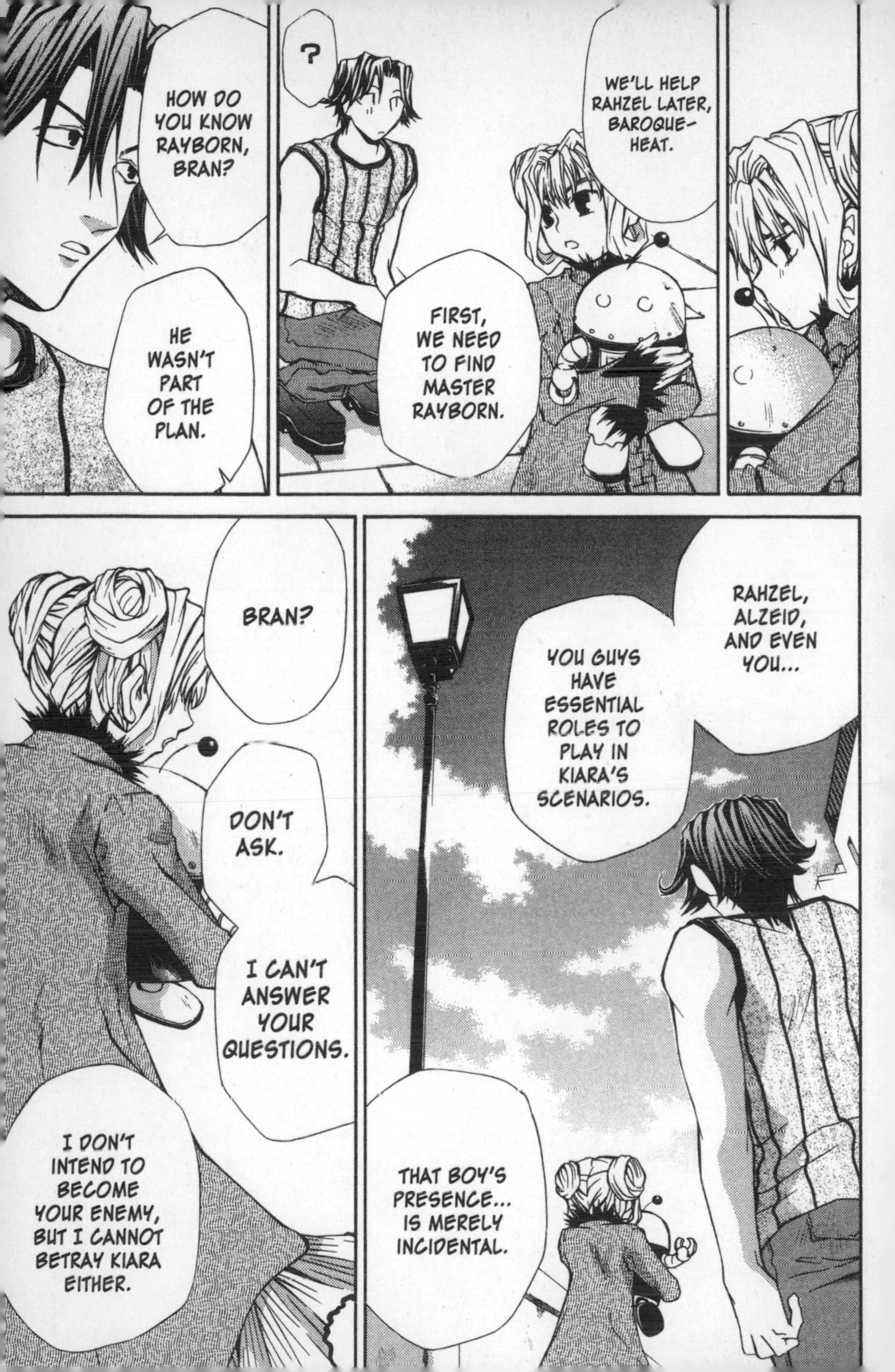
WE'LL HELP RAHZEL LATER, BAROQUE-HEAT.
FIRST, WE NEED TO FIND MASTER RAYBORN.
?
HOW DO YOU KNOW RAYBORN, BRAN?
HE WASN'T PART OF THE PLAN.
RAHZEL, ALZEID, AND EVEN YOU...
YOU GUYS HAVE ESSENTIAL ROLES TO PLAY IN KIARA'S SCENARIOS.
THAT BOY'S PRESENCE... IS MERELY INCIDENTAL.
BRAN?
DON'T ASK.
I CAN'T ANSWER YOUR QUESTIONS.
I DON'T INTEND TO BECOME YOUR ENEMY, BUT I CANNOT BETRAY KIARA EITHER.

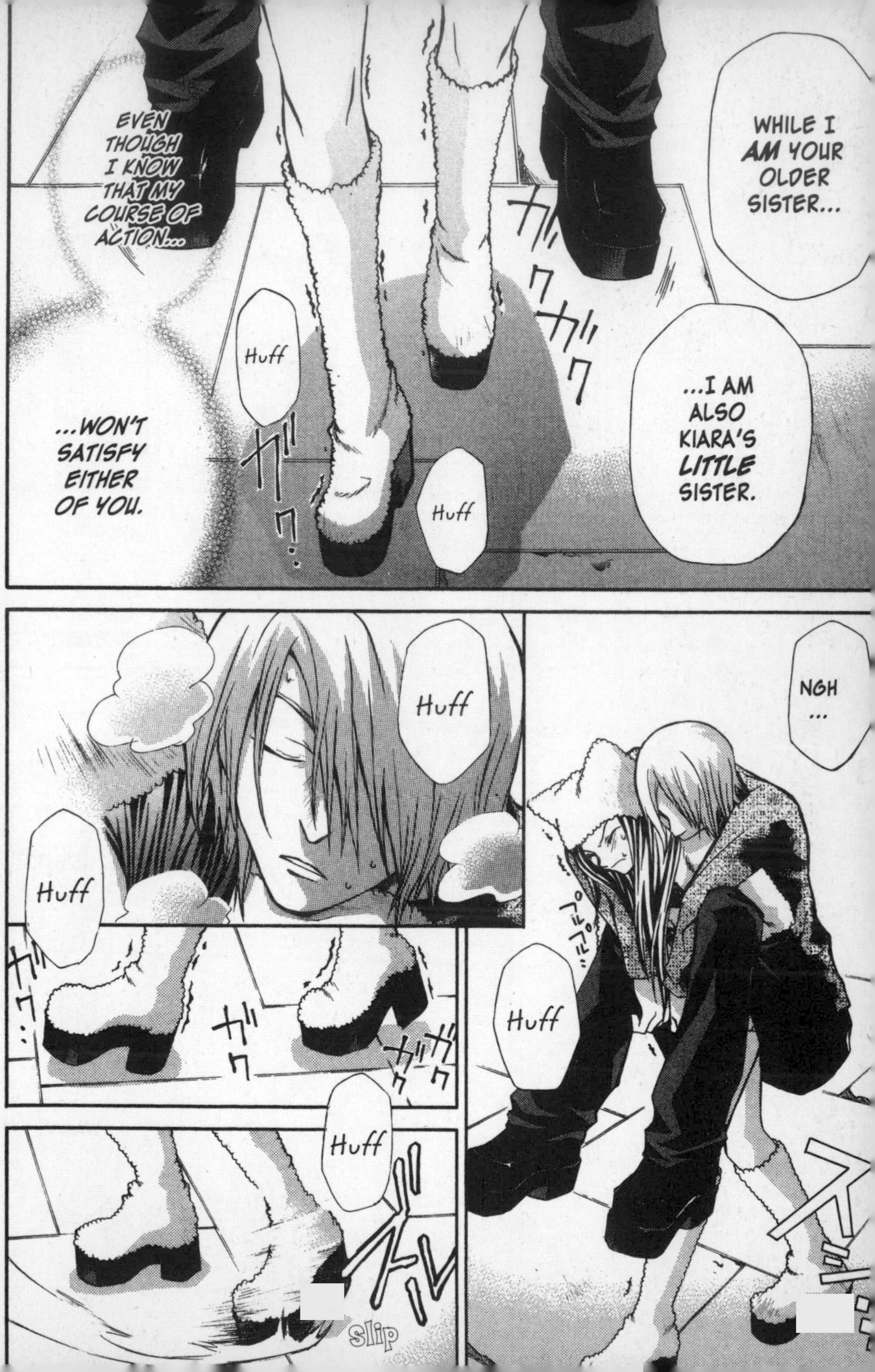

WHILE I AM YOUR OLDER SISTER...
...I AM ALSO KIARA'S LITTLE SISTER.
EVEN THOUGH I KNOW THAT MY COURSE OF ACTION...
Huff
Huff
...WON'T SATISFY EITHER OF YOU.
NGH ...
Huff
Huff
Huff
Huff
slip

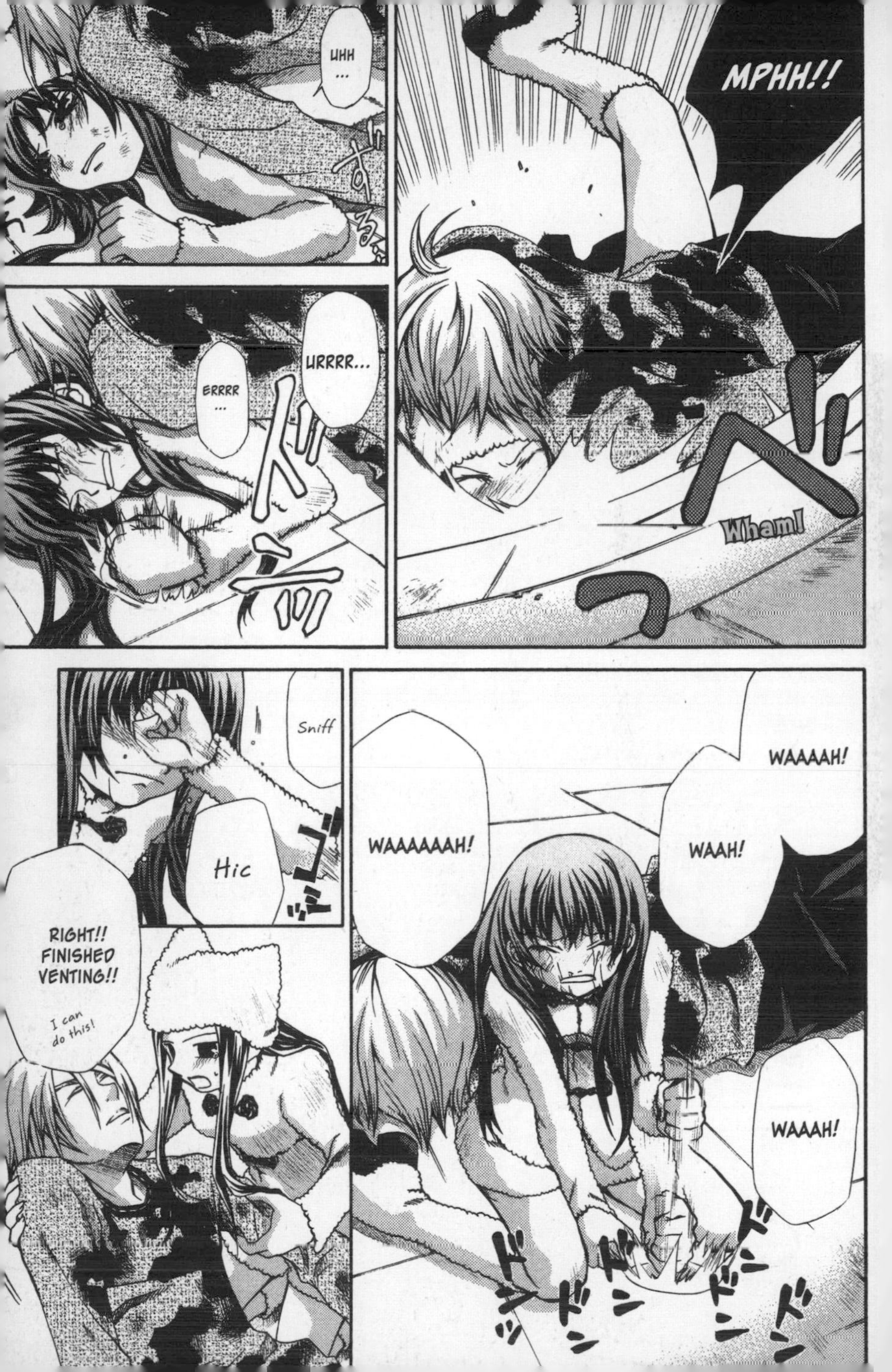
MPHH!!
Wham!
UHH ...
URRRR...
ERRRR ...
WAAAAH!
WAAH!
WAAAAAAH!
WAAAH!
Sniff
Hic
RIGHT!! FINISHED VENTING!!
I can do this!

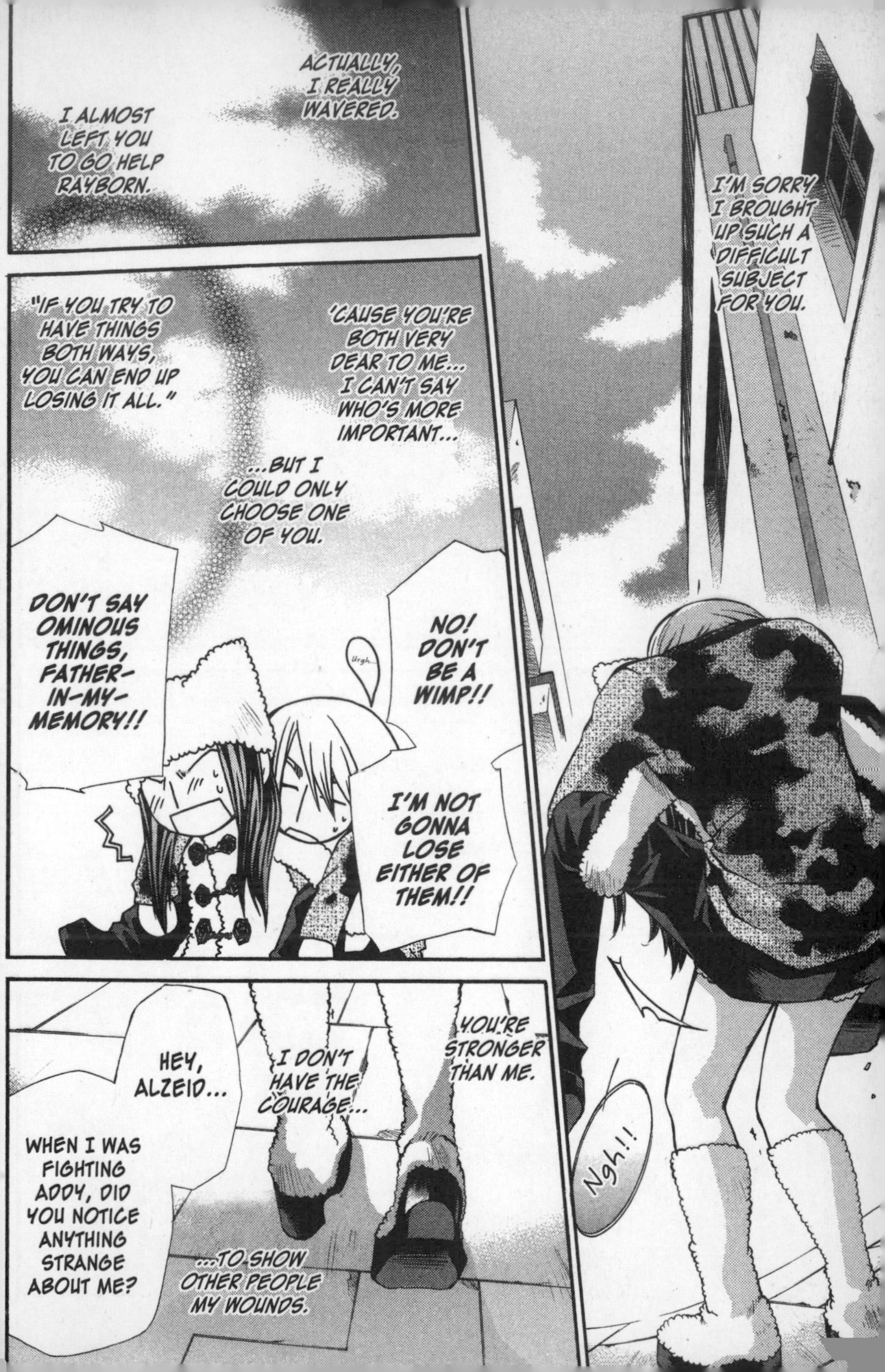
I'M SORRY I BROUGHT UP SUCH A DIFFICULT SUBJECT FOR YOU.
Ngh!!
ACTUALLY, I REALLY WAVERED.
I ALMOST LEFT YOU TO GO HELP RAYBORN.
'CAUSE YOU'RE BOTH VERY DEAR TO ME... I CAN'T SAY WHO'S MORE IMPORTANT...
...BUT I COULD ONLY CHOOSE ONE OF YOU.
"IF YOU TRY TO HAVE THINGS BOTH WAYS, YOU CAN END UP LOSING IT ALL."
NO! DON'T BE A WIMP!!
I'M NOT GONNA LOSE EITHER OF THEM!!
Urgh...
DON'T SAY OMINOUS THINGS, FATHER-IN-MY-MEMORY!!
YOU'RE STRONGER THAN ME.
I DON'T HAVE THE COURAGE...
...TO SHOW OTHER PEOPLE MY WOUNDS.
HEY, ALZEID...
WHEN I WAS FIGHTING ADDY, DID YOU NOTICE ANYTHING STRANGE ABOUT ME?

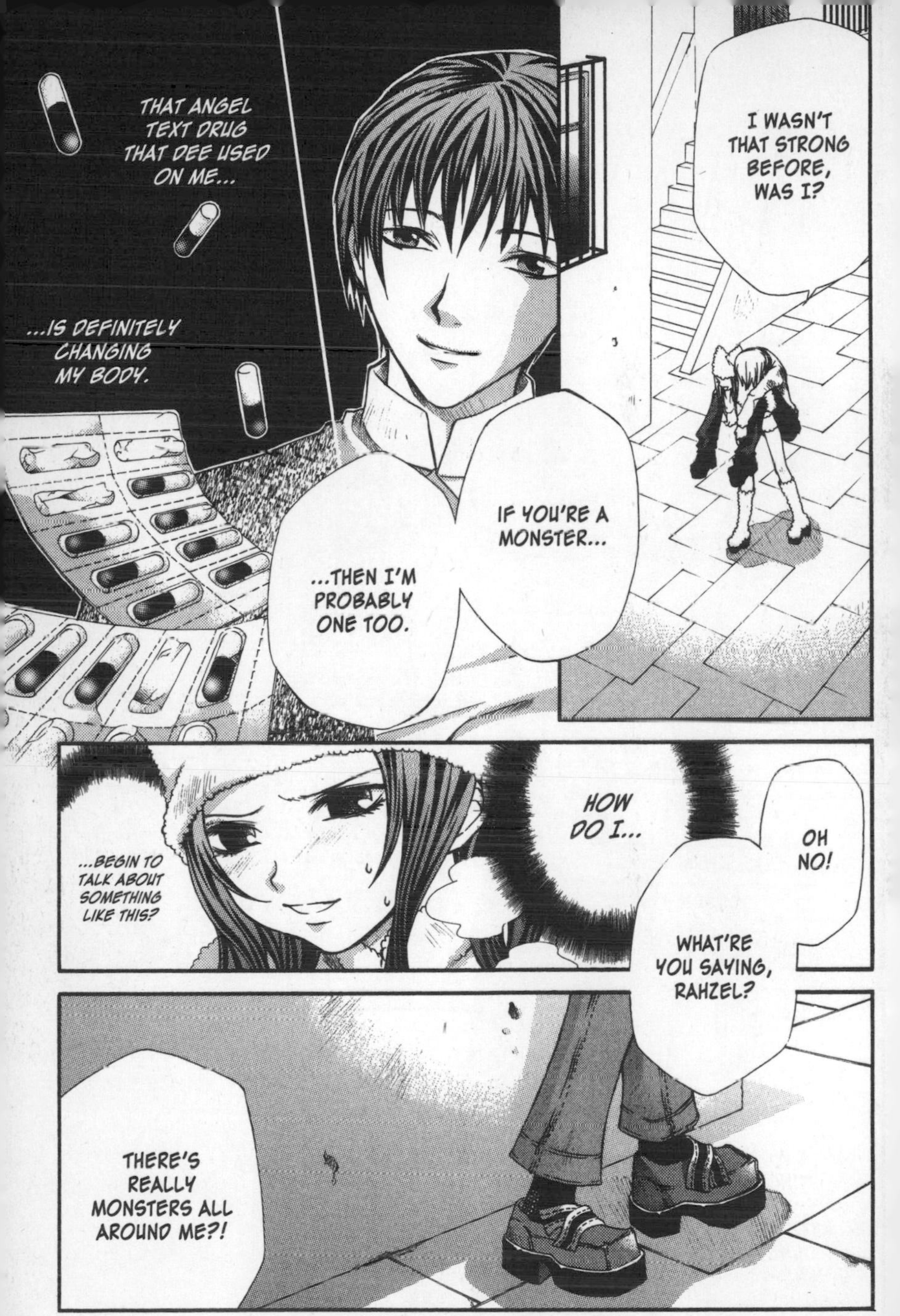
I WASN'T THAT STRONG BEFORE, WAS I?
THAT ANGEL TEXT DRUG THAT DEE USED ON ME...
...IS DEFINITELY CHANGING MY BODY.
IF YOU'RE A MONSTER...
...THEN I'M PROBABLY ONE TOO.
OH NO!
WHAT'RE YOU SAYING, RAHZEL?
HOW DO I...
...BEGIN TO TALK ABOUT SOMETHING LIKE THIS?
THERE'S REALLY MONSTERS ALL AROUND ME?!

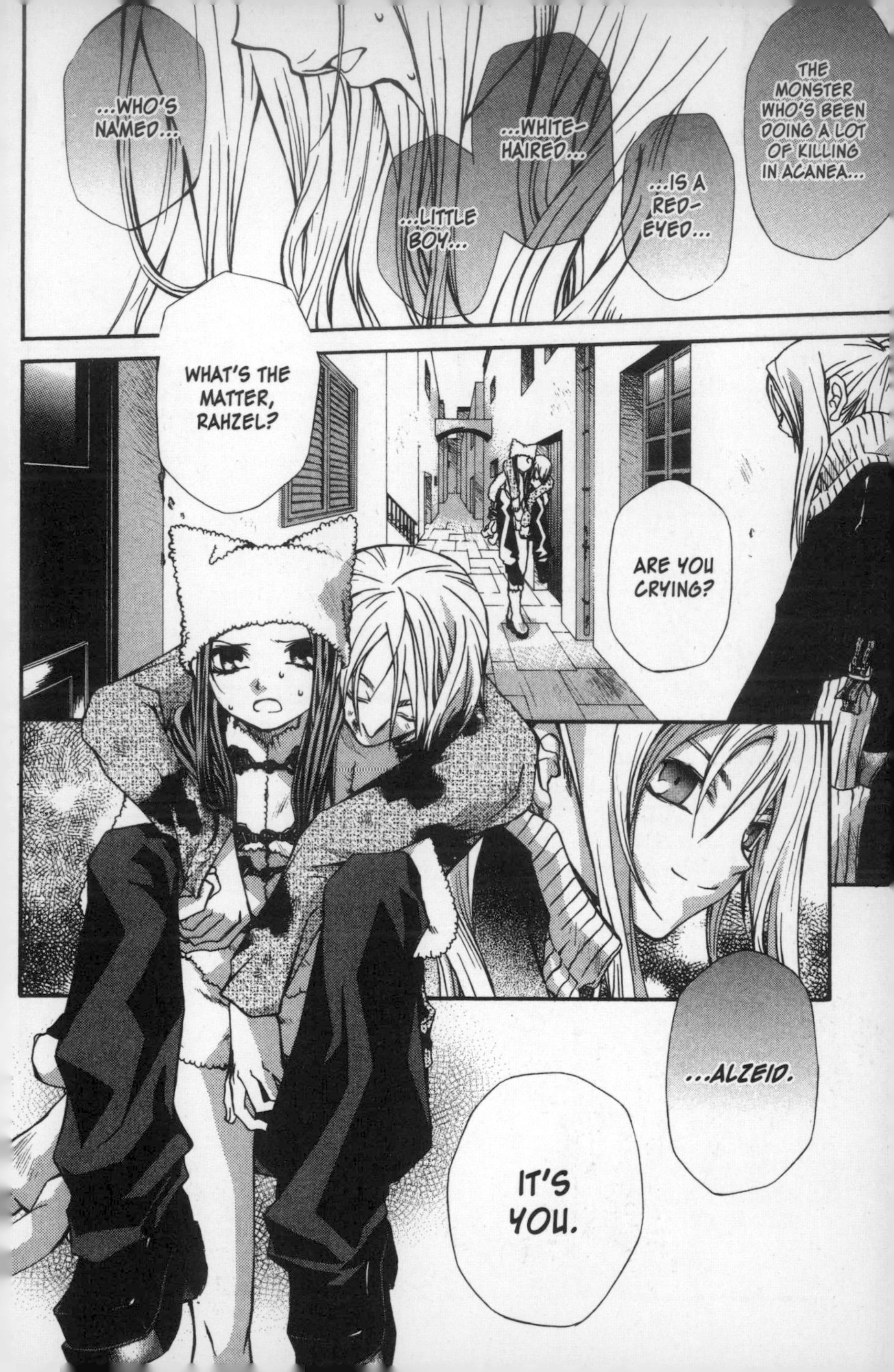
THE MONSTER WHO'S BEEN DOING A LOT OF KILLING IN ACANEA...
...IS A RED-EYED...
...WHITE-HAIRED...
...LITTLE BOY...
...WHO'S NAMED...
WHAT'S THE MATTER, RAHZEL?
ARE YOU CRYING?
...ALZEID.
IT'S YOU.

Chapter 43: The Ephemeral Proposition--Part 8: The Name Rules

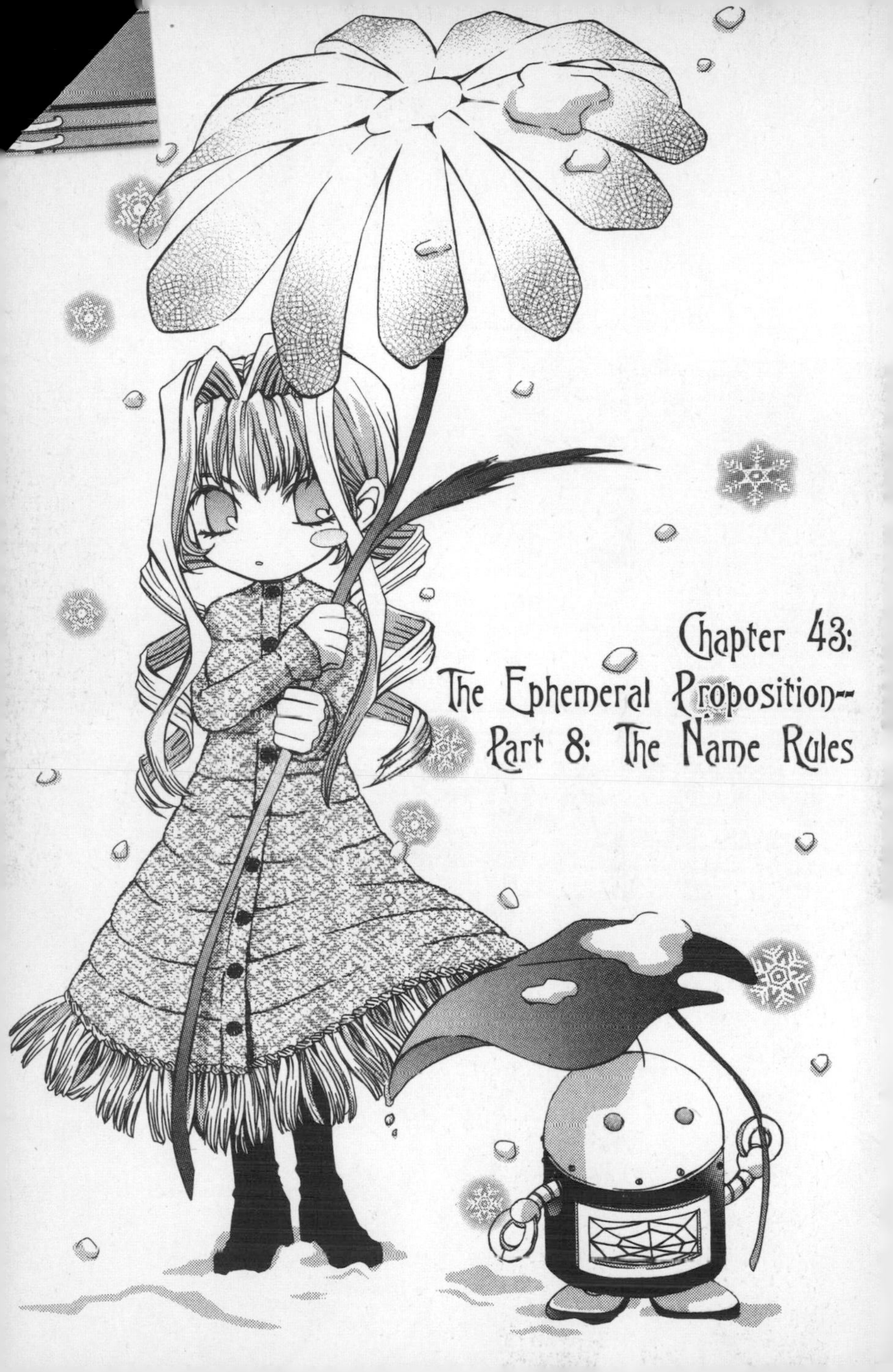

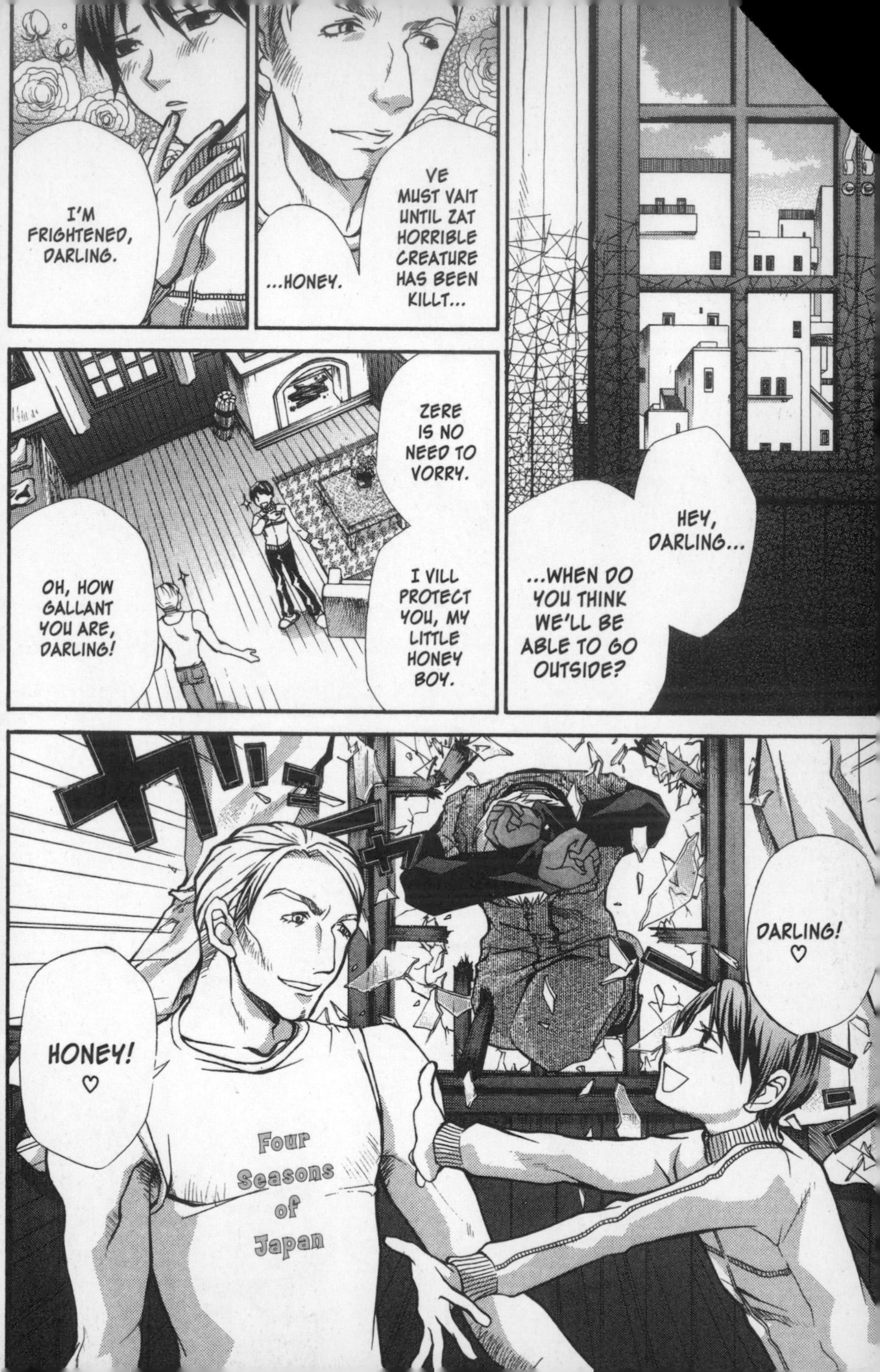
HEY, DARLING...
...WHEN DO YOU THINK WE'LL BE ABLE TO GO OUTSIDE?
VE MUST VAIT UNTIL ZAT HORRIBLE CREATURE HAS BEEN KILLT...
...HONEY.
I'M FRIGHTENED, DARLING.
ZERE IS NO NEED TO VORRY.
I VILL PROTECT YOU, MY LITTLE HONEY BOY.
OH, HOW GALLANT YOU ARE, DARLING!
DARLING! ♡
HONEY! ♡
Four Seasons of Japan

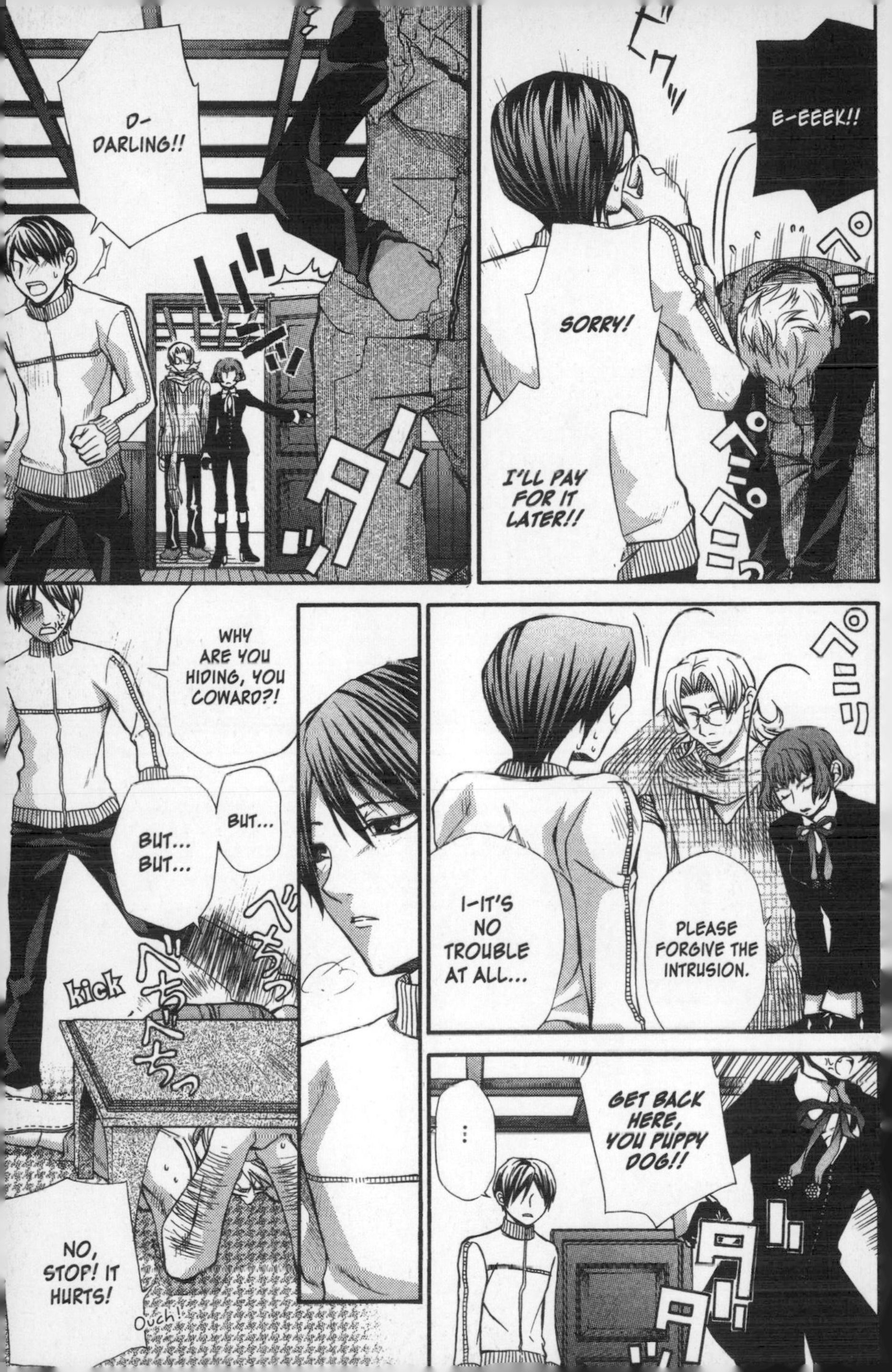
E-EEEK!!
SORRY!
I'LL PAY FOR IT LATER!!
D-DARLING!!
PLEASE FORGIVE THE INTRUSION.
I-IT'S NO TROUBLE AT ALL...
GET BACK HERE, YOU PUPPY DOG!!
...
WHY ARE YOU HIDING, YOU COWARD?!
BUT...
BUT... BUT...
kick
NO, STOP! IT HURTS!
Ouch!

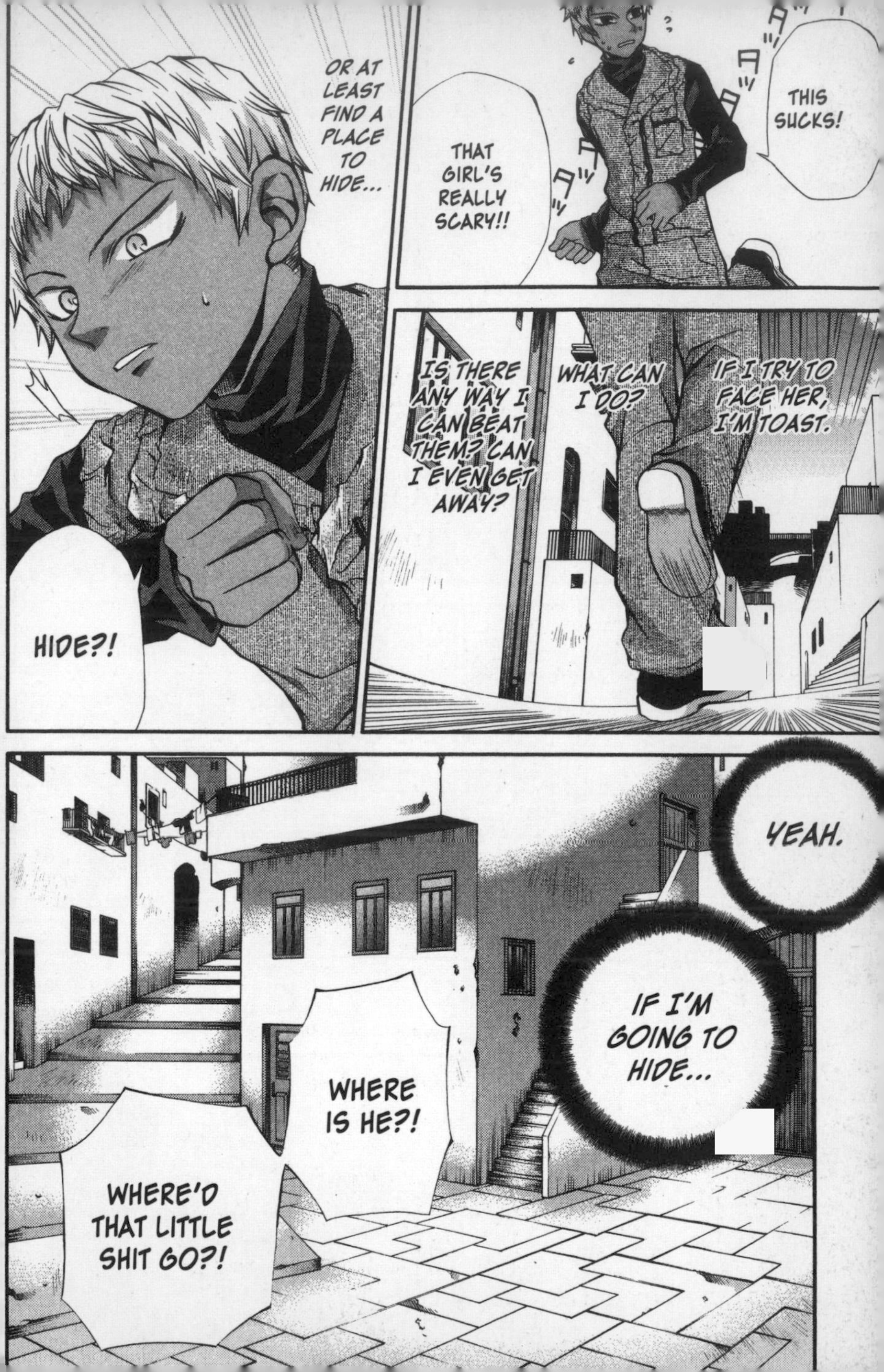
THIS SUCKS!
THAT GIRL'S REALLY SCARY!!
IF I TRY TO FACE HER, I'M TOAST.
WHAT CAN I DO?
IS THERE ANY WAY I CAN BEAT THEM? CAN I EVEN GET AWAY?
OR AT LEAST FIND A PLACE TO HIDE...
HIDE?!
YEAH.
IF I'M GOING TO HIDE...
WHERE IS HE?!
WHERE'D THAT LITTLE SHIT GO?!

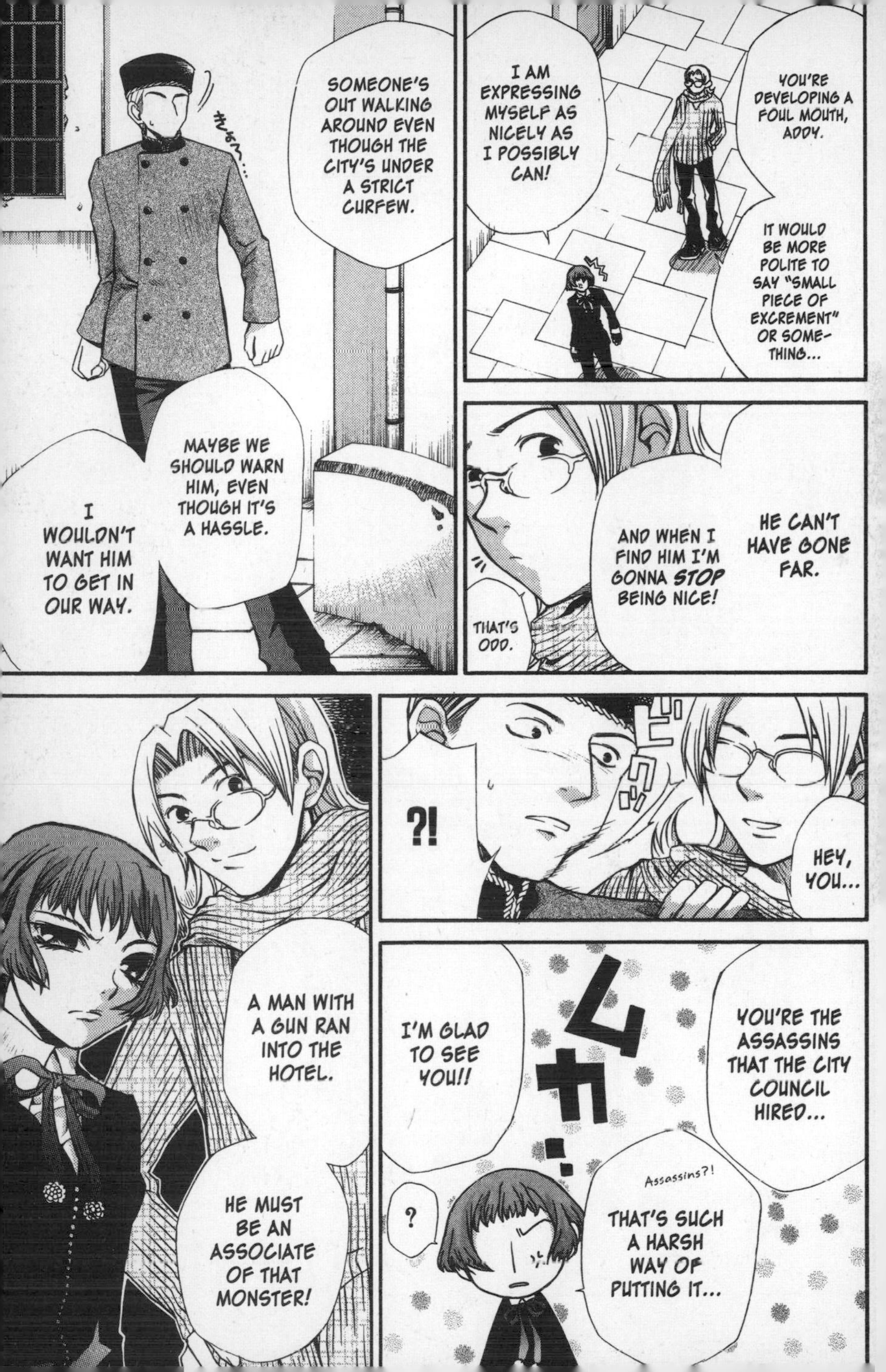
YOU'RE DEVELOPING A FOUL MOUTH, ADDY.
IT WOULD BE MORE POLITE TO SAY "SMALL PIECE OF EXCREMENT" OR SOME-THING...
I AM EXPRESSING MYSELF AS NICELY AS I POSSIBLY CAN!
HE CAN'T HAVE GONE FAR.
AND WHEN I FIND HIM I'M GONNA *STOP* BEING NICE!
THAT'S ODD.
SOMEONE'S OUT WALKING AROUND EVEN THOUGH THE CITY'S UNDER A STRICT CURFEW.
MAYBE WE SHOULD WARN HIM, EVEN THOUGH IT'S A HASSLE.
I WOULDN'T WANT HIM TO GET IN OUR WAY.
HEY, YOU...
?!
YOU'RE THE ASSASSINS THAT THE CITY COUNCIL HIRED...
I'M GLAD TO SEE YOU!!
Assassins?!
THAT'S SUCH A HARSH WAY OF PUTTING IT...
?
A MAN WITH A GUN RAN INTO THE HOTEL.
HE MUST BE AN ASSOCIATE OF THAT MONSTER!

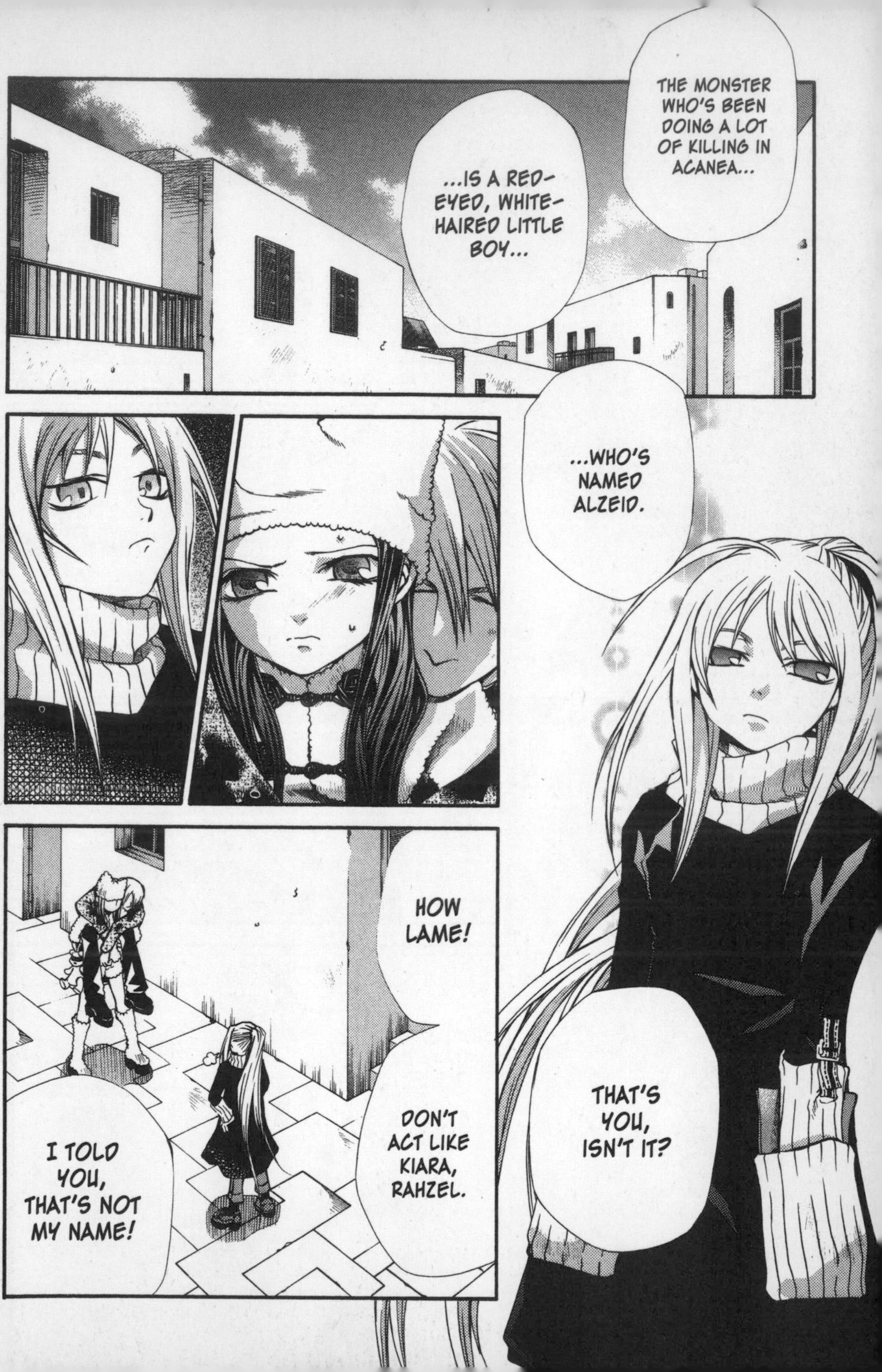
THE MONSTER WHO'S BEEN DOING A LOT OF KILLING IN ACANEA...
...IS A RED-EYED, WHITE-HAIRED LITTLE BOY...
...WHO'S NAMED ALZEID.
THAT'S YOU, ISN'T IT?
HOW LAME!
DON'T ACT LIKE KIARA, RAHZEL.
I TOLD YOU, THAT'S NOT MY NAME!

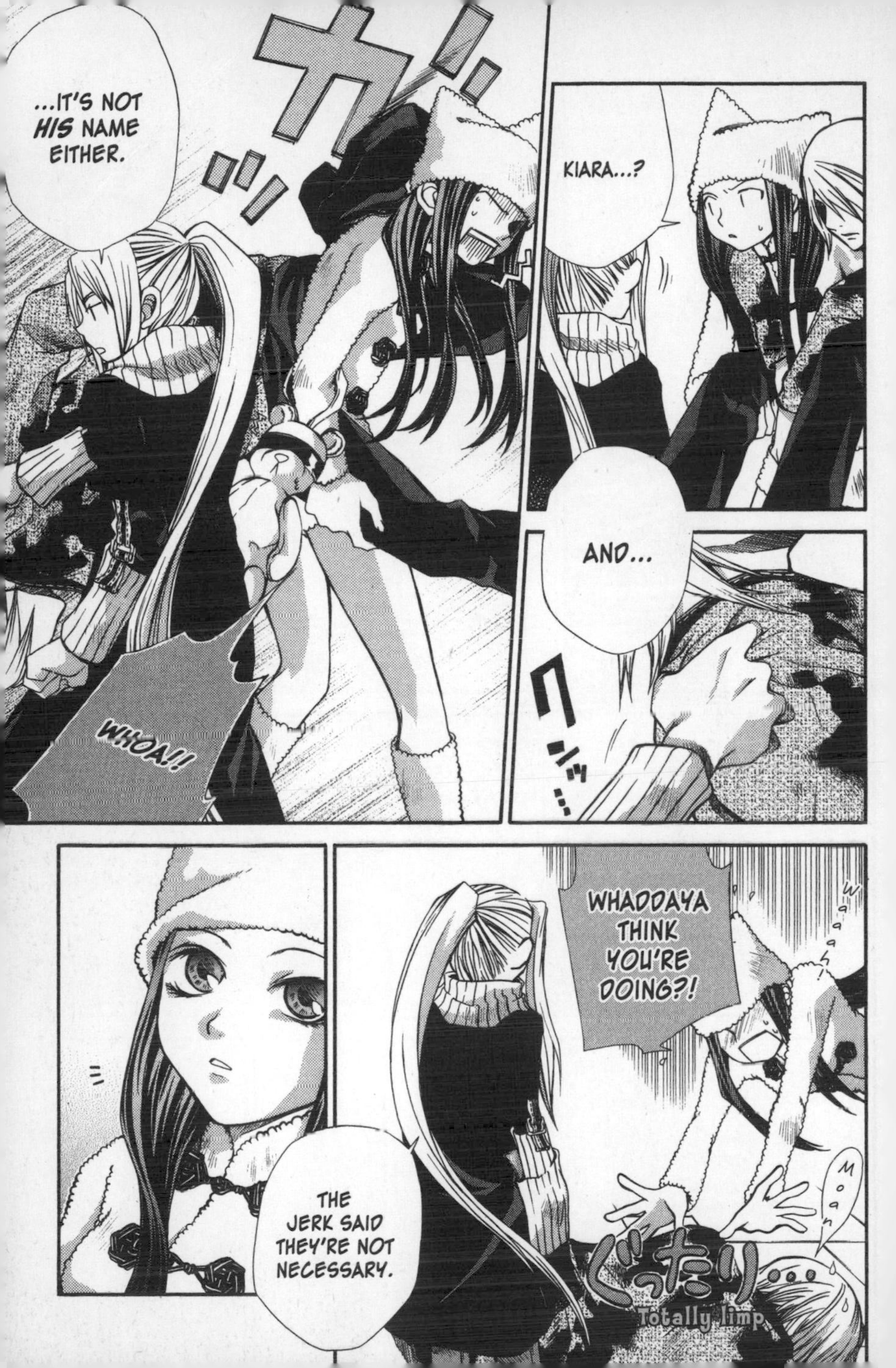
KIARA...?
AND...
...IT'S NOT HIS NAME EITHER.
WHOA!!
WHADDAYA THINK YOU'RE DOING?!
Waaah!
Moan
ぐったり...
Totally limp
THE JERK SAID THEY'RE NOT NECESSARY.

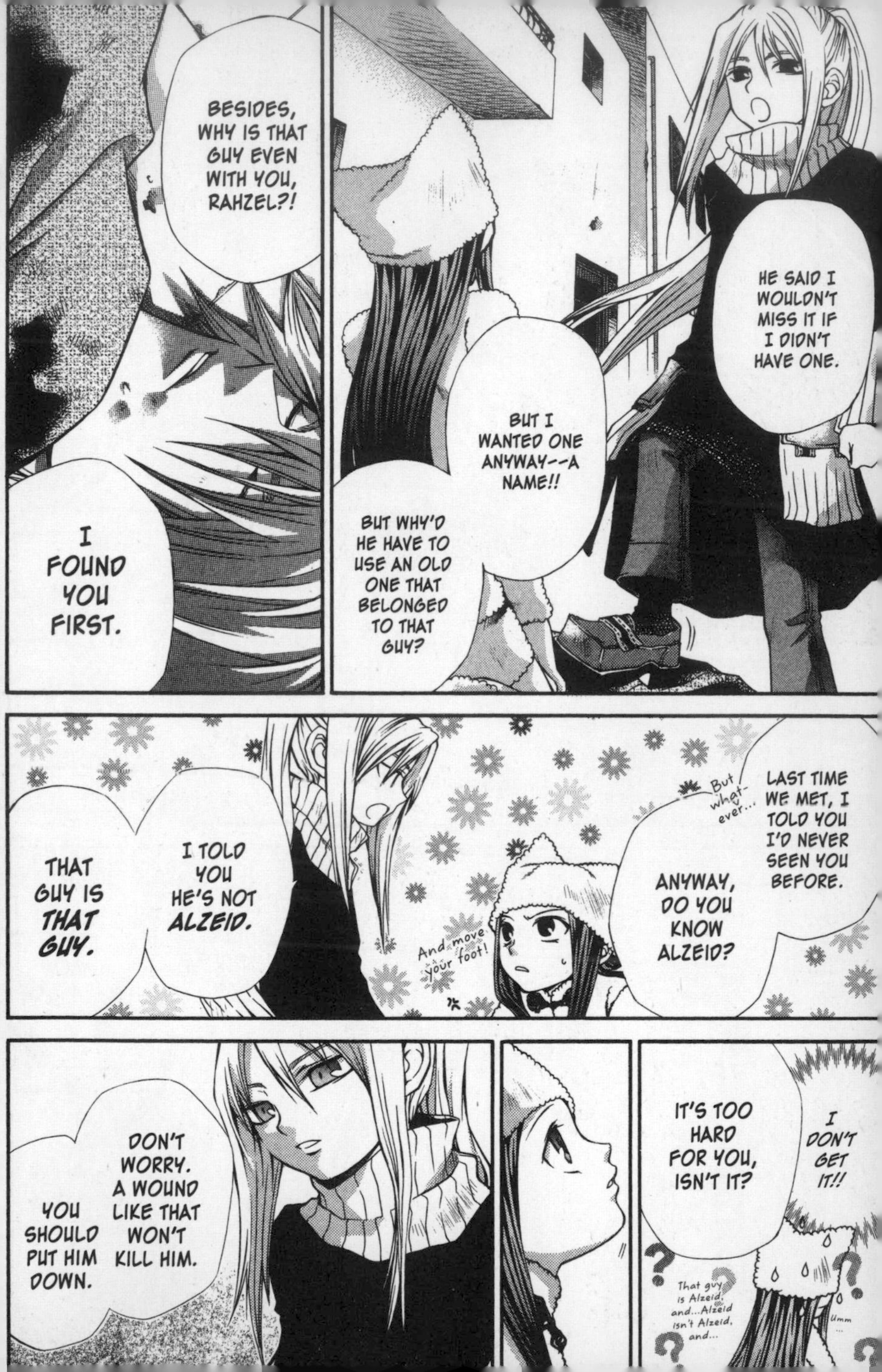
HE SAID I WOULDN'T MISS IT IF I DIDN'T HAVE ONE.
BUT I WANTED ONE ANYWAY--A NAME!!
BUT WHY'D HE HAVE TO USE AN OLD ONE THAT BELONGED TO THAT GUY?
BESIDES, WHY IS THAT GUY EVEN WITH YOU, RAHZEL?!
I FOUND YOU FIRST.
LAST TIME WE MET, I TOLD YOU I'D NEVER SEEN YOU BEFORE.
But whatever...
ANYWAY, DO YOU KNOW ALZEID?
And move your foot!
I TOLD YOU HE'S NOT ALZEID.
THAT GUY IS THAT GUY.
I DON'T GET IT!!
IT'S TOO HARD FOR YOU, ISN'T IT?
That guy is Alzeid, and...Alzeid isn't Alzeid, and...
Umm...
DON'T WORRY. A WOUND LIKE THAT WON'T KILL HIM.
YOU SHOULD PUT HIM DOWN.

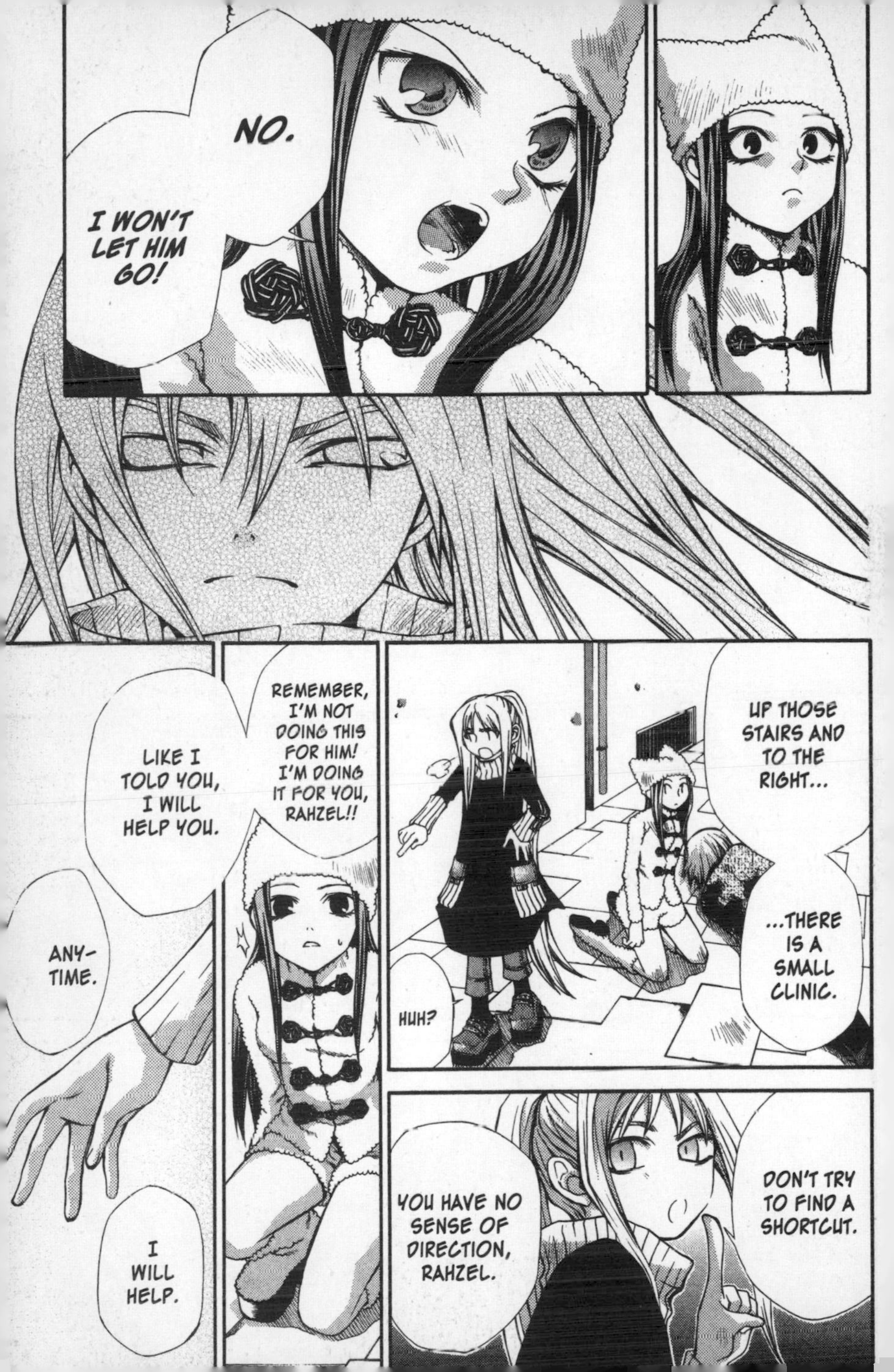

NO.
I WON'T LET HIM GO!
UP THOSE STAIRS AND TO THE RIGHT...
...THERE IS A SMALL CLINIC.
HUH?
DON'T TRY TO FIND A SHORTCUT.
YOU HAVE NO SENSE OF DIRECTION, RAHZEL.
REMEMBER, I'M NOT DOING THIS FOR HIM! I'M DOING IT FOR YOU, RAHZEL!!
LIKE I TOLD YOU, I WILL HELP YOU.
ANY-TIME.
I WILL HELP.

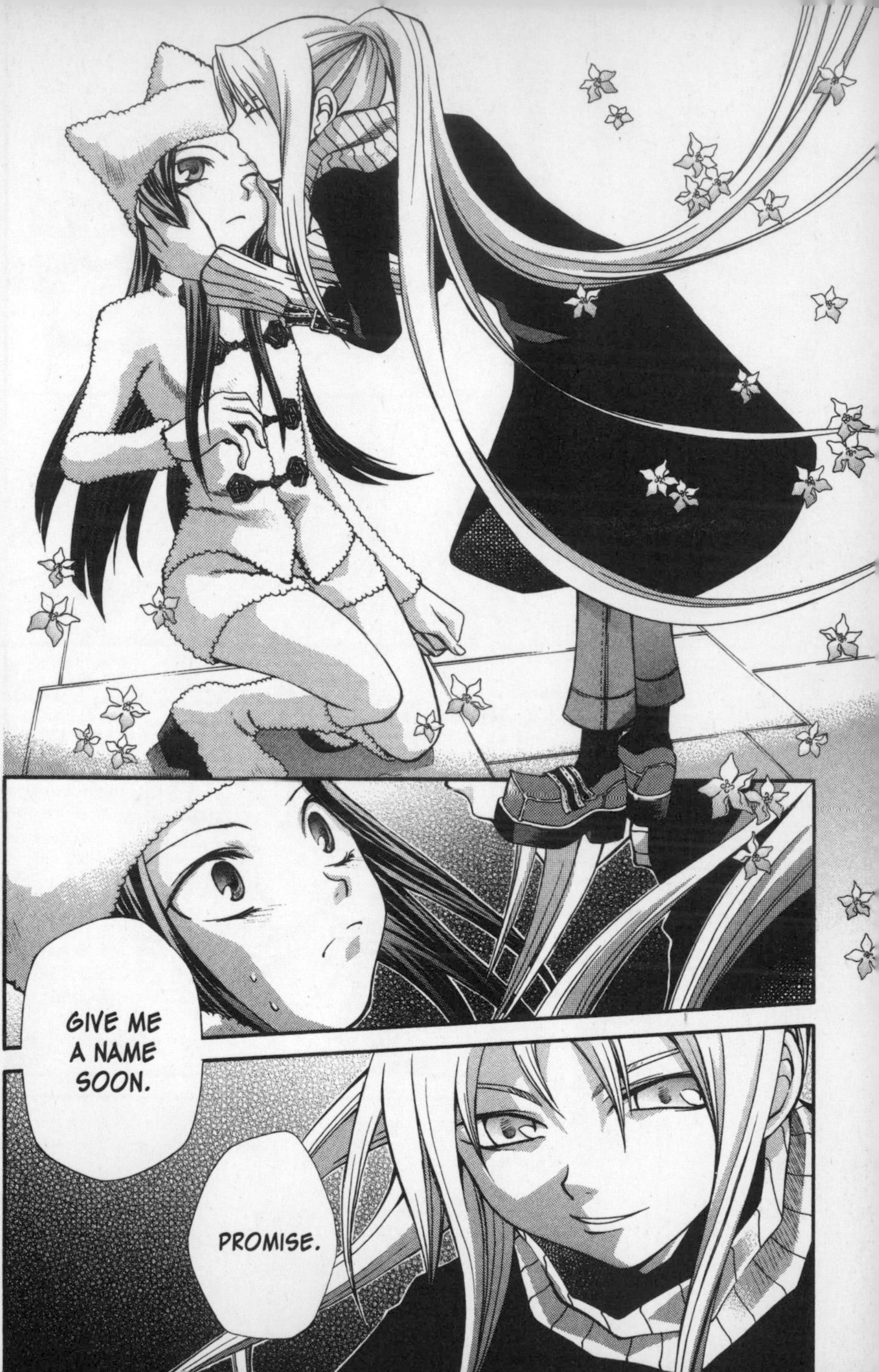
GIVE ME A NAME SOON.
PROMISE.

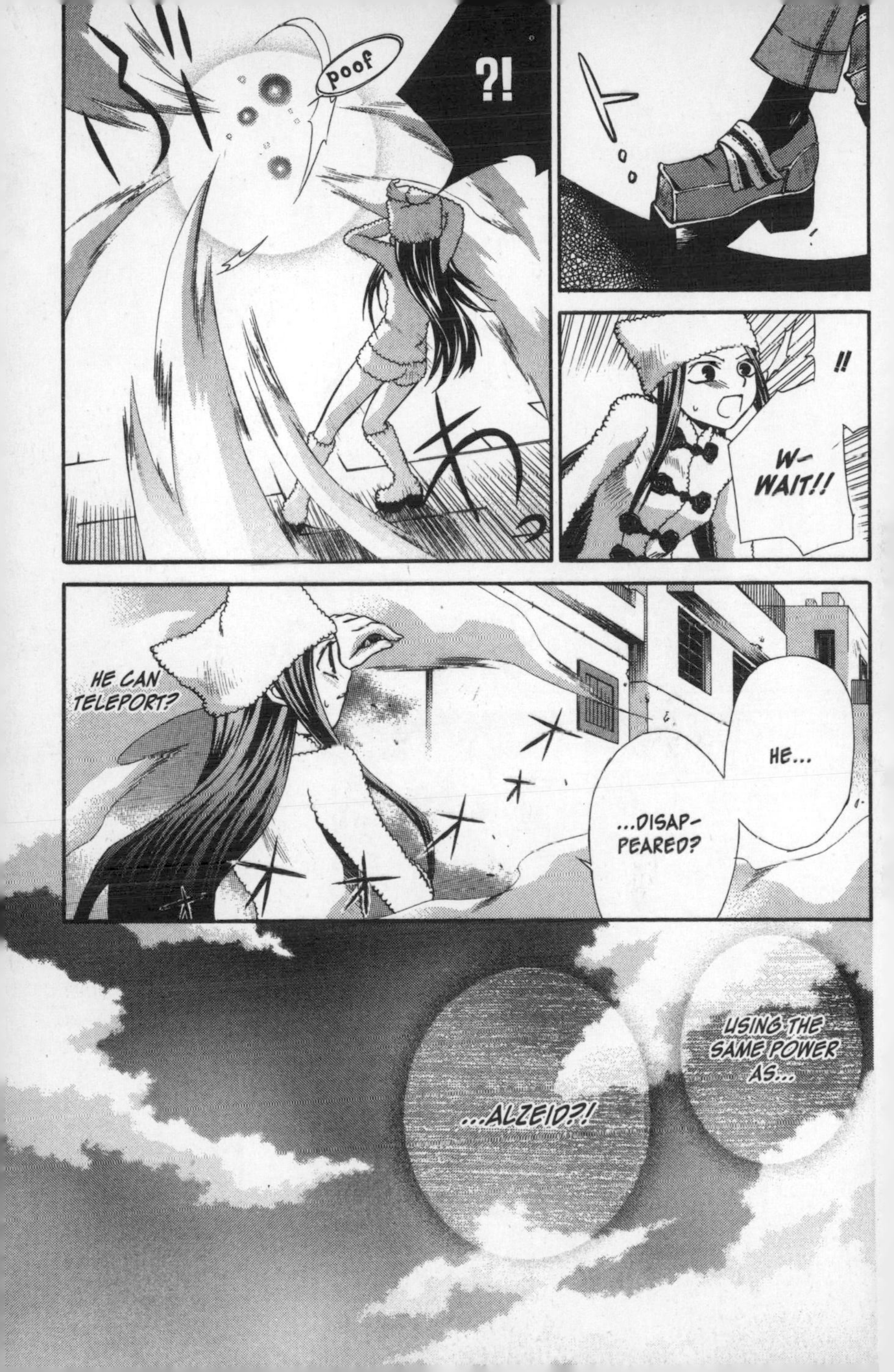

!!
W-WAIT!!
?!
poof
HE...
...DISAP-PEARED?
HE CAN TELEPORT?
USING THE SAME POWER AS...
...ALZEID?!

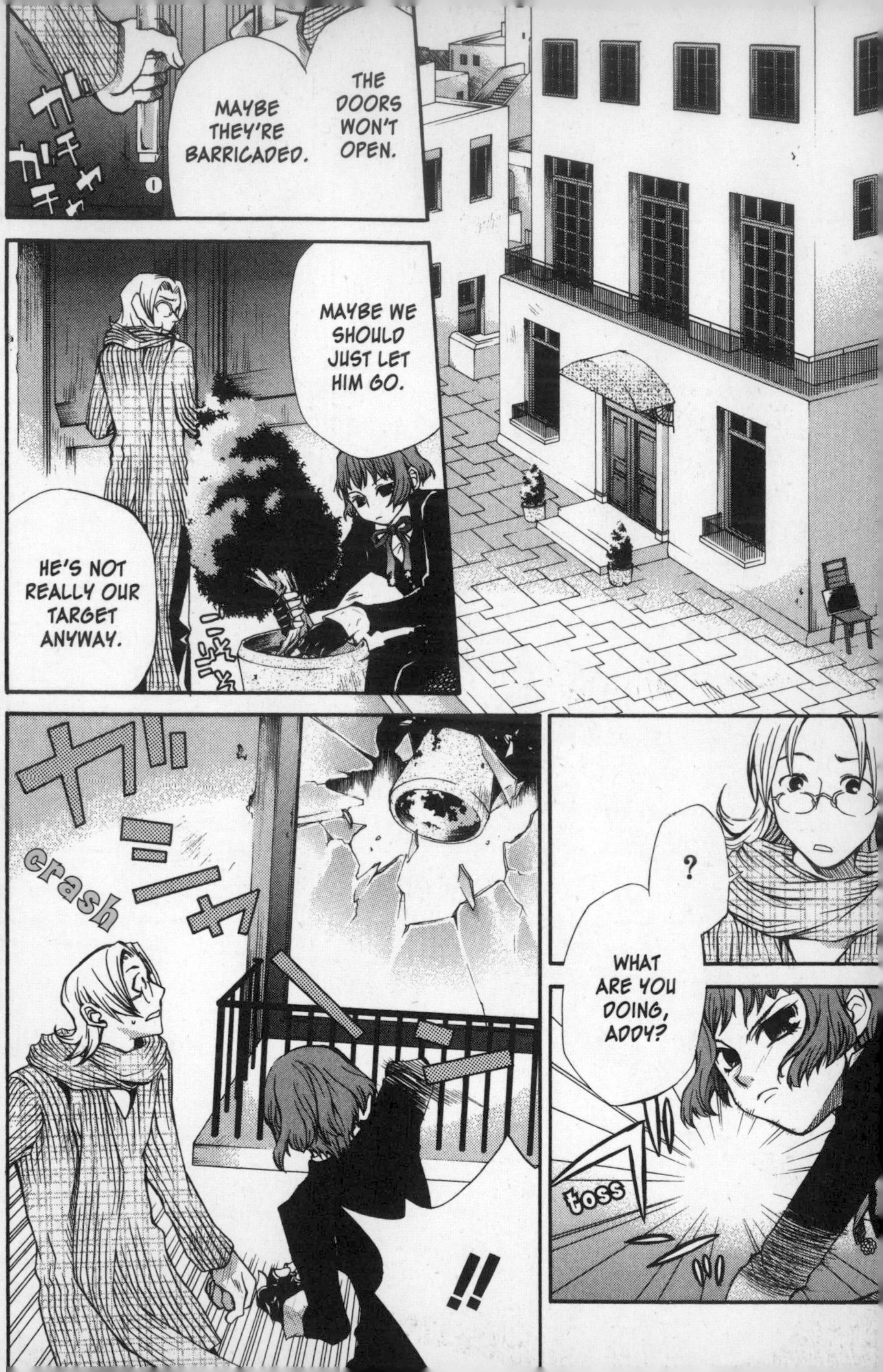
THE DOORS WON'T OPEN.
MAYBE THEY'RE BARRICADED.
MAYBE WE SHOULD JUST LET HIM GO.
HE'S NOT REALLY OUR TARGET ANYWAY.
?
WHAT ARE YOU DOING, ADDY?
toss
crash
!!

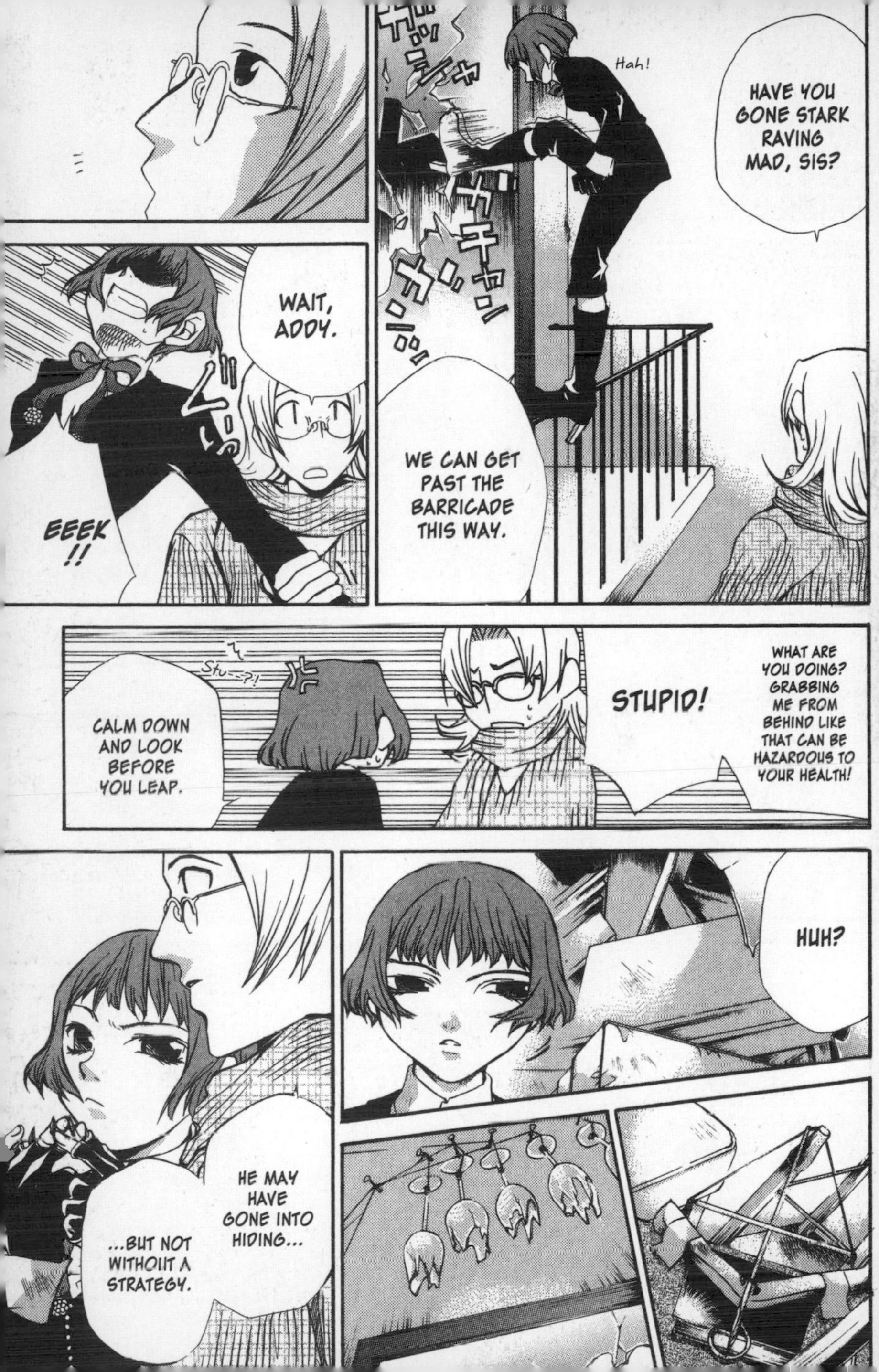
Hah!
HAVE YOU GONE STARK RAVING MAD, SIS?
WE CAN GET PAST THE BARRICADE THIS WAY.
WAIT, ADDY.
EEEK !!
WHAT ARE YOU DOING? GRABBING ME FROM BEHIND LIKE THAT CAN BE HAZARDOUS TO YOUR HEALTH!
STUPID!
Stu--?!
CALM DOWN AND LOOK BEFORE YOU LEAP.
HUH?
HE MAY HAVE GONE INTO HIDING...
...BUT NOT WITHOUT A STRATEGY.

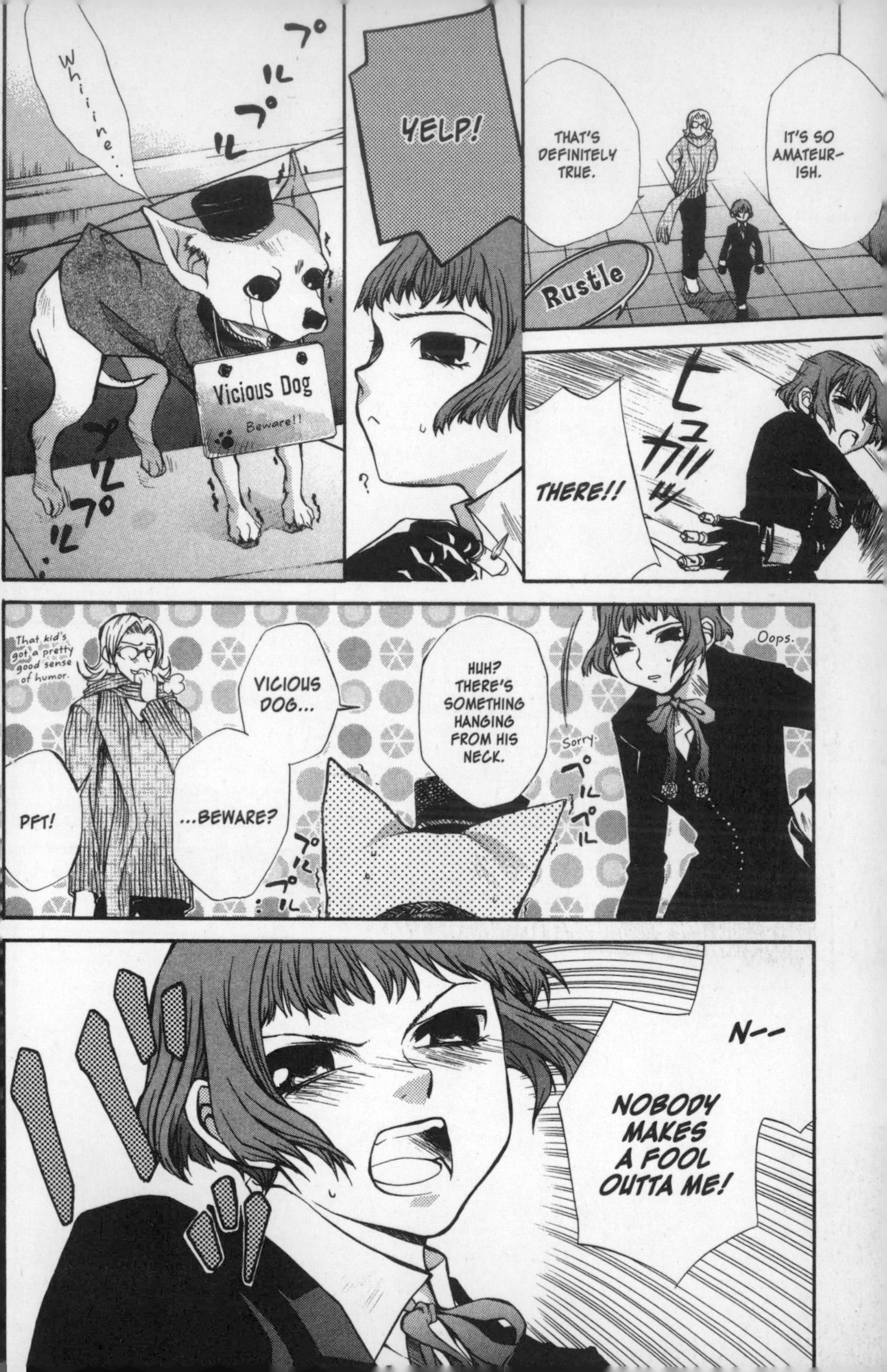

IT'S SO AMATEUR-ISH.
THAT'S DEFINITELY TRUE.
Rustle
ヒュカッ
THERE!!
YELP!
?
プルプル
Whiiine...
Vicious Dog
Beware!!
プルプル
Oops.
Sorry.
プルプル
HUH? THERE'S SOMETHING HANGING FROM HIS NECK.
VICIOUS DOG...
...BEWARE?
プルプル
That kid's got a pretty good sense of humor.
PFT!
N--
NOBODY MAKES A FOOL OUTTA ME!

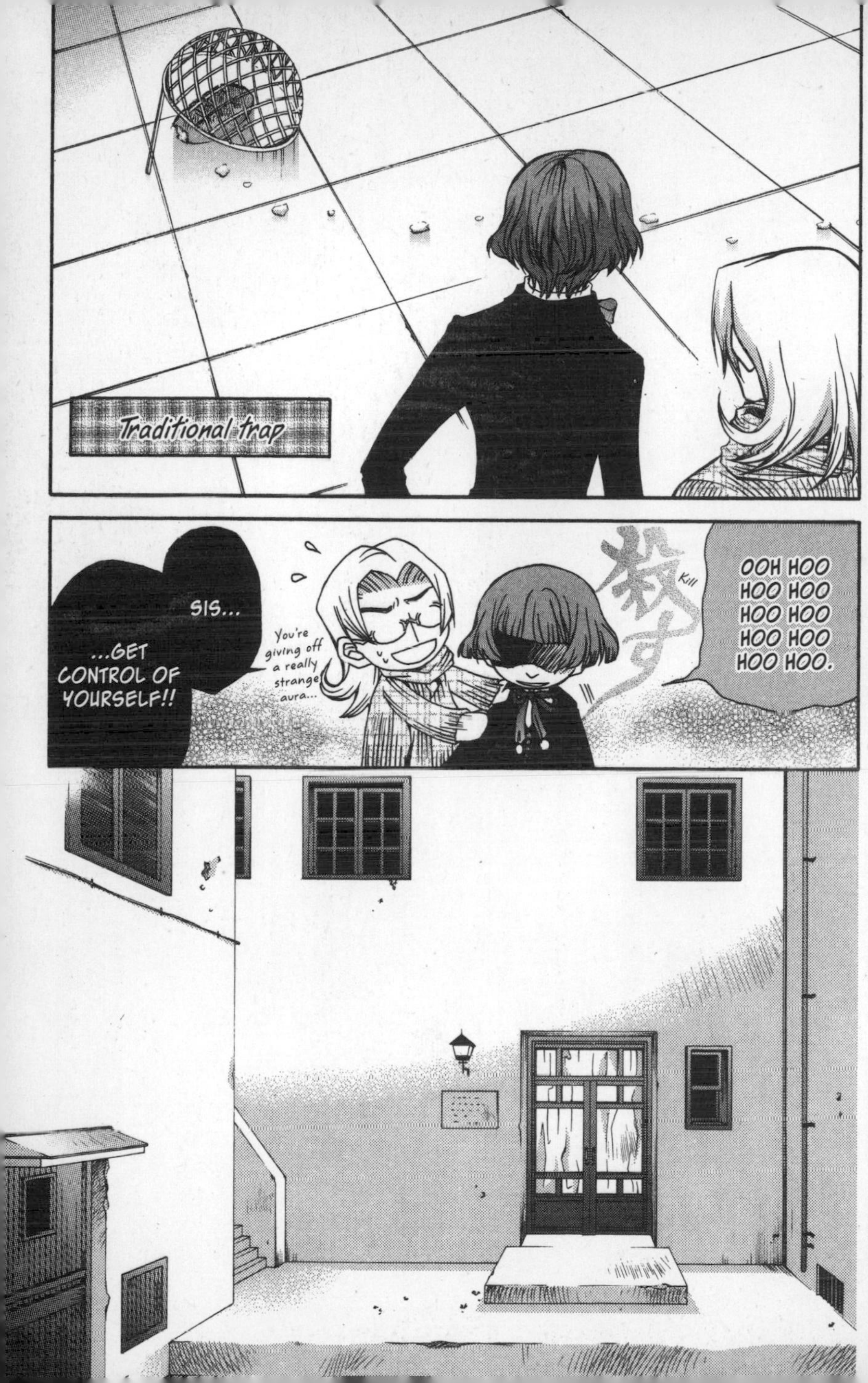
Traditional trap
OOH HOO HOO HOO HOO HOO HOO HOO HOO HOO.
殺す
Kill
You're giving off a really strange aura...
SIS...
...GET CONTROL OF YOURSELF!!

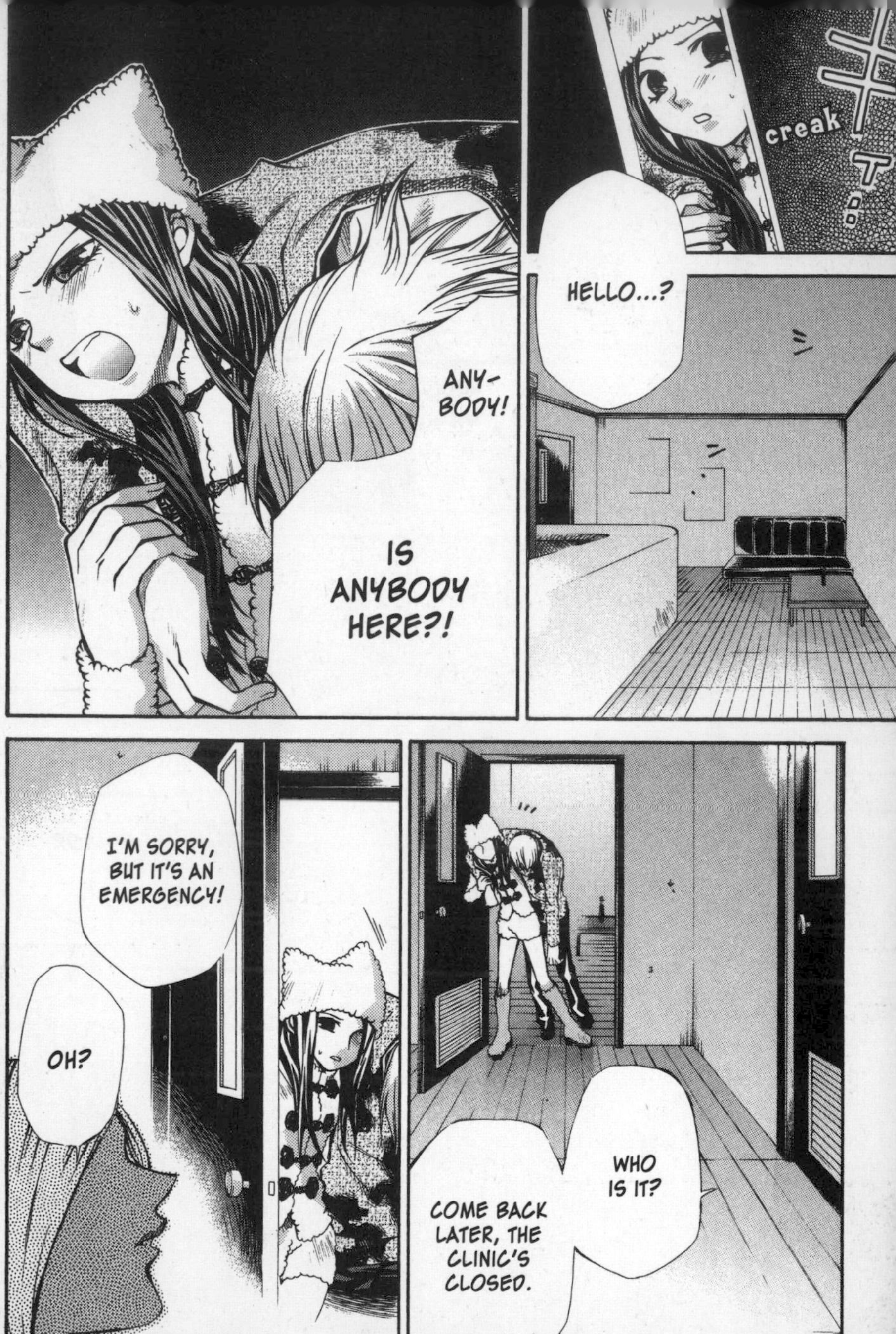
creak
HELLO...?
ANY-BODY!
IS ANYBODY HERE?!
WHO IS IT?
COME BACK LATER, THE CLINIC'S CLOSED.
I'M SORRY, BUT IT'S AN EMERGENCY!
OH?

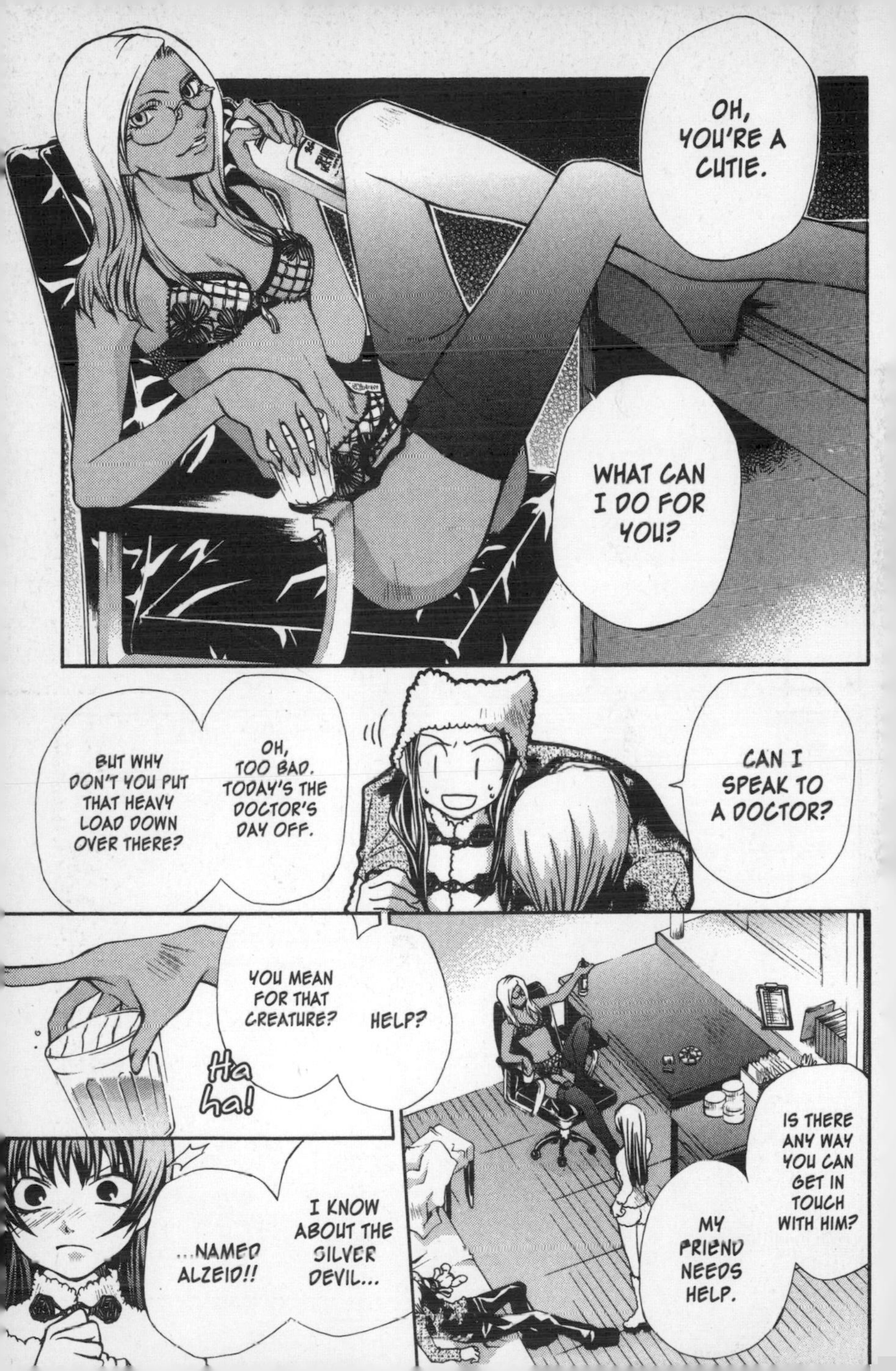
OH, YOU'RE A CUTIE.
WHAT CAN I DO FOR YOU?
CAN I SPEAK TO A DOCTOR?
OH, TOO BAD. TODAY'S THE DOCTOR'S DAY OFF.
BUT WHY DON'T YOU PUT THAT HEAVY LOAD DOWN OVER THERE?
IS THERE ANY WAY YOU CAN GET IN TOUCH WITH HIM?
MY FRIEND NEEDS HELP.
HELP?
YOU MEAN FOR THAT CREATURE?
Ha ha!
I KNOW ABOUT THE SILVER DEVIL...
...NAMED ALZEID!!

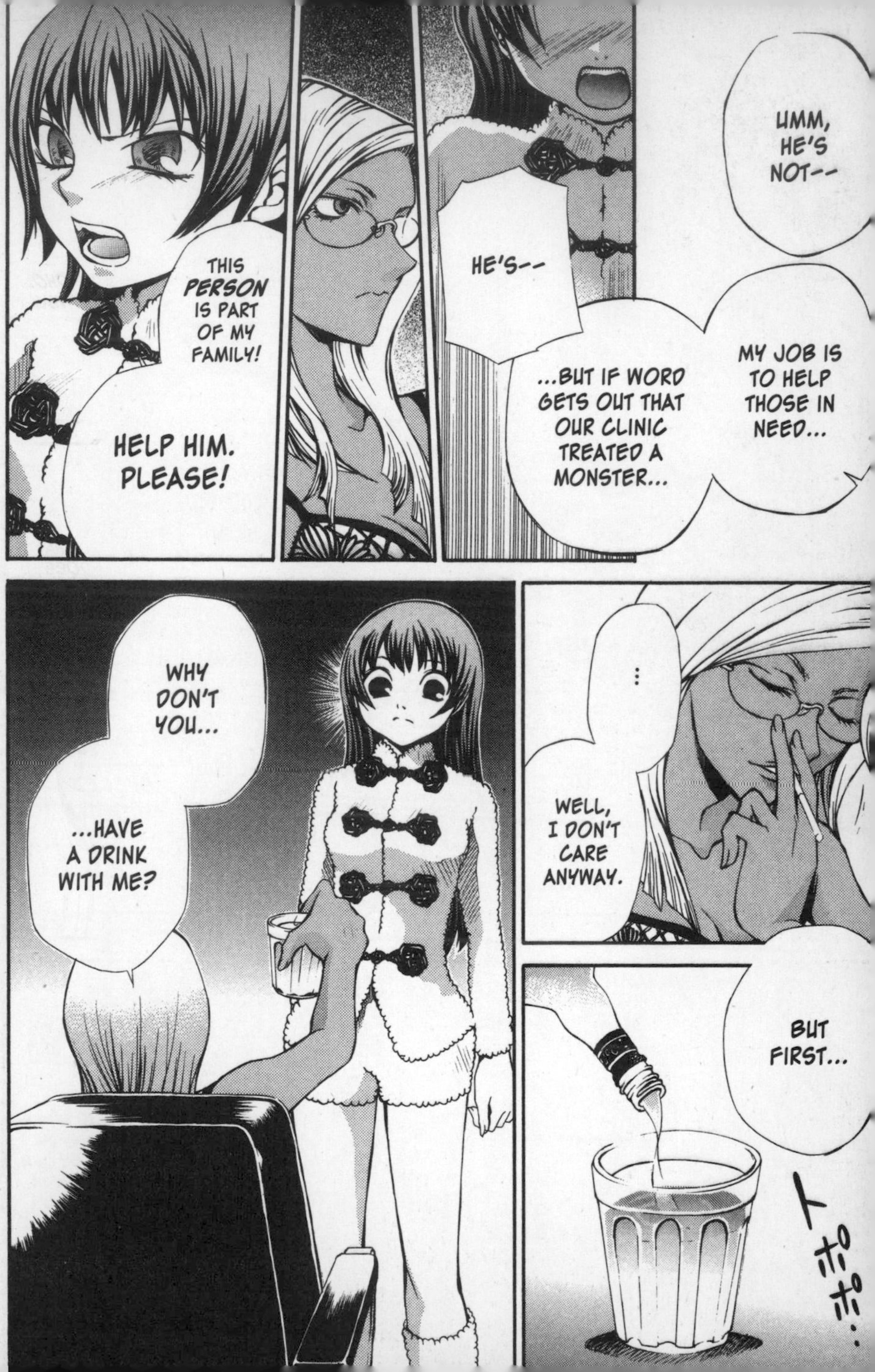

UMM, HE'S NOT--
HE'S--
MY JOB IS TO HELP THOSE IN NEED...
...BUT IF WORD GETS OUT THAT OUR CLINIC TREATED A MONSTER...
THIS *PERSON* IS PART OF MY FAMILY!
HELP HIM. PLEASE!
...
WELL, I DON'T CARE ANYWAY.
BUT FIRST...
トポポ・・
WHY DON'T YOU...
...HAVE A DRINK WITH ME?

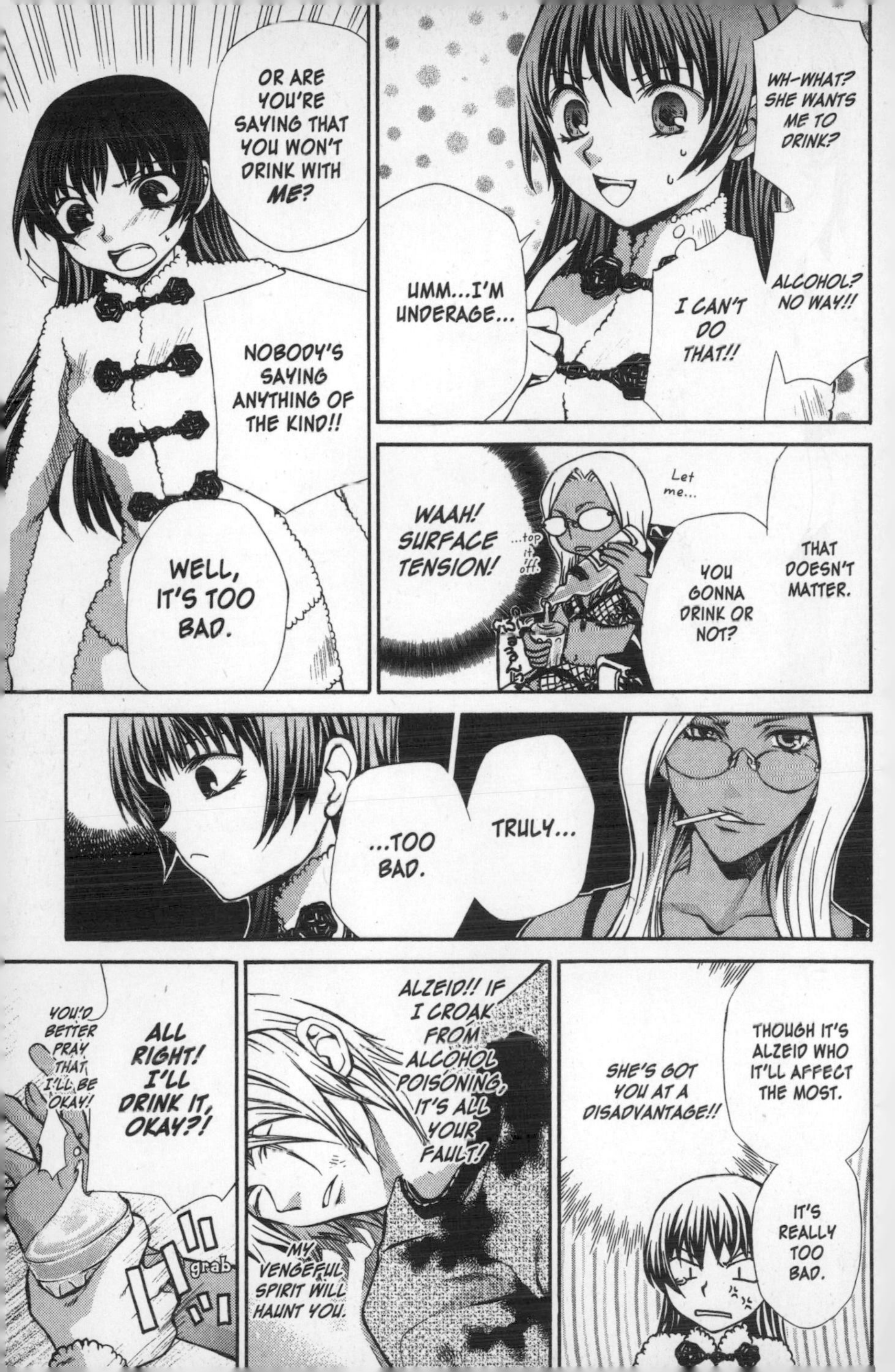
WH-WHAT? SHE WANTS ME TO DRINK?
ALCOHOL? NO WAY!!
I CAN'T DO THAT!!
UMM...I'M UNDERAGE...
THAT DOESN'T MATTER.
YOU GONNA DRINK OR NOT?
Let me...
...top it off.
WAAH! SURFACE TENSION!
OR ARE YOU'RE SAYING THAT YOU WON'T DRINK WITH ME?
NOBODY'S SAYING ANYTHING OF THE KIND!!
WELL, IT'S TOO BAD.
TRULY...
...TOO BAD.
THOUGH IT'S ALZEID WHO IT'LL AFFECT THE MOST.
SHE'S GOT YOU AT A DISADVANTAGE!!
IT'S REALLY TOO BAD.
ALZEID!! IF I CROAK FROM ALCOHOL POISONING, IT'S ALL YOUR FAULT!
MY VENGEFUL SPIRIT WILL HAUNT YOU.
ALL RIGHT! I'LL DRINK IT, OKAY?!
YOU'D BETTER PRAY THAT I'LL BE OKAY!
grab

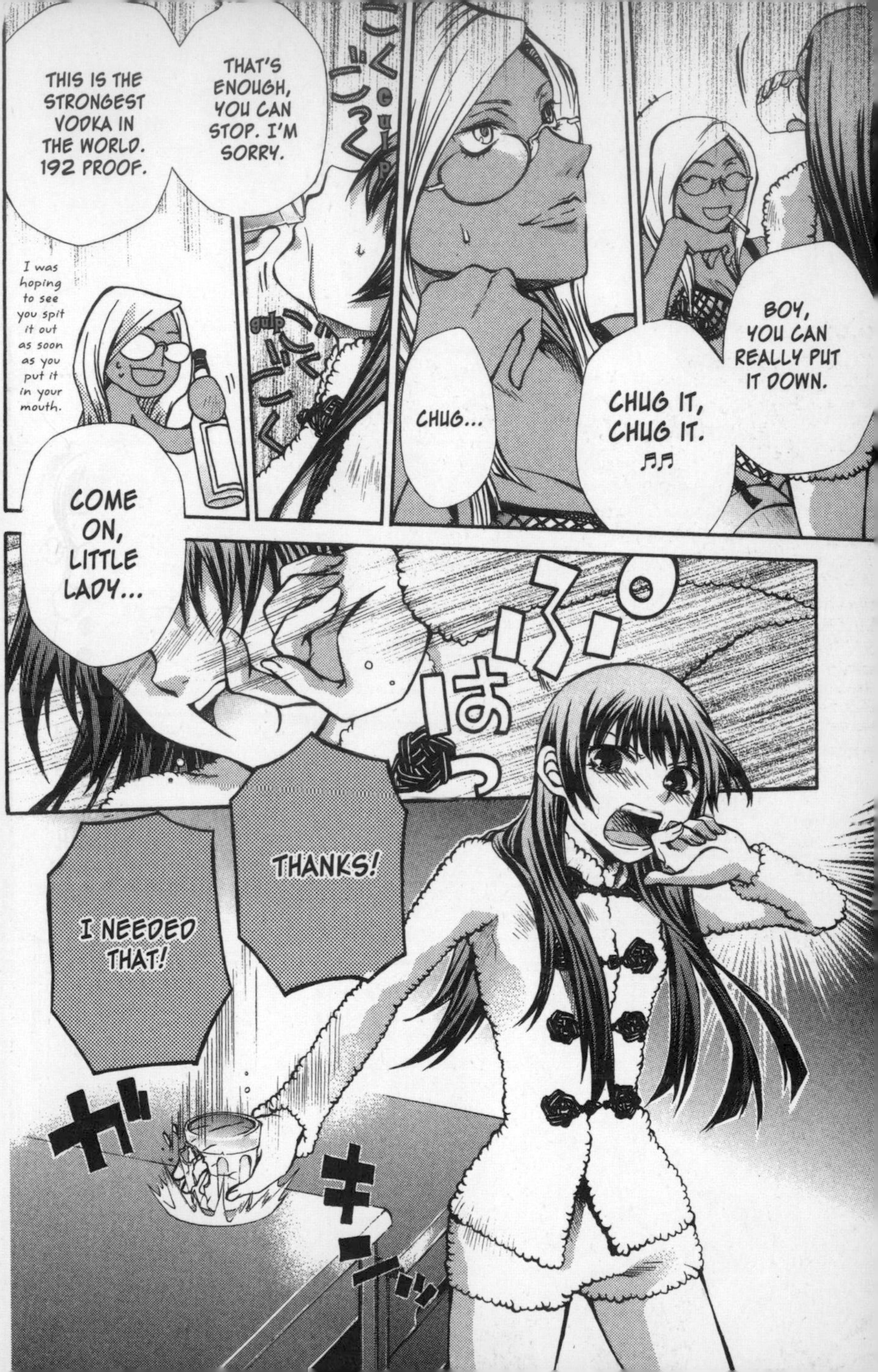
BOY, YOU CAN REALLY PUT IT DOWN.
CHUG IT, CHUG IT. ♫♫
CHUG...
gulp
gulp
THAT'S ENOUGH, YOU CAN STOP. I'M SORRY.
THIS IS THE STRONGEST VODKA IN THE WORLD. 192 PROOF.
I was hoping to see you spit it out as soon as you put it in your mouth.
COME ON, LITTLE LADY...
ぷはっ
THANKS!
I NEEDED THAT!

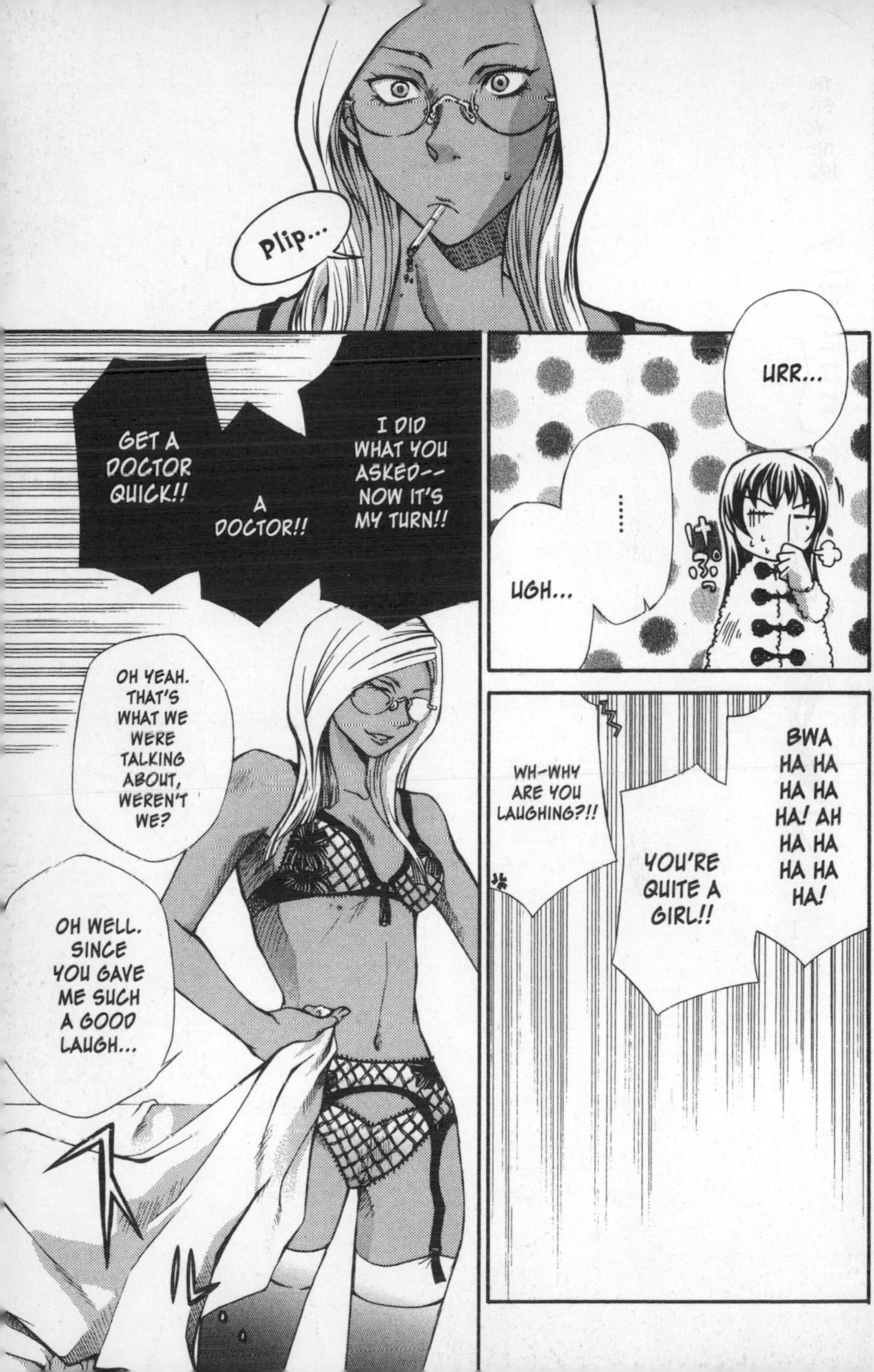

Plip...
URR...
......
UGH...
I DID WHAT YOU ASKED--NOW IT'S MY TURN!!
A DOCTOR!!
GET A DOCTOR QUICK!!
BWA HA HA HA HA HA! AH HA HA HA HA HA!
YOU'RE QUITE A GIRL!!
WH-WHY ARE YOU LAUGHING?!!
OH YEAH. THAT'S WHAT WE WERE TALKING ABOUT, WEREN'T WE?
OH WELL. SINCE YOU GAVE ME SUCH A GOOD LAUGH...

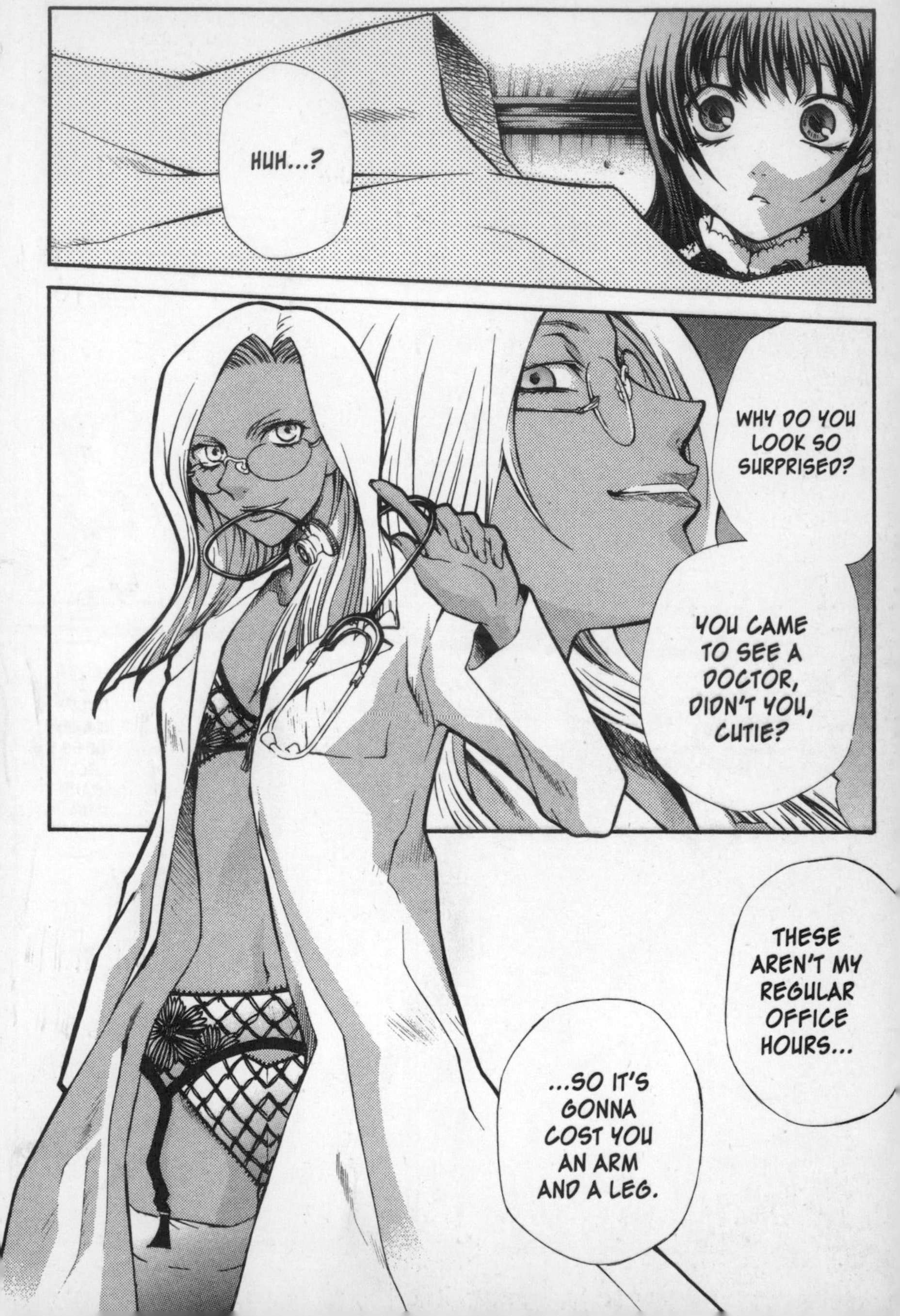
HUH...?
WHY DO YOU LOOK SO SURPRISED?
YOU CAME TO SEE A DOCTOR, DIDN'T YOU, CUTIE?
THESE AREN'T MY REGULAR OFFICE HOURS...
...SO IT'S GONNA COST YOU AN ARM AND A LEG.

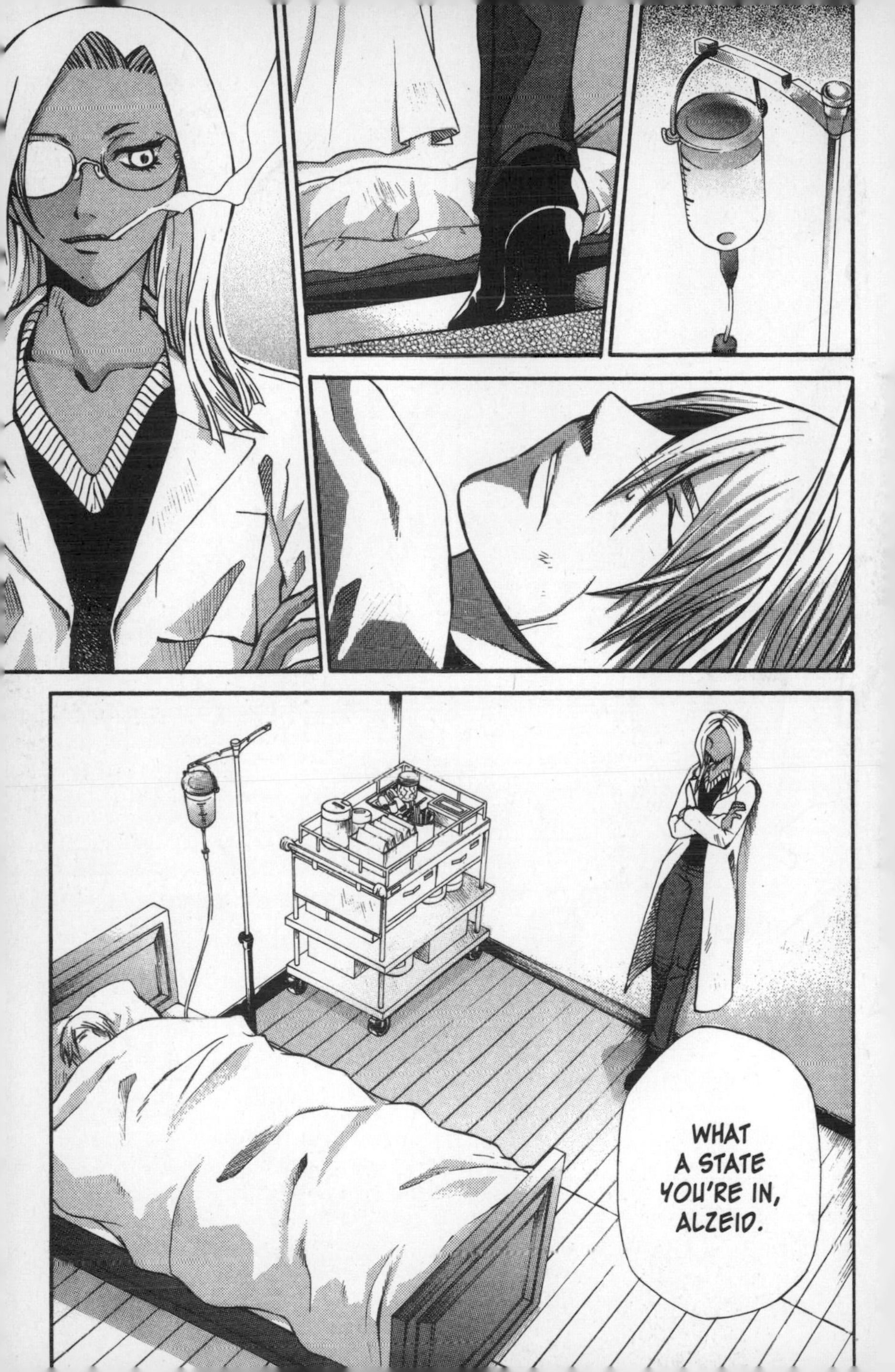
WHAT A STATE YOU'RE IN, ALZEID.

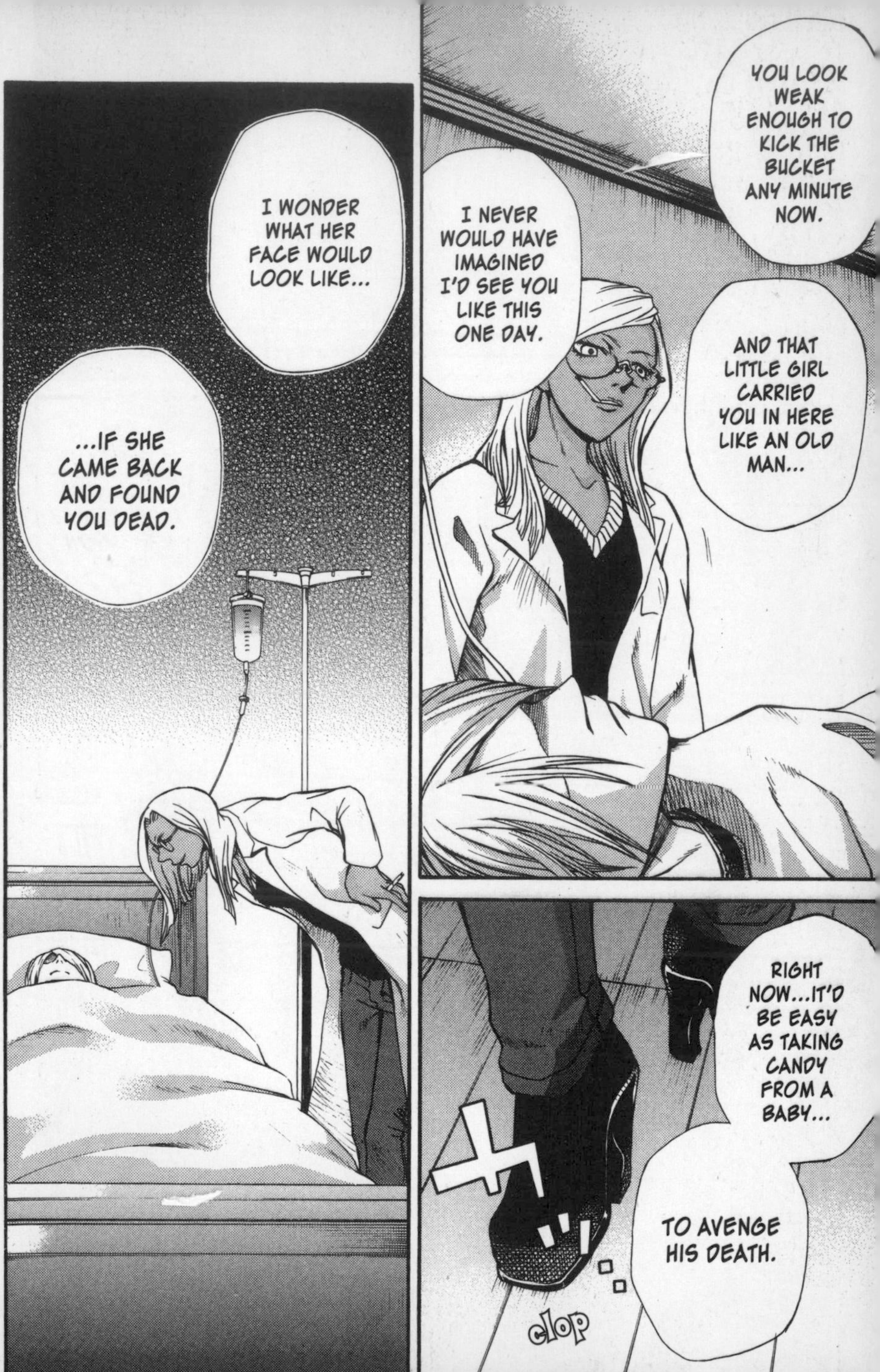
YOU LOOK WEAK ENOUGH TO KICK THE BUCKET ANY MINUTE NOW.
I NEVER WOULD HAVE IMAGINED I'D SEE YOU LIKE THIS ONE DAY.
AND THAT LITTLE GIRL CARRIED YOU IN HERE LIKE AN OLD MAN...
RIGHT NOW...IT'D BE EASY AS TAKING CANDY FROM A BABY...
clop
TO AVENGE HIS DEATH.
I WONDER WHAT HER FACE WOULD LOOK LIKE...
...IF SHE CAME BACK AND FOUND YOU DEAD.

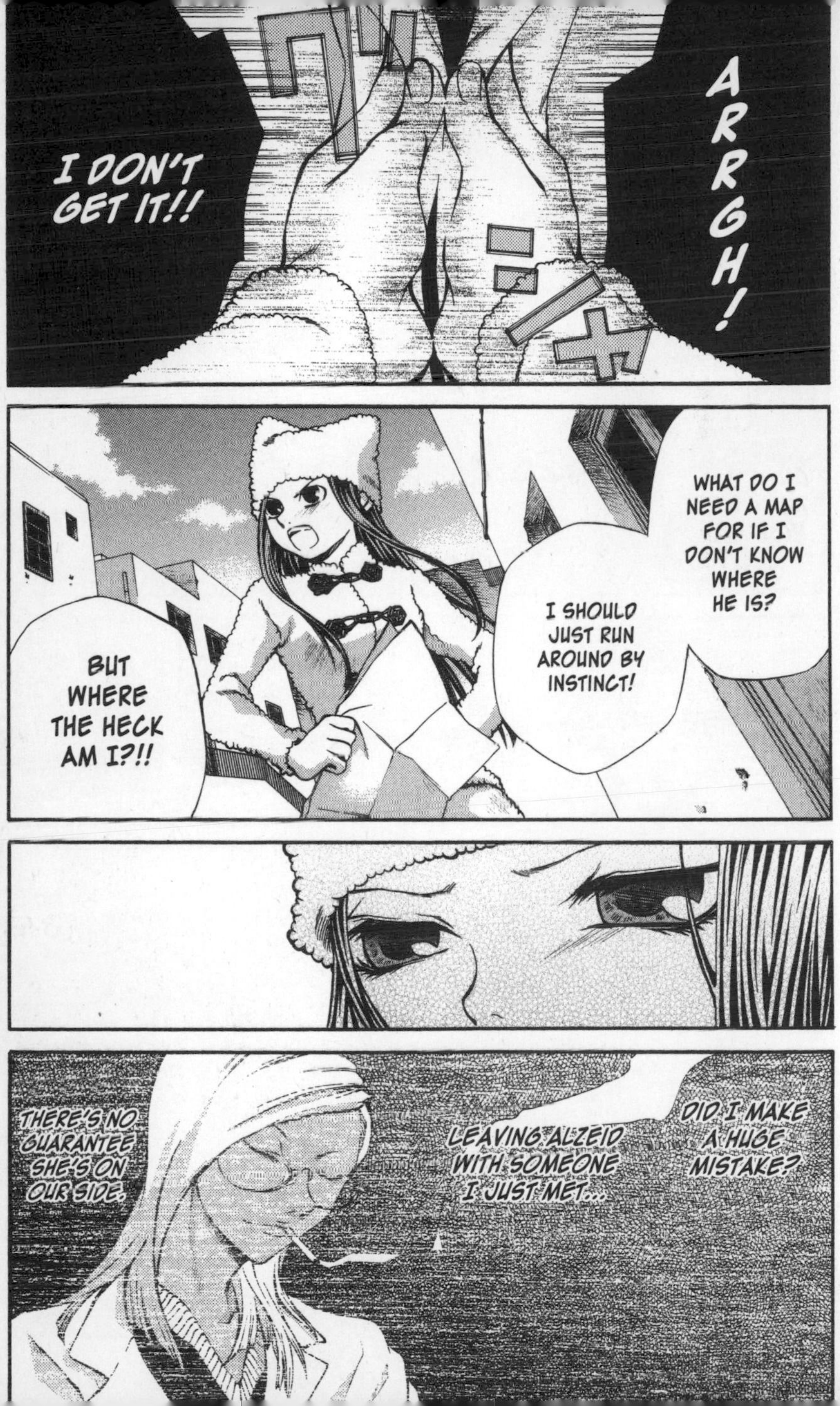
ARRGH!
I DON'T GET IT!!
WHAT DO I NEED A MAP FOR IF I DON'T KNOW WHERE HE IS?
I SHOULD JUST RUN AROUND BY INSTINCT!
BUT WHERE THE HECK AM I?!!
DID I MAKE A HUGE MISTAKE?
LEAVING ALZEID WITH SOMEONE I JUST MET...
THERE'S NO GUARANTEE SHE'S ON OUR SIDE.

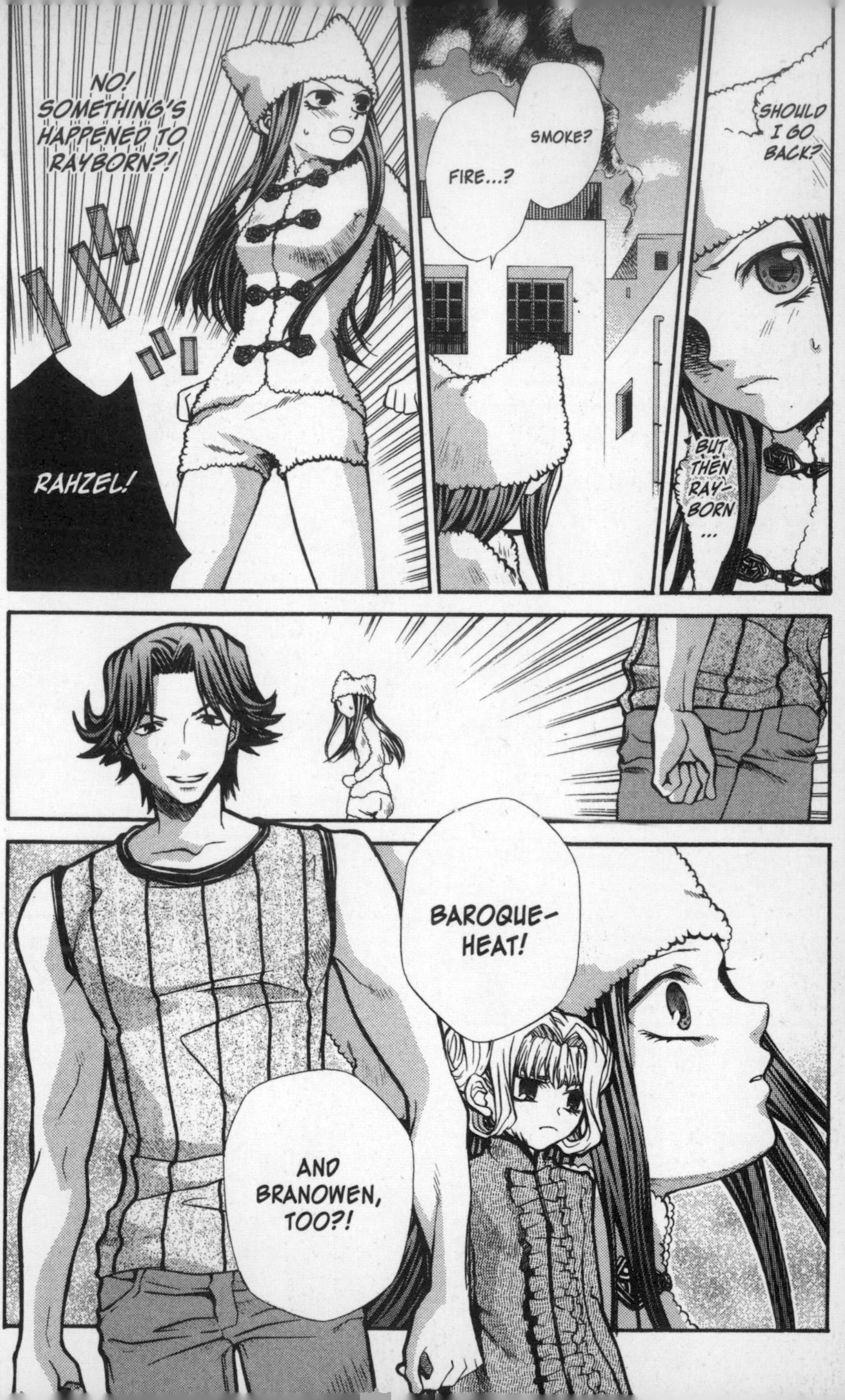
SHOULD I GO BACK?
BUT THEN RAY-BORN...
SMOKE?
FIRE...?
NO! SOMETHING'S HAPPENED TO RAYBORN?!
RAHZEL!
BAROQUE-HEAT!
AND BRANOWEN, TOO?!

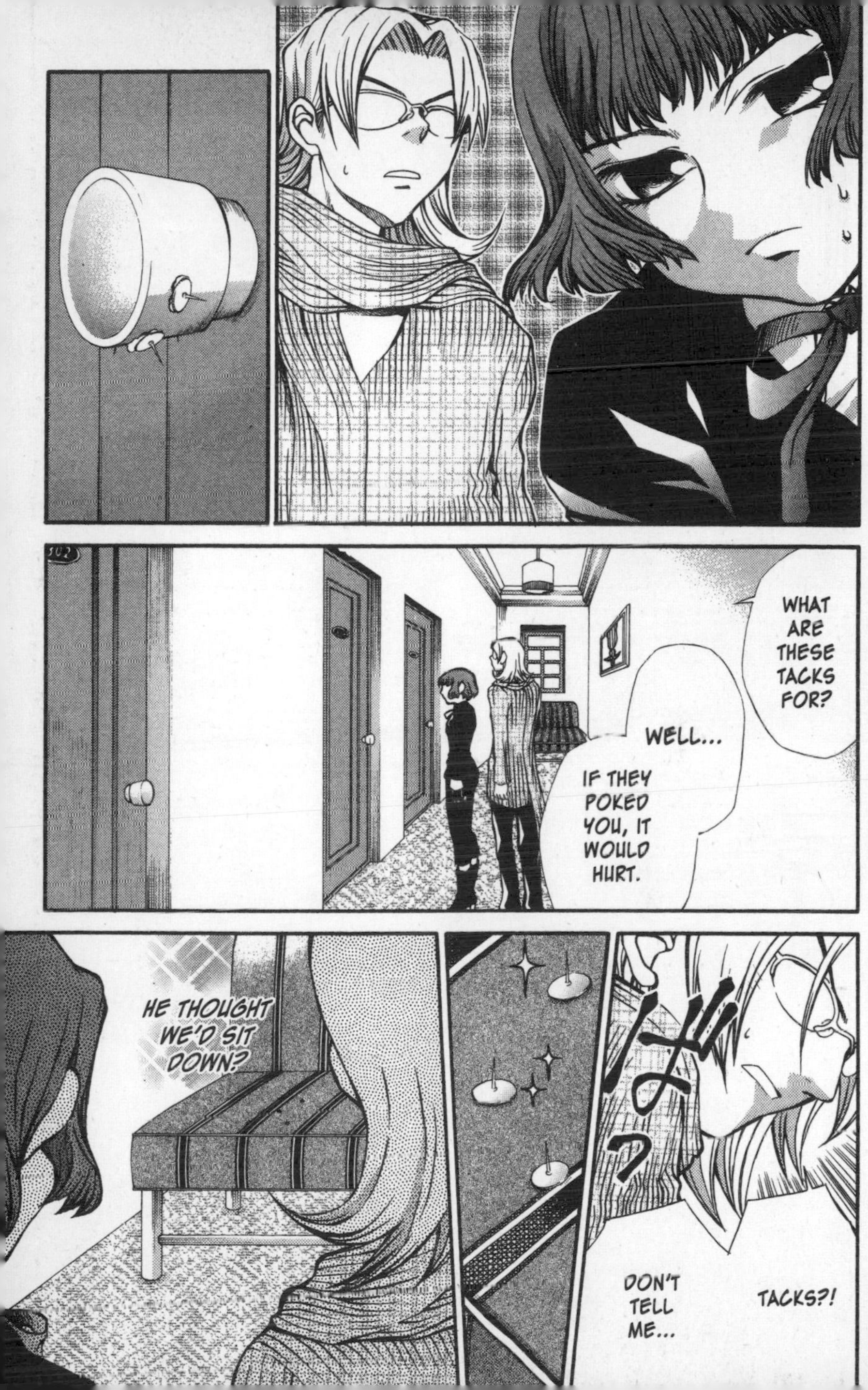
WHAT ARE THESE TACKS FOR?
WELL...
IF THEY POKED YOU, IT WOULD HURT.
TACKS?!
DON'T TELL ME...
HE THOUGHT WE'D SIT DOWN?

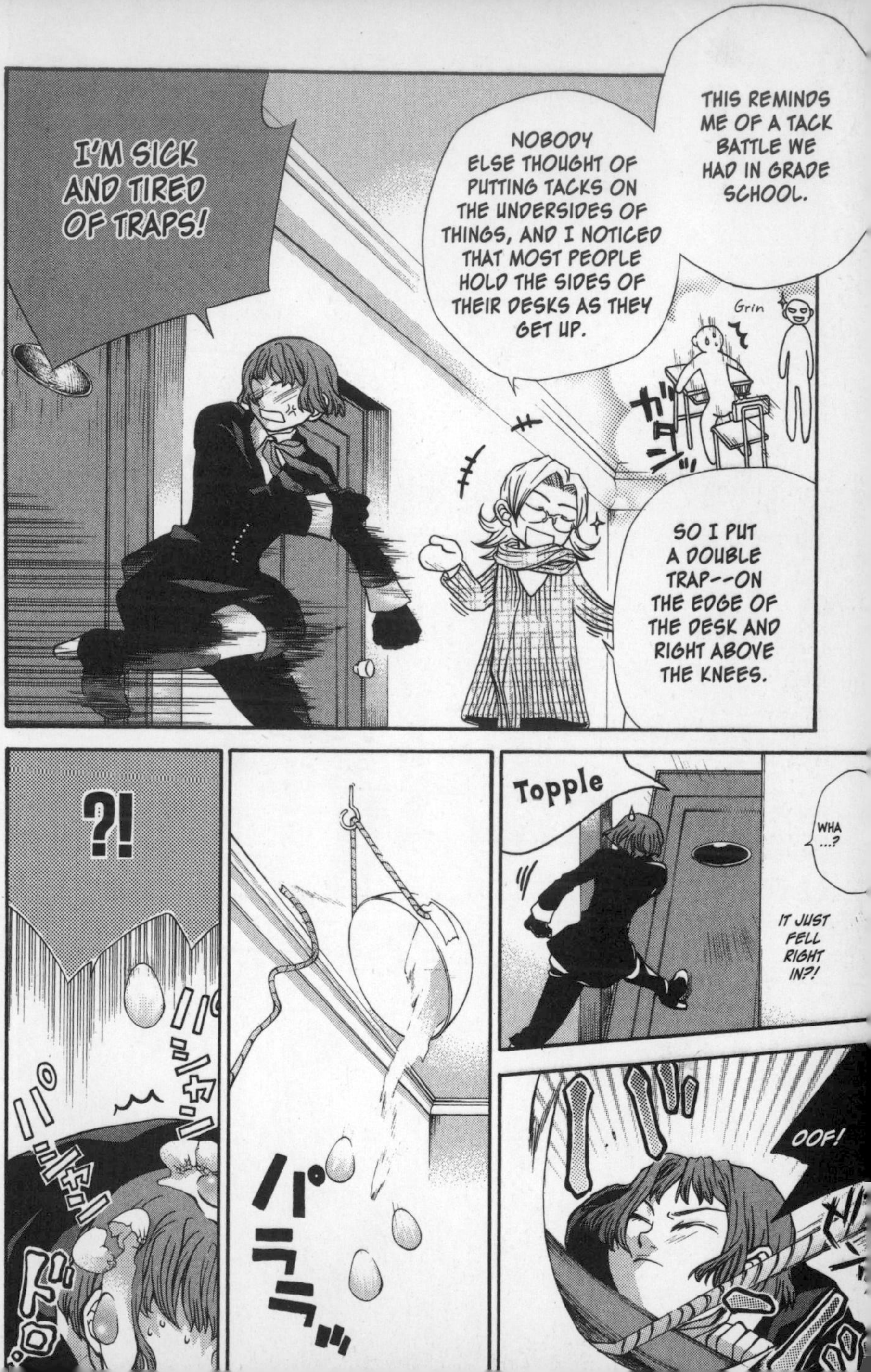
THIS REMINDS ME OF A TACK BATTLE WE HAD IN GRADE SCHOOL.
NOBODY ELSE THOUGHT OF PUTTING TACKS ON THE UNDERSIDES OF THINGS, AND I NOTICED THAT MOST PEOPLE HOLD THE SIDES OF THEIR DESKS AS THEY GET UP.
Grin
SO I PUT A DOUBLE TRAP--ON THE EDGE OF THE DESK AND RIGHT ABOVE THE KNEES.
I'M SICK AND TIRED OF TRAPS!
WHA ...?
Topple
IT JUST FELL RIGHT IN?!
OOF!
?!

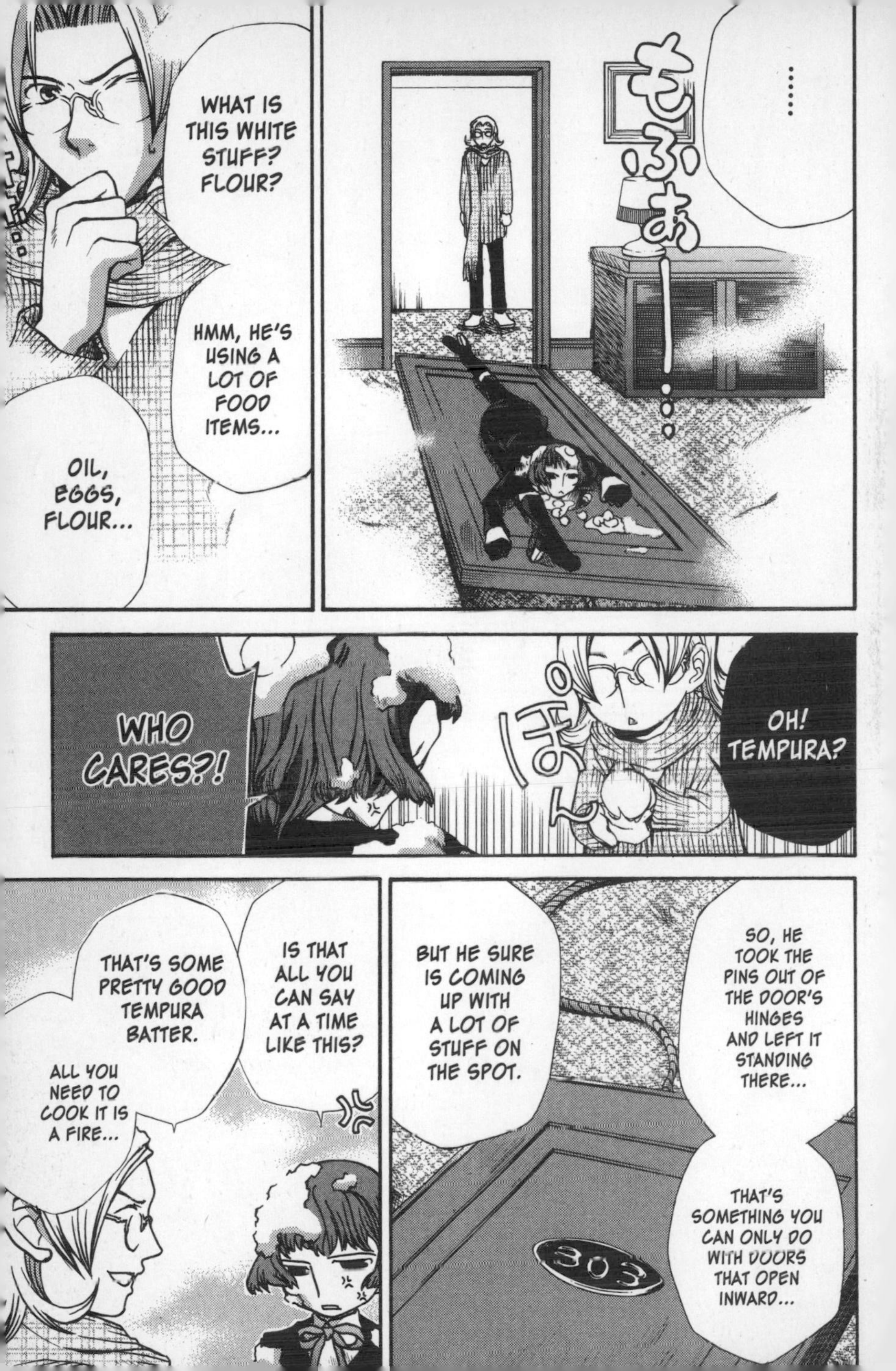

......
もふぁー…
WHAT IS THIS WHITE STUFF? FLOUR?
HMM, HE'S USING A LOT OF FOOD ITEMS...
OIL, EGGS, FLOUR...
OH! TEMPURA?
ぽん
WHO CARES?!
SO, HE TOOK THE PINS OUT OF THE DOOR'S HINGES AND LEFT IT STANDING THERE...
BUT HE SURE IS COMING UP WITH A LOT OF STUFF ON THE SPOT.
THAT'S SOMETHING YOU CAN ONLY DO WITH DOORS THAT OPEN INWARD...
303
THAT'S SOME PRETTY GOOD TEMPURA BATTER.
ALL YOU NEED TO COOK IT IS A FIRE...
IS THAT ALL YOU CAN SAY AT A TIME LIKE THIS?

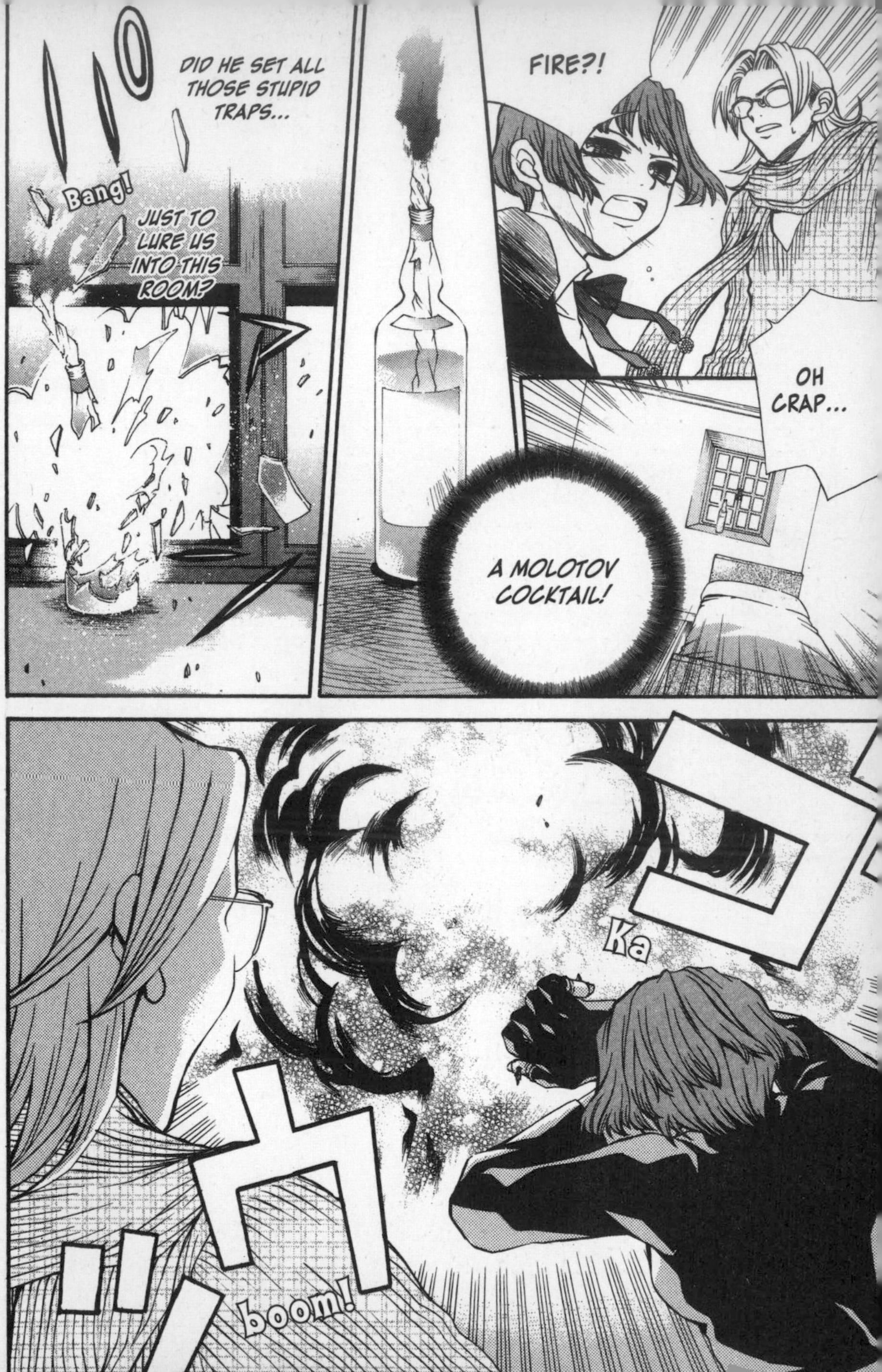
FIRE?!
OH CRAP...
A MOLOTOV COCKTAIL!
DID HE SET ALL THOSE STUPID TRAPS...
Bang!
JUST TO LURE US INTO THIS ROOM?
Ka
boom!

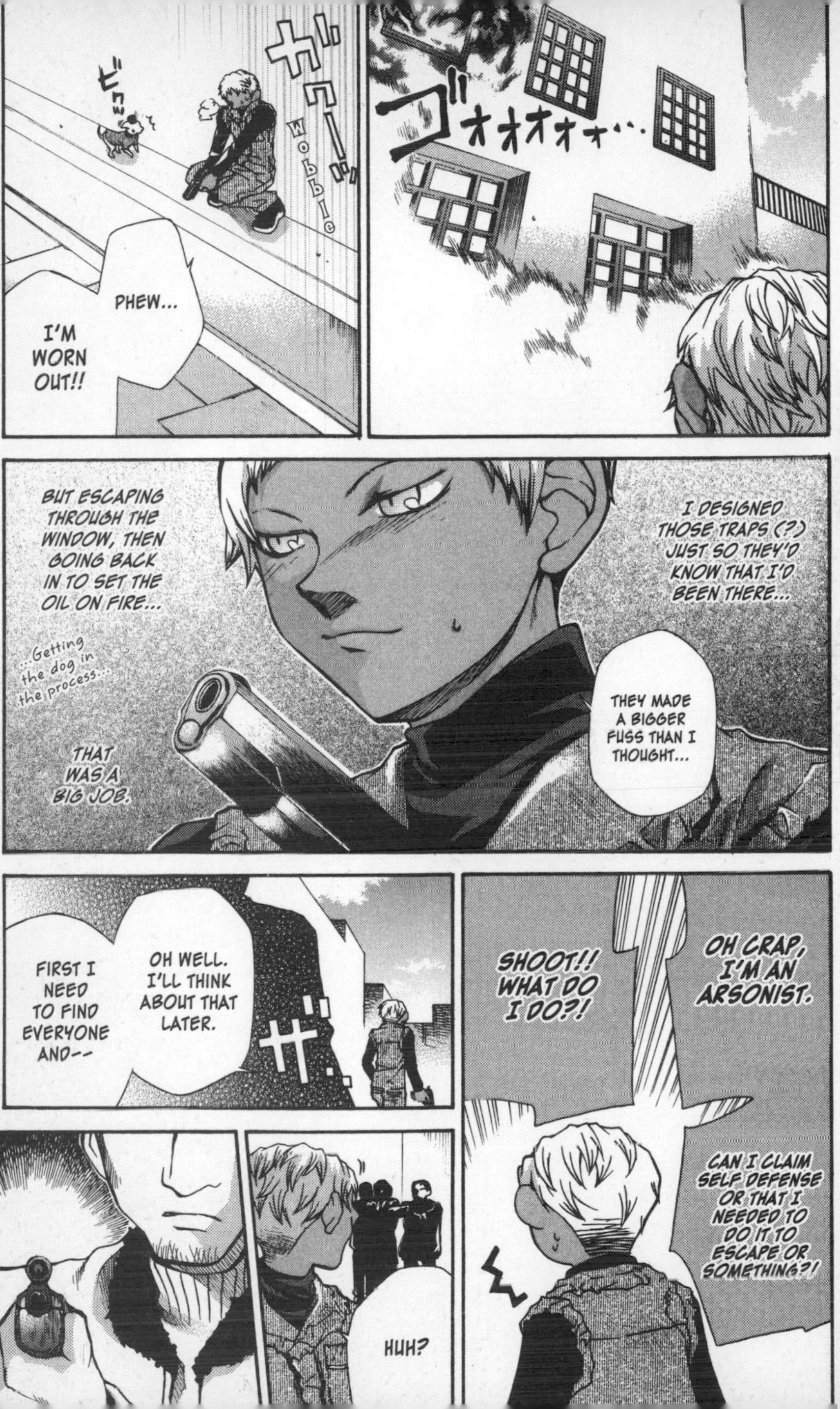
ゴォオオオォ…
wobble
PHEW...
I'M WORN OUT!!
I DESIGNED THOSE TRAPS (?) JUST SO THEY'D KNOW THAT I'D BEEN THERE...
THEY MADE A BIGGER FUSS THAN I THOUGHT...
BUT ESCAPING THROUGH THE WINDOW, THEN GOING BACK IN TO SET THE OIL ON FIRE...
...Getting the dog in the process...
THAT WAS A BIG JOB.
OH CRAP, I'M AN ARSONIST.
SHOOT!! WHAT DO I DO?!
CAN I CLAIM SELF DEFENSE OR THAT I NEEDED TO DO IT TO ESCAPE OR SOMETHING?!
OH WELL. I'LL THINK ABOUT THAT LATER.
FIRST I NEED TO FIND EVERYONE AND--
HUH?

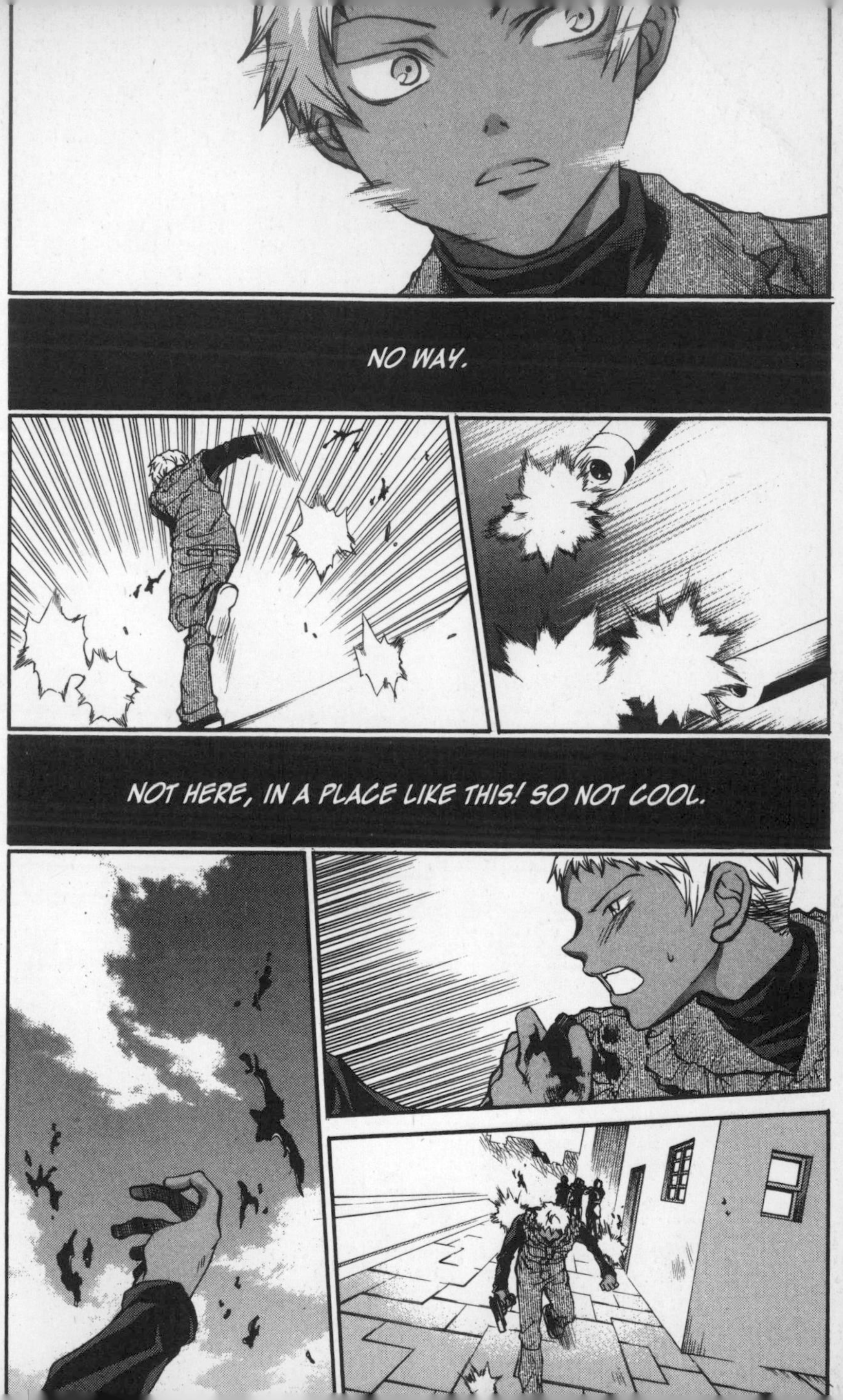
NO WAY.
NOT HERE, IN A PLACE LIKE THIS! SO NOT COOL.

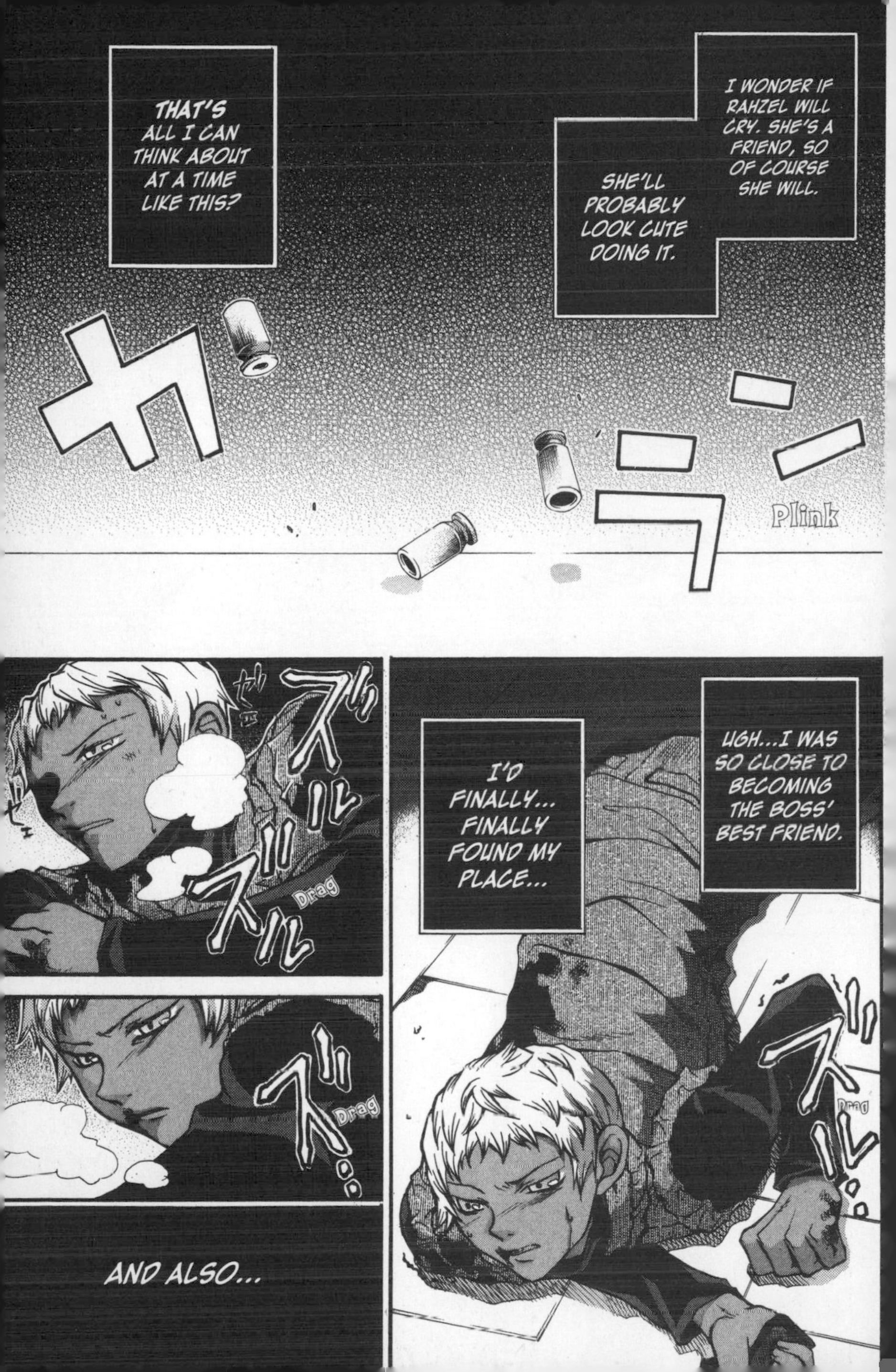
I WONDER IF RAHZEL WILL CRY. SHE'S A FRIEND, SO OF COURSE SHE WILL.
SHE'LL PROBABLY LOOK CUTE DOING IT.
THAT'S ALL I CAN THINK ABOUT AT A TIME LIKE THIS?
Plink
UGH...I WAS SO CLOSE TO BECOMING THE BOSS' BEST FRIEND.
I'D FINALLY... FINALLY FOUND MY PLACE...
Drag
Drag
Drag
AND ALSO...

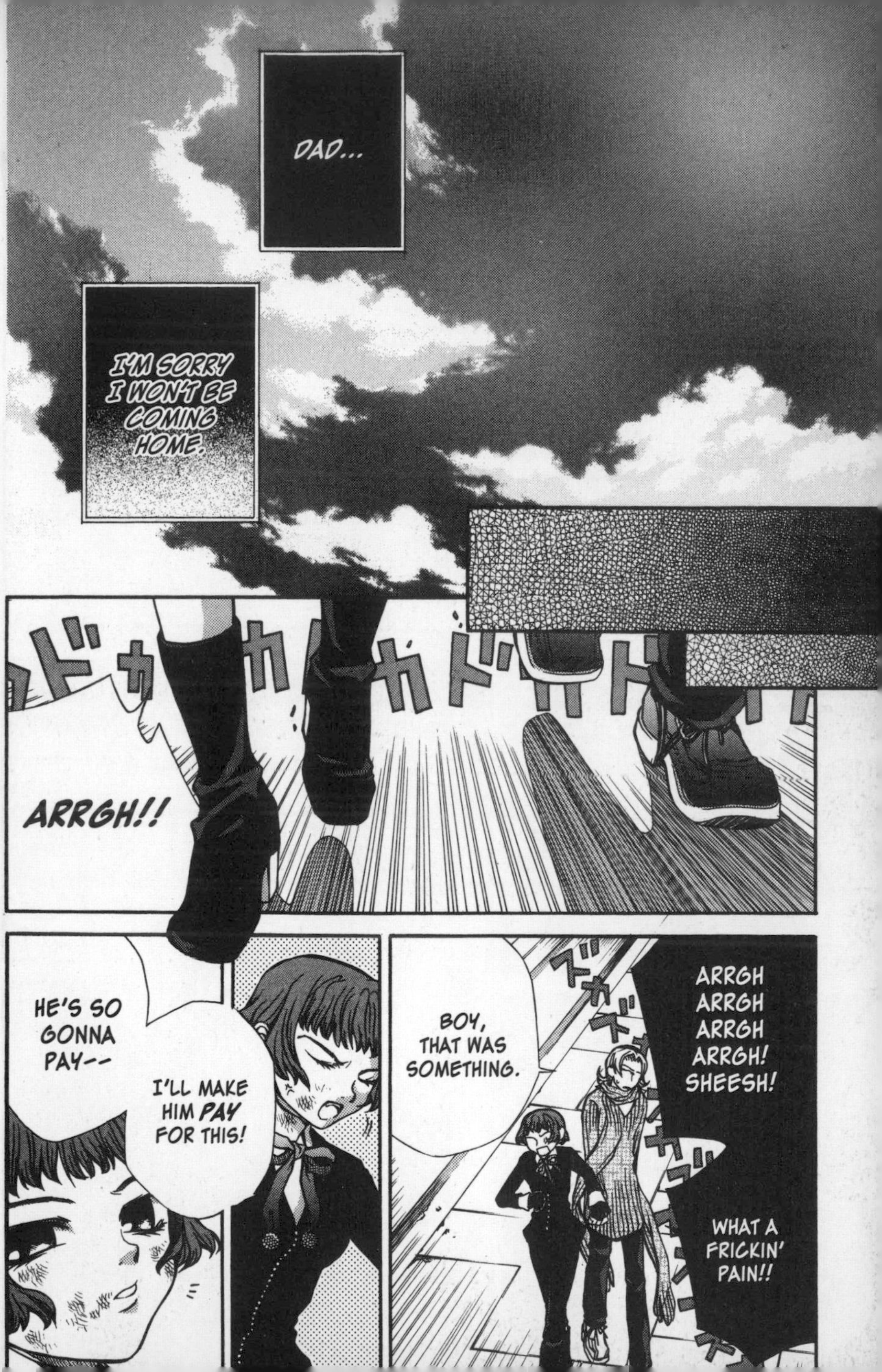
DAD...
I'M SORRY I WON'T BE COMING HOME.
ARRGH!!
ARRGH ARRGH ARRGH ARRGH! SHEESH!
BOY, THAT WAS SOMETHING.
WHAT A FRICKIN' PAIN!!
HE'S SO GONNA PAY--
I'LL MAKE HIM PAY FOR THIS!

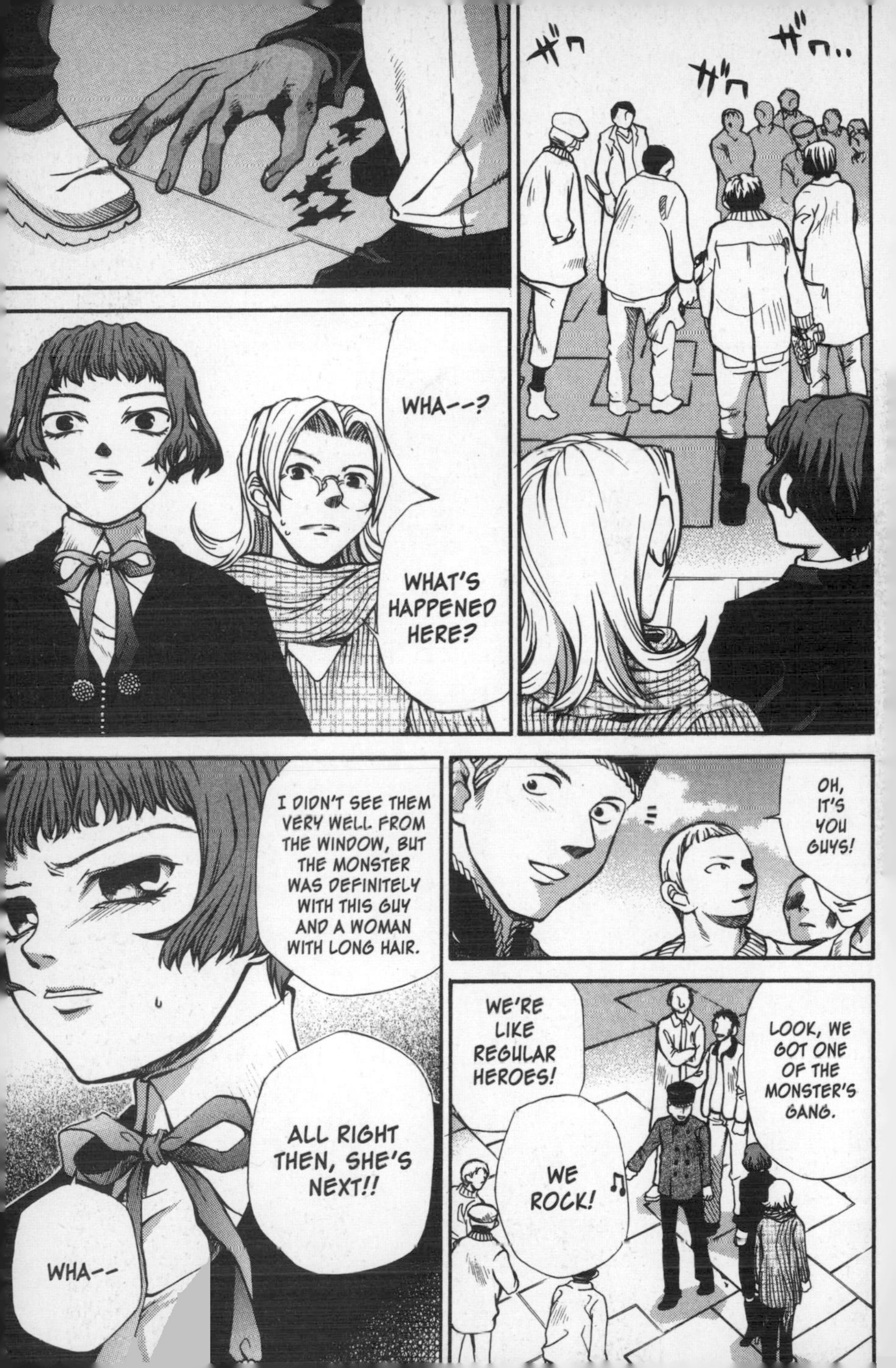
ザワ
ザワ..
ザワ
WHA--?
WHAT'S HAPPENED HERE?
OH, IT'S YOU GUYS!
LOOK, WE GOT ONE OF THE MONSTER'S GANG.
WE'RE LIKE REGULAR HEROES!
WE ROCK!
I DIDN'T SEE THEM VERY WELL FROM THE WINDOW, BUT THE MONSTER WAS DEFINITELY WITH THIS GUY AND A WOMAN WITH LONG HAIR.
ALL RIGHT THEN, SHE'S NEXT!!
WHA--

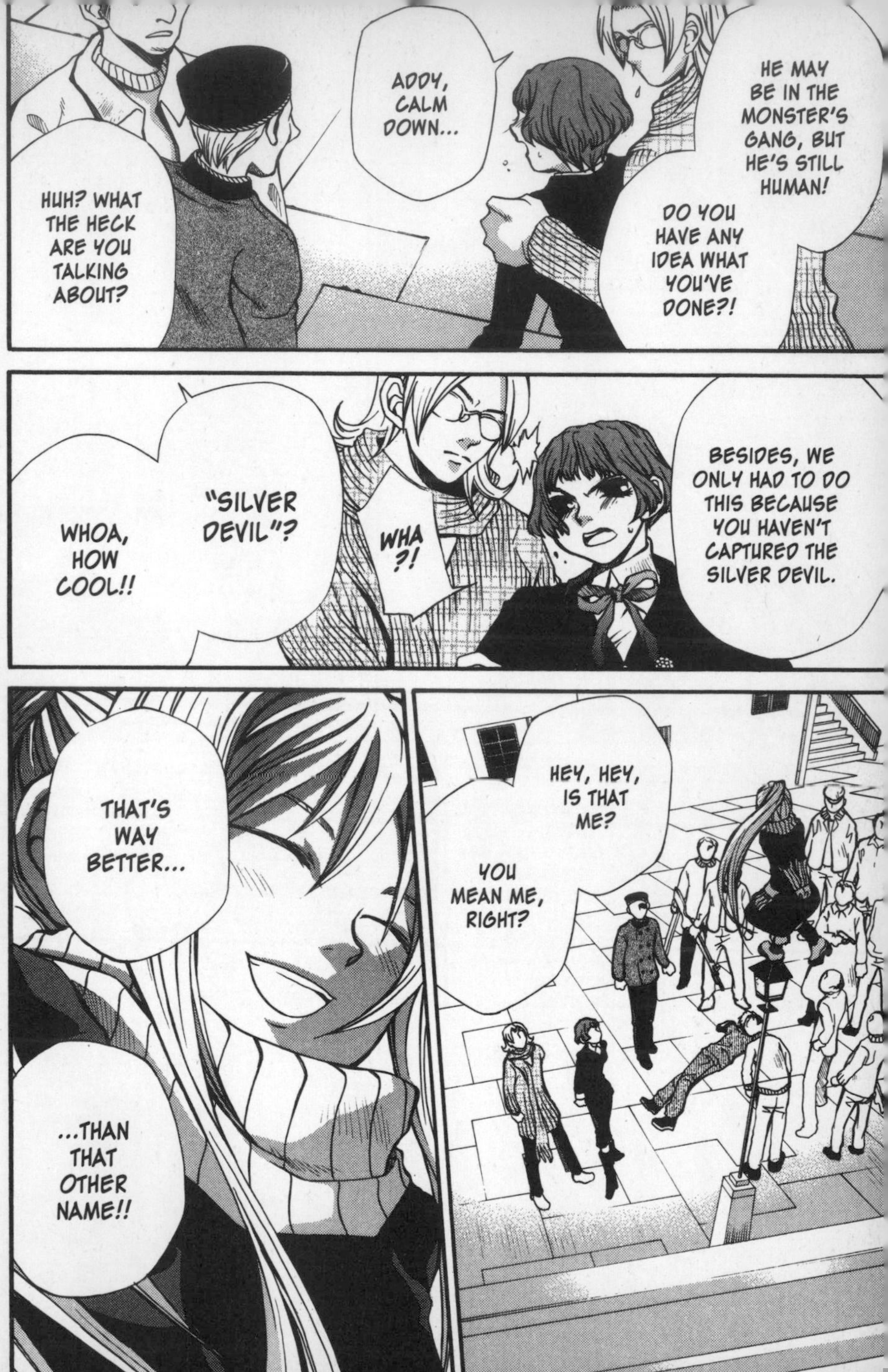
HE MAY BE IN THE MONSTER'S GANG, BUT HE'S STILL HUMAN!
DO YOU HAVE ANY IDEA WHAT YOU'VE DONE?!
ADDY, CALM DOWN...
HUH? WHAT THE HECK ARE YOU TALKING ABOUT?
BESIDES, WE ONLY HAD TO DO THIS BECAUSE YOU HAVEN'T CAPTURED THE SILVER DEVIL.
WHA?!
"SILVER DEVIL"?
WHOA, HOW COOL!!
HEY, HEY, IS THAT ME?
YOU MEAN ME, RIGHT?
THAT'S WAY BETTER...
...THAN THAT OTHER NAME!!

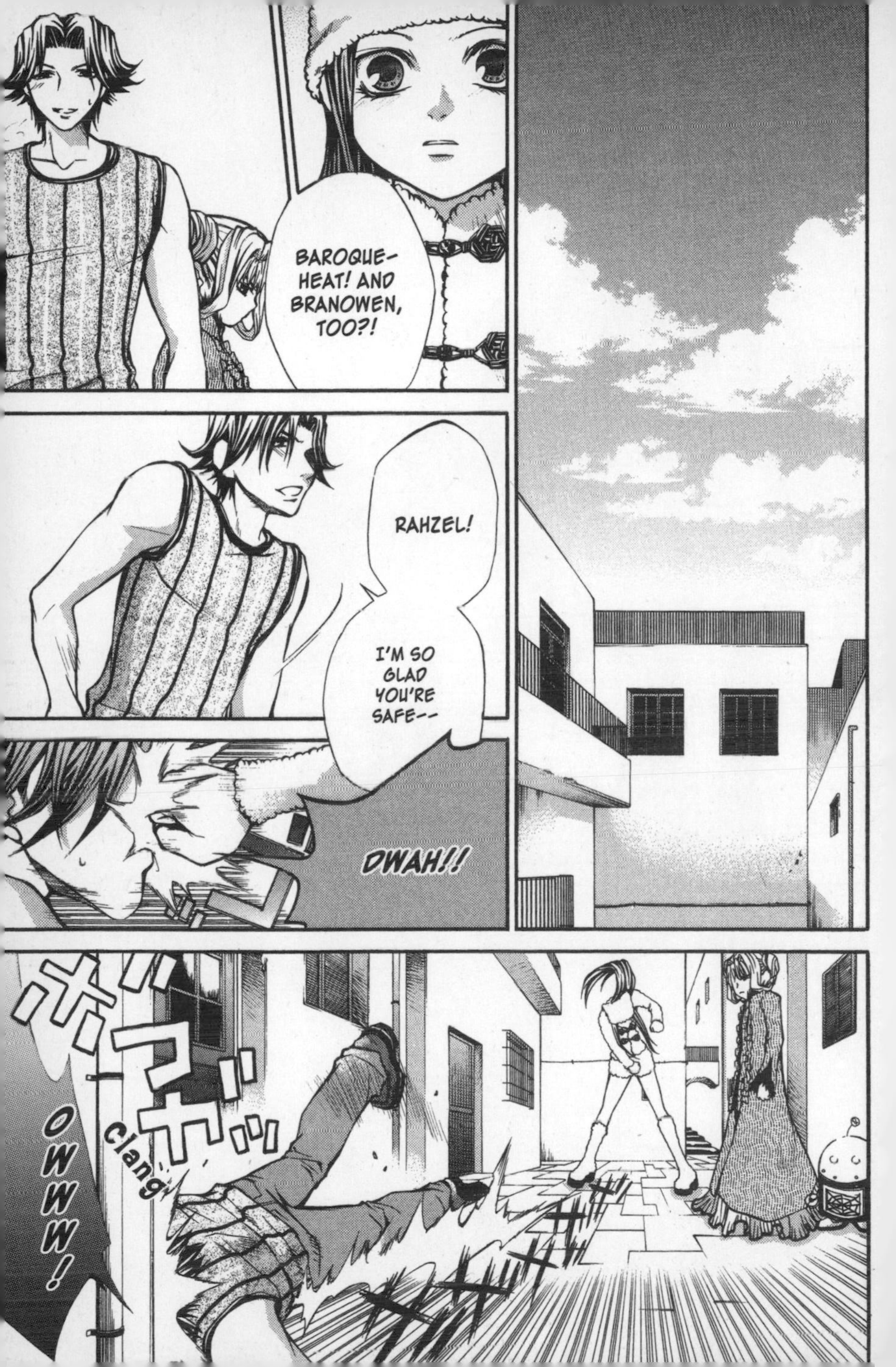
BAROQUE-HEAT! AND BRANOWEN, TOO?!
RAHZEL!
I'M SO GLAD YOU'RE SAFE--
DWAH!!
clang
OWWW!

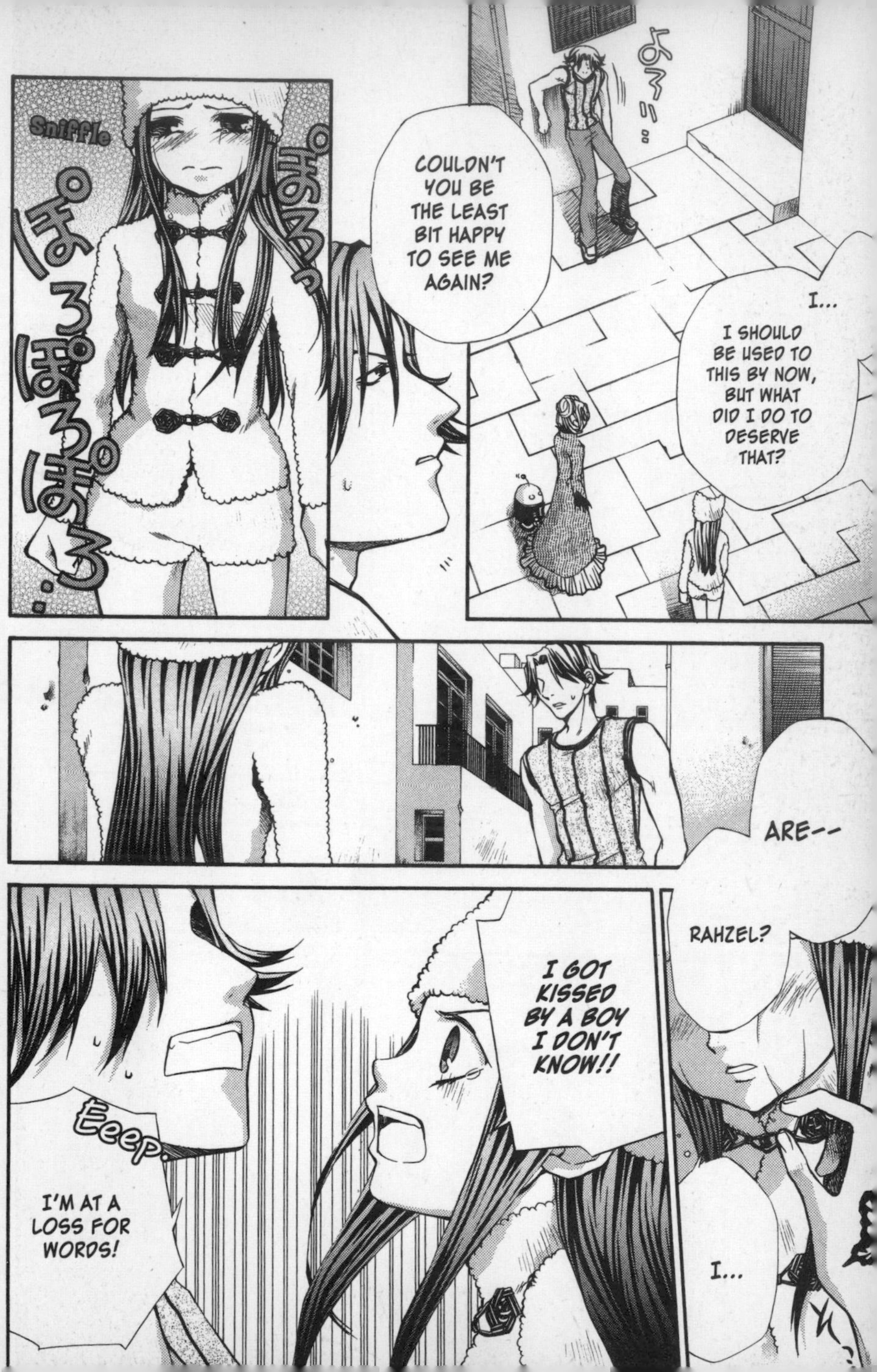
よろ…
I...
I SHOULD BE USED TO THIS BY NOW, BUT WHAT DID I DO TO DESERVE THAT?
COULDN'T YOU BE THE LEAST BIT HAPPY TO SEE ME AGAIN?
Sniffle
ぽろっ
ぽろぽろぽろ..
ARE--
RAHZEL?
I...
I GOT KISSED BY A BOY I DON'T KNOW!!
Eeep.
I'M AT A LOSS FOR WORDS!

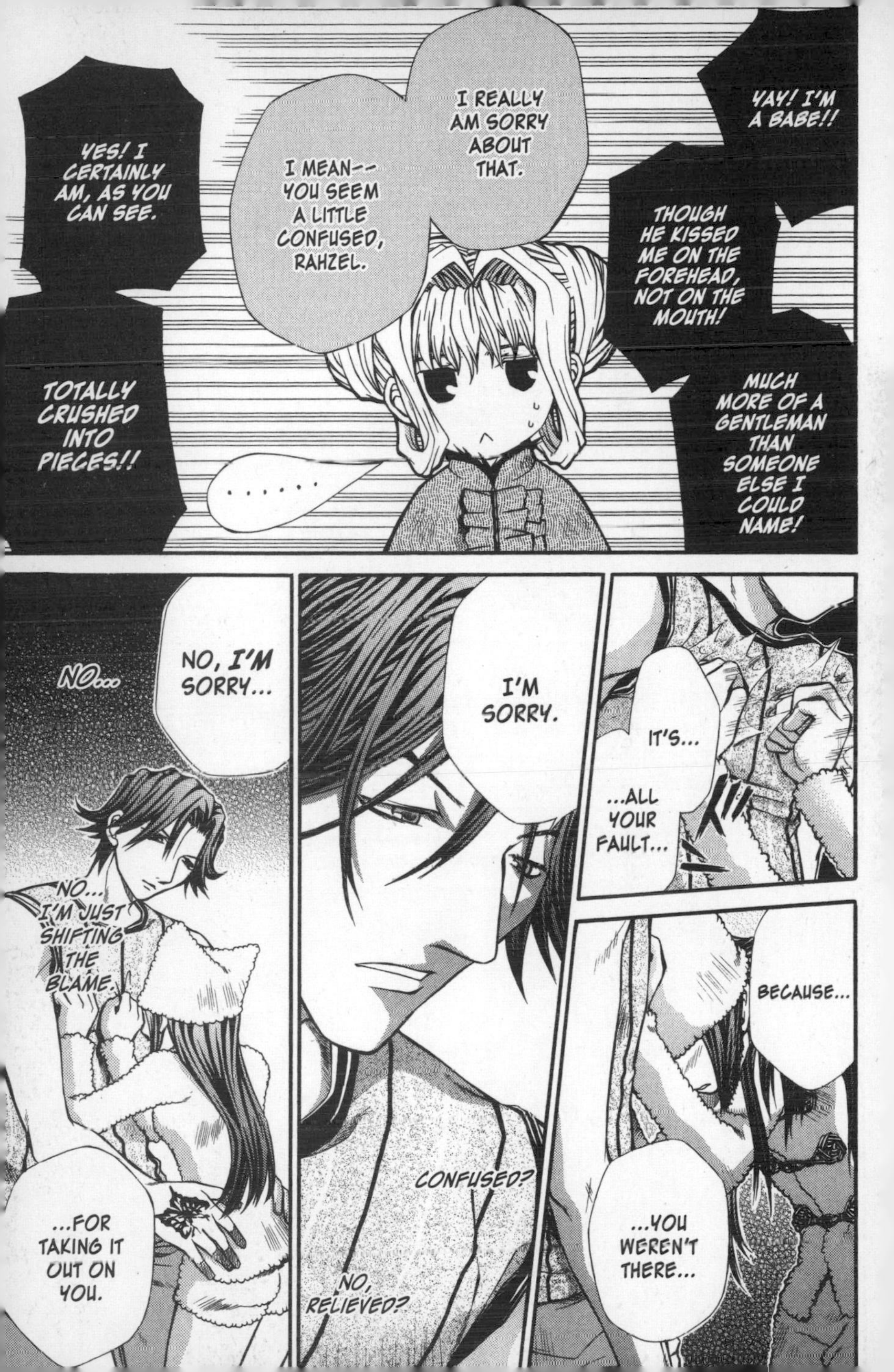
YAY! I'M A BABE!!
THOUGH HE KISSED ME ON THE FOREHEAD, NOT ON THE MOUTH!
MUCH MORE OF A GENTLEMAN THAN SOMEONE ELSE I COULD NAME!
I REALLY AM SORRY ABOUT THAT.
I MEAN-- YOU SEEM A LITTLE CONFUSED, RAHZEL.
YES! I CERTAINLY AM, AS YOU CAN SEE.
TOTALLY CRUSHED INTO PIECES!!
......
IT'S...
...ALL YOUR FAULT...
BECAUSE...
...YOU WEREN'T THERE...
I'M SORRY.
CONFUSED?
NO, RELIEVED?
NO, I'M SORRY...
NO...
NO... I'M JUST SHIFTING THE BLAME.
...FOR TAKING IT OUT ON YOU.

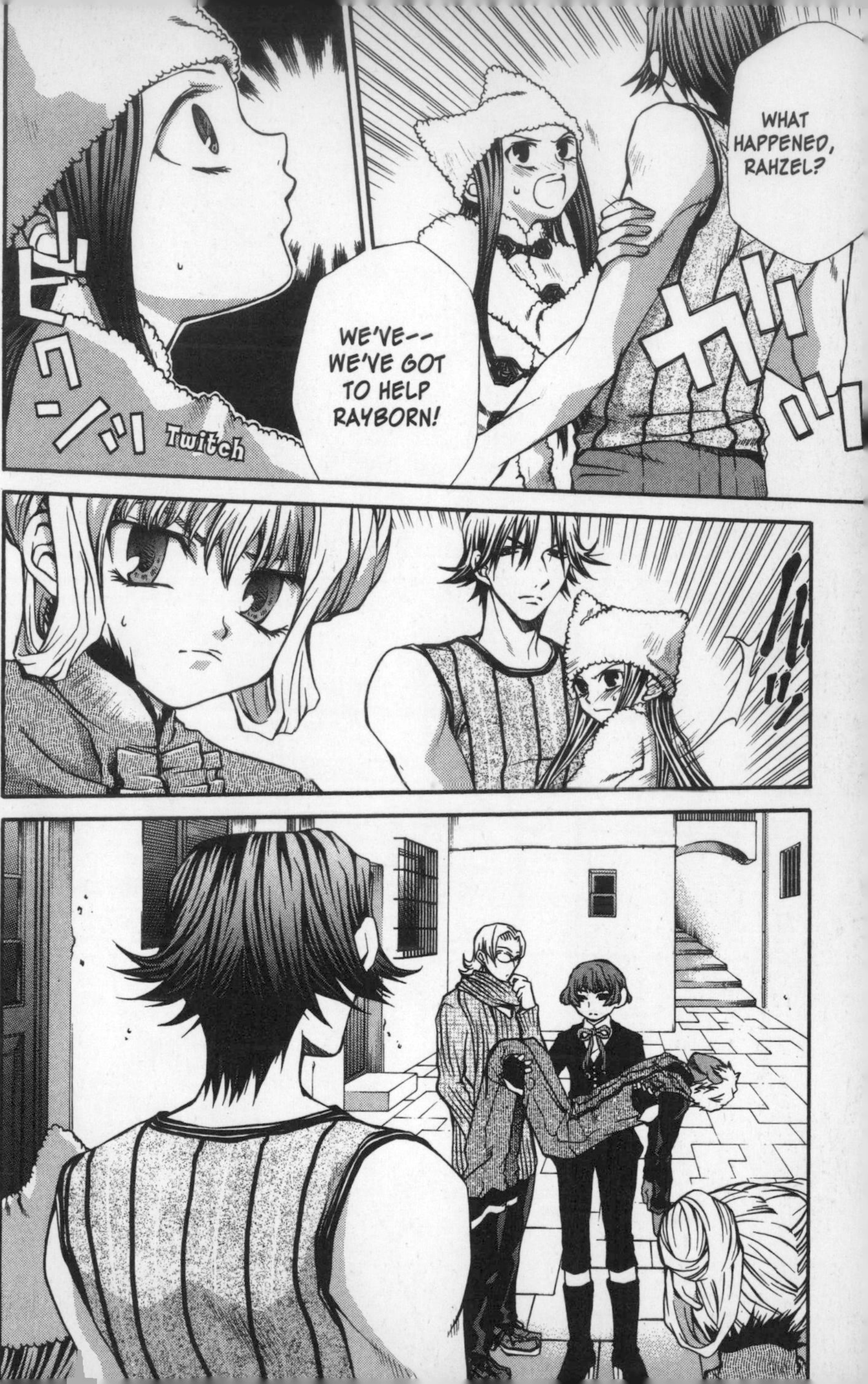
WHAT HAPPENED, RAHZEL?
WE'VE-- WE'VE GOT TO HELP RAYBORN!
Twitch

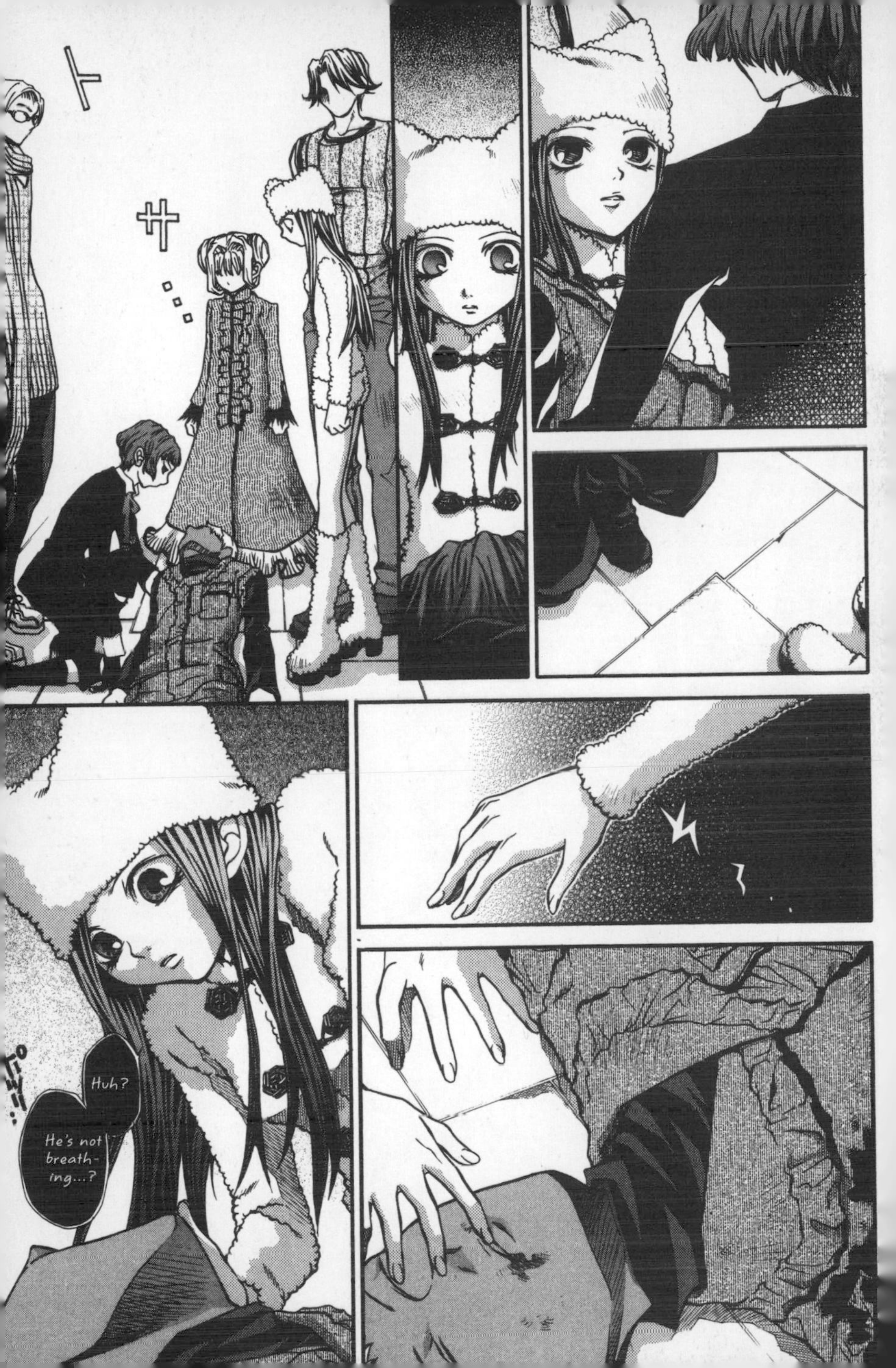
ト
サ
Huh?
He's not breath-ing...?

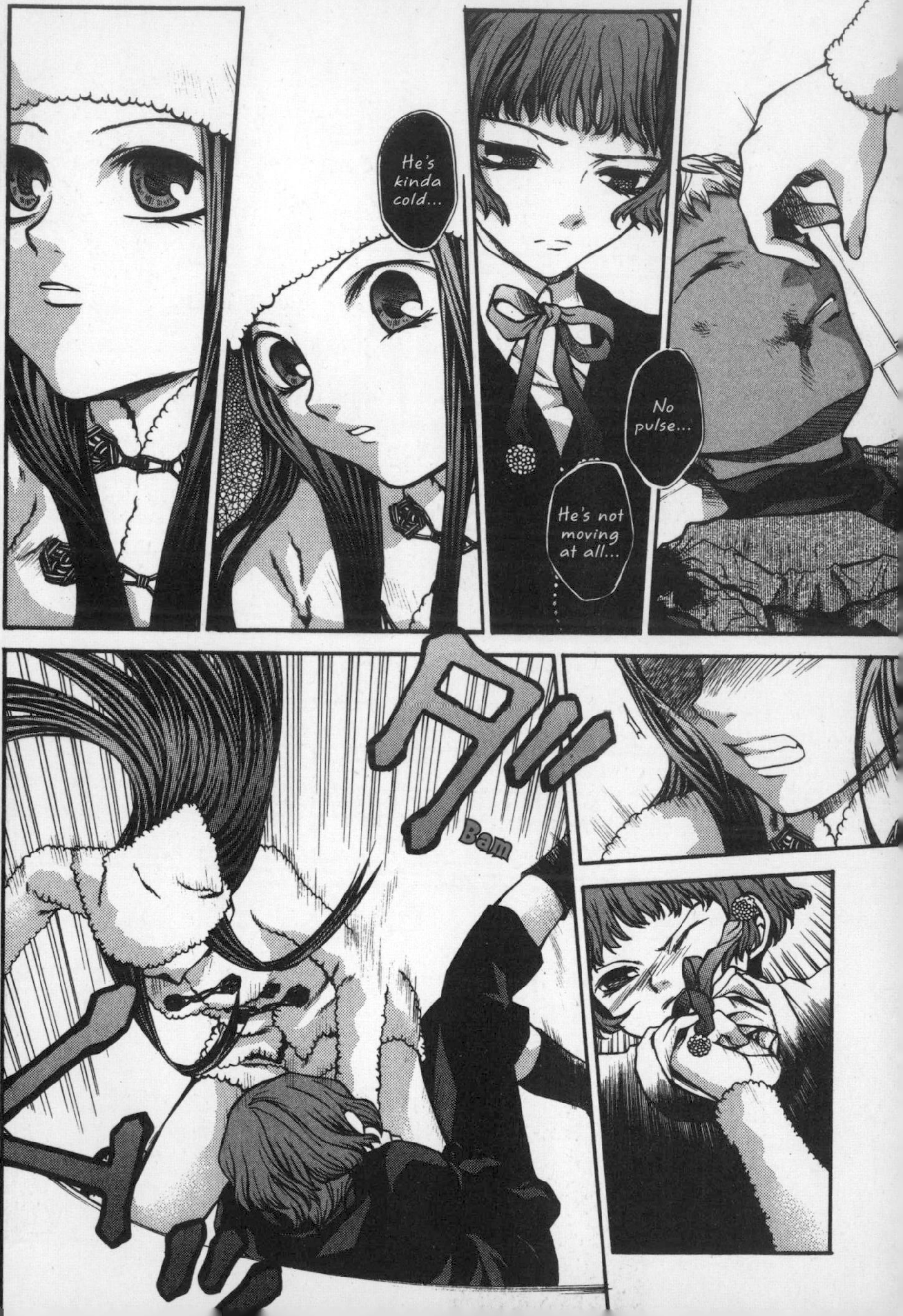
No pulse...
He's not moving at all...
He's kinda cold...
Bam

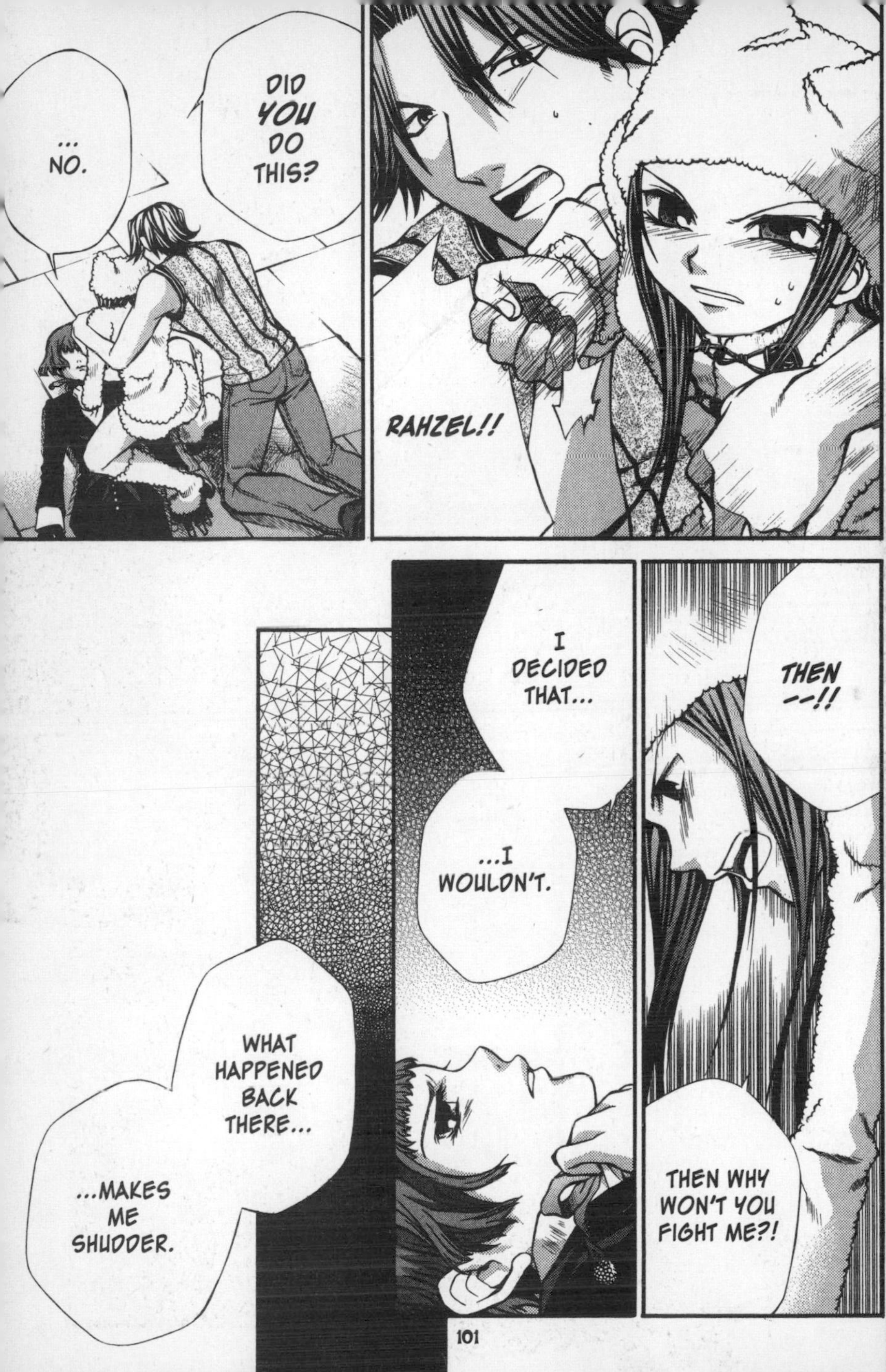

RAHZEL!!
DID YOU DO THIS?
... NO.
THEN --!!
THEN WHY WON'T YOU FIGHT ME?!
I DECIDED THAT...
...I WOULDN'T.
WHAT HAPPENED BACK THERE...
...MAKES ME SHUDDER.

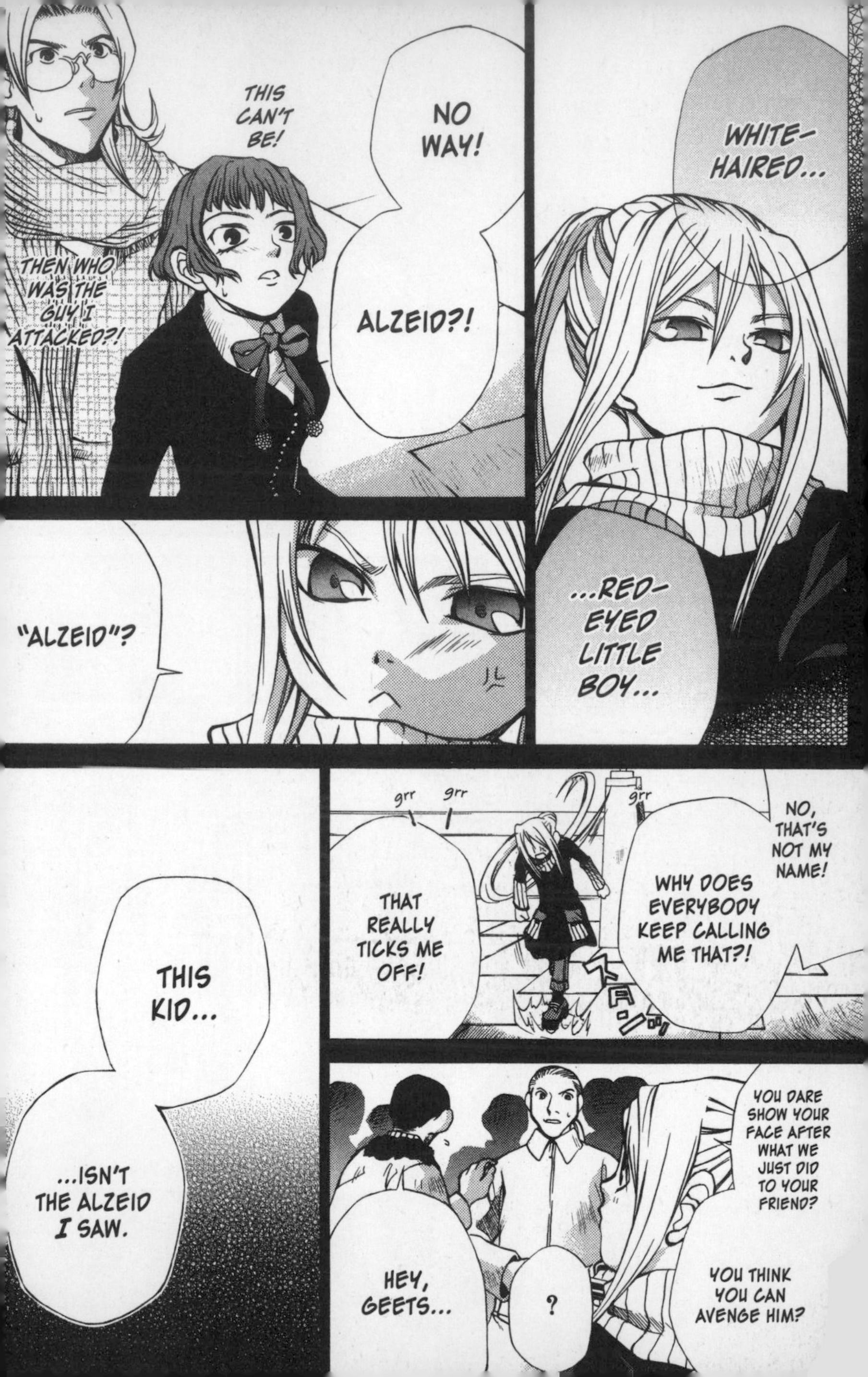
WHITE-HAIRED...
...RED-EYED LITTLE BOY...
NO WAY!
ALZEID?!
THIS CAN'T BE!
THEN WHO WAS THE GUY I ATTACKED?!
"ALZEID"?
grr
NO, THAT'S NOT MY NAME!
WHY DOES EVERYBODY KEEP CALLING ME THAT?!
grr grr
THAT REALLY TICKS ME OFF!
YOU DARE SHOW YOUR FACE AFTER WHAT WE JUST DID TO YOUR FRIEND?
YOU THINK YOU CAN AVENGE HIM?
?
HEY, GEETS...
THIS KID...
...ISN'T THE ALZEID I SAW.

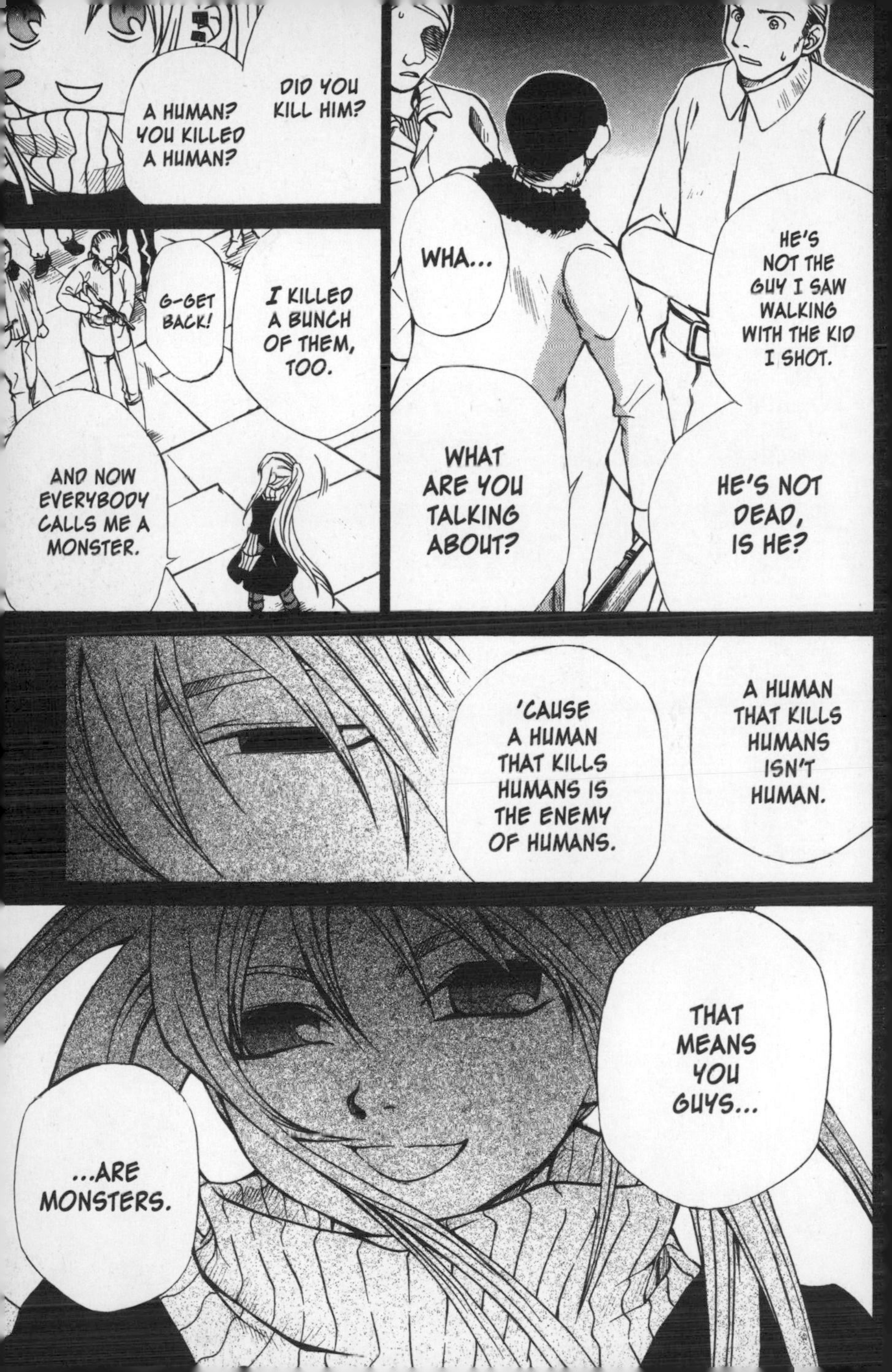
HE'S NOT THE GUY I SAW WALKING WITH THE KID I SHOT.
WHA...
HE'S NOT DEAD, IS HE?
WHAT ARE YOU TALKING ABOUT?
DID YOU KILL HIM?
A HUMAN? YOU KILLED A HUMAN?
I KILLED A BUNCH OF THEM, TOO.
G-GET BACK!
AND NOW EVERYBODY CALLS ME A MONSTER.
A HUMAN THAT KILLS HUMANS ISN'T HUMAN.
'CAUSE A HUMAN THAT KILLS HUMANS IS THE ENEMY OF HUMANS.
THAT MEANS YOU GUYS...
...ARE MONSTERS.

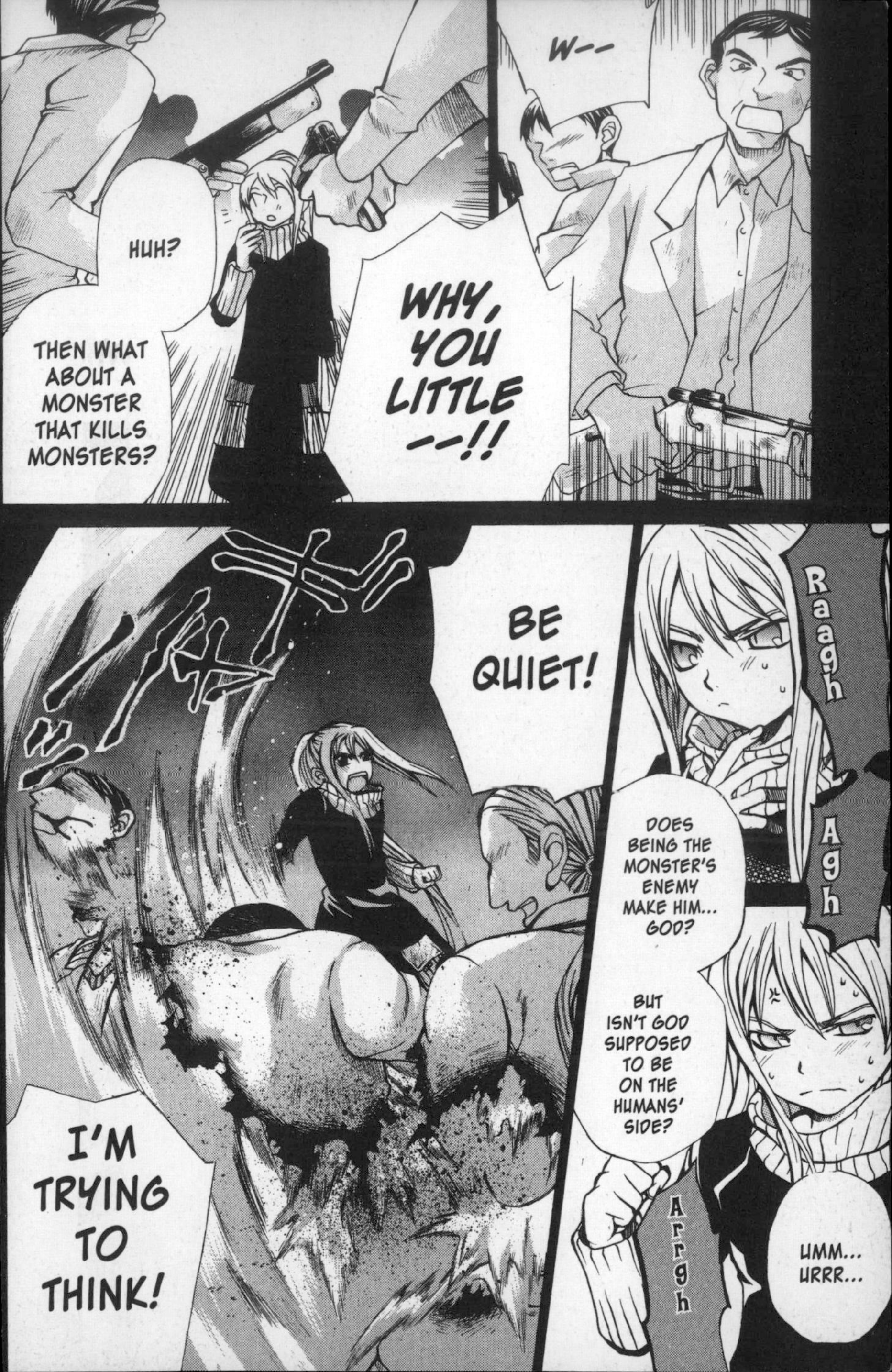

W--
WHY, YOU LITTLE --!!
HUH?
THEN WHAT ABOUT A MONSTER THAT KILLS MONSTERS?
Raagh
Agh
DOES BEING THE MONSTER'S ENEMY MAKE HIM... GOD?
BUT ISN'T GOD SUPPOSED TO BE ON THE HUMANS' SIDE?
Arrgh
UMM... URRR...
BE QUIET!
I'M TRYING TO THINK!

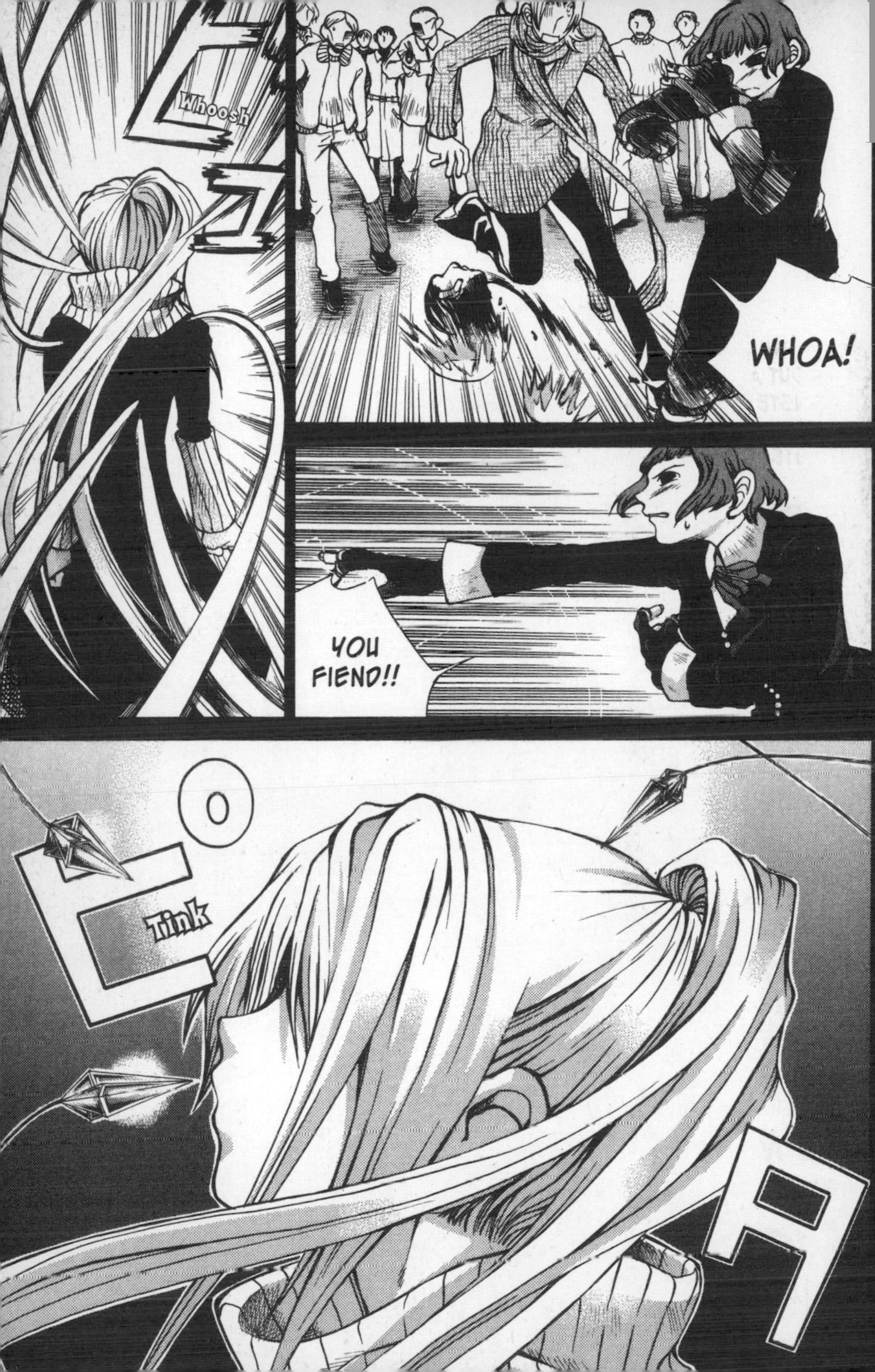
WHOA!
YOU FIEND!!
Whoosh
Tink

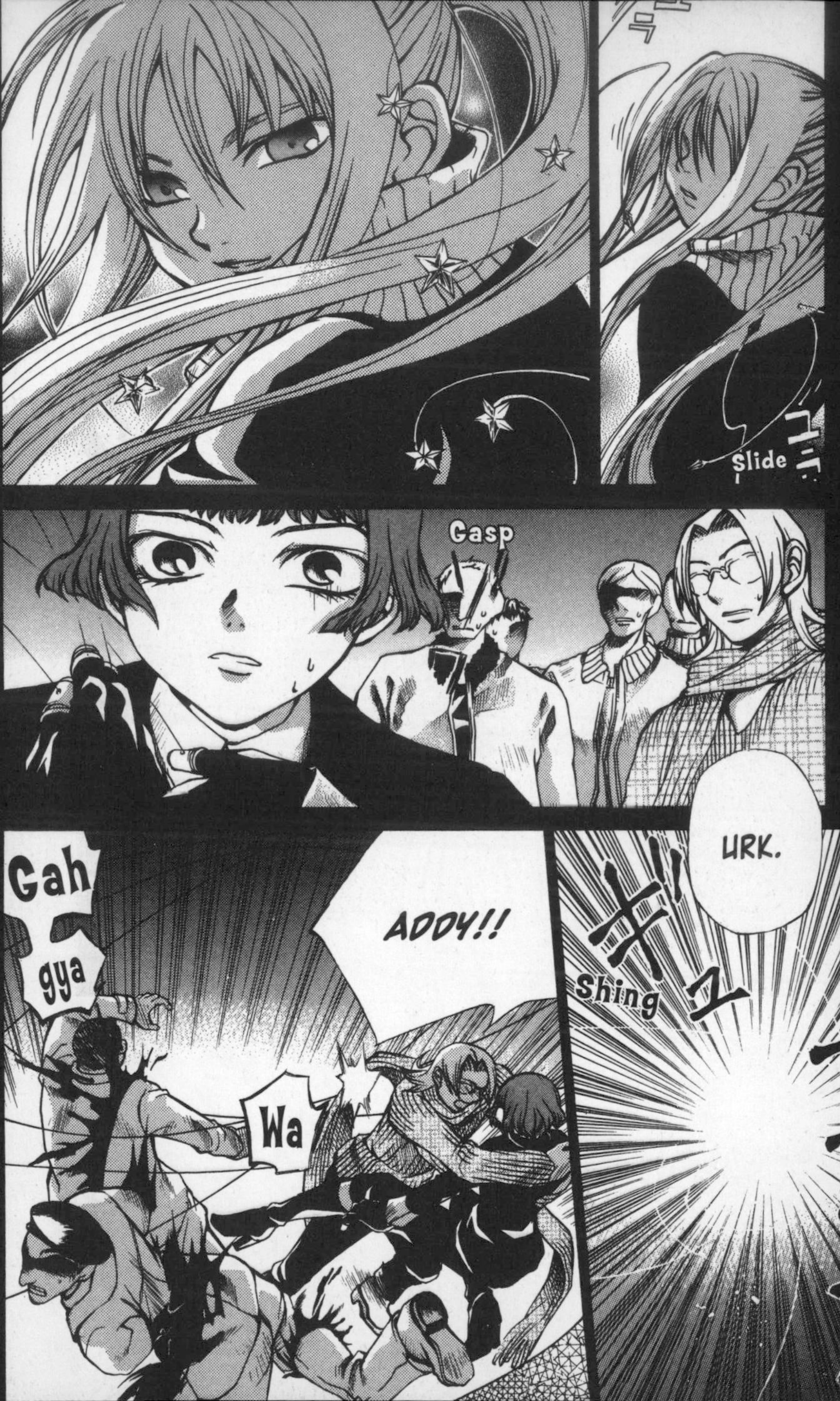
Slide
Gasp
URK.
Shing
Gah
gya
ADDY!!
Wa

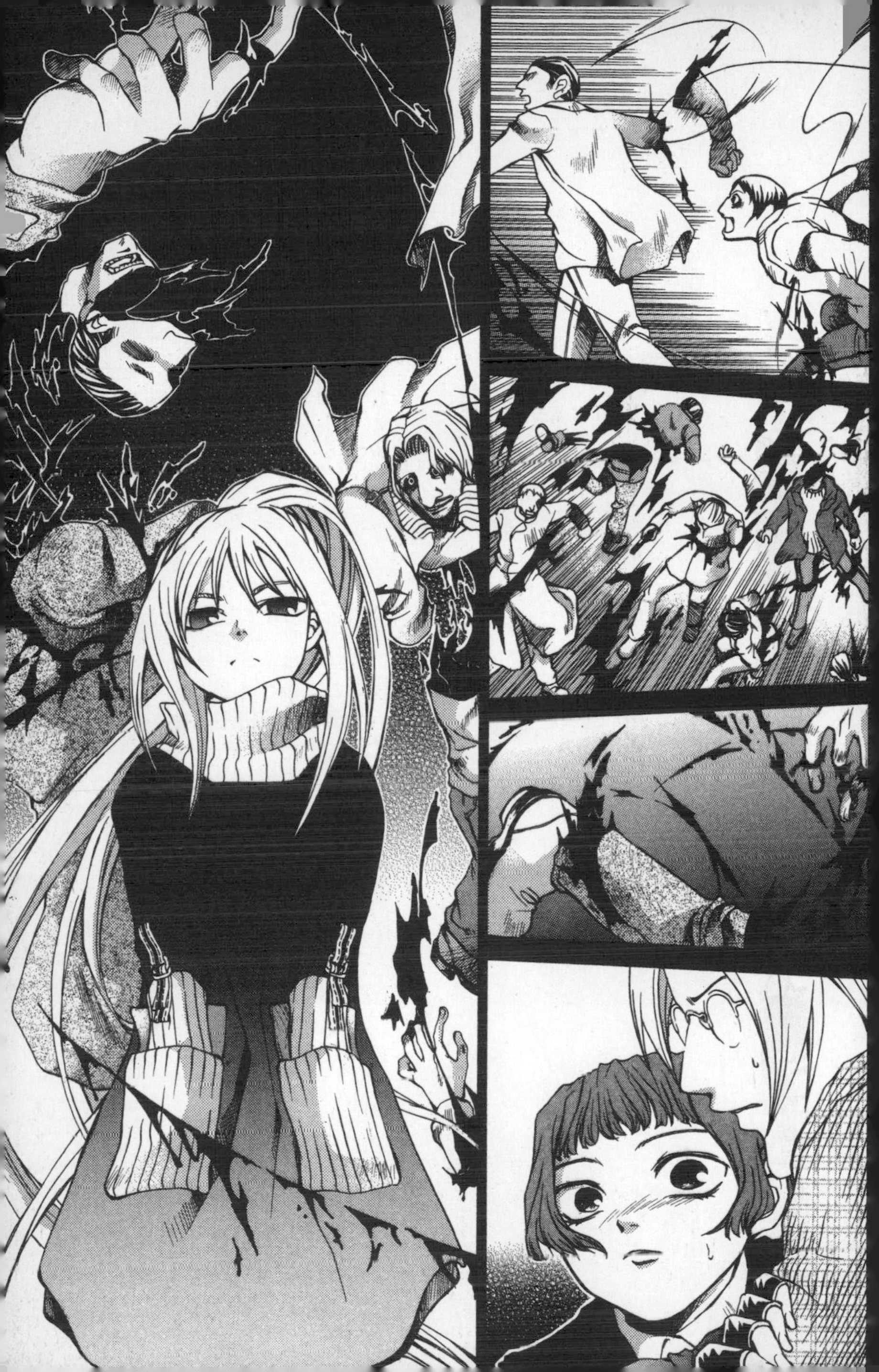

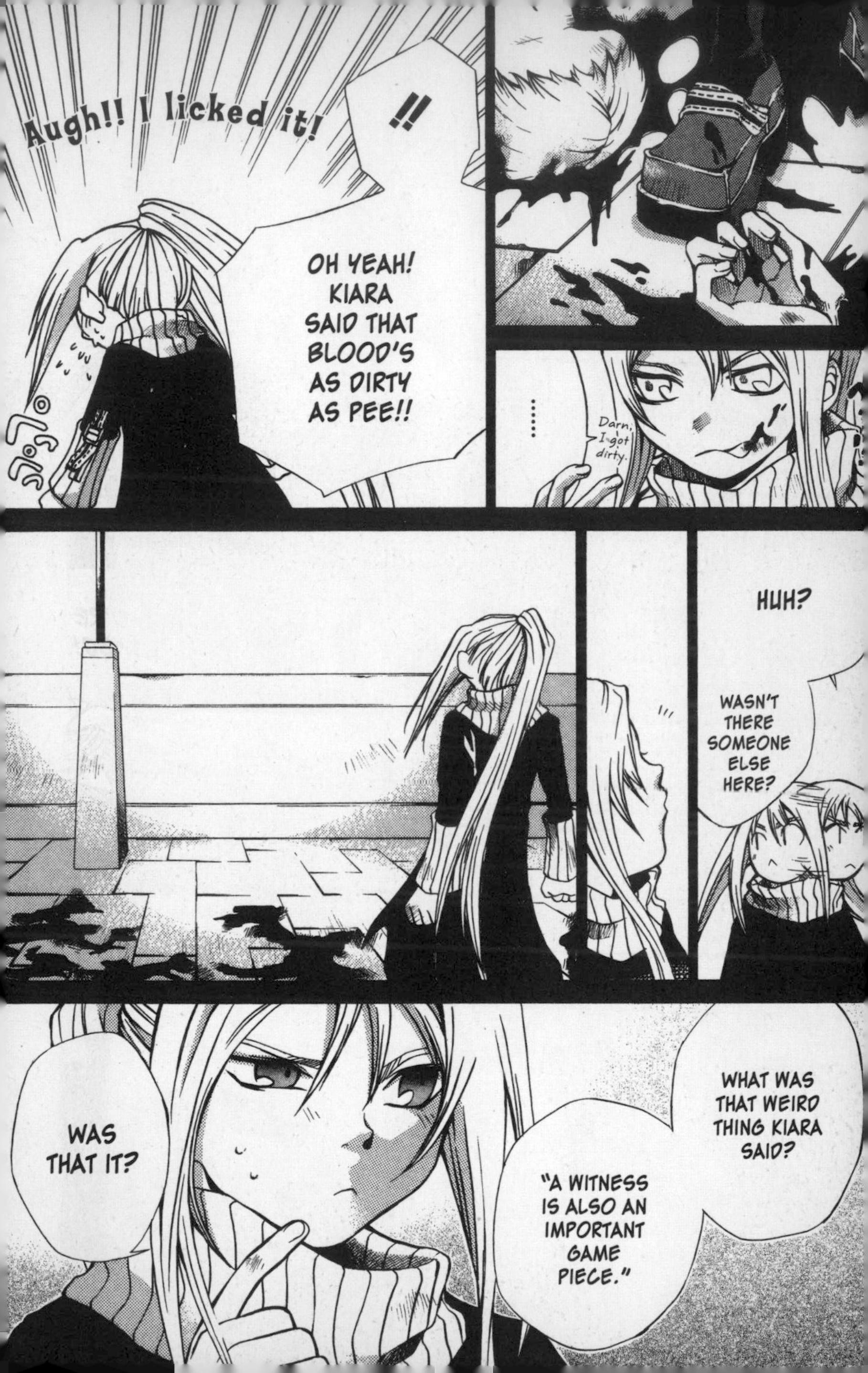
Darn, I got dirty.
......
!!
Augh!! I licked it!
OH YEAH! KIARA SAID THAT BLOOD'S AS DIRTY AS PEE!!
HUH?
WASN'T THERE SOMEONE ELSE HERE?
WHAT WAS THAT WEIRD THING KIARA SAID?
"A WITNESS IS ALSO AN IMPORTANT GAME PIECE."
WAS THAT IT?

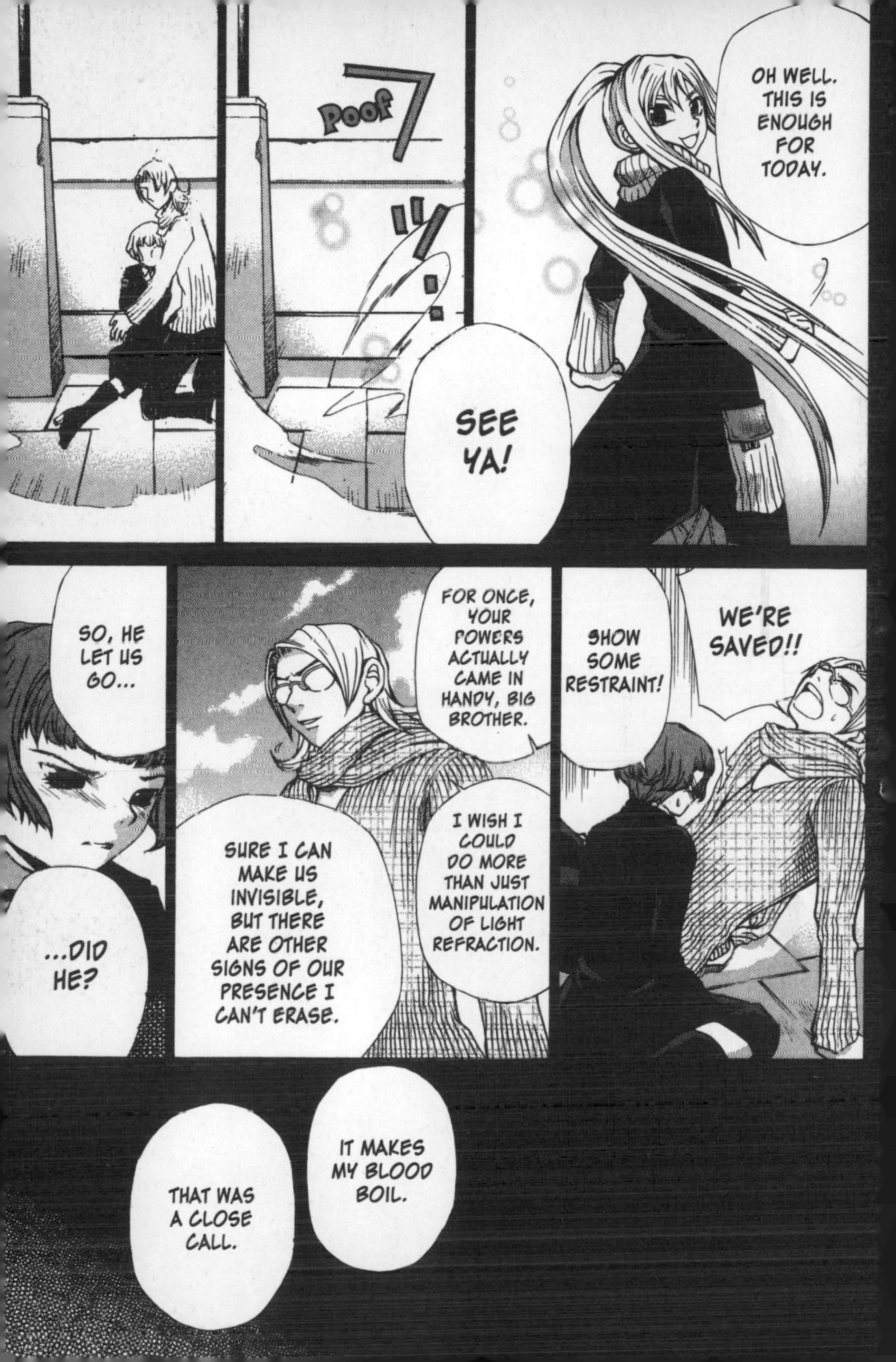
OH WELL. THIS IS ENOUGH FOR TODAY.
SEE YA!
Poof
WE'RE SAVED!!
SHOW SOME RESTRAINT!
FOR ONCE, YOUR POWERS ACTUALLY CAME IN HANDY, BIG BROTHER.
I WISH I COULD DO MORE THAN JUST MANIPULATION OF LIGHT REFRACTION.
SURE I CAN MAKE US INVISIBLE, BUT THERE ARE OTHER SIGNS OF OUR PRESENCE I CAN'T ERASE.
SO, HE LET US GO...
...DID HE?
IT MAKES MY BLOOD BOIL.
THAT WAS A CLOSE CALL.

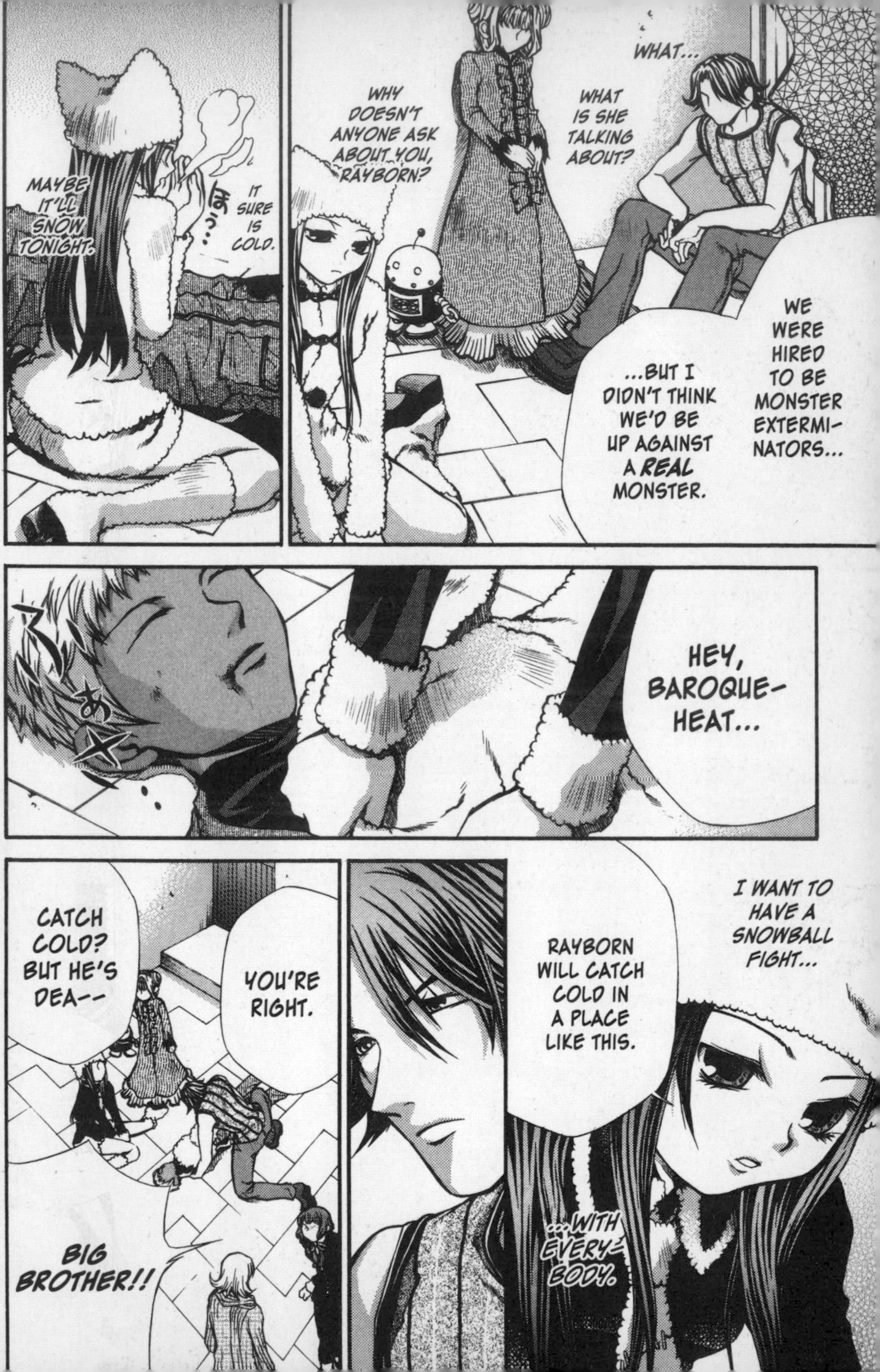
WHAT...
WHAT IS SHE TALKING ABOUT?
WHY DOESN'T ANYONE ASK ABOUT YOU, RAYBORN?
WE WERE HIRED TO BE MONSTER EXTERMI-NATORS...
...BUT I DIDN'T THINK WE'D BE UP AGAINST A REAL MONSTER.
IT SURE IS COLD.
MAYBE IT'LL SNOW TONIGHT.
HEY, BAROQUE-HEAT...
I WANT TO HAVE A SNOWBALL FIGHT...
RAYBORN WILL CATCH COLD IN A PLACE LIKE THIS.
...WITH EVERY-BODY.
YOU'RE RIGHT.
CATCH COLD? BUT HE'S DEA--
BIG BROTHER!!

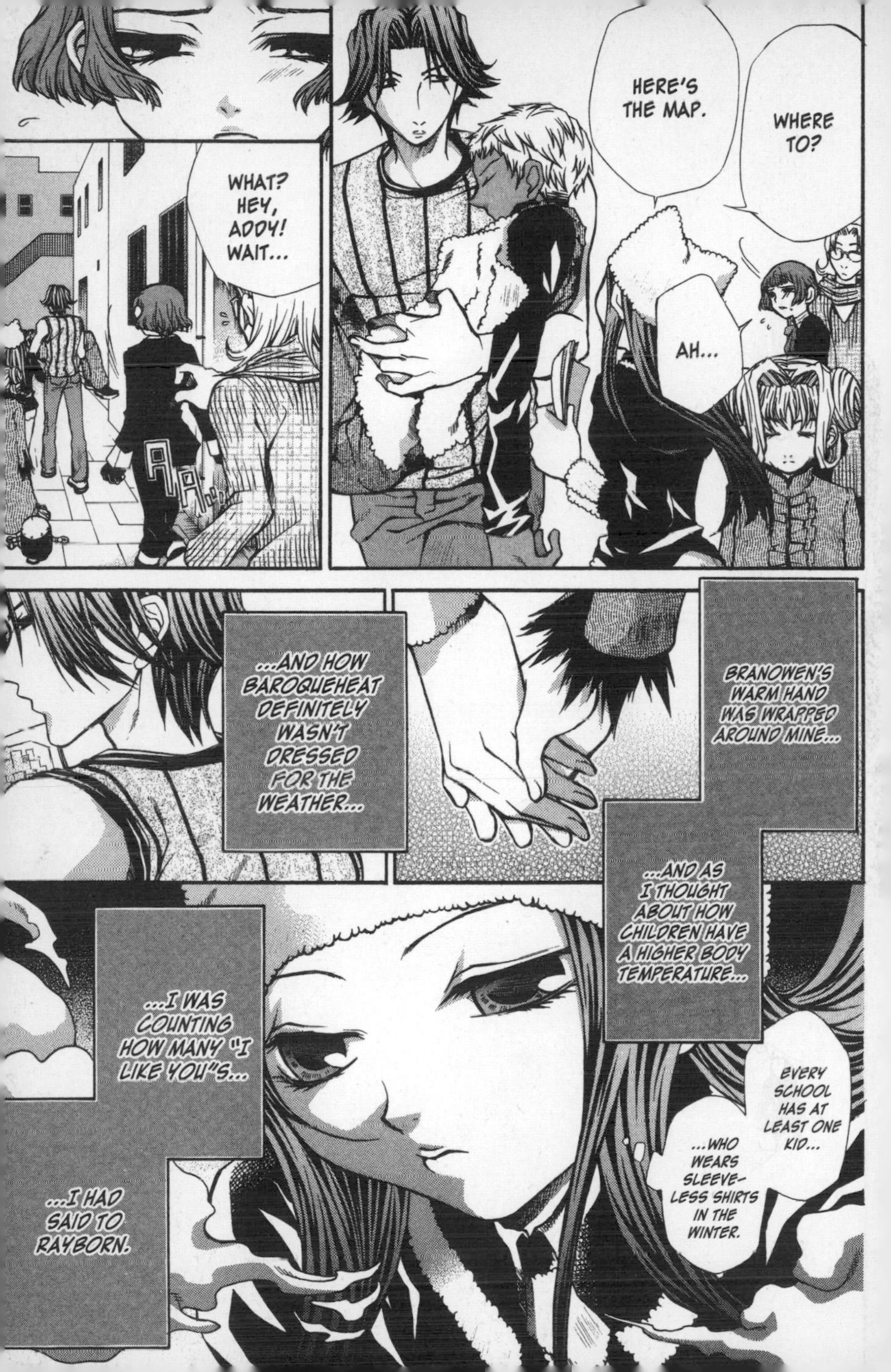
WHERE TO?
HERE'S THE MAP.
AH...
WHAT? HEY, ADDY! WAIT...
BRANOWEN'S WARM HAND WAS WRAPPED AROUND MINE...
...AND HOW BAROQUEHEAT DEFINITELY WASN'T DRESSED FOR THE WEATHER...
...AND AS I THOUGHT ABOUT HOW CHILDREN HAVE A HIGHER BODY TEMPERATURE...
EVERY SCHOOL HAS AT LEAST ONE KID...
...WHO WEARS SLEEVE-LESS SHIRTS IN THE WINTER.
...I WAS COUNTING HOW MANY "I LIKE YOU"S...
...I HAD SAID TO RAYBORN.

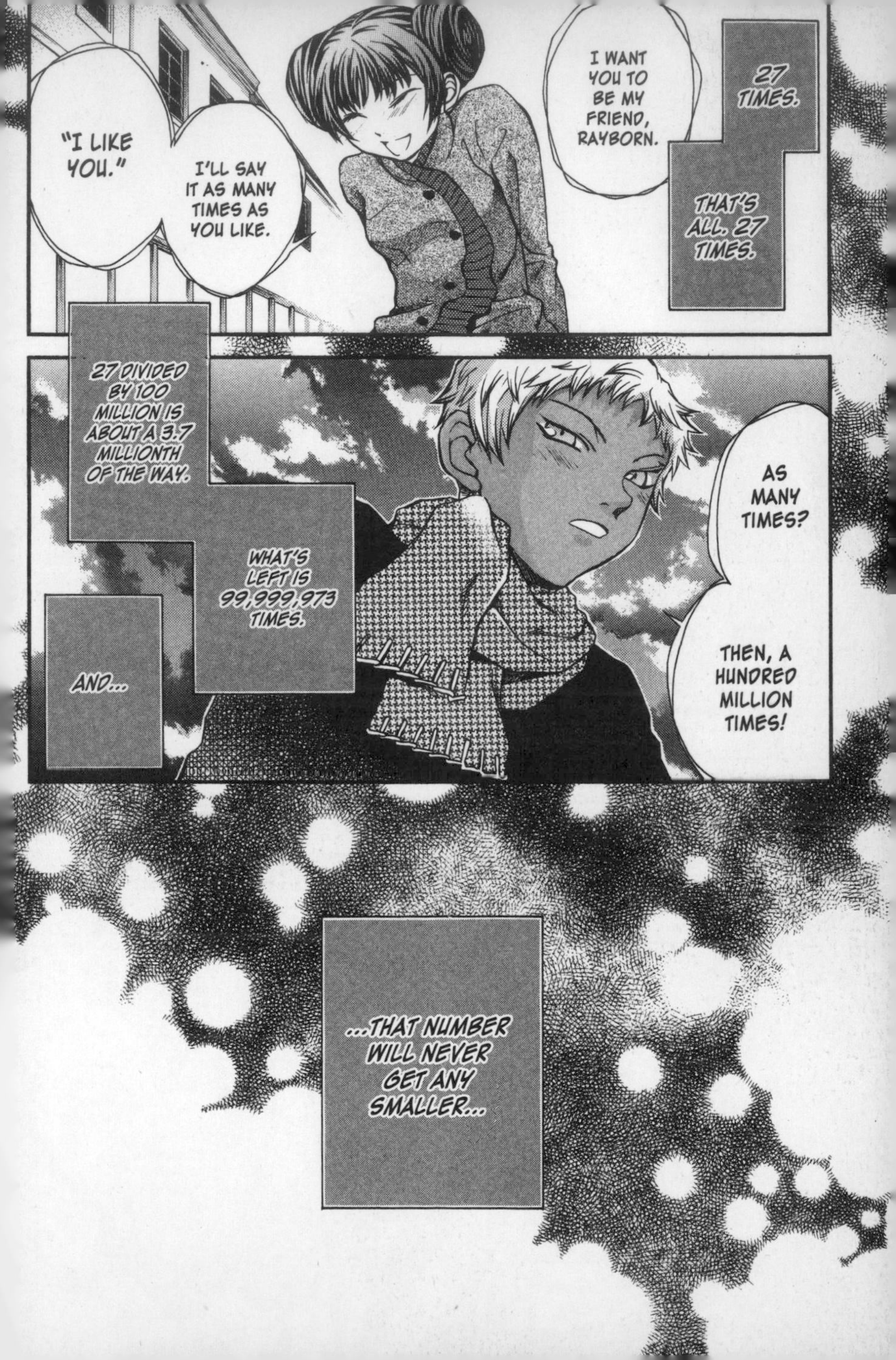

I WANT YOU TO BE MY FRIEND, RAYBORN.
27 TIMES.
THAT'S ALL. 27 TIMES.
"I LIKE YOU."
I'LL SAY IT AS MANY TIMES AS YOU LIKE.
AS MANY TIMES?
THEN, A HUNDRED MILLION TIMES!
27 DIVIDED BY 100 MILLION IS ABOUT A 3.7 MILLIONTH OF THE WAY.
WHAT'S LEFT IS 99,999,973 TIMES.
AND...
...THAT NUMBER WILL NEVER GET ANY SMALLER...

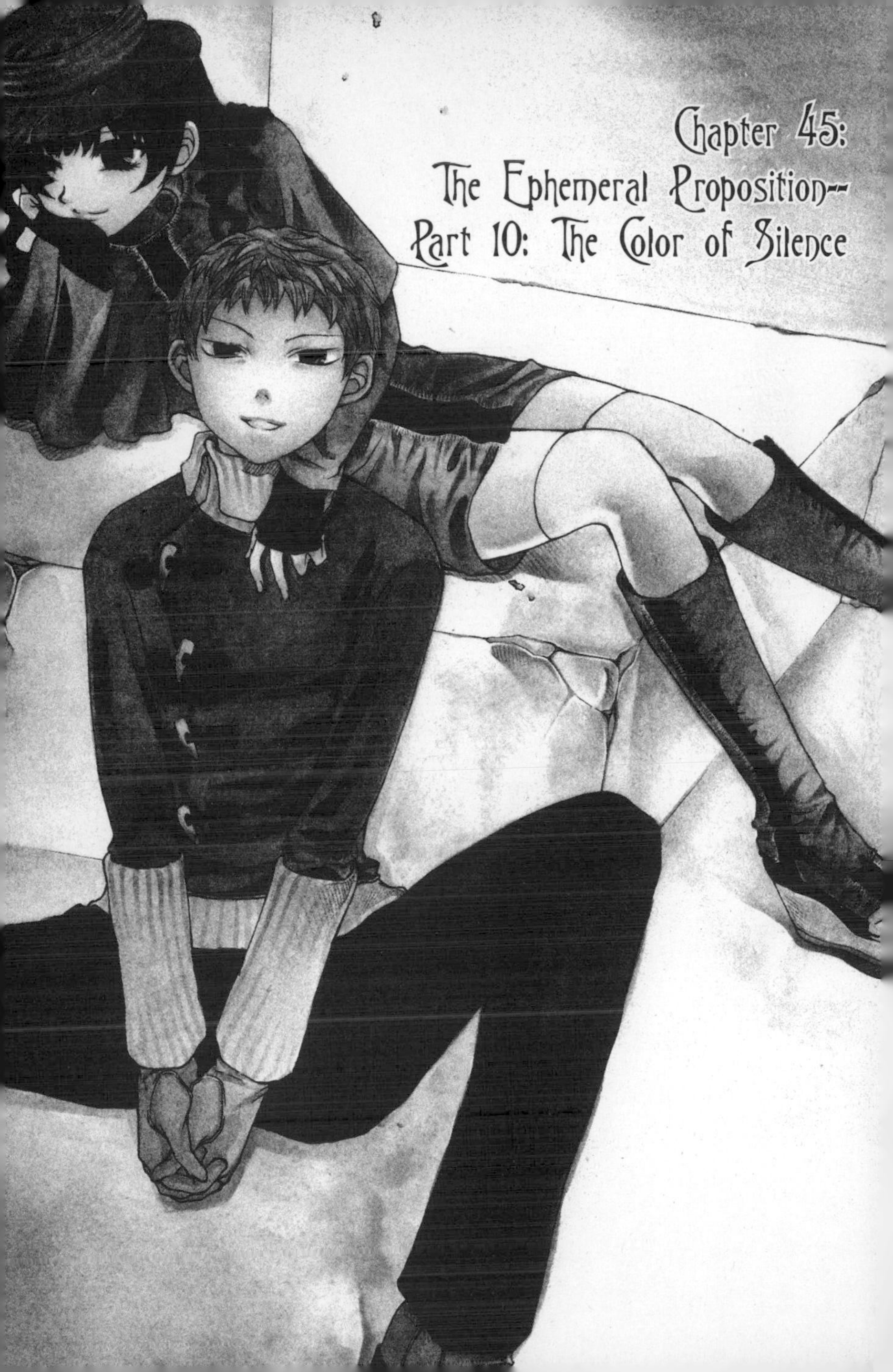
Chapter 45:
The Ephemeral Proposition--
Part 10: The Color of Silence

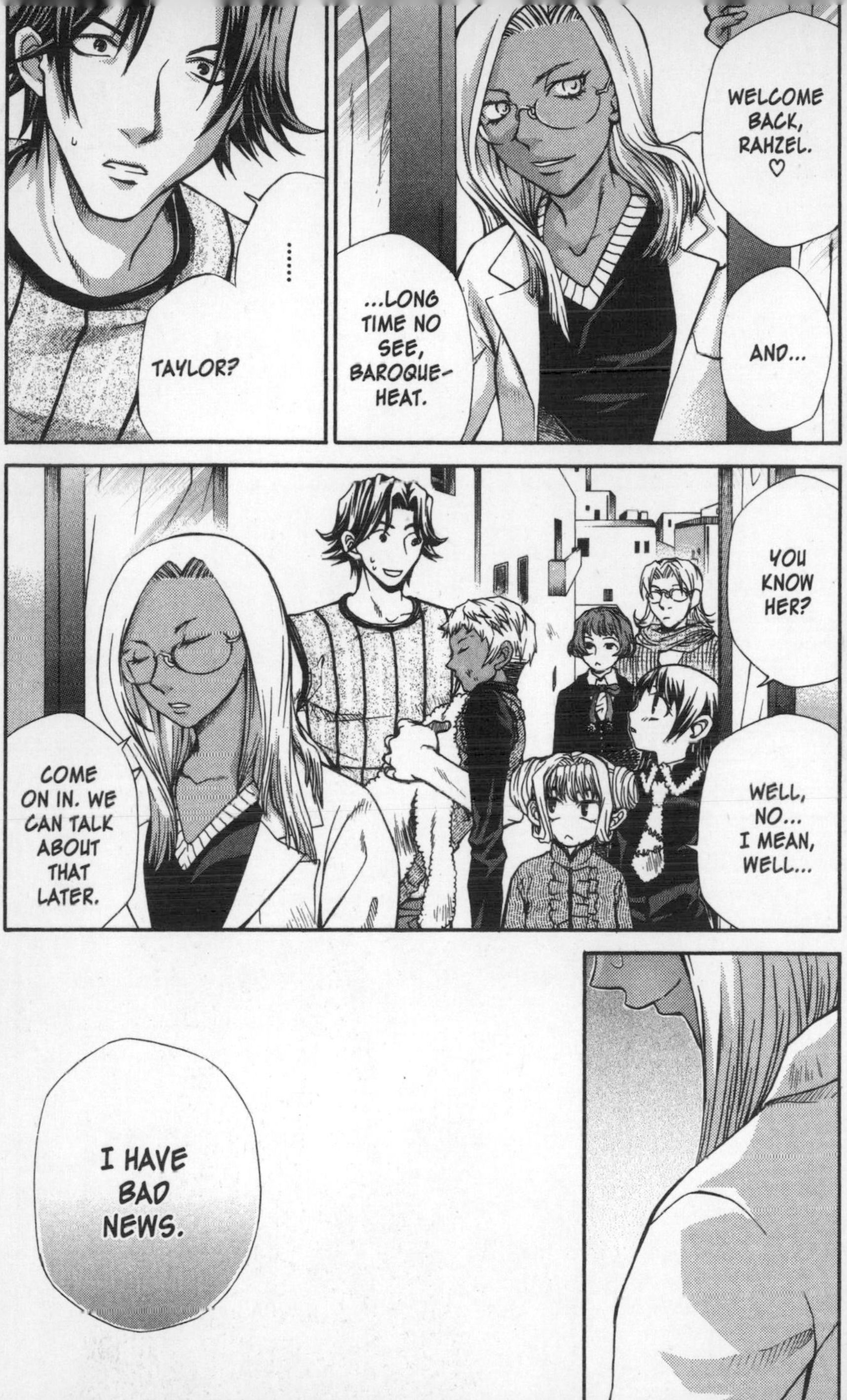
WELCOME BACK, RAHZEL. ♡
AND...
...LONG TIME NO SEE, BAROQUE-HEAT.
......
TAYLOR?
YOU KNOW HER?
WELL, NO... I MEAN, WELL...
COME ON IN. WE CAN TALK ABOUT THAT LATER.
I HAVE BAD NEWS.

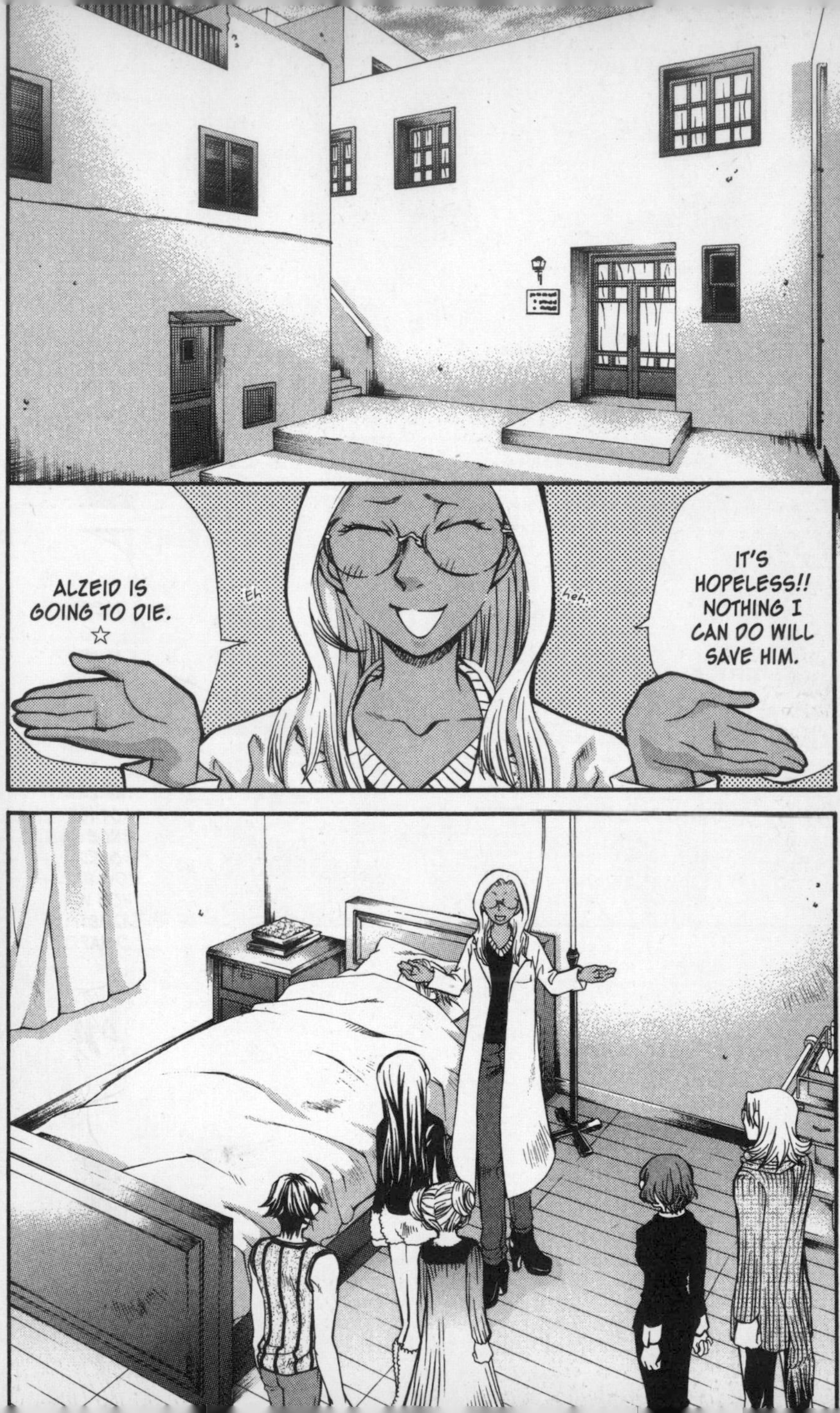
IT'S HOPELESS!! NOTHING I CAN DO WILL SAVE HIM.
heh.
Eh.
ALZEID IS GOING TO DIE. ☆

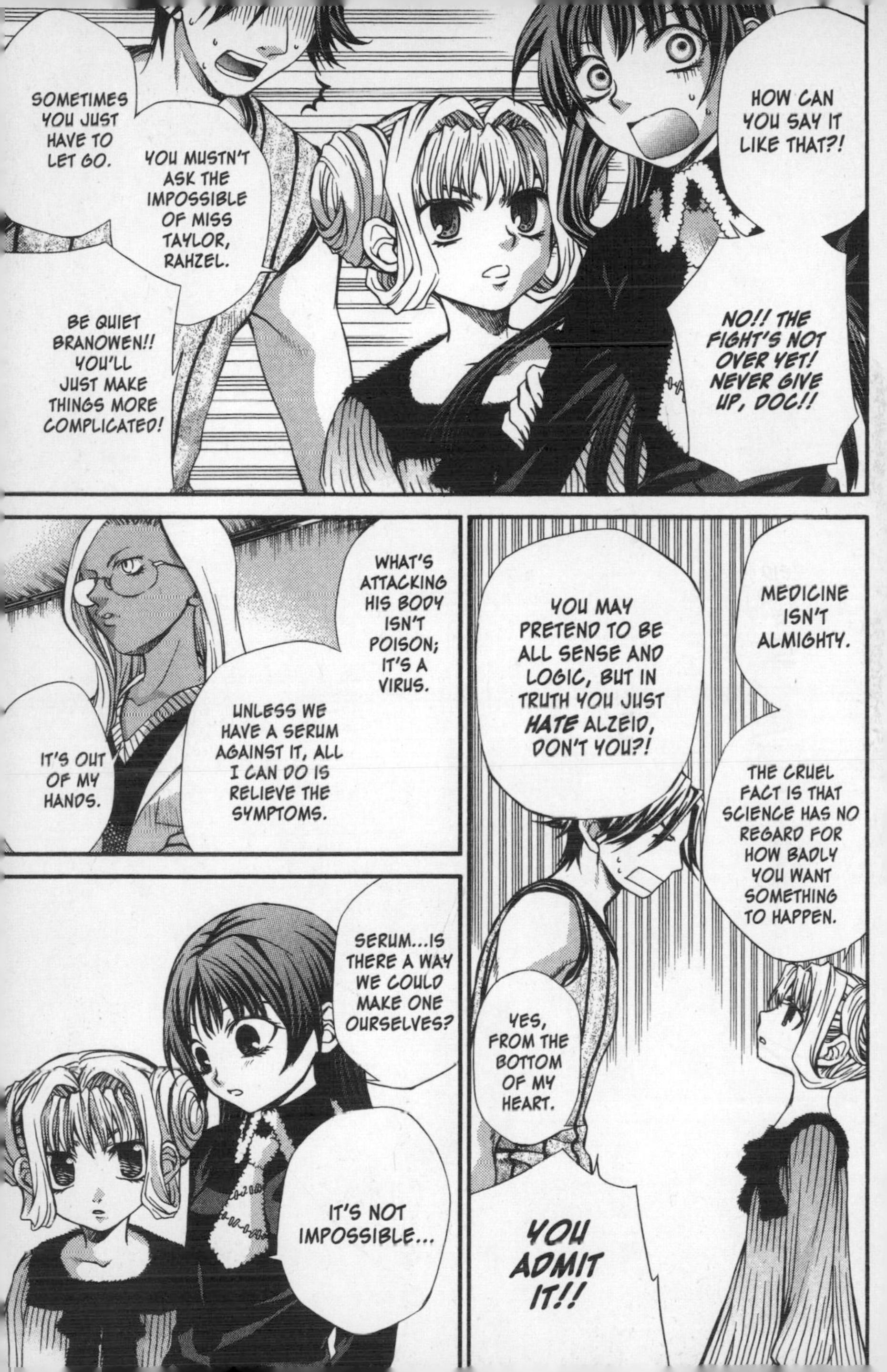
HOW CAN YOU SAY IT LIKE THAT?!
SOMETIMES YOU JUST HAVE TO LET GO.
YOU MUSTN'T ASK THE IMPOSSIBLE OF MISS TAYLOR, RAHZEL.
NO!! THE FIGHT'S NOT OVER YET! NEVER GIVE UP, DOC!!
BE QUIET BRANOWEN!! YOU'LL JUST MAKE THINGS MORE COMPLICATED!
MEDICINE ISN'T ALMIGHTY.
THE CRUEL FACT IS THAT SCIENCE HAS NO REGARD FOR HOW BADLY YOU WANT SOMETHING TO HAPPEN.
YOU MAY PRETEND TO BE ALL SENSE AND LOGIC, BUT IN TRUTH YOU JUST HATE ALZEID, DON'T YOU?!
YES, FROM THE BOTTOM OF MY HEART.
YOU ADMIT IT!!
WHAT'S ATTACKING HIS BODY ISN'T POISON; IT'S A VIRUS.
UNLESS WE HAVE A SERUM AGAINST IT, ALL I CAN DO IS RELIEVE THE SYMPTOMS.
IT'S OUT OF MY HANDS.
SERUM...IS THERE A WAY WE COULD MAKE ONE OURSELVES?
IT'S NOT IMPOSSIBLE...

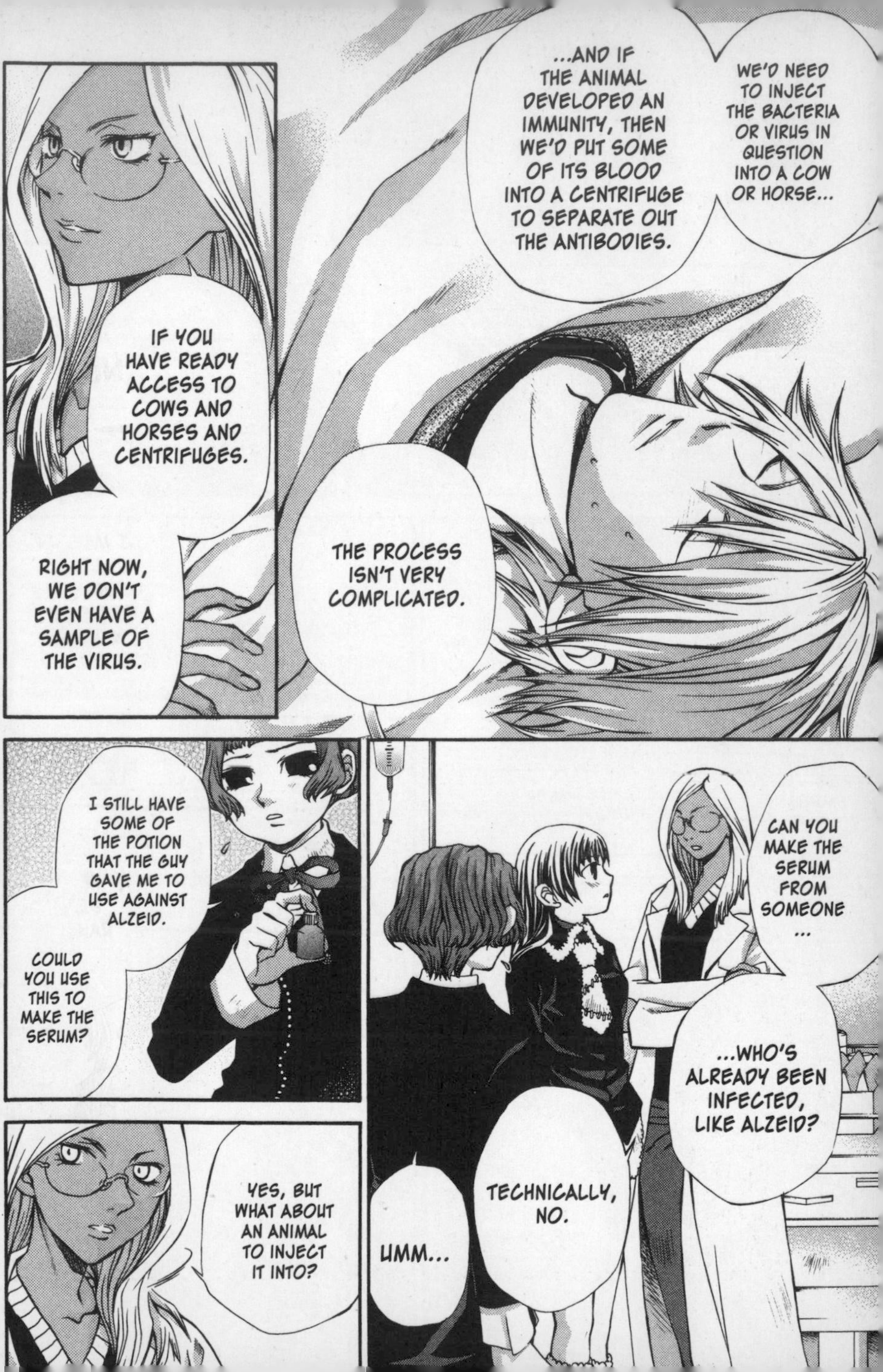
WE'D NEED TO INJECT THE BACTERIA OR VIRUS IN QUESTION INTO A COW OR HORSE...
...AND IF THE ANIMAL DEVELOPED AN IMMUNITY, THEN WE'D PUT SOME OF ITS BLOOD INTO A CENTRIFUGE TO SEPARATE OUT THE ANTIBODIES.
THE PROCESS ISN'T VERY COMPLICATED.
IF YOU HAVE READY ACCESS TO COWS AND HORSES AND CENTRIFUGES.
RIGHT NOW, WE DON'T EVEN HAVE A SAMPLE OF THE VIRUS.
CAN YOU MAKE THE SERUM FROM SOMEONE ...
...WHO'S ALREADY BEEN INFECTED, LIKE ALZEID?
TECHNICALLY, NO.
UMM...
I STILL HAVE SOME OF THE POTION THAT THE GUY GAVE ME TO USE AGAINST ALZEID.
COULD YOU USE THIS TO MAKE THE SERUM?
YES, BUT WHAT ABOUT AN ANIMAL TO INJECT IT INTO?

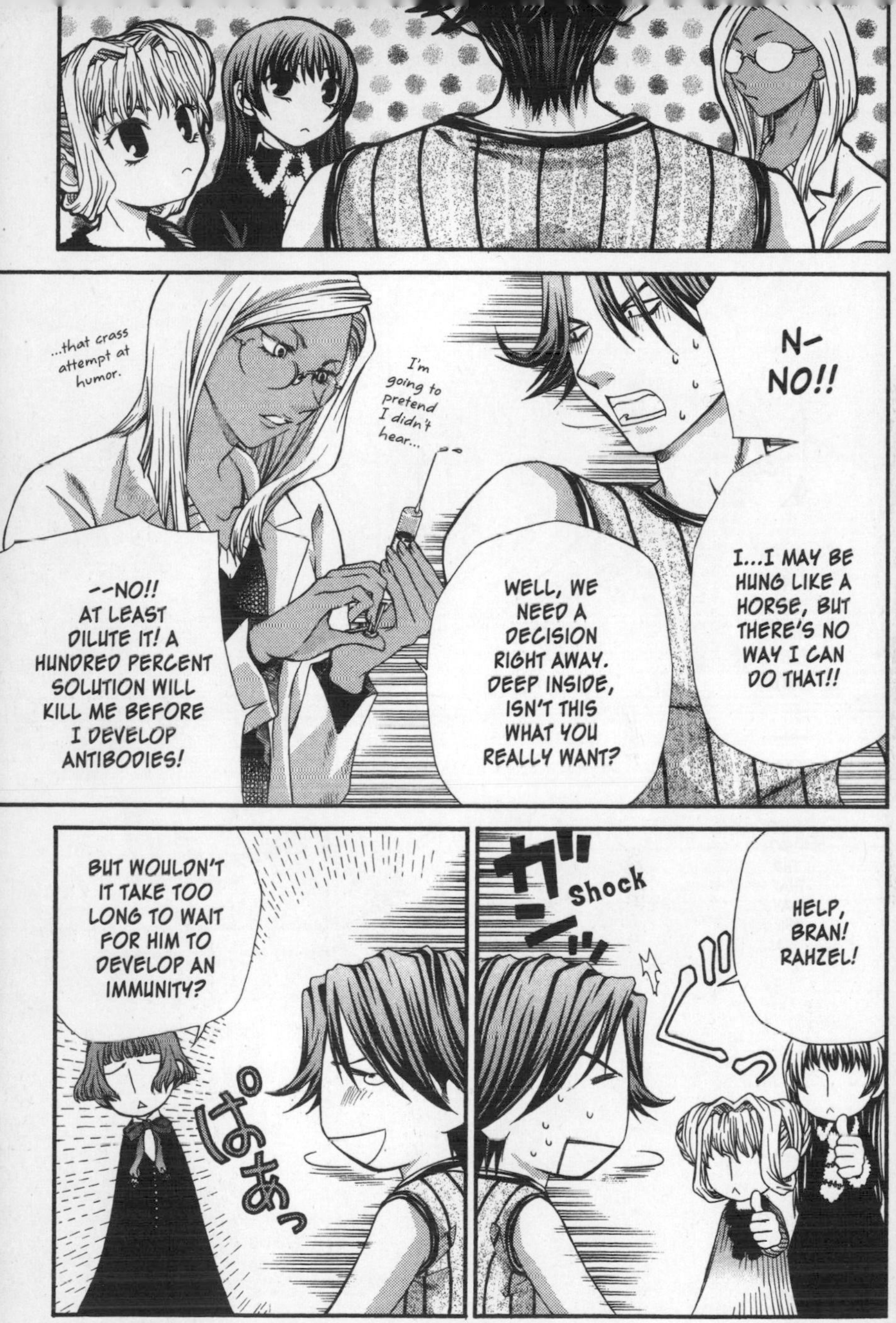
N-NO!!
I...I MAY BE HUNG LIKE A HORSE, BUT THERE'S NO WAY I CAN DO THAT!!
WELL, WE NEED A DECISION RIGHT AWAY. DEEP INSIDE, ISN'T THIS WHAT YOU REALLY WANT?
I'm going to pretend I didn't hear...
...that crass attempt at humor.
--NO!! AT LEAST DILUTE IT! A HUNDRED PERCENT SOLUTION WILL KILL ME BEFORE I DEVELOP ANTIBODIES!
HELP, BRAN! RAHZEL!
Shock
BUT WOULDN'T IT TAKE TOO LONG TO WAIT FOR HIM TO DEVELOP AN IMMUNITY?
ぱぁっ

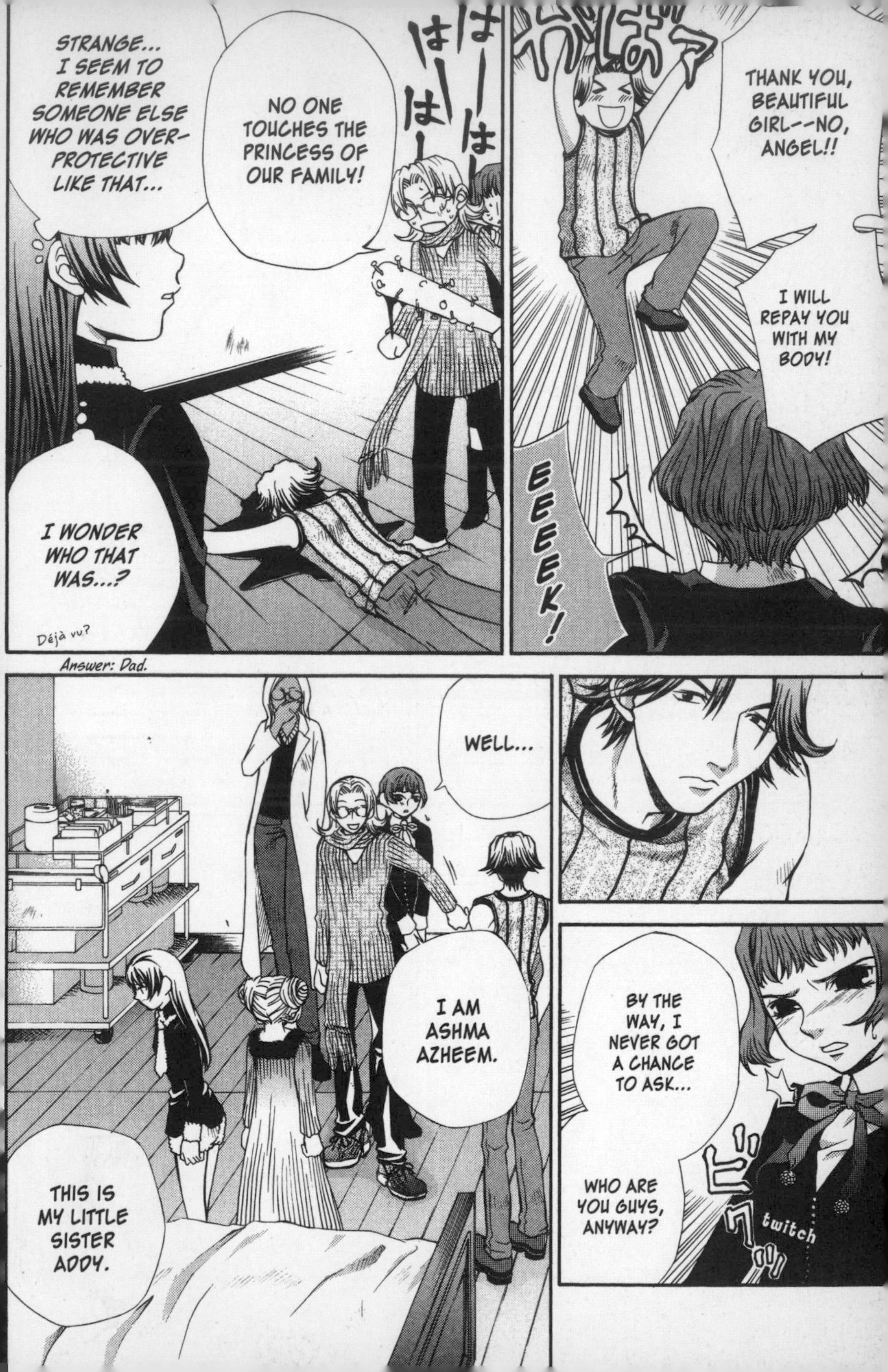
THANK YOU, BEAUTIFUL GIRL--NO, ANGEL!!
I WILL REPAY YOU WITH MY BODY!
EEEEEK!
はーはーはー
NO ONE TOUCHES THE PRINCESS OF OUR FAMILY!
STRANGE... I SEEM TO REMEMBER SOMEONE ELSE WHO WAS OVER-PROTECTIVE LIKE THAT...
I WONDER WHO THAT WAS...?
Déjà vu?
Answer: Dad.
BY THE WAY, I NEVER GOT A CHANCE TO ASK...
WHO ARE YOU GUYS, ANYWAY?
twitch
WELL...
I AM ASHMA AZHEEM.
THIS IS MY LITTLE SISTER ADDY.

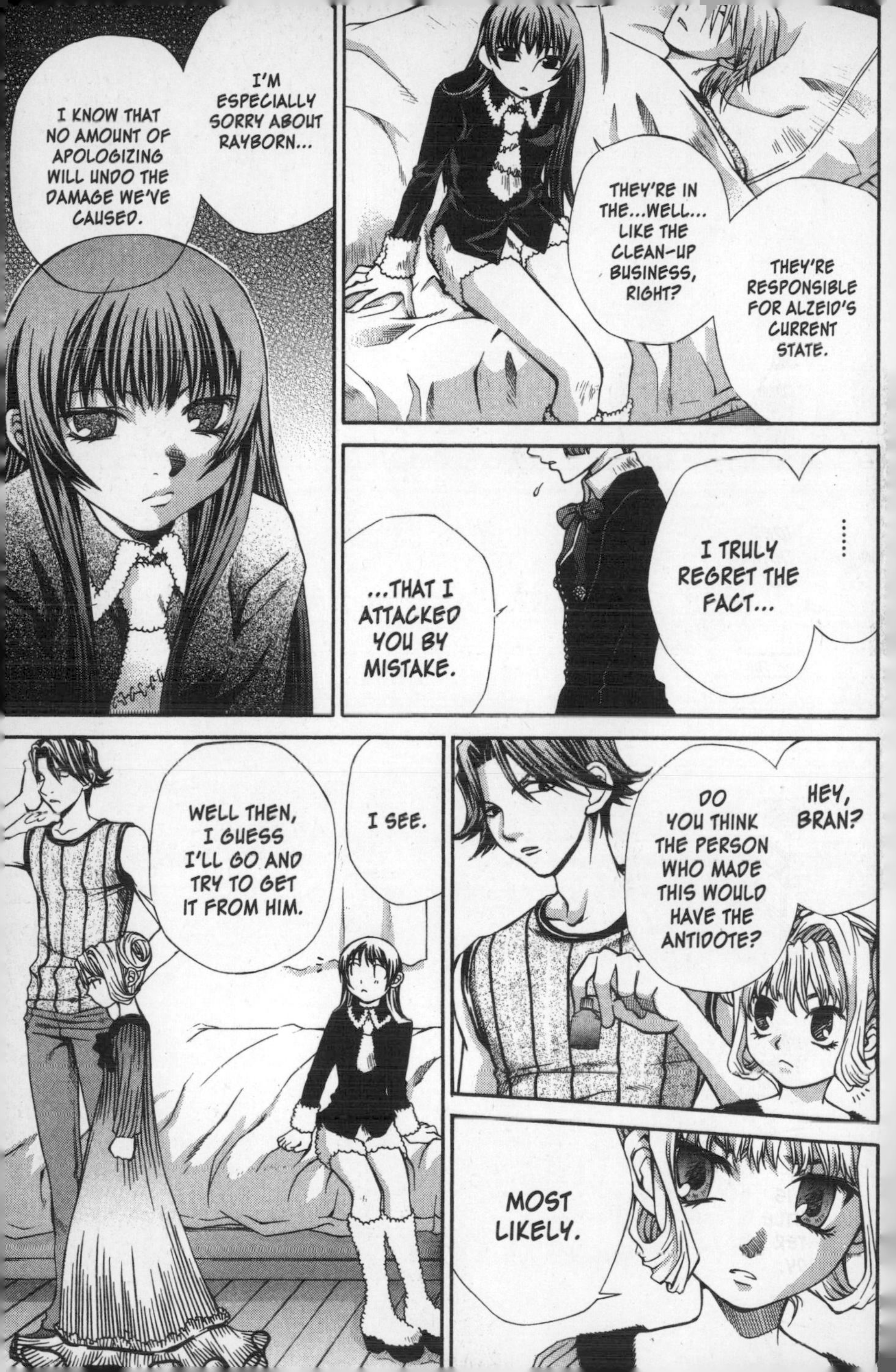
THEY'RE RESPONSIBLE FOR ALZEID'S CURRENT STATE.
THEY'RE IN THE...WELL... LIKE THE CLEAN-UP BUSINESS, RIGHT?
......
I TRULY REGRET THE FACT...
...THAT I ATTACKED YOU BY MISTAKE.
I'M ESPECIALLY SORRY ABOUT RAYBORN...
I KNOW THAT NO AMOUNT OF APOLOGIZING WILL UNDO THE DAMAGE WE'VE CAUSED.
HEY, BRAN?
DO YOU THINK THE PERSON WHO MADE THIS WOULD HAVE THE ANTIDOTE?
MOST LIKELY.
I SEE.
WELL THEN, I GUESS I'LL GO AND TRY TO GET IT FROM HIM.

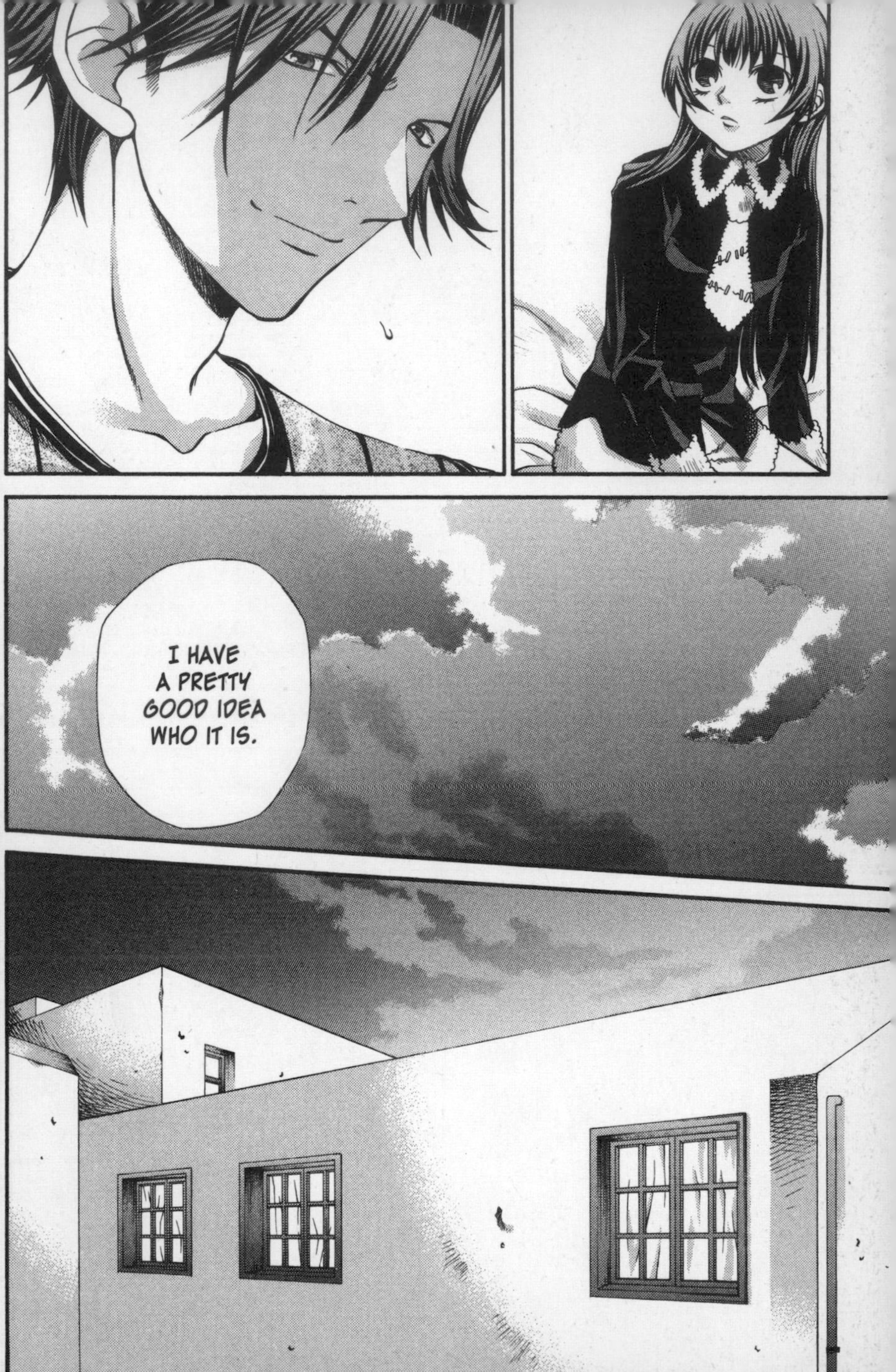
I HAVE A PRETTY GOOD IDEA WHO IT IS.

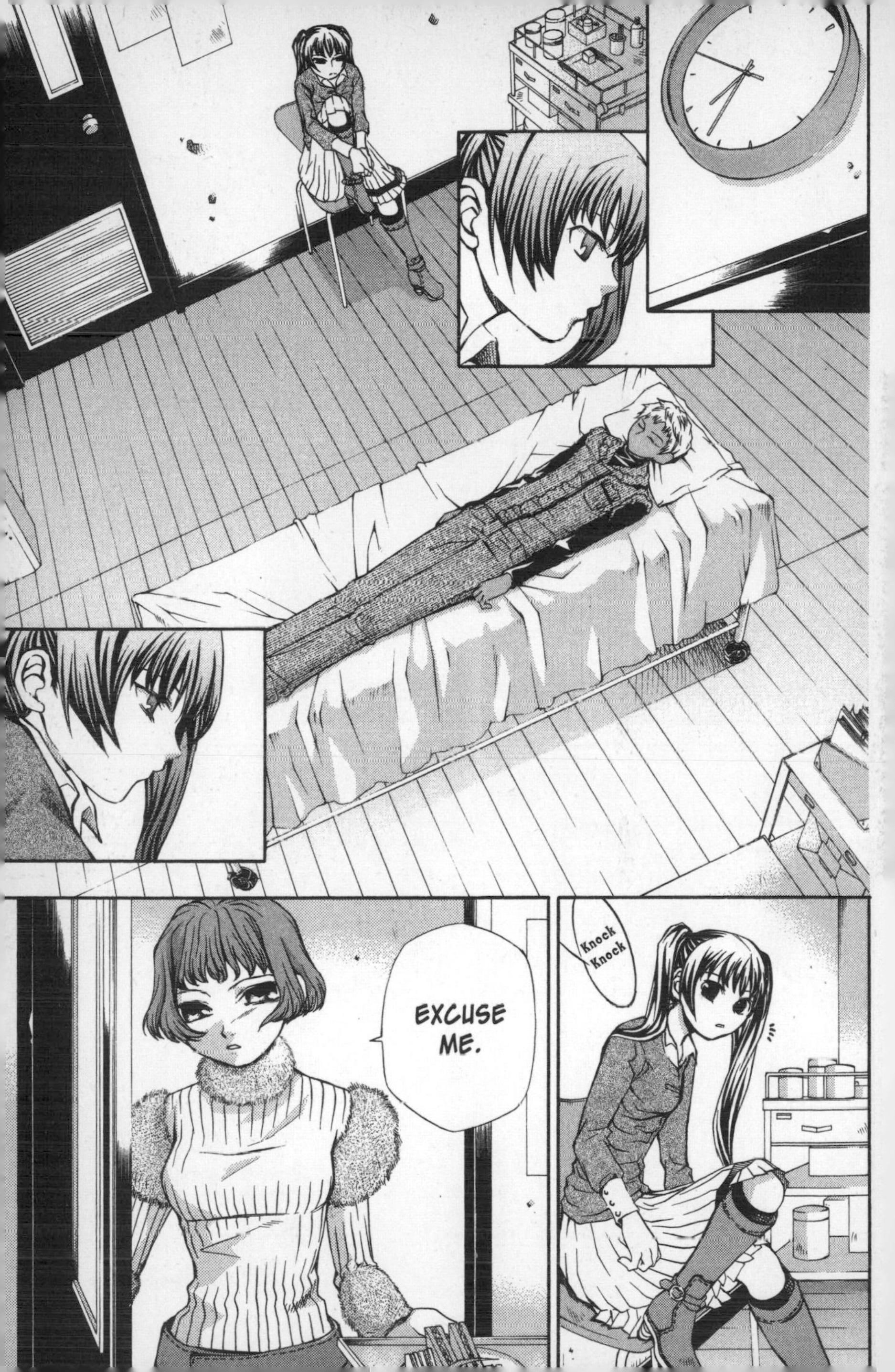
Knock Knock
EXCUSE ME.

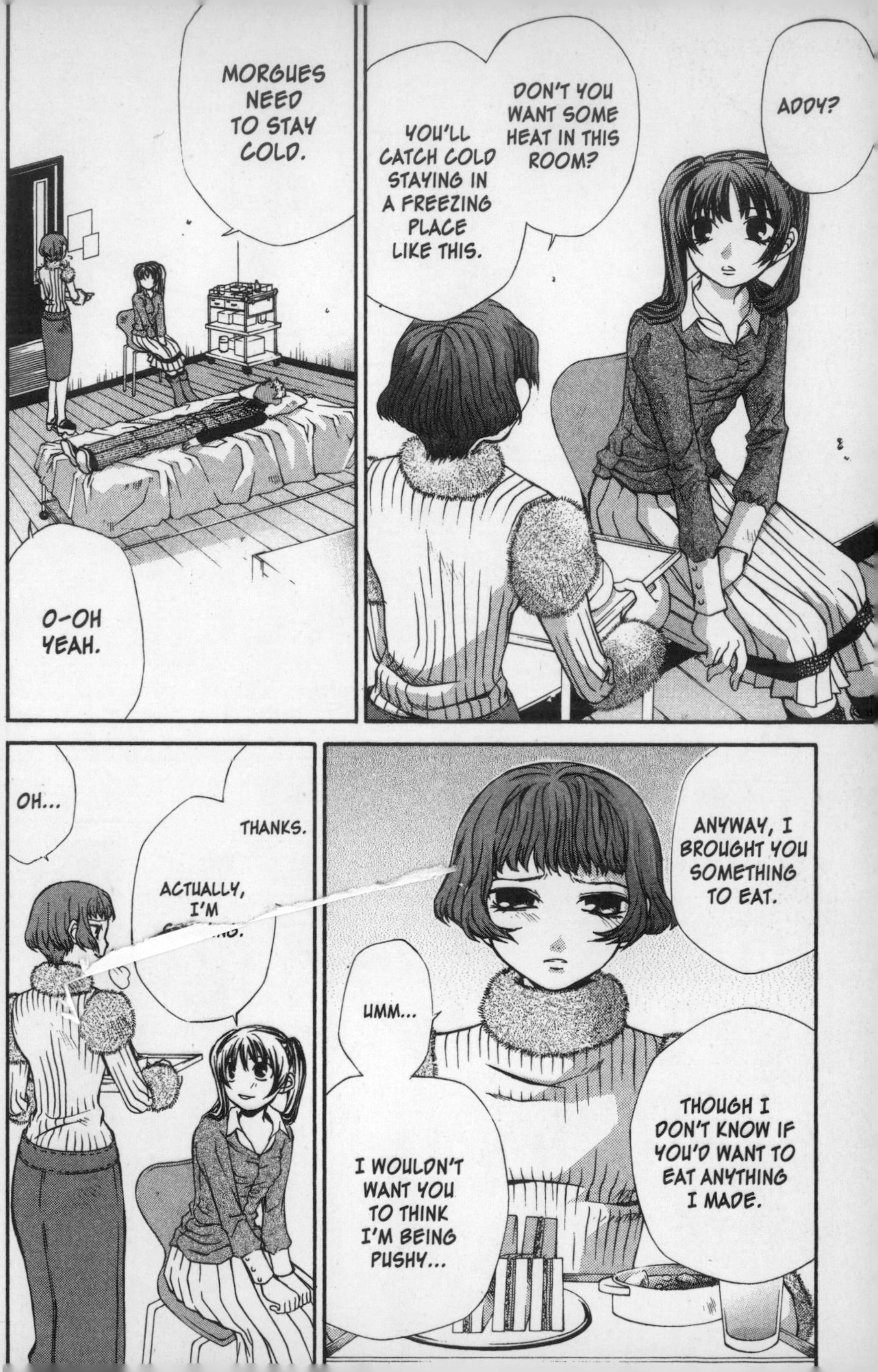
ADDY?
DON'T YOU WANT SOME HEAT IN THIS ROOM?
YOU'LL CATCH COLD STAYING IN A FREEZING PLACE LIKE THIS.
MORGUES NEED TO STAY COLD.
O-OH YEAH.
ANYWAY, I BROUGHT YOU SOMETHING TO EAT.
THOUGH I DON'T KNOW IF YOU'D WANT TO EAT ANYTHING I MADE.
UMM...
I WOULDN'T WANT YOU TO THINK I'M BEING PUSHY...
OH...
THANKS.
ACTUALLY, I'M

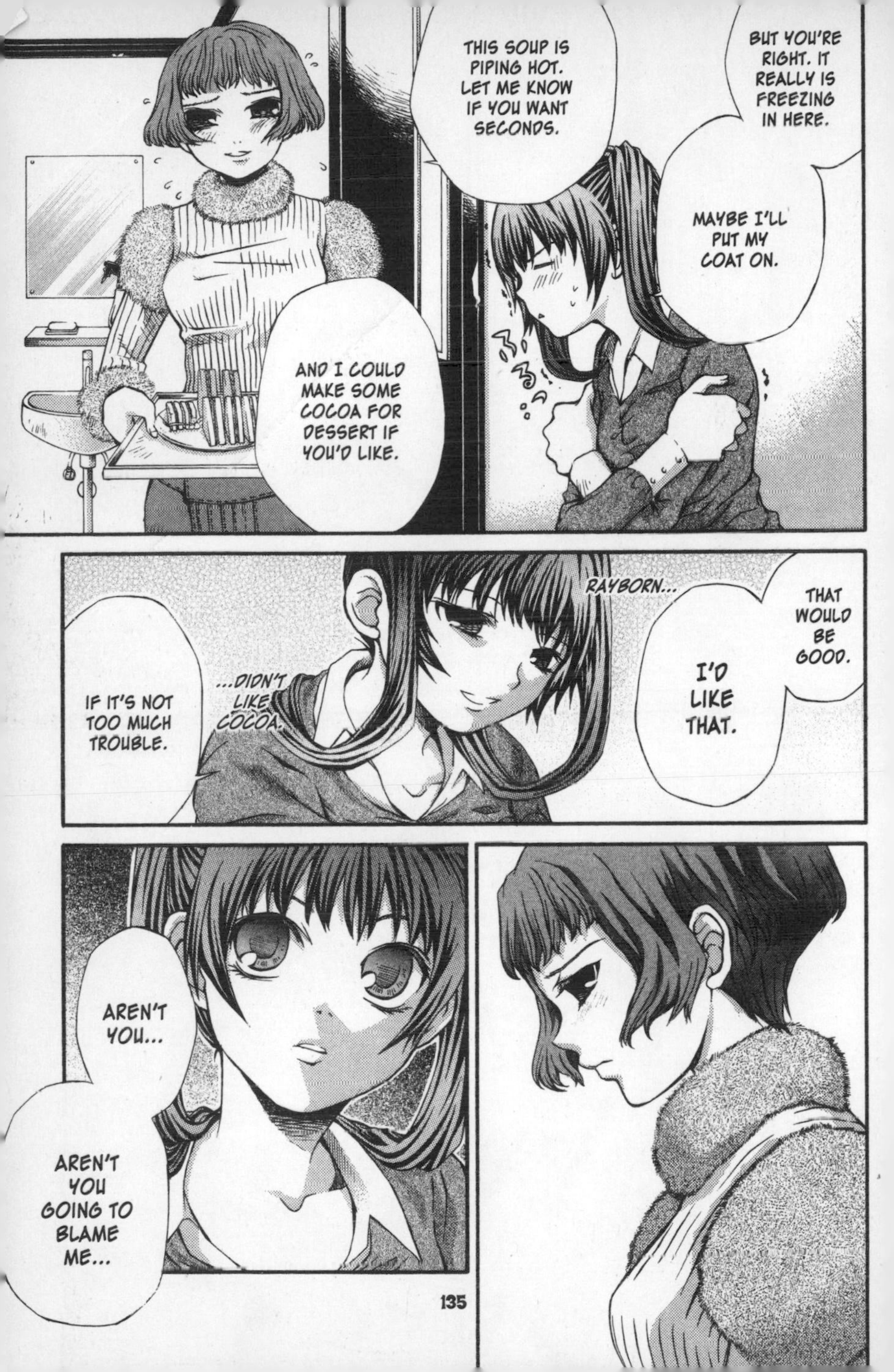
THIS SOUP IS PIPING HOT. LET ME KNOW IF YOU WANT SECONDS.
BUT YOU'RE RIGHT. IT REALLY IS FREEZING IN HERE.
MAYBE I'LL PUT MY COAT ON.
AND I COULD MAKE SOME COCOA FOR DESSERT IF YOU'D LIKE.
THAT WOULD BE GOOD.
I'D LIKE THAT.
RAYBORN...
...DIDN'T LIKE COCOA.
IF IT'S NOT TOO MUCH TROUBLE.
AREN'T YOU...
AREN'T YOU GOING TO BLAME ME...

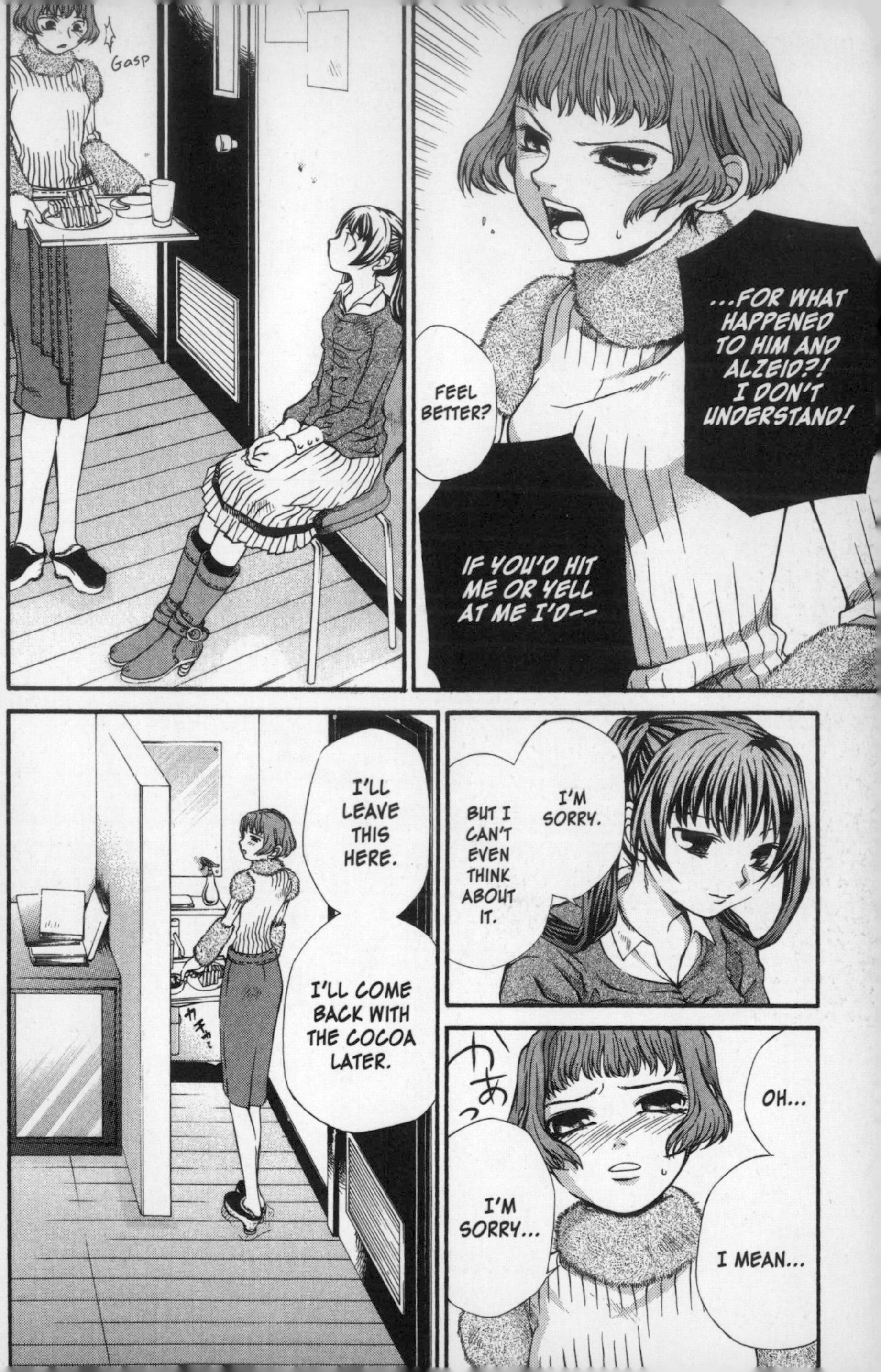
...FOR WHAT HAPPENED TO HIM AND ALZEID?! I DON'T UNDERSTAND!
FEEL BETTER?
IF YOU'D HIT ME OR YELL AT ME I'D--
Gasp
I'M SORRY.
BUT I CAN'T EVEN THINK ABOUT IT.
OH...
かあっ
I'M SORRY...
I MEAN...
I'LL LEAVE THIS HERE.
I'LL COME BACK WITH THE COCOA LATER.

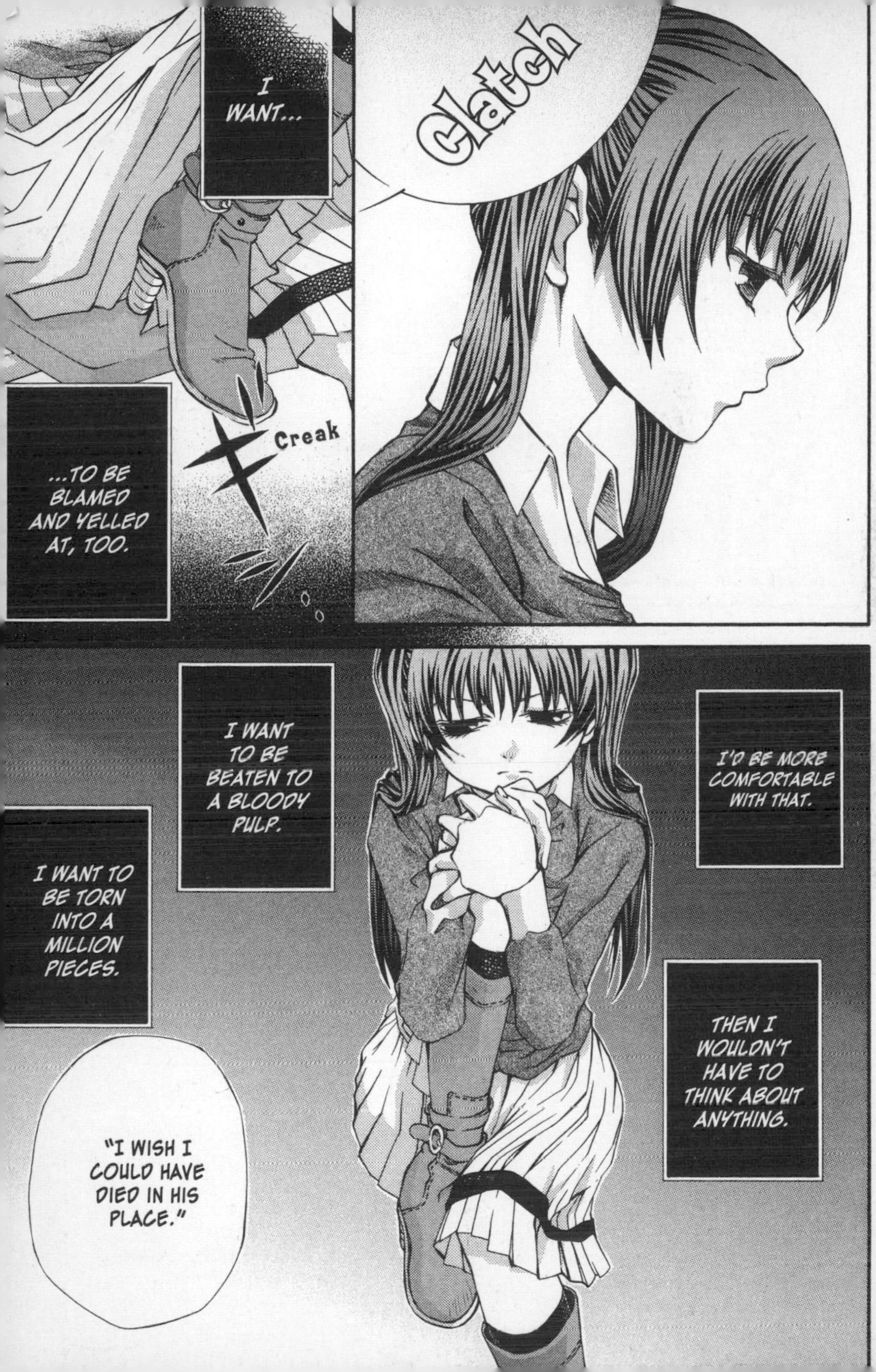

Clatch
I WANT...
...TO BE BLAMED AND YELLED AT, TOO.
Creak
I'D BE MORE COMFORTABLE WITH THAT.
I WANT TO BE BEATEN TO A BLOODY PULP.
I WANT TO BE TORN INTO A MILLION PIECES.
THEN I WOULDN'T HAVE TO THINK ABOUT ANYTHING.
"I WISH I COULD HAVE DIED IN HIS PLACE."

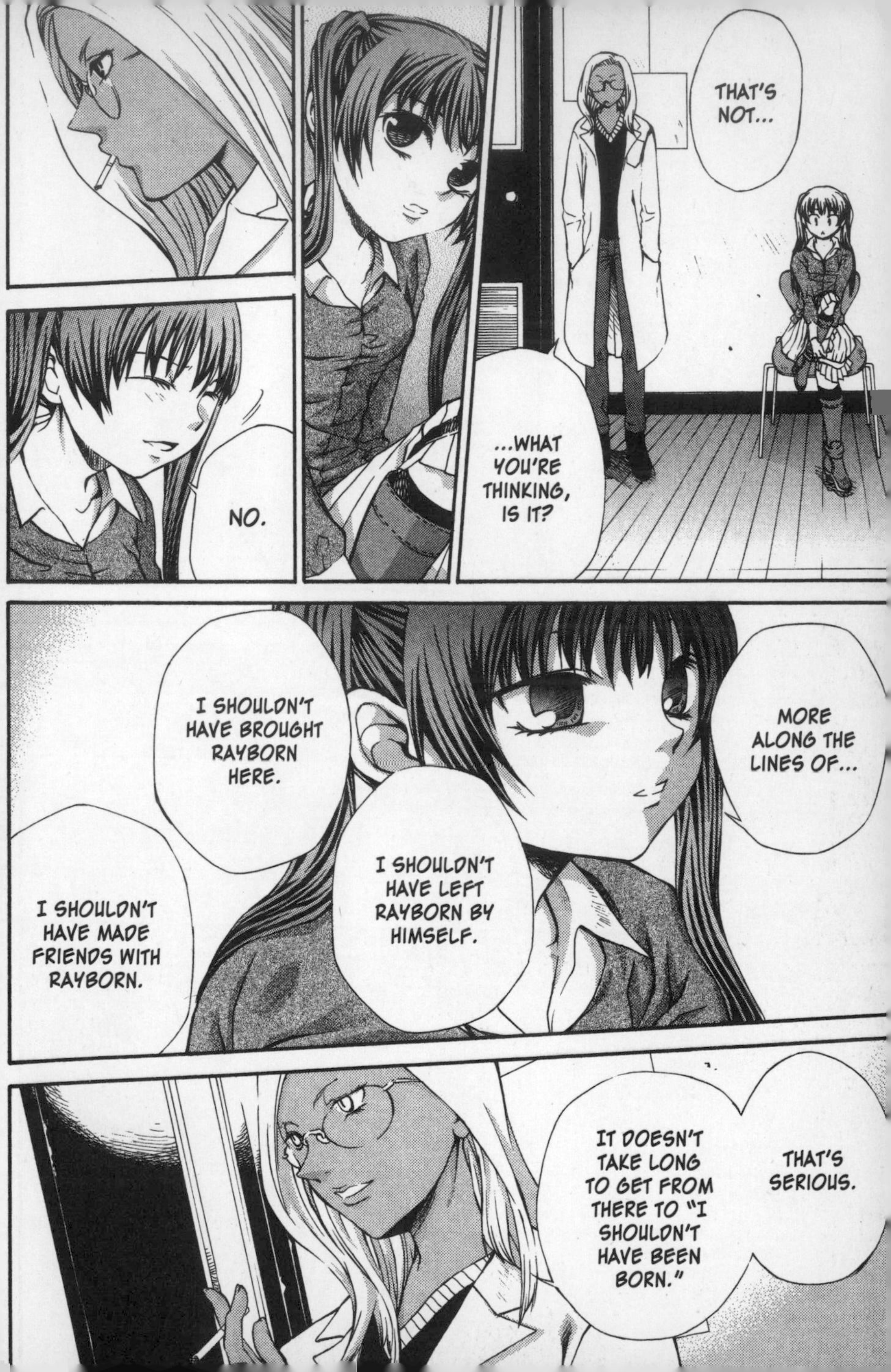
THAT'S NOT...
...WHAT YOU'RE THINKING, IS IT?
NO.
MORE ALONG THE LINES OF...
I SHOULDN'T HAVE BROUGHT RAYBORN HERE.
I SHOULDN'T HAVE LEFT RAYBORN BY HIMSELF.
I SHOULDN'T HAVE MADE FRIENDS WITH RAYBORN.
THAT'S SERIOUS.
IT DOESN'T TAKE LONG TO GET FROM THERE TO "I SHOULDN'T HAVE BEEN BORN."

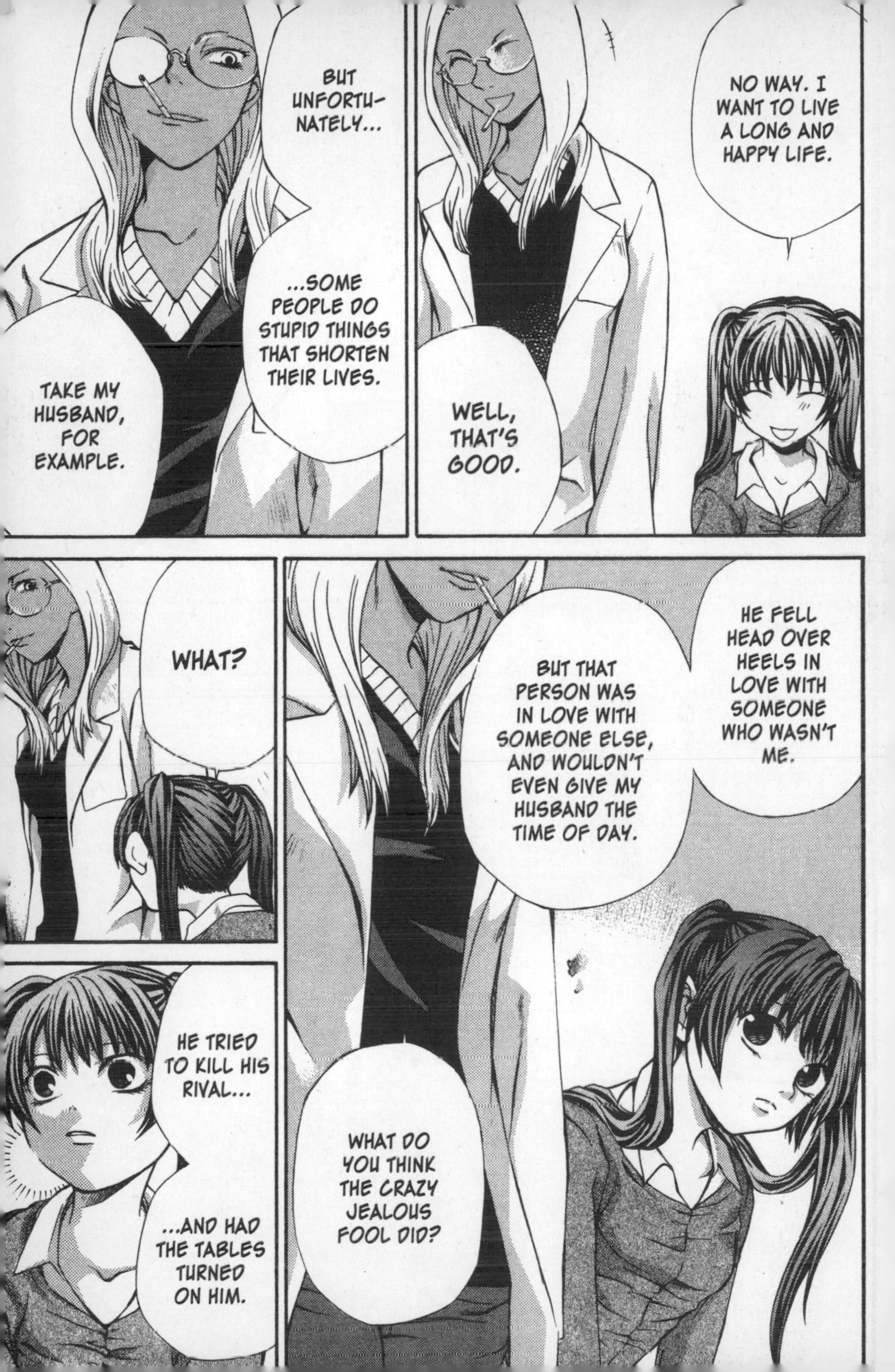
NO WAY. I WANT TO LIVE A LONG AND HAPPY LIFE.
WELL, THAT'S GOOD.
BUT UNFORTUNATELY...
...SOME PEOPLE DO STUPID THINGS THAT SHORTEN THEIR LIVES.
TAKE MY HUSBAND, FOR EXAMPLE.
HE FELL HEAD OVER HEELS IN LOVE WITH SOMEONE WHO WASN'T ME.
BUT THAT PERSON WAS IN LOVE WITH SOMEONE ELSE, AND WOULDN'T EVEN GIVE MY HUSBAND THE TIME OF DAY.
WHAT DO YOU THINK THE CRAZY JEALOUS FOOL DID?
WHAT?
HE TRIED TO KILL HIS RIVAL...
...AND HAD THE TABLES TURNED ON HIM.

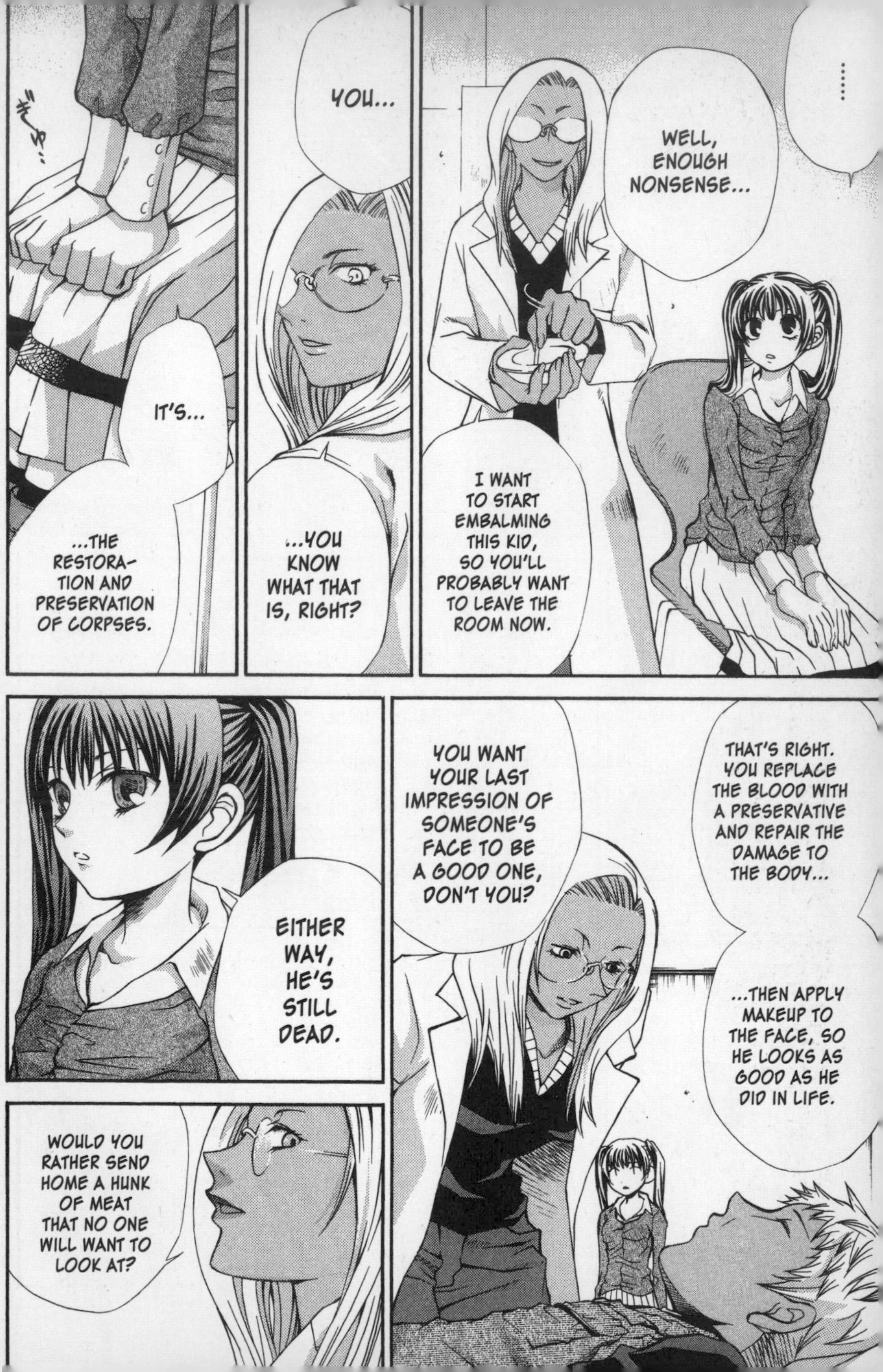
......
WELL, ENOUGH NONSENSE...
I WANT TO START EMBALMING THIS KID, SO YOU'LL PROBABLY WANT TO LEAVE THE ROOM NOW.
YOU...
...YOU KNOW WHAT THAT IS, RIGHT?
ぎゅ…
IT'S...
...THE RESTORATION AND PRESERVATION OF CORPSES.
THAT'S RIGHT. YOU REPLACE THE BLOOD WITH A PRESERVATIVE AND REPAIR THE DAMAGE TO THE BODY...
...THEN APPLY MAKEUP TO THE FACE, SO HE LOOKS AS GOOD AS HE DID IN LIFE.
YOU WANT YOUR LAST IMPRESSION OF SOMEONE'S FACE TO BE A GOOD ONE, DON'T YOU?
EITHER WAY, HE'S STILL DEAD.
WOULD YOU RATHER SEND HOME A HUNK OF MEAT THAT NO ONE WILL WANT TO LOOK AT?

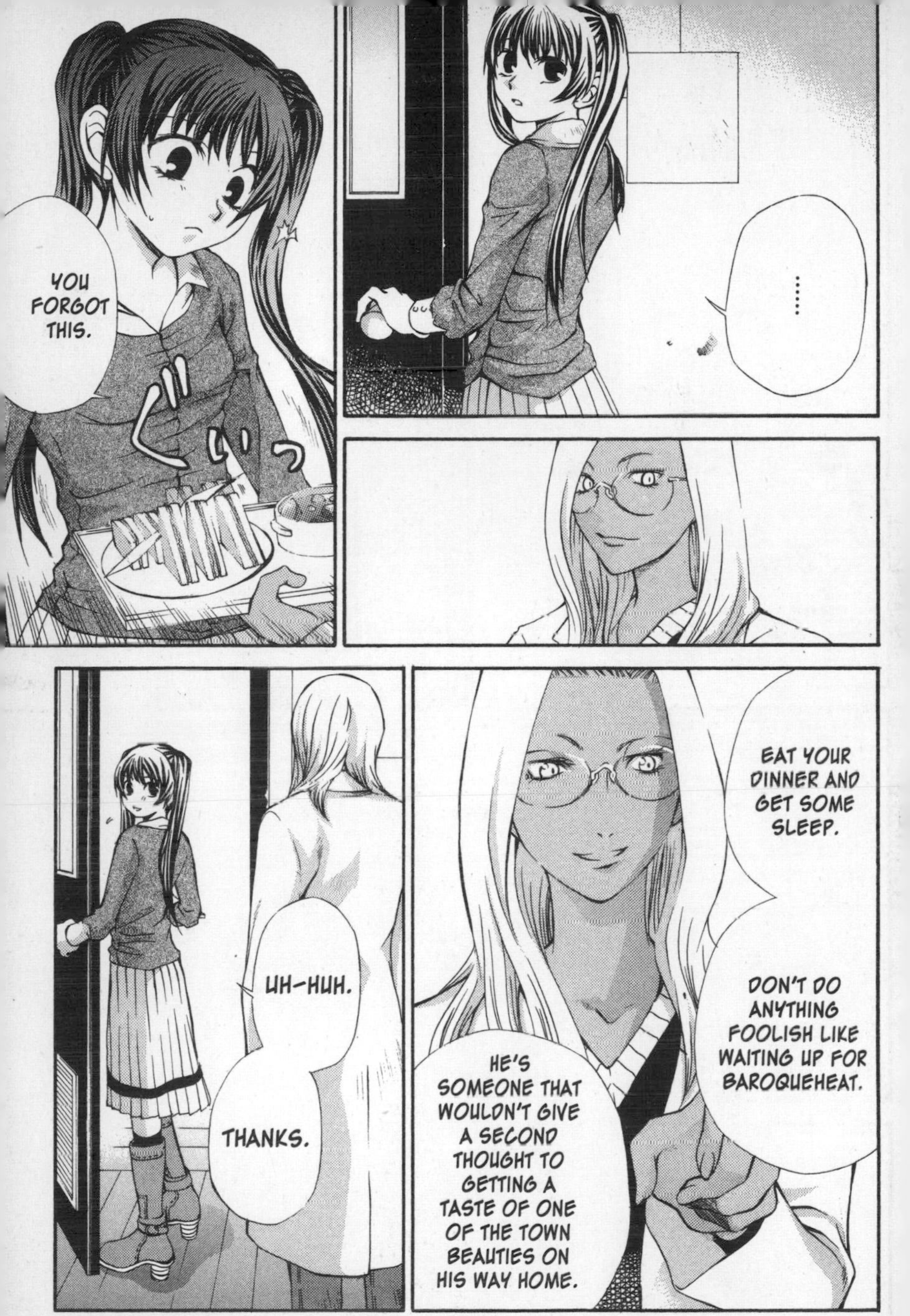
......
YOU FORGOT THIS.
EAT YOUR DINNER AND GET SOME SLEEP.
DON'T DO ANYTHING FOOLISH LIKE WAITING UP FOR BAROQUEHEAT.
HE'S SOMEONE THAT WOULDN'T GIVE A SECOND THOUGHT TO GETTING A TASTE OF ONE OF THE TOWN BEAUTIES ON HIS WAY HOME.
UH-HUH.
THANKS.

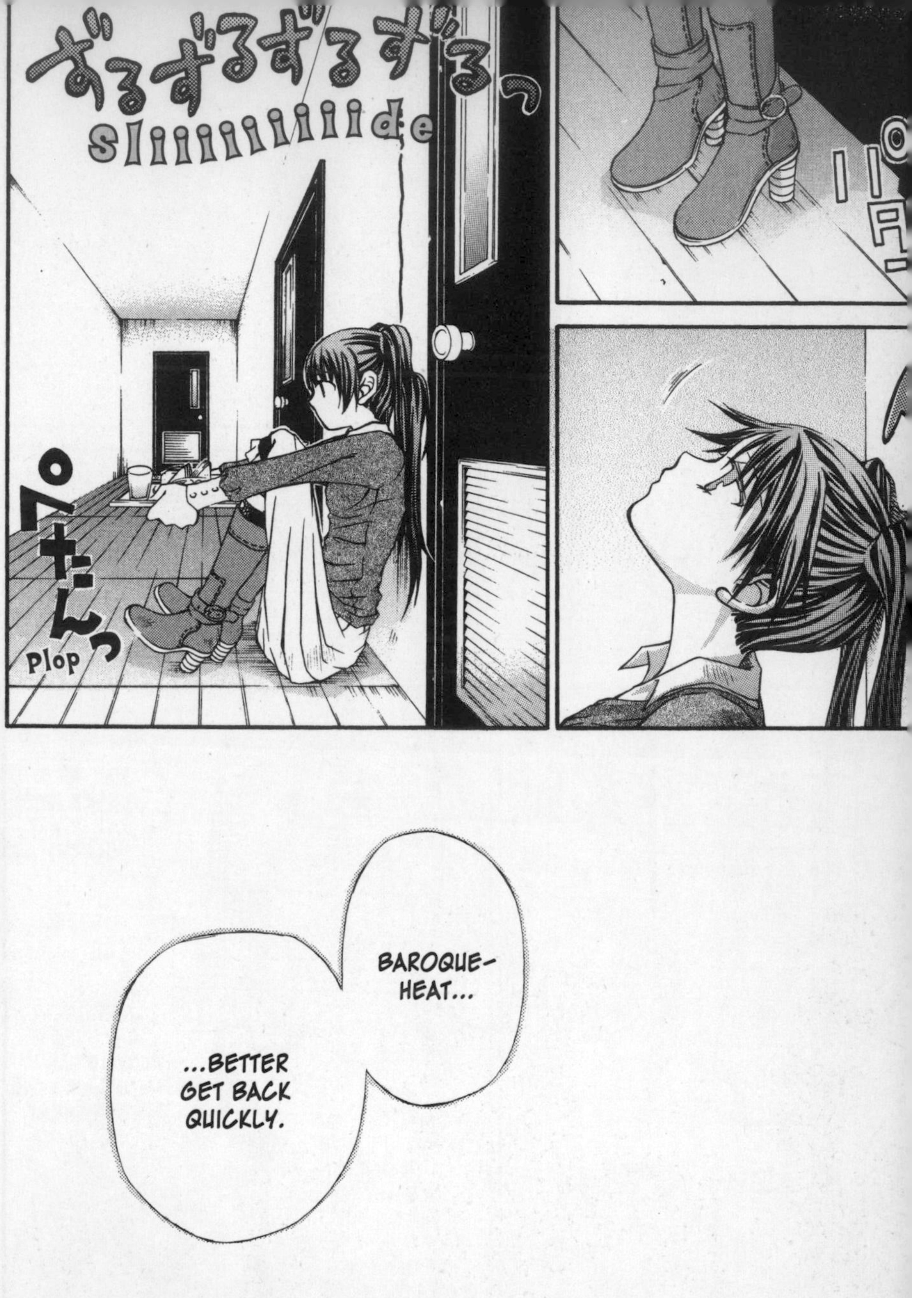
ずるずるずるずるっ
sliiiiiiiiiide
ぺたんっ
Plop
BAROQUE-HEAT...
...BETTER GET BACK QUICKLY.

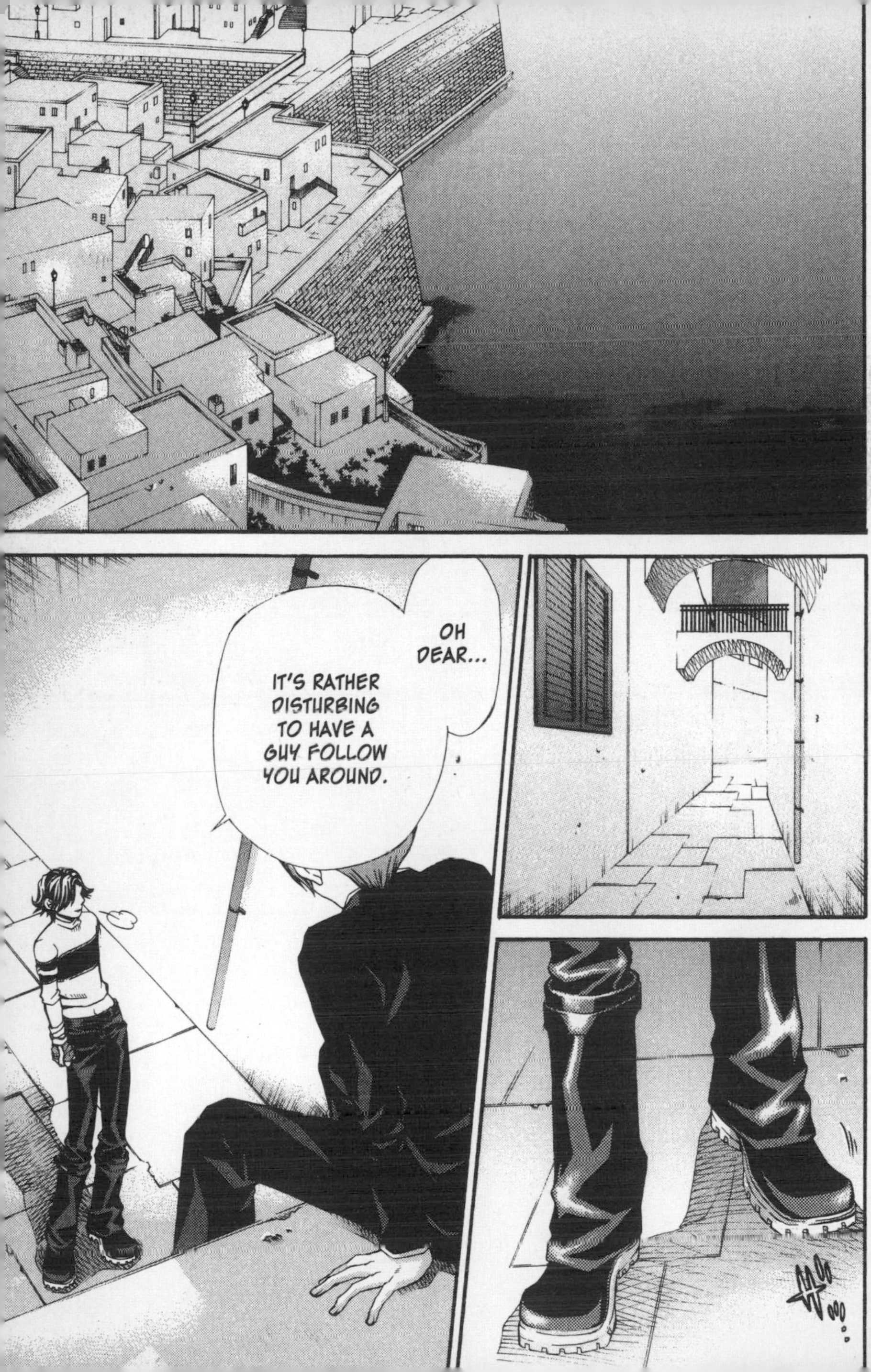
OH DEAR...
IT'S RATHER DISTURBING TO HAVE A GUY FOLLOW YOU AROUND.

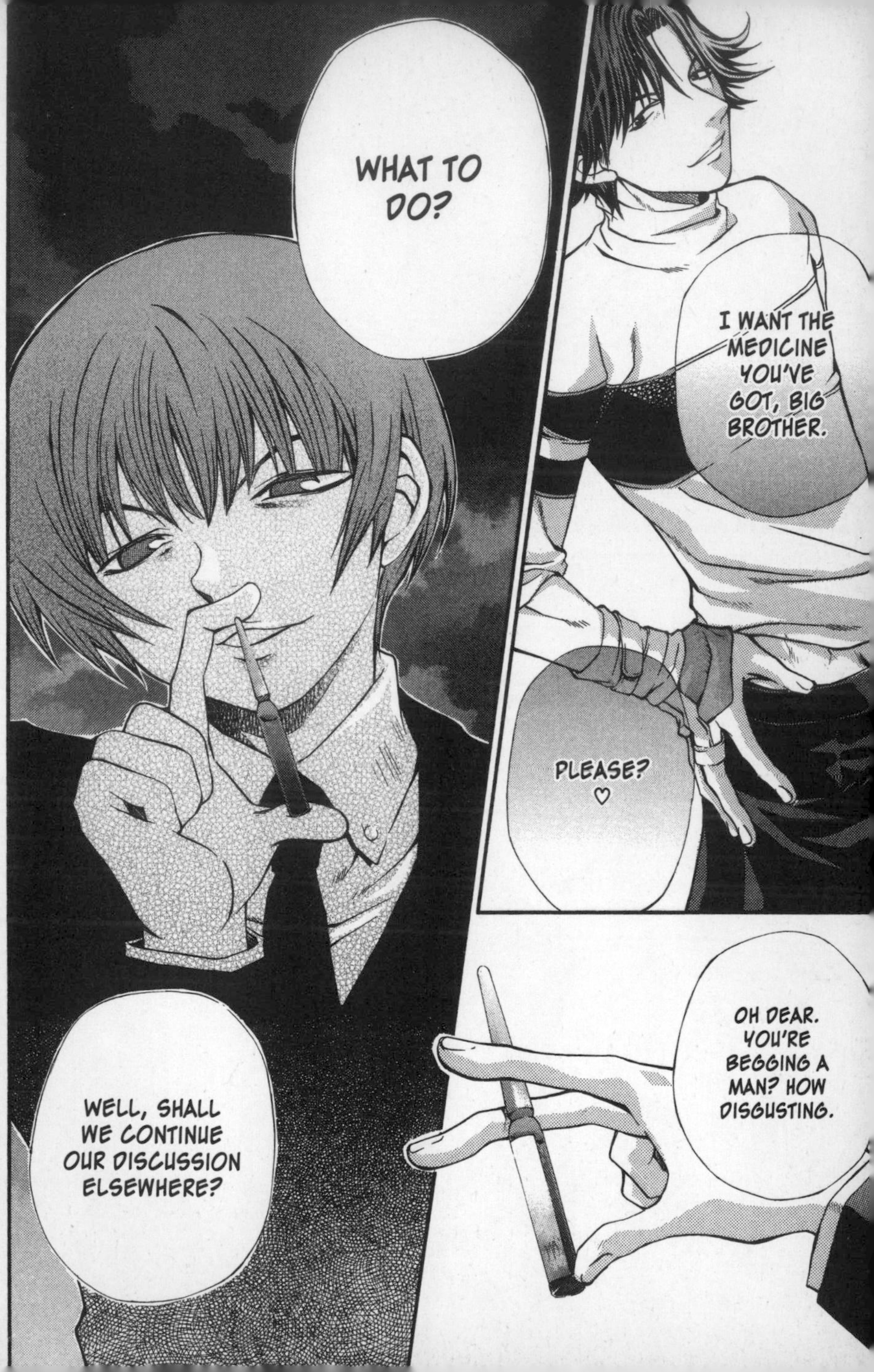
I WANT THE MEDICINE YOU'VE GOT, BIG BROTHER.
PLEASE? ♡
OH DEAR. YOU'RE BEGGING A MAN? HOW DISGUSTING.
WHAT TO DO?
WELL, SHALL WE CONTINUE OUR DISCUSSION ELSEWHERE?

Chapter 46: The Ephemeral Proposition--Part II: I Don't Have Words to Fill the Gap

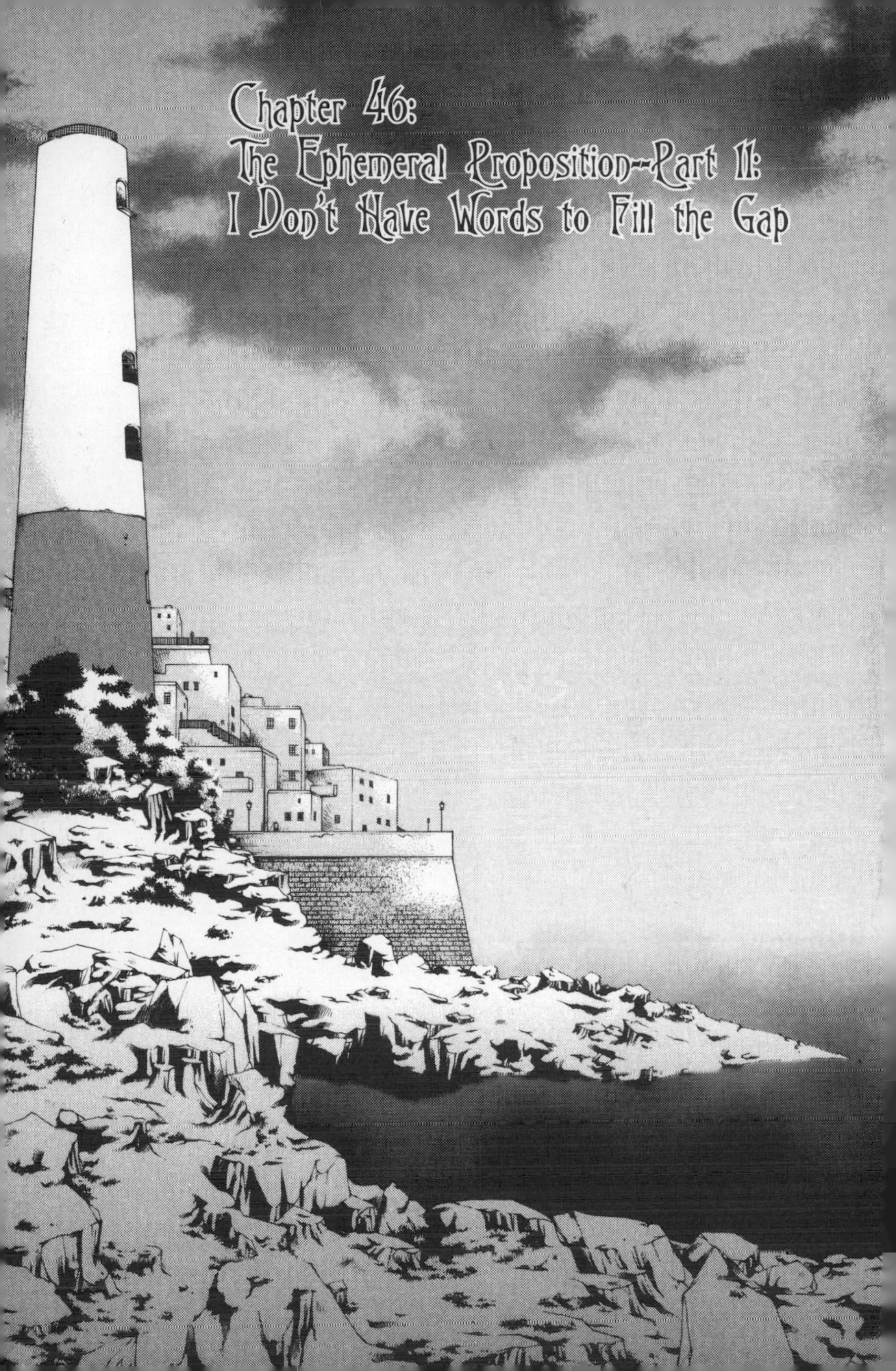

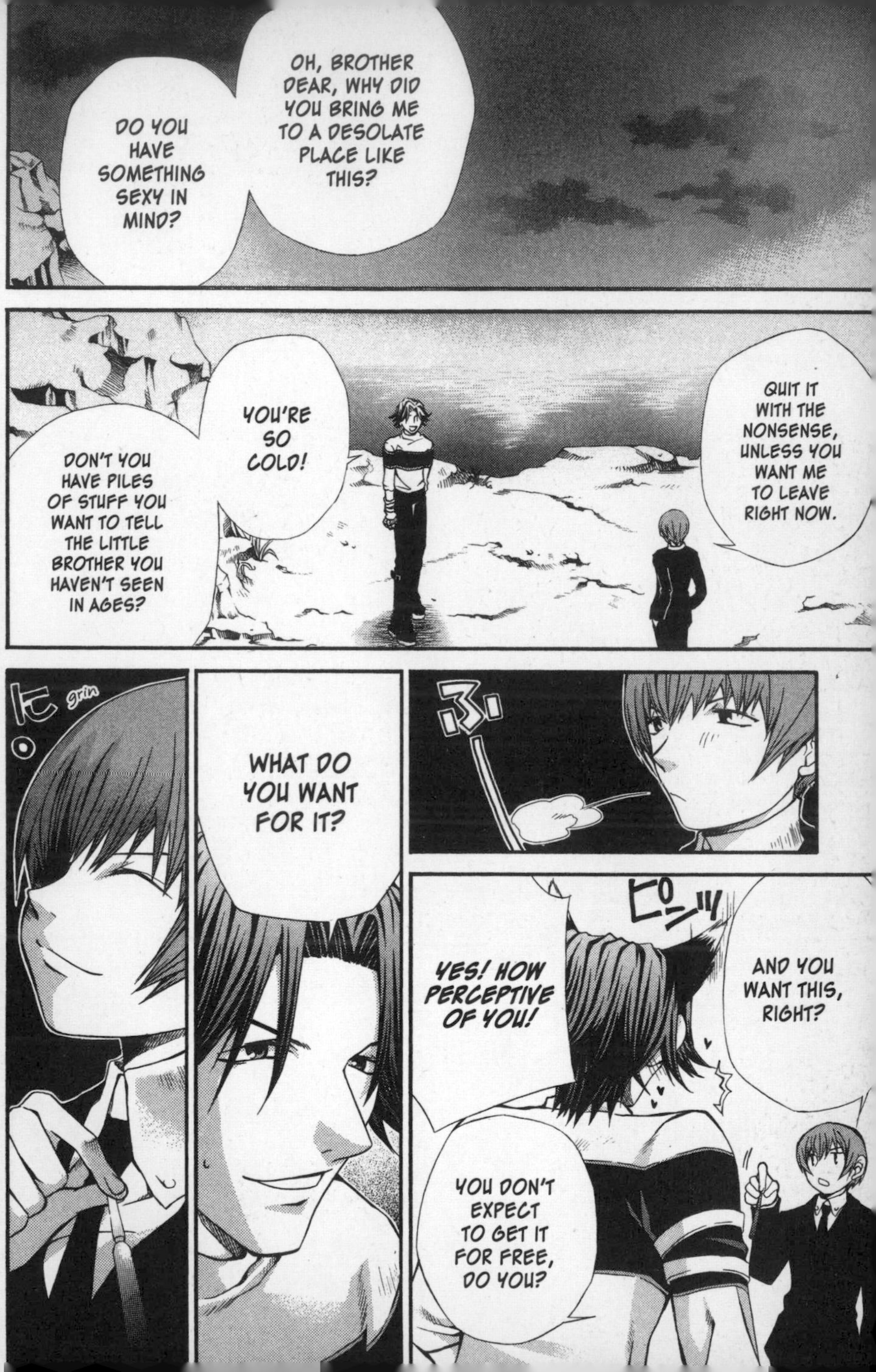
OH, BROTHER DEAR, WHY DID YOU BRING ME TO A DESOLATE PLACE LIKE THIS?
DO YOU HAVE SOMETHING SEXY IN MIND?
QUIT IT WITH THE NONSENSE, UNLESS YOU WANT ME TO LEAVE RIGHT NOW.
YOU'RE SO COLD!
DON'T YOU HAVE PILES OF STUFF YOU WANT TO TELL THE LITTLE BROTHER YOU HAVEN'T SEEN IN AGES?
ふ
AND YOU WANT THIS, RIGHT?
YES! HOW PERCEPTIVE OF YOU!
YOU DON'T EXPECT TO GET IT FOR FREE, DO YOU?
WHAT DO YOU WANT FOR IT?
に
grin

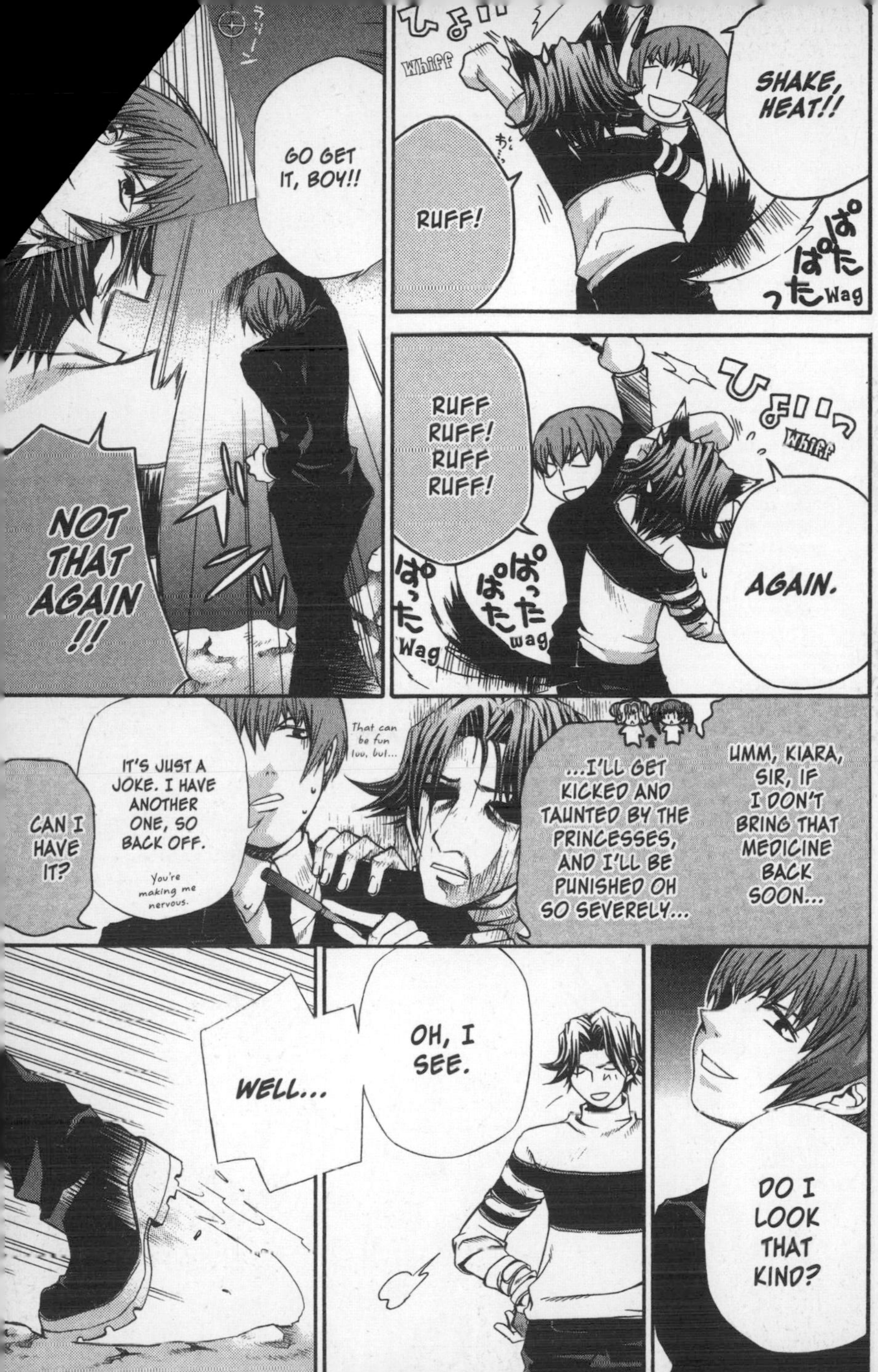

SHAKE, HEAT!!
ひょいっ
Whiff
RUFF!
ぱたぱたっ
Wag
AGAIN.
ひょいっ
Whiff
RUFF RUFF! RUFF RUFF!
ぱったぱった
wag
ぱった
Wag
GO GET IT, BOY!!
NOT THAT AGAIN!!
UMM, KIARA, SIR, IF I DON'T BRING THAT MEDICINE BACK SOON...
...I'LL GET KICKED AND TAUNTED BY THE PRINCESSES, AND I'LL BE PUNISHED OH SO SEVERELY...
That can be fun too, but...
IT'S JUST A JOKE. I HAVE ANOTHER ONE, SO BACK OFF.
You're making me nervous.
CAN I HAVE IT?
DO I LOOK THAT KIND?
OH, I SEE.
WELL...

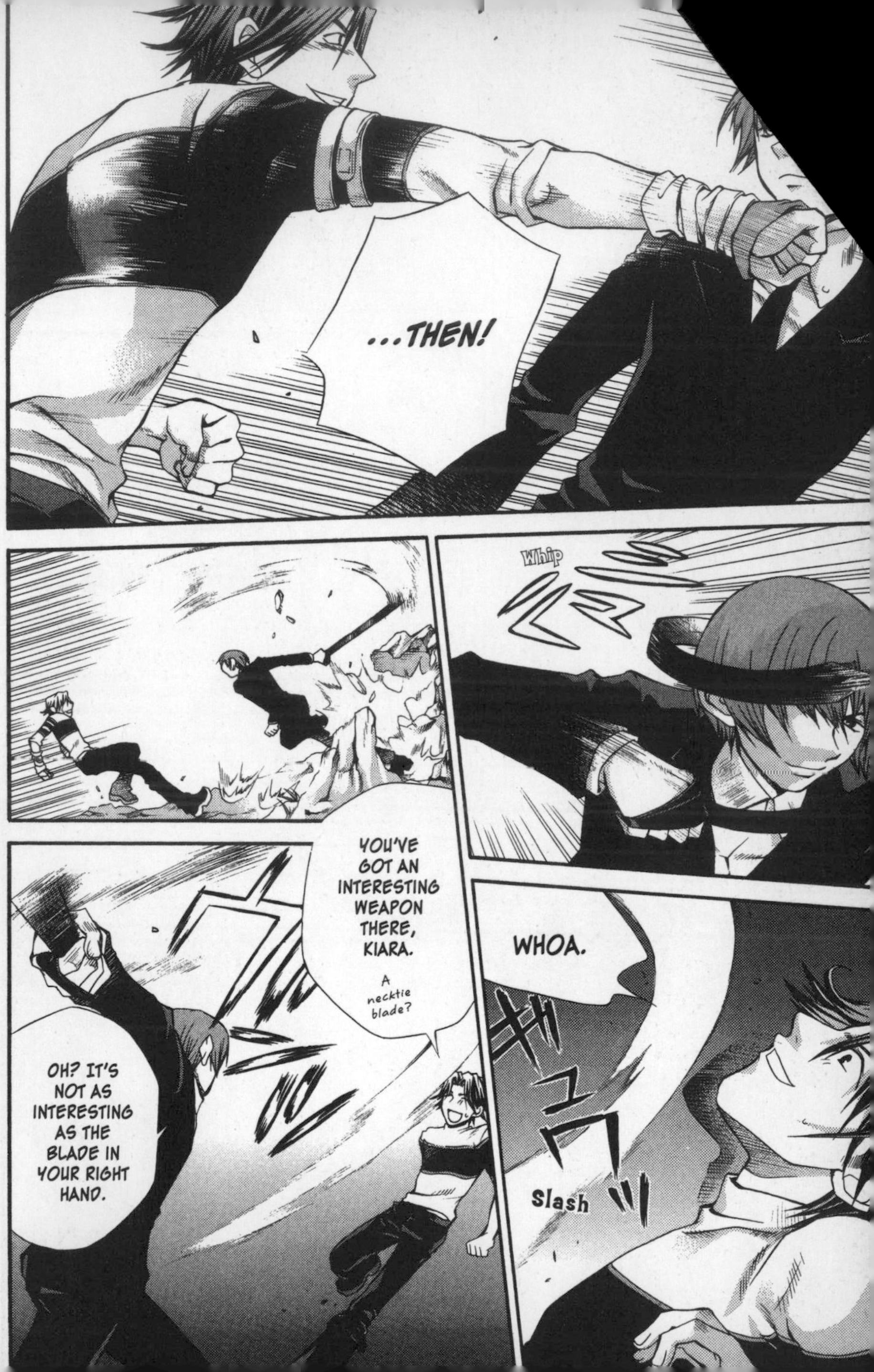
...THEN!
Whip
WHOA.
Slash
YOU'VE GOT AN INTERESTING WEAPON THERE, KIARA.
A necktie blade?
OH? IT'S NOT AS INTERESTING AS THE BLADE IN YOUR RIGHT HAND.

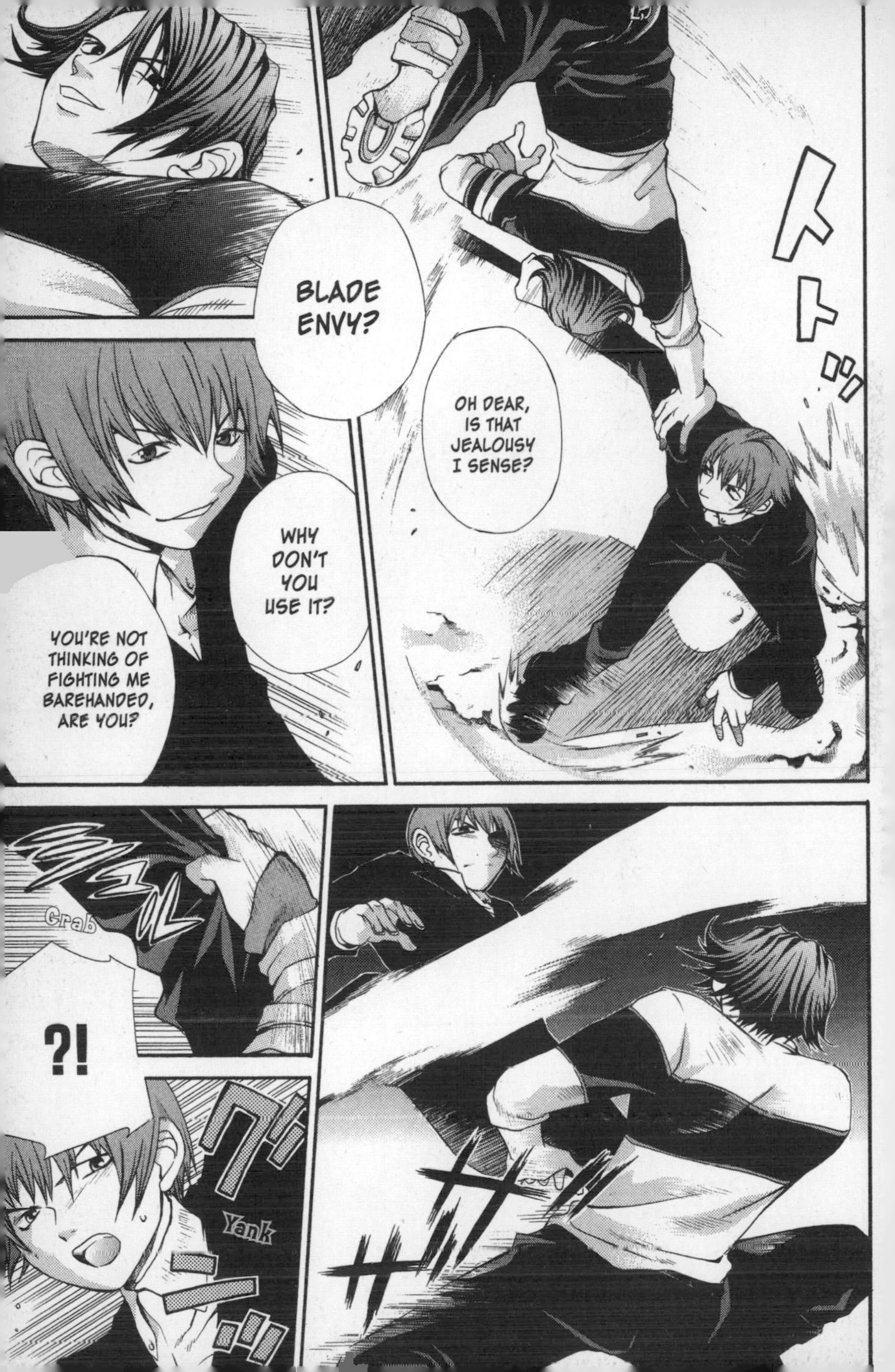

OH DEAR, IS THAT JEALOUSY I SENSE?
BLADE ENVY?
WHY DON'T YOU USE IT?
YOU'RE NOT THINKING OF FIGHTING ME BAREHANDED, ARE YOU?
Grab
?!
Yank

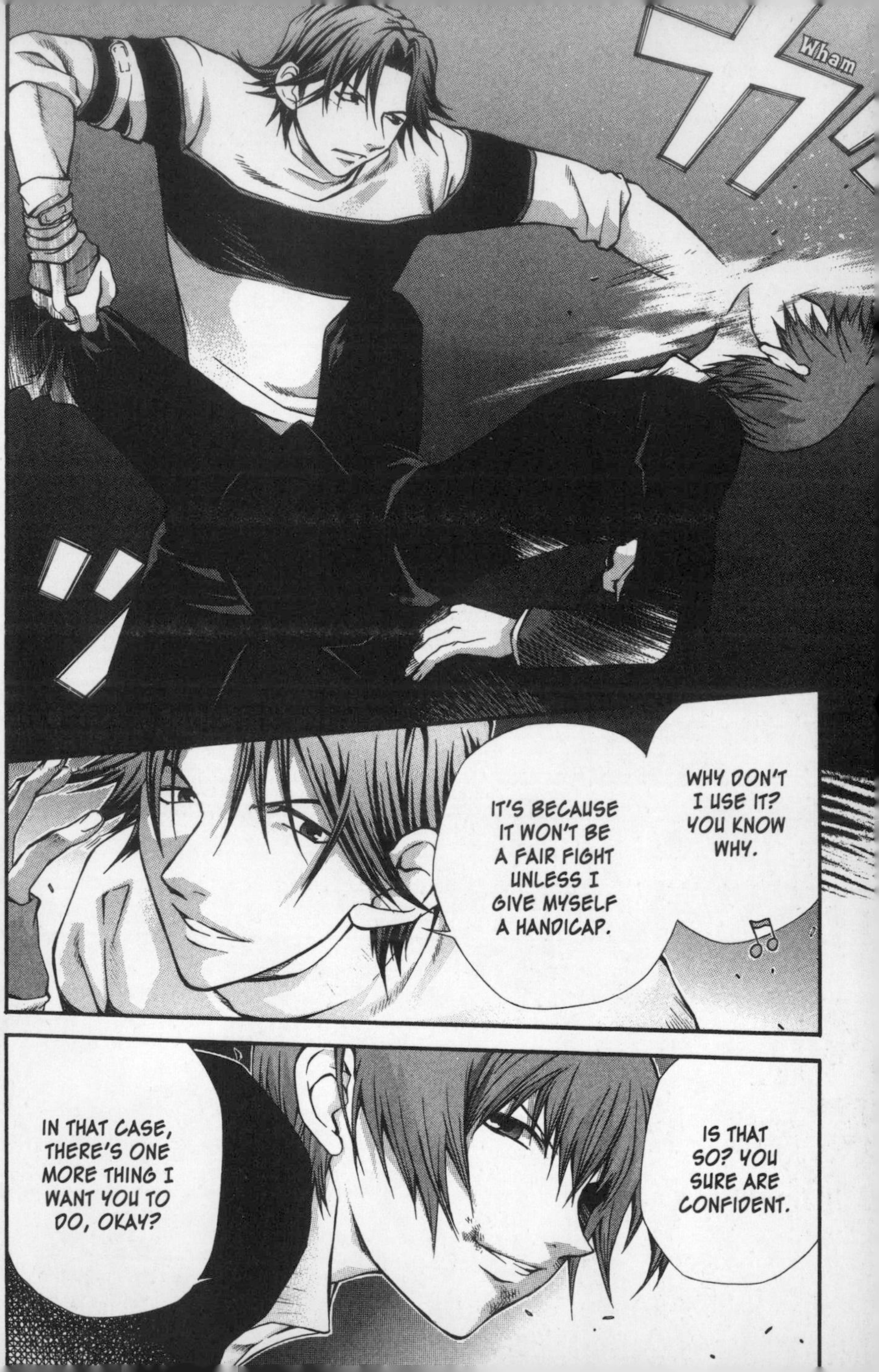
Wham
WHY DON'T I USE IT? YOU KNOW WHY.
IT'S BECAUSE IT WON'T BE A FAIR FIGHT UNLESS I GIVE MYSELF A HANDICAP.
IS THAT SO? YOU SURE ARE CONFIDENT.
IN THAT CASE, THERE'S ONE MORE THING I WANT YOU TO DO, OKAY?

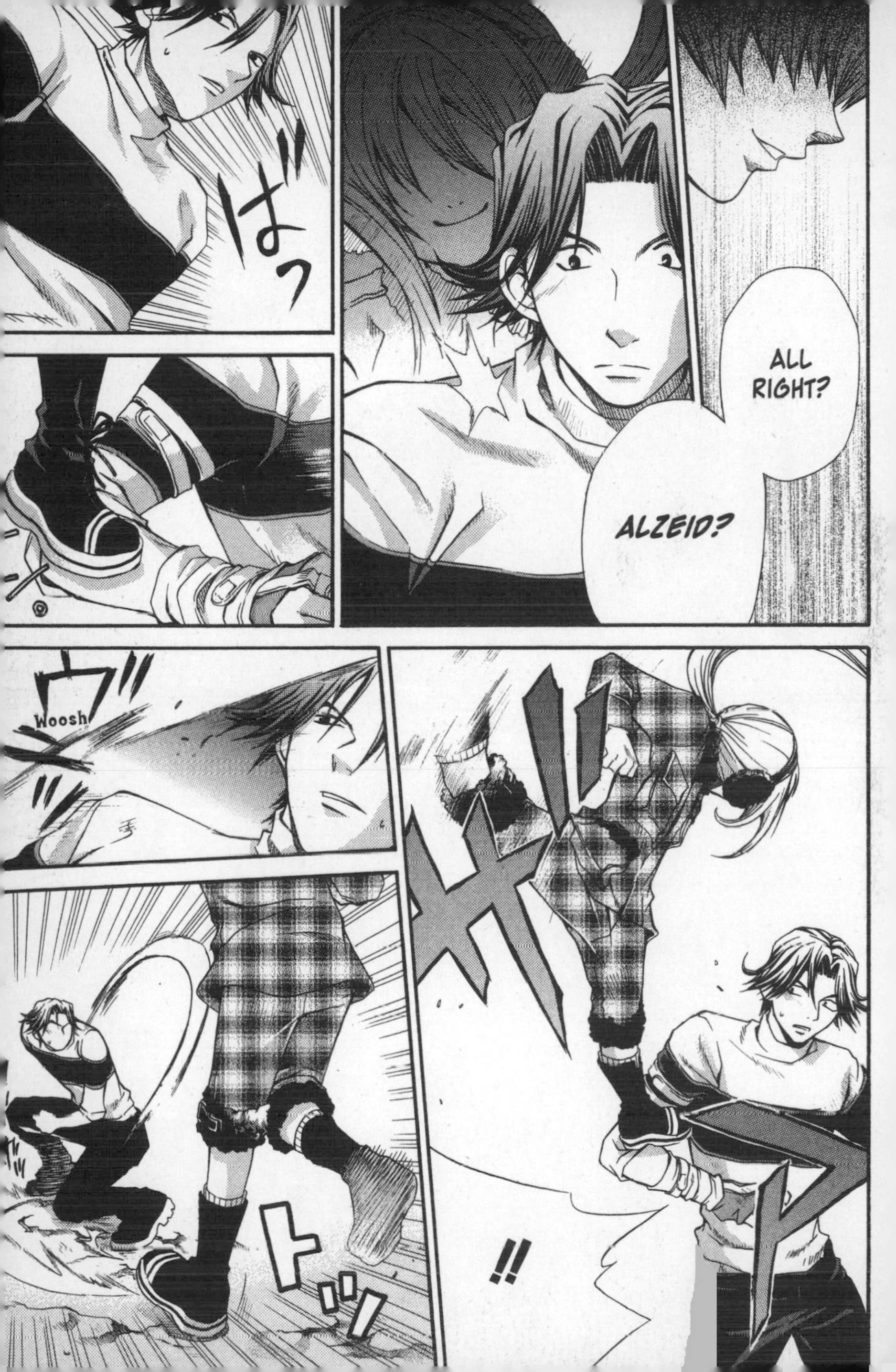
ALL RIGHT?
ALZEID?
ばっ
ヴ
Woosh
!!

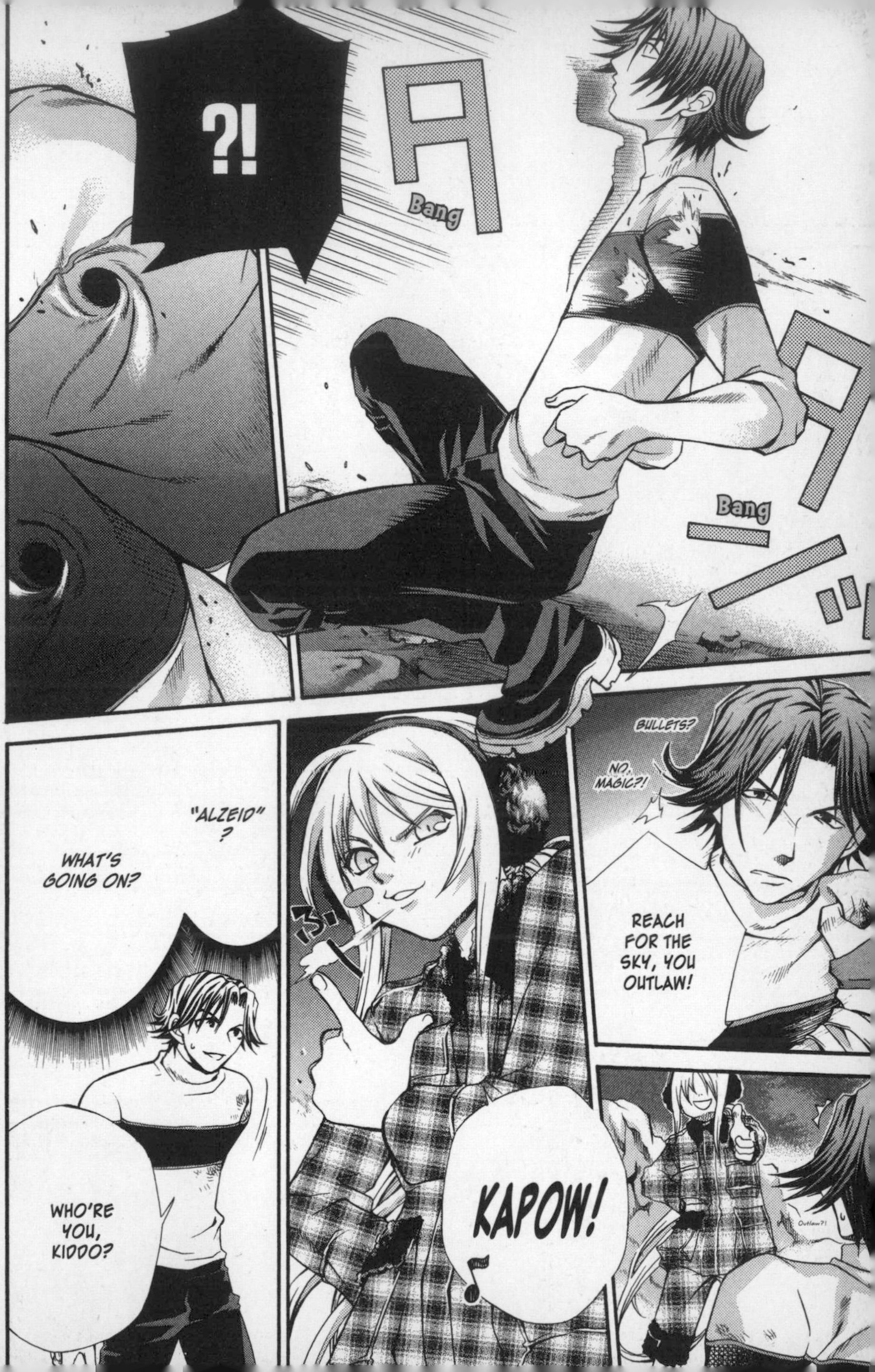
Bang
Bang
?!
BULLETS?
NO, MAGIC?!
REACH FOR THE SKY, YOU OUTLAW!
Outlaw?!
KAPOW!
"ALZEID"?
WHAT'S GOING ON?
WHO'RE YOU, KIDDO?

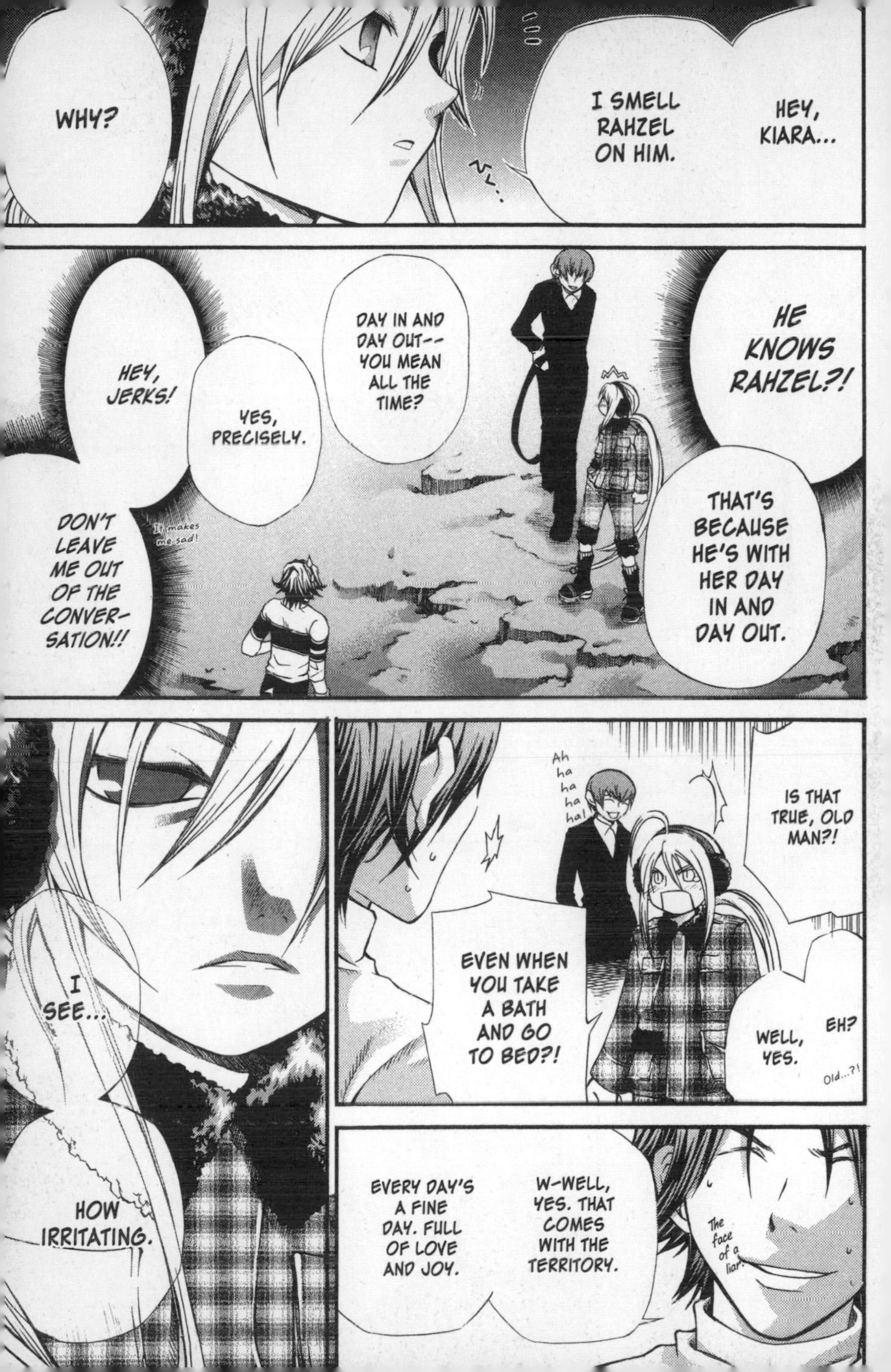
HEY, KIARA...
I SMELL RAHZEL ON HIM.
WHY?
HE KNOWS RAHZEL?!
THAT'S BECAUSE HE'S WITH HER DAY IN AND DAY OUT.
DAY IN AND DAY OUT-- YOU MEAN ALL THE TIME?
YES, PRECISELY.
HEY, JERKS!
DON'T LEAVE ME OUT OF THE CONVER-SATION!!
It makes me sad!
IS THAT TRUE, OLD MAN?!
Ah ha ha ha ha!
EH?
WELL, YES.
Old...?!
EVEN WHEN YOU TAKE A BATH AND GO TO BED?!
The face of a liar.
W-WELL, YES. THAT COMES WITH THE TERRITORY.
EVERY DAY'S A FINE DAY. FULL OF LOVE AND JOY.
I SEE...
HOW IRRITATING.

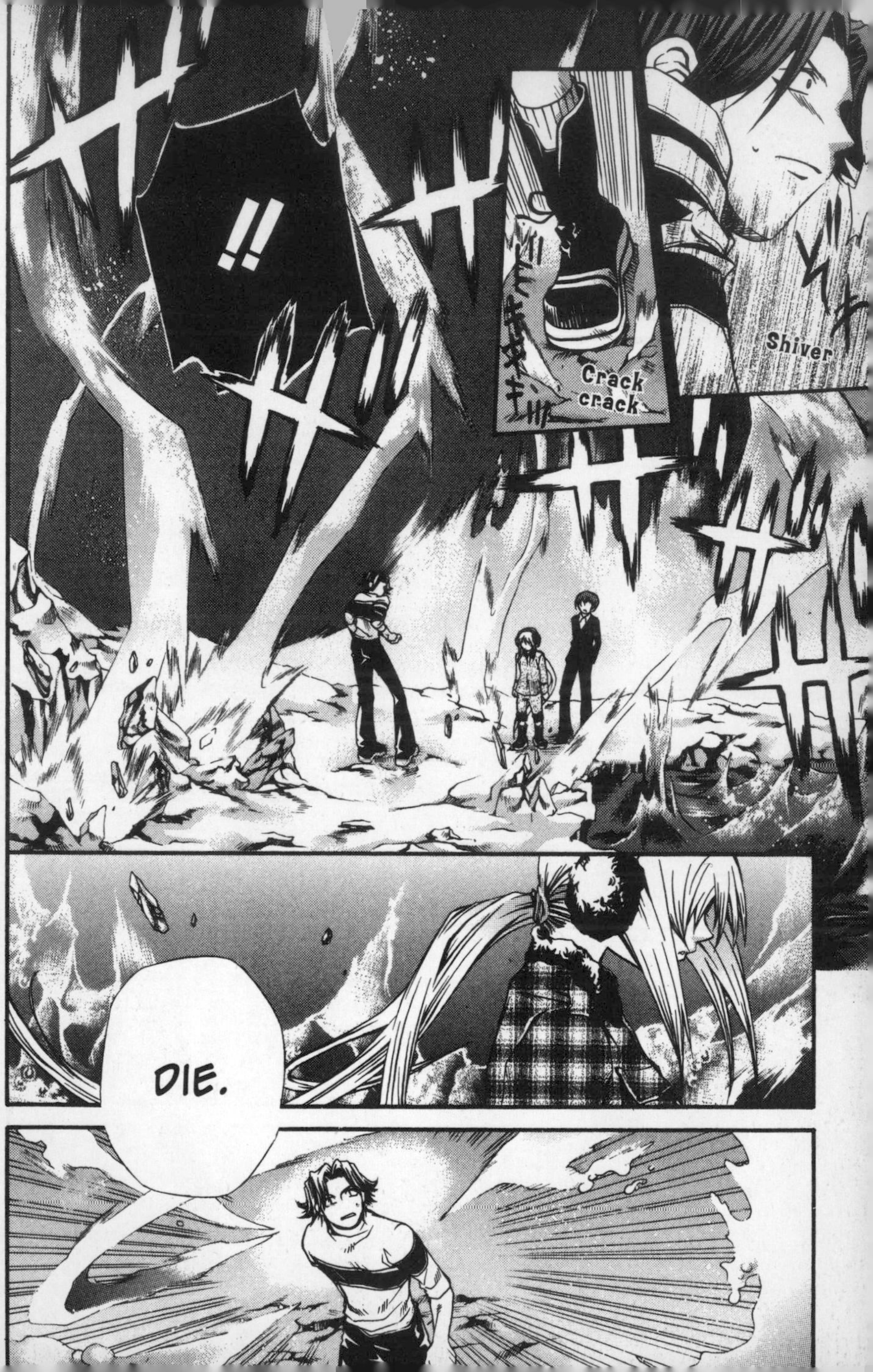
Shiver
Crack crack
!!
DIE.

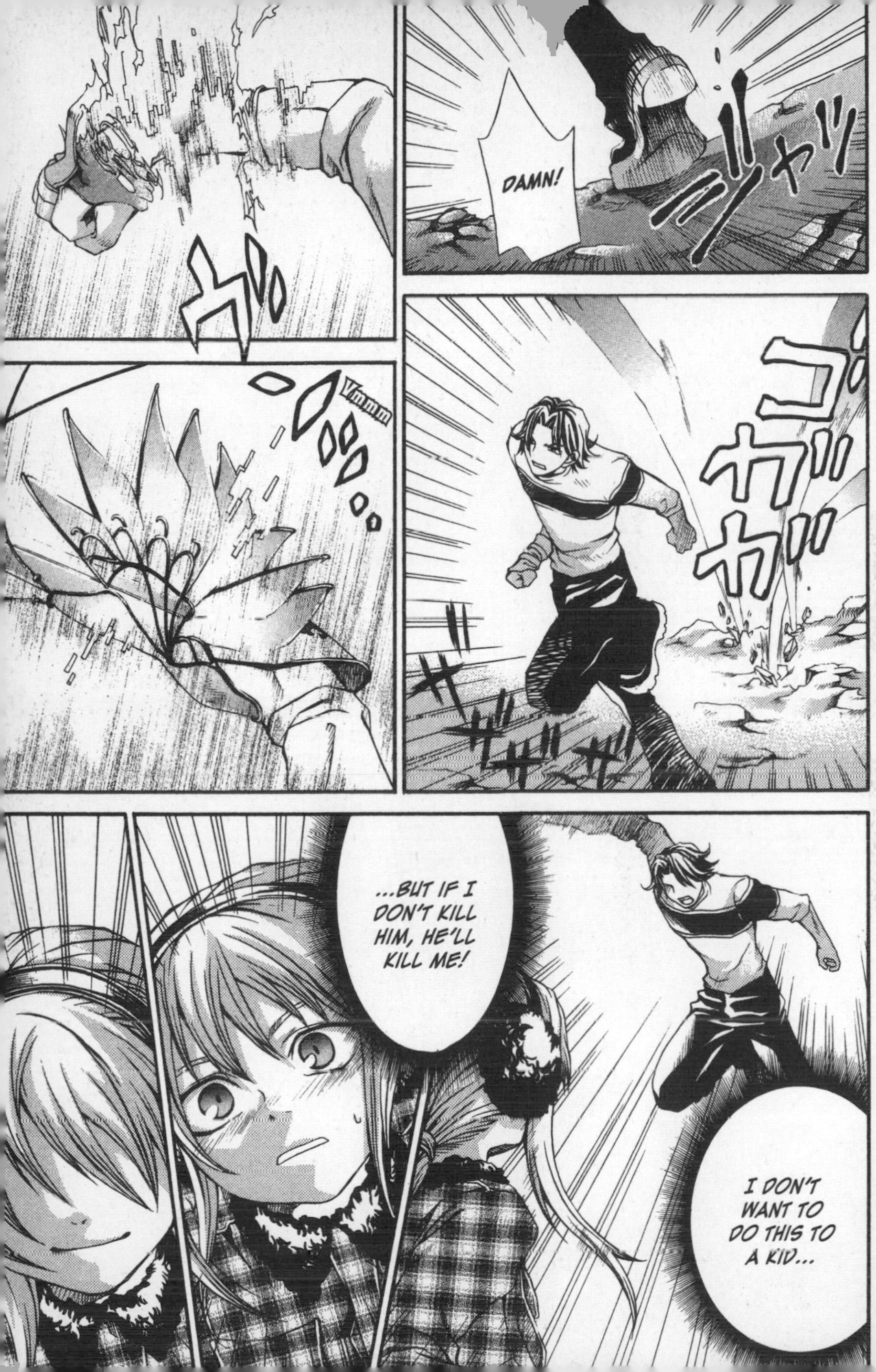
DAMN!
Vmmm
I DON'T WANT TO DO THIS TO A KID...
...BUT IF I DON'T KILL HIM, HE'LL KILL ME!

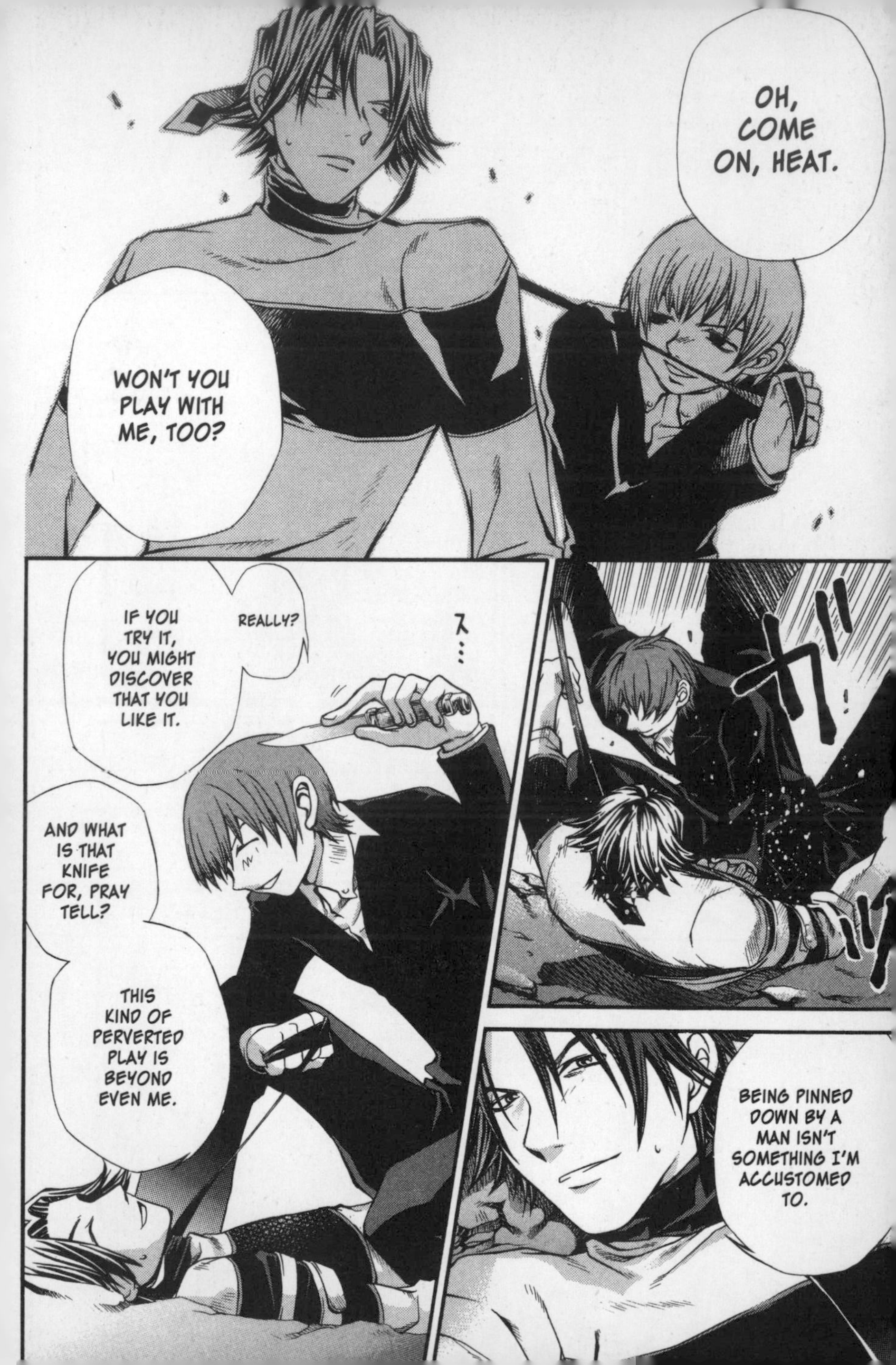
OH, COME ON, HEAT.
WON'T YOU PLAY WITH ME, TOO?
BEING PINNED DOWN BY A MAN ISN'T SOMETHING I'M ACCUSTOMED TO.
REALLY?
IF YOU TRY IT, YOU MIGHT DISCOVER THAT YOU LIKE IT.
ス…
AND WHAT IS THAT KNIFE FOR, PRAY TELL?
THIS KIND OF PERVERTED PLAY IS BEYOND EVEN ME.

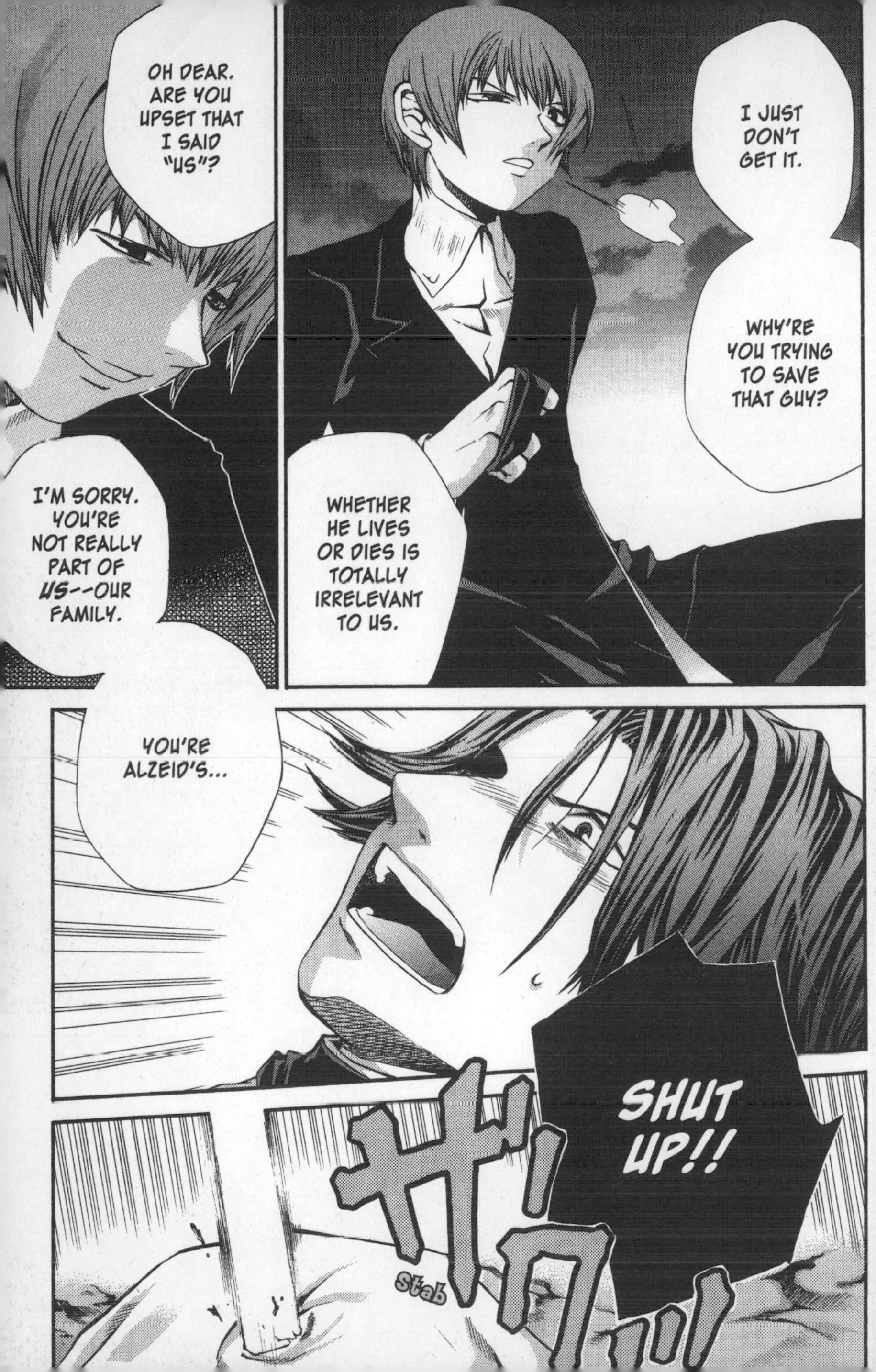
I JUST DON'T GET IT.
WHY'RE YOU TRYING TO SAVE THAT GUY?
WHETHER HE LIVES OR DIES IS TOTALLY IRRELEVANT TO US.
OH DEAR. ARE YOU UPSET THAT I SAID "US"?
I'M SORRY. YOU'RE NOT REALLY PART OF US--OUR FAMILY.
YOU'RE ALZEID'S...
SHUT UP!!
Stab

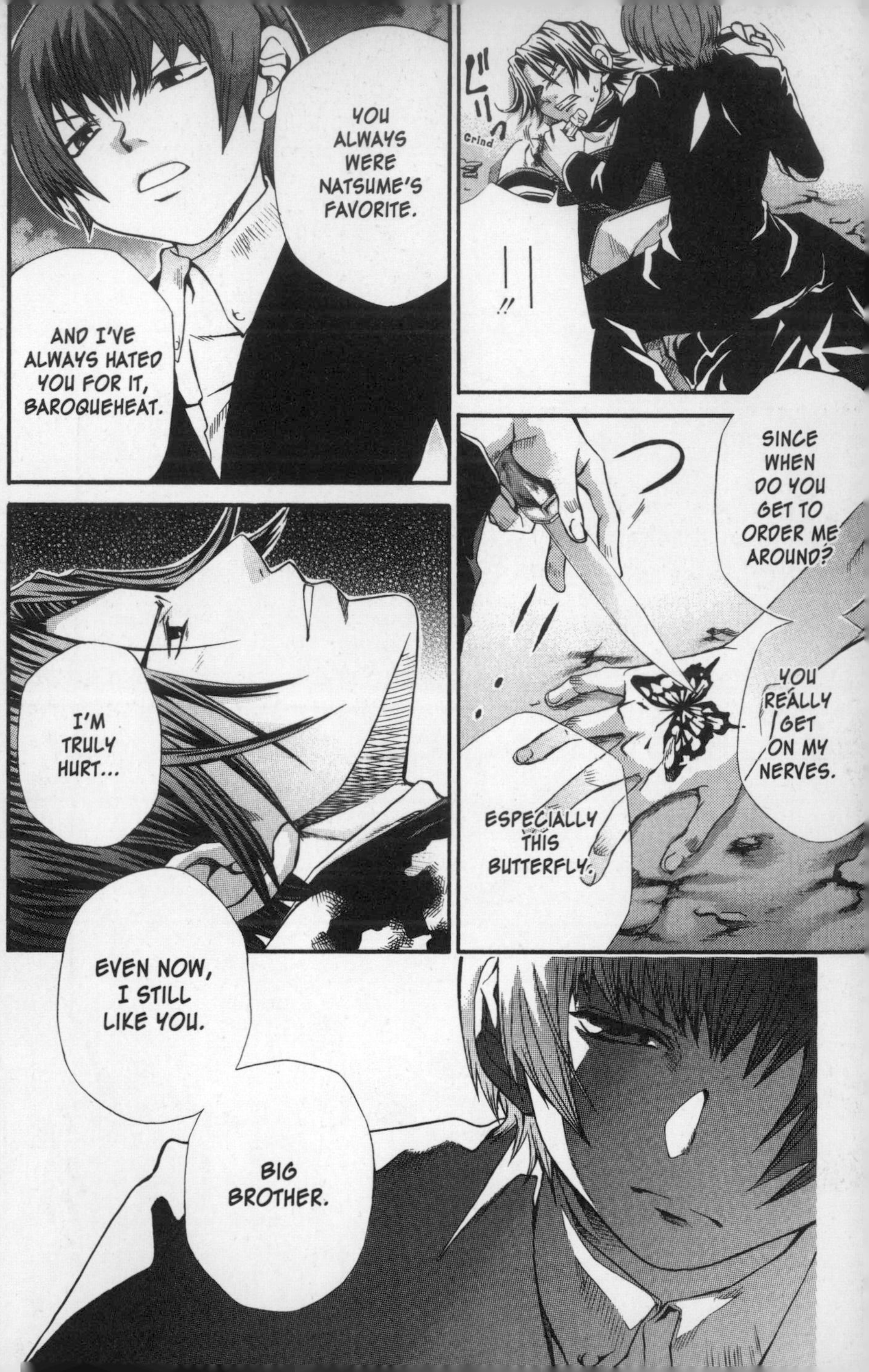
Grind
!!
YOU ALWAYS WERE NATSUME'S FAVORITE.
AND I'VE ALWAYS HATED YOU FOR IT, BAROQUEHEAT.
SINCE WHEN DO YOU GET TO ORDER ME AROUND?
YOU REALLY GET ON MY NERVES.
ESPECIALLY THIS BUTTERFLY.
I'M TRULY HURT...
EVEN NOW, I STILL LIKE YOU.
BIG BROTHER.

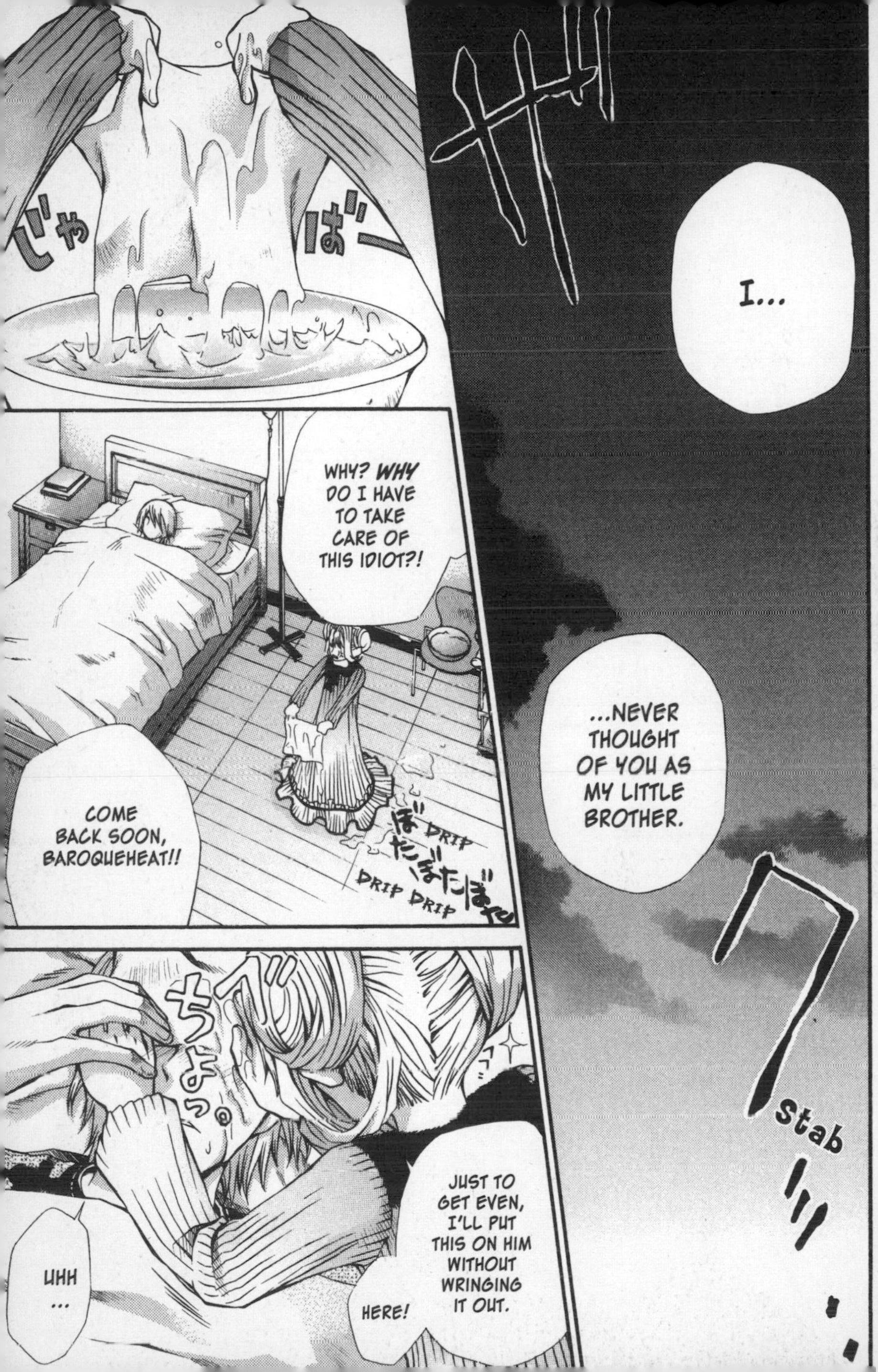
ザ
I...
...NEVER THOUGHT OF YOU AS MY LITTLE BROTHER.
ク
Stab
じゃばー
WHY? WHY DO I HAVE TO TAKE CARE OF THIS IDIOT?!
COME BACK SOON, BAROQUEHEAT!!
ぼたぼたぼたぼた
DRIP
DRIP DRIP
べちょっ
JUST TO GET EVEN, I'LL PUT THIS ON HIM WITHOUT WRINGING IT OUT.
HERE!
UHH ...

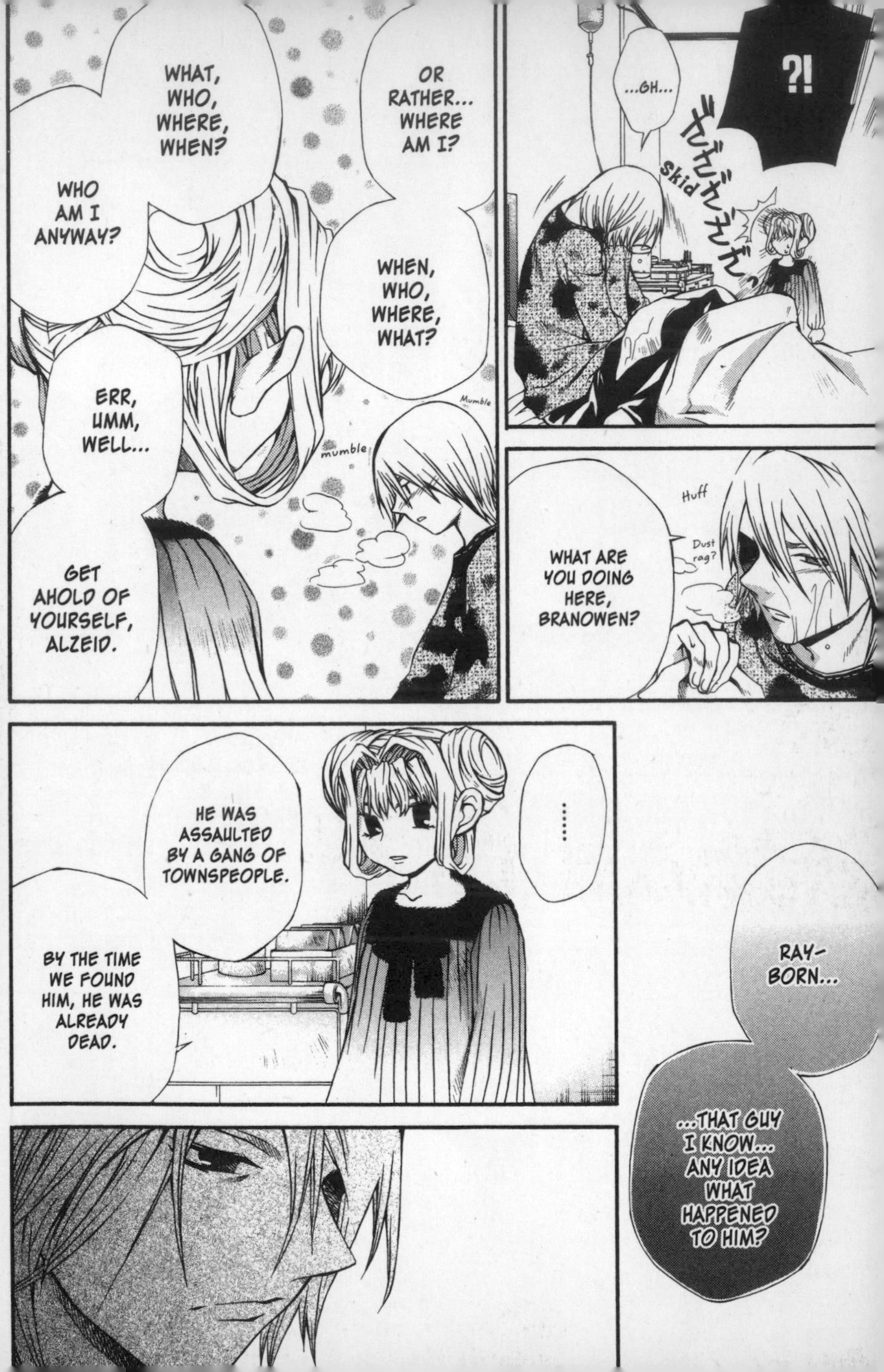

...GH...
?!
skid
Huff
Dust rag?
WHAT ARE YOU DOING HERE, BRANOWEN?
OR RATHER... WHERE AM I?
WHAT, WHO, WHERE, WHEN?
WHEN, WHO, WHERE, WHAT?
WHO AM I ANYWAY?
Mumble
mumble
ERR, UMM, WELL...
GET AHOLD OF YOURSELF, ALZEID.
RAY-BORN...
...THAT GUY I KNOW... ANY IDEA WHAT HAPPENED TO HIM?
......
HE WAS ASSAULTED BY A GANG OF TOWNSPEOPLE.
BY THE TIME WE FOUND HIM, HE WAS ALREADY DEAD.

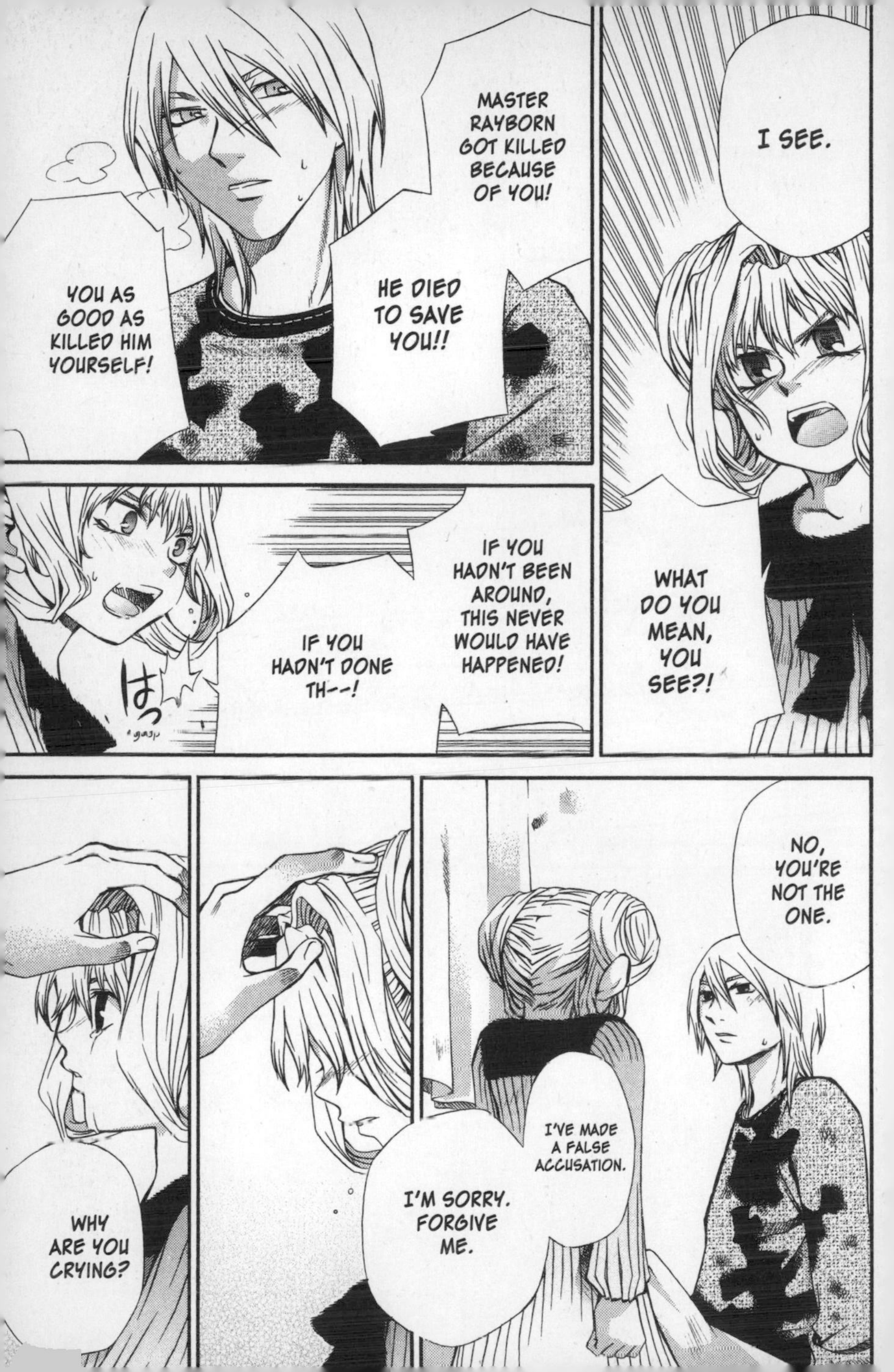
I SEE.
WHAT DO YOU MEAN, YOU SEE?!
MASTER RAYBORN GOT KILLED BECAUSE OF YOU!
HE DIED TO SAVE YOU!!
YOU AS GOOD AS KILLED HIM YOURSELF!
IF YOU HADN'T BEEN AROUND, THIS NEVER WOULD HAVE HAPPENED!
IF YOU HADN'T DONE TH--!
はっ
*gasp
NO, YOU'RE NOT THE ONE.
I'VE MADE A FALSE ACCUSATION.
I'M SORRY. FORGIVE ME.
WHY ARE YOU CRYING?

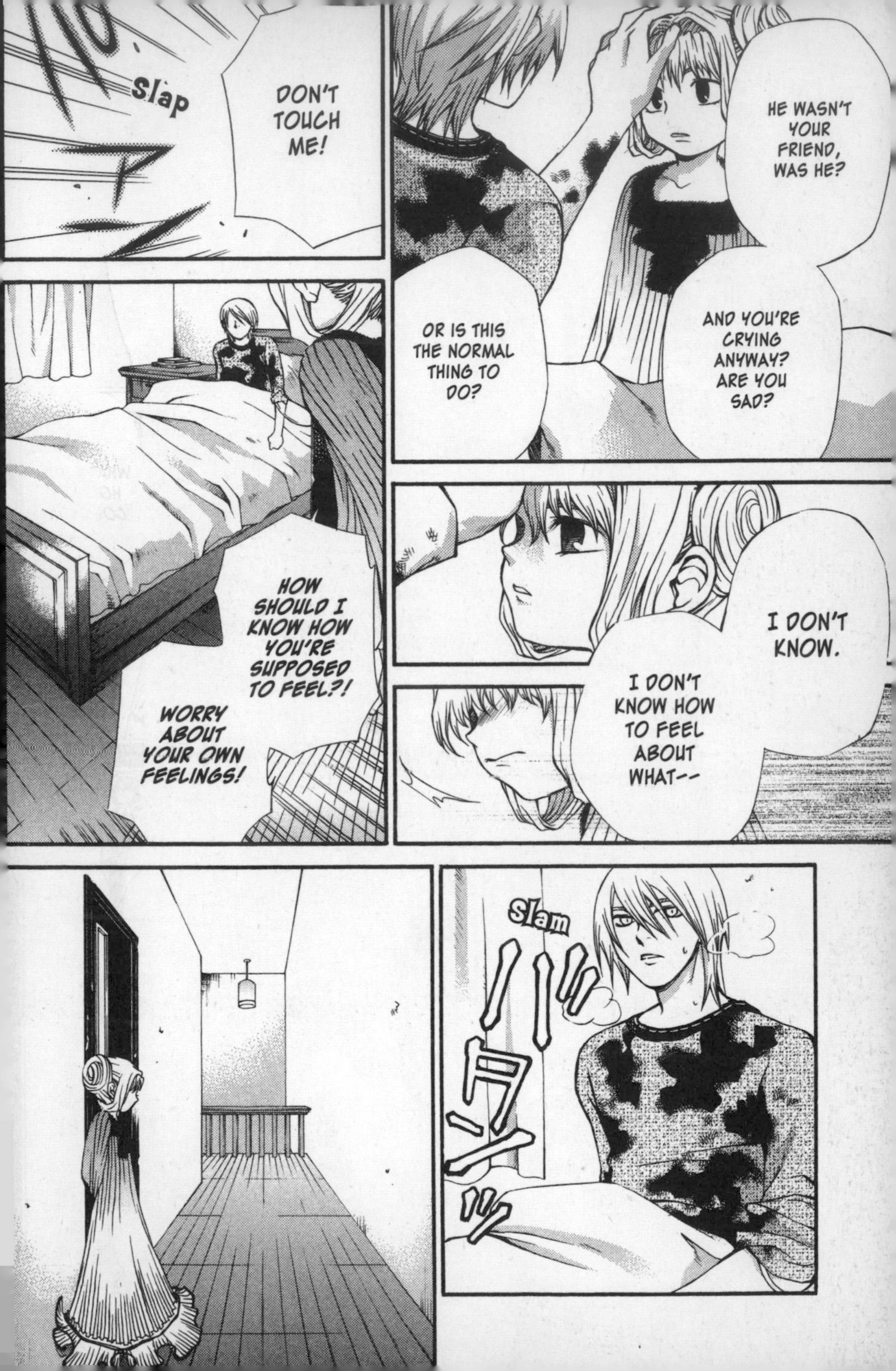
HE WASN'T YOUR FRIEND, WAS HE?
AND YOU'RE CRYING ANYWAY? ARE YOU SAD?
OR IS THIS THE NORMAL THING TO DO?
I DON'T KNOW.
I DON'T KNOW HOW TO FEEL ABOUT WHAT--
Slap
DON'T TOUCH ME!
HOW SHOULD I KNOW HOW YOU'RE SUPPOSED TO FEEL?!
WORRY ABOUT YOUR OWN FEELINGS!
Slam

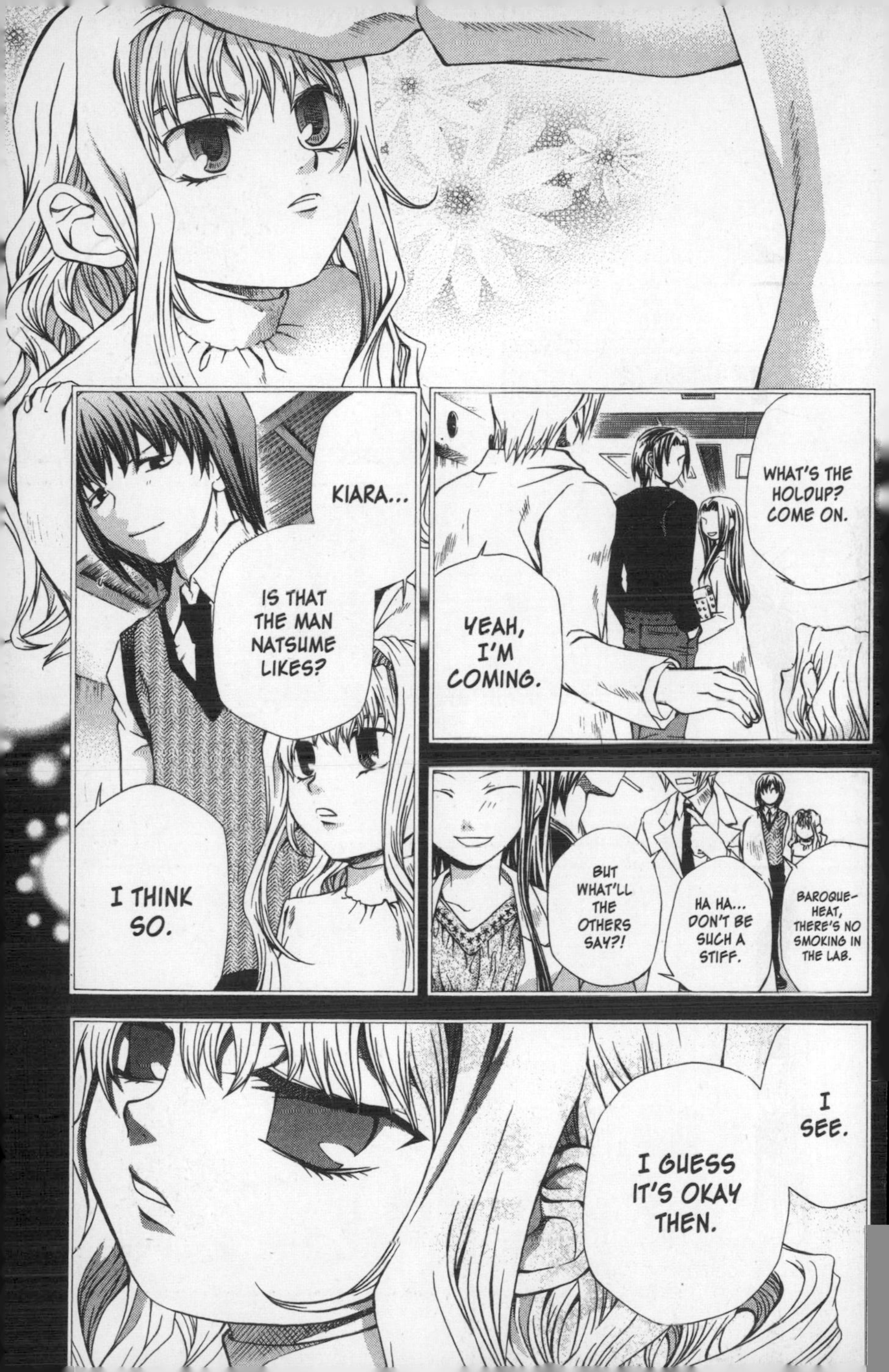
WHAT'S THE HOLDUP? COME ON.
YEAH, I'M COMING.
BAROQUE-HEAT, THERE'S NO SMOKING IN THE LAB.
HA HA... DON'T BE SUCH A STIFF.
BUT WHAT'LL THE OTHERS SAY?!
KIARA...
IS THAT THE MAN NATSUME LIKES?
I THINK SO.
I SEE.
I GUESS IT'S OKAY THEN.

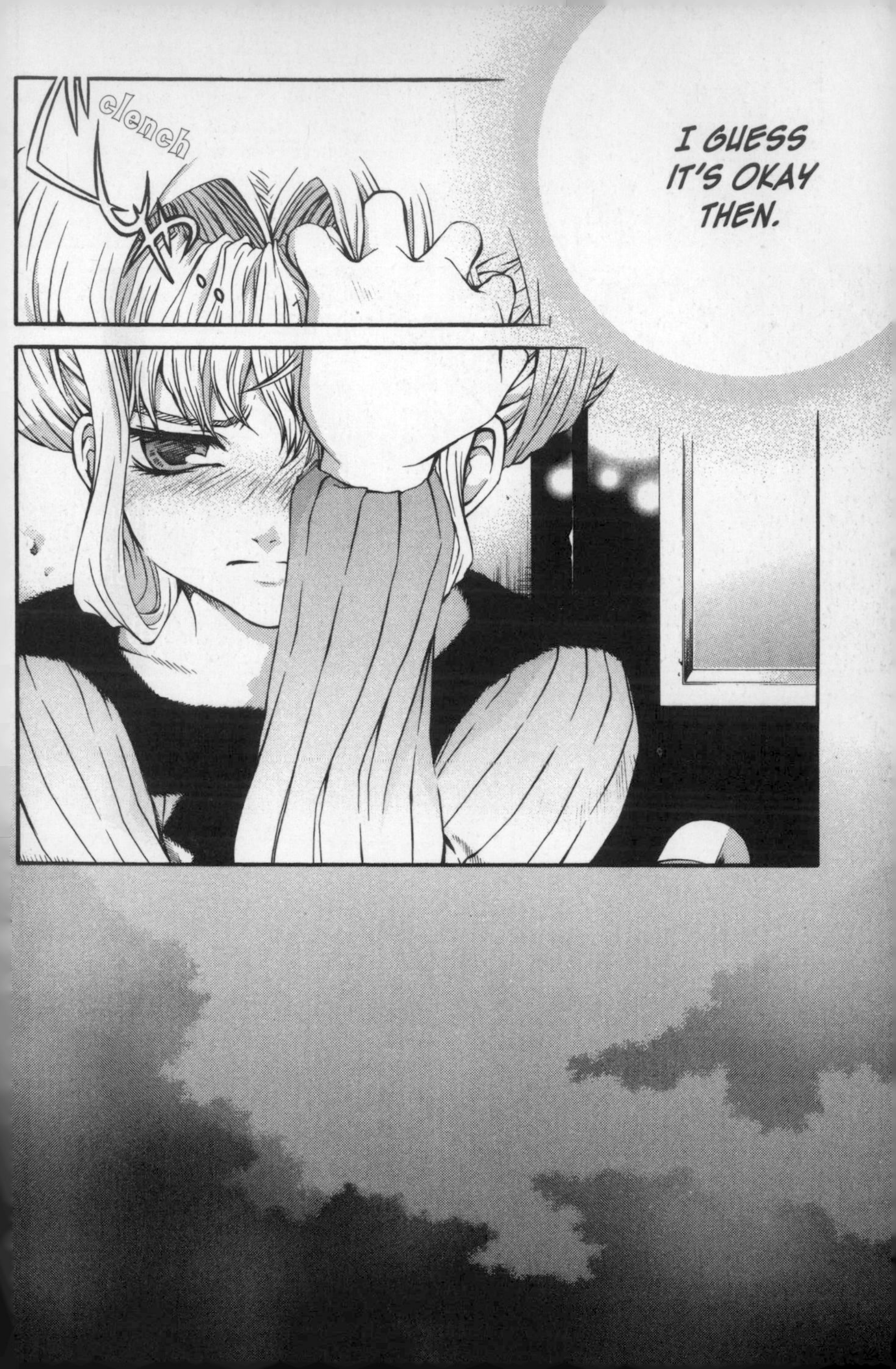
I GUESS IT'S OKAY THEN.
clench

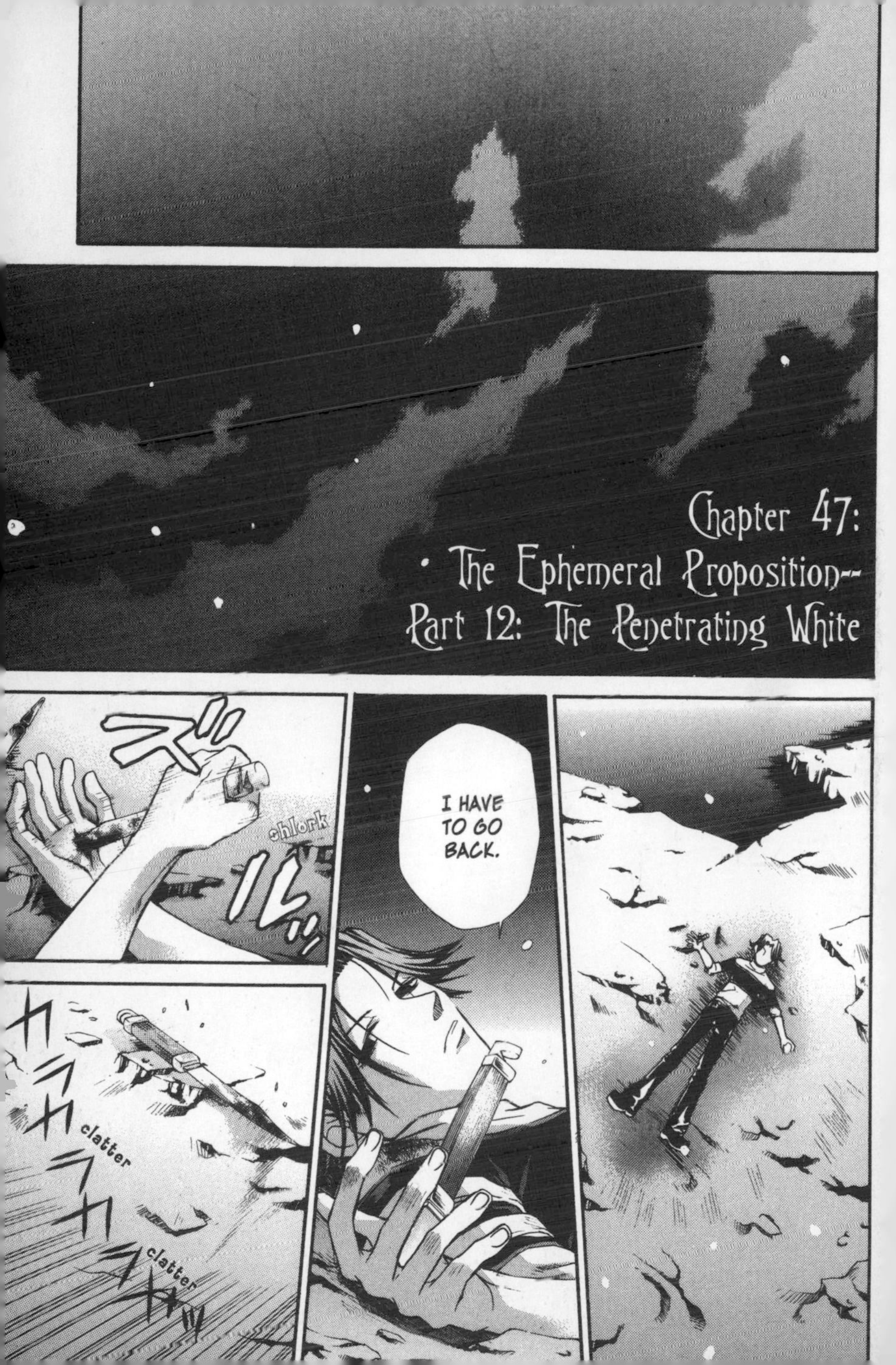
Chapter 47:
The Ephemeral Proposition--
Part 12: The Penetrating White
I HAVE TO GO BACK.
chlork
clatter
clatter

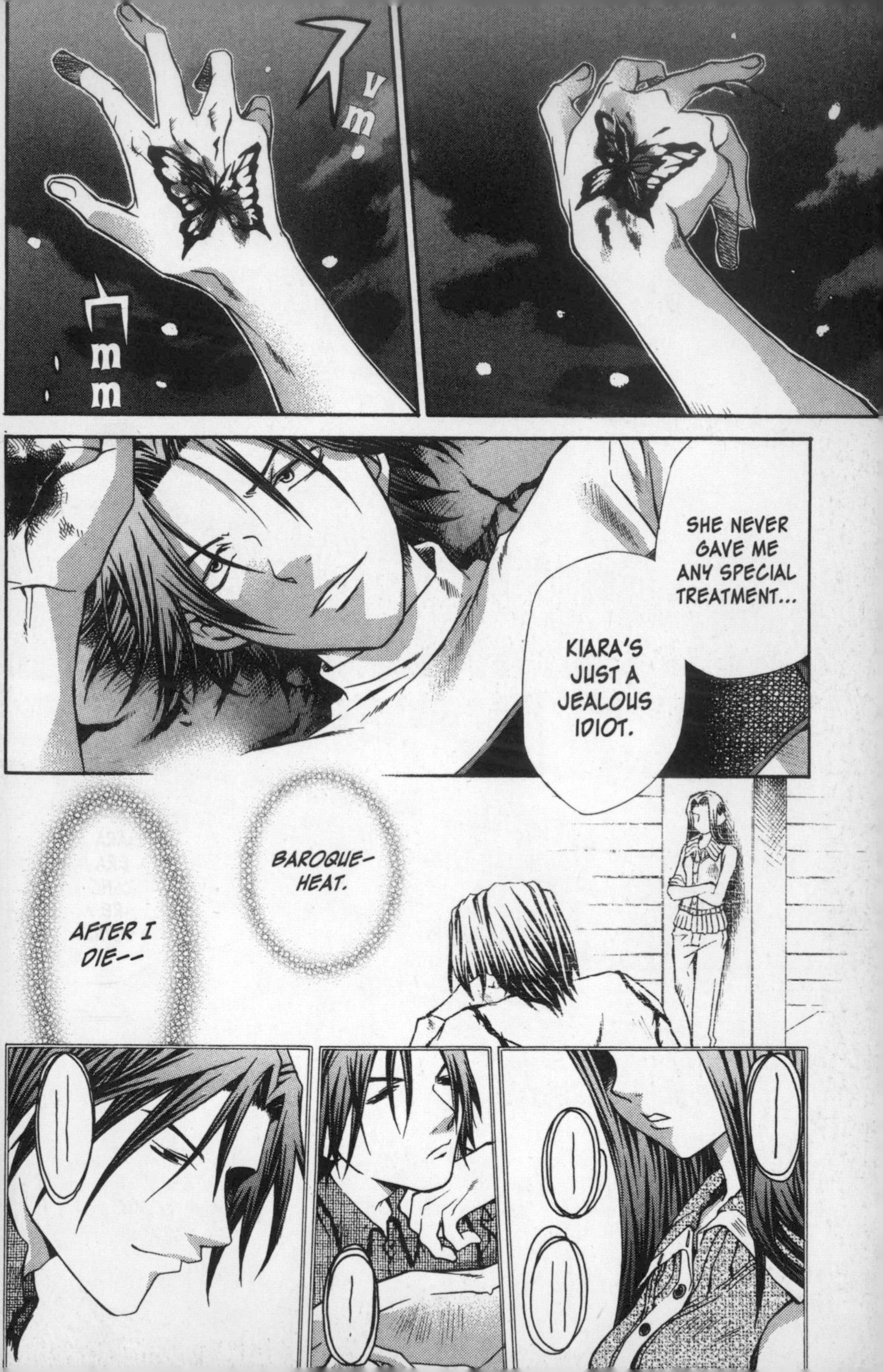
vm
mm
SHE NEVER GAVE ME ANY SPECIAL TREATMENT...
KIARA'S JUST A JEALOUS IDIOT.
BAROQUE-HEAT.
AFTER I DIE--

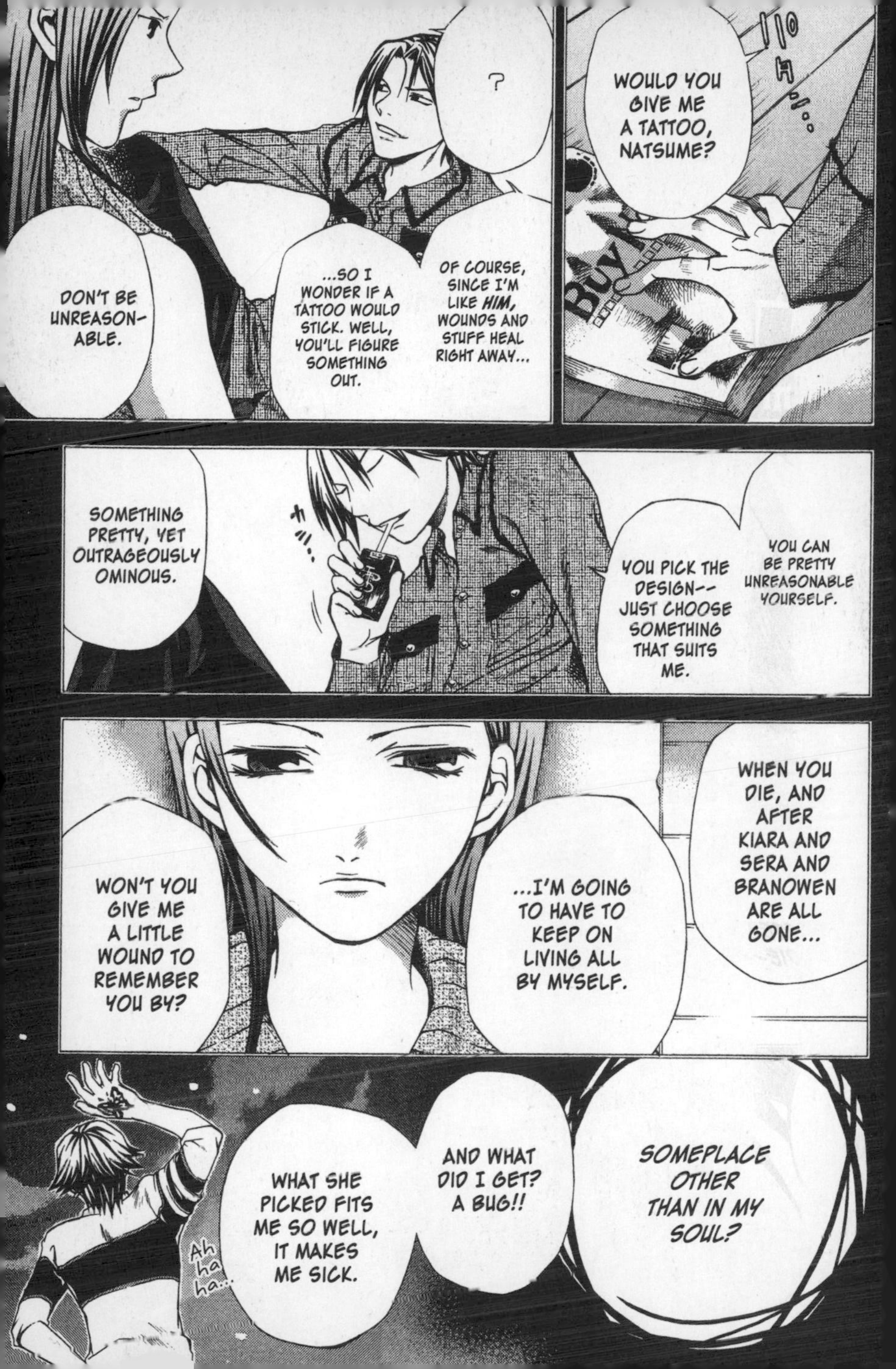
WOULD YOU GIVE ME A TATTOO, NATSUME?
?
OF COURSE, SINCE I'M LIKE *HIM*, WOUNDS AND STUFF HEAL RIGHT AWAY...
...SO I WONDER IF A TATTOO WOULD STICK. WELL, YOU'LL FIGURE SOMETHING OUT.
DON'T BE UNREASONABLE.
YOU CAN BE PRETTY UNREASONABLE YOURSELF.
YOU PICK THE DESIGN-- JUST CHOOSE SOMETHING THAT SUITS ME.
SOMETHING PRETTY, YET OUTRAGEOUSLY OMINOUS.
WHEN YOU DIE, AND AFTER KIARA AND SERA AND BRANOWEN ARE ALL GONE...
...I'M GOING TO HAVE TO KEEP ON LIVING ALL BY MYSELF.
WON'T YOU GIVE ME A LITTLE WOUND TO REMEMBER YOU BY?
SOMEPLACE OTHER THAN IN MY SOUL?
AND WHAT DID I GET? A BUG!!
WHAT SHE PICKED FITS ME SO WELL, IT MAKES ME SICK.
Ah ha ha...

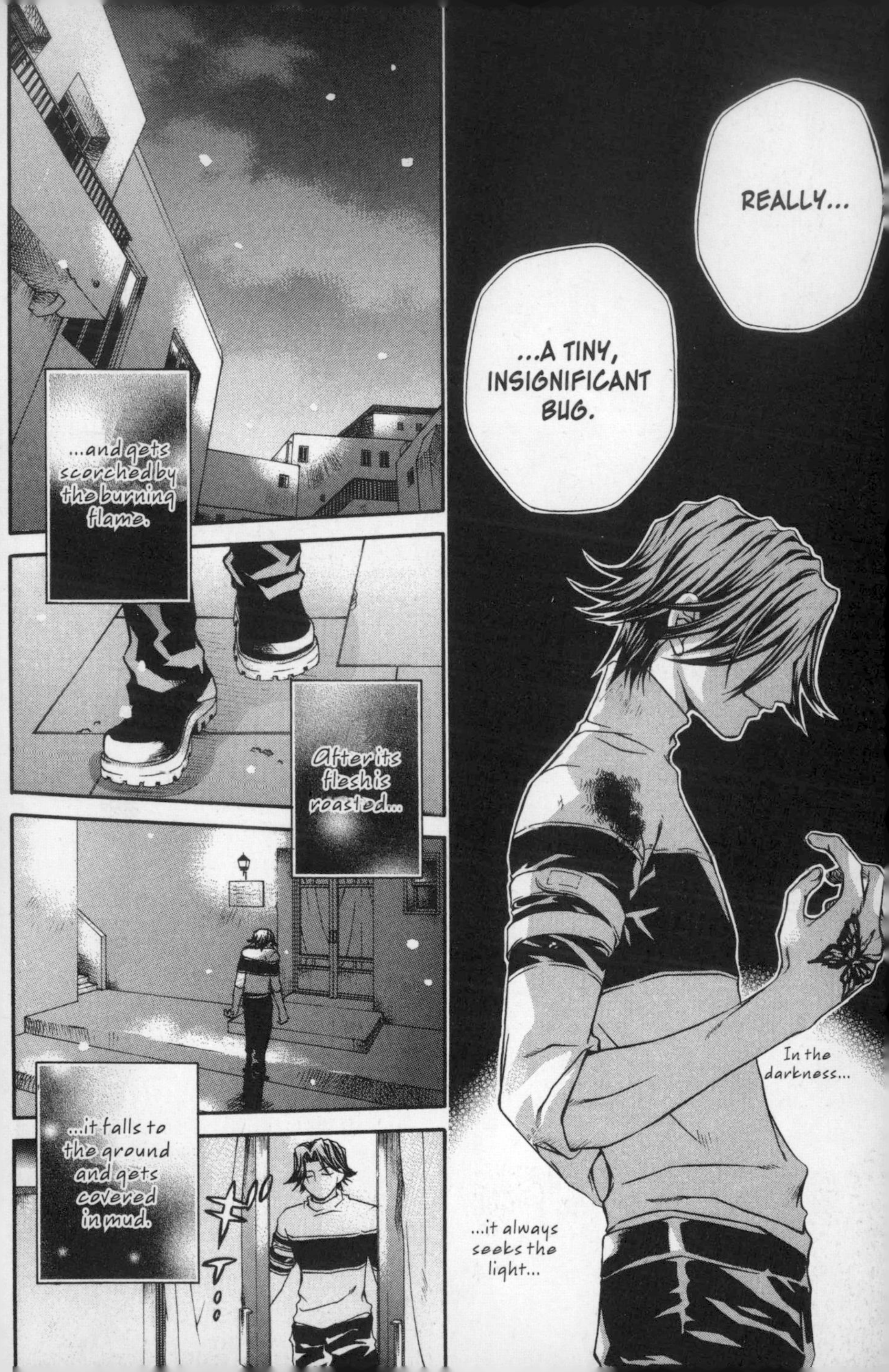
REALLY...
...A TINY, INSIGNIFICANT BUG.
In the darkness...
...it always seeks the light...
...and gets scorched by the burning flame.
After its flesh is roasted...
...it falls to the ground and gets covered in mud.

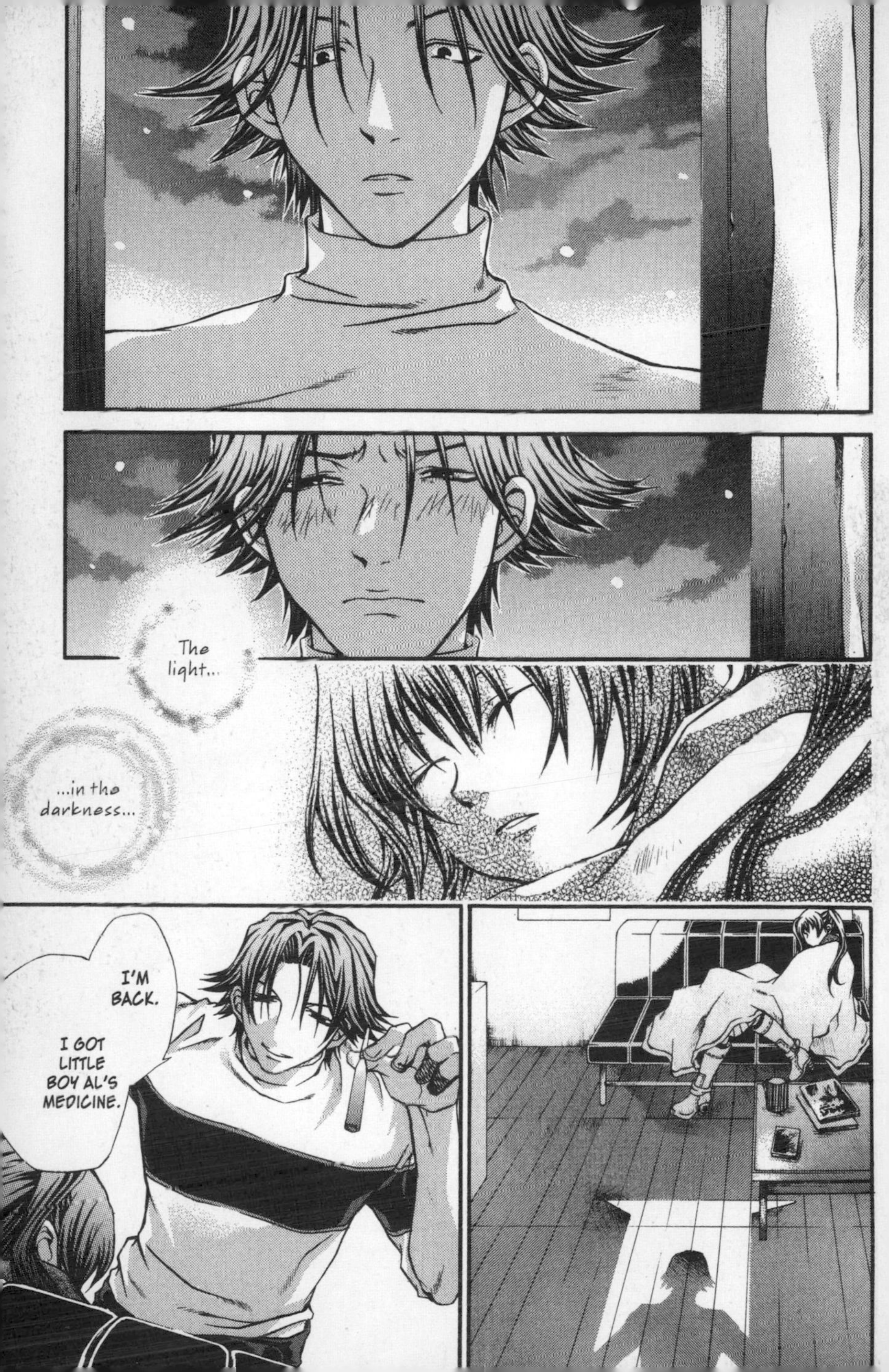
The light...
...in the darkness...
I'M BACK.
I GOT LITTLE BOY AL'S MEDICINE.

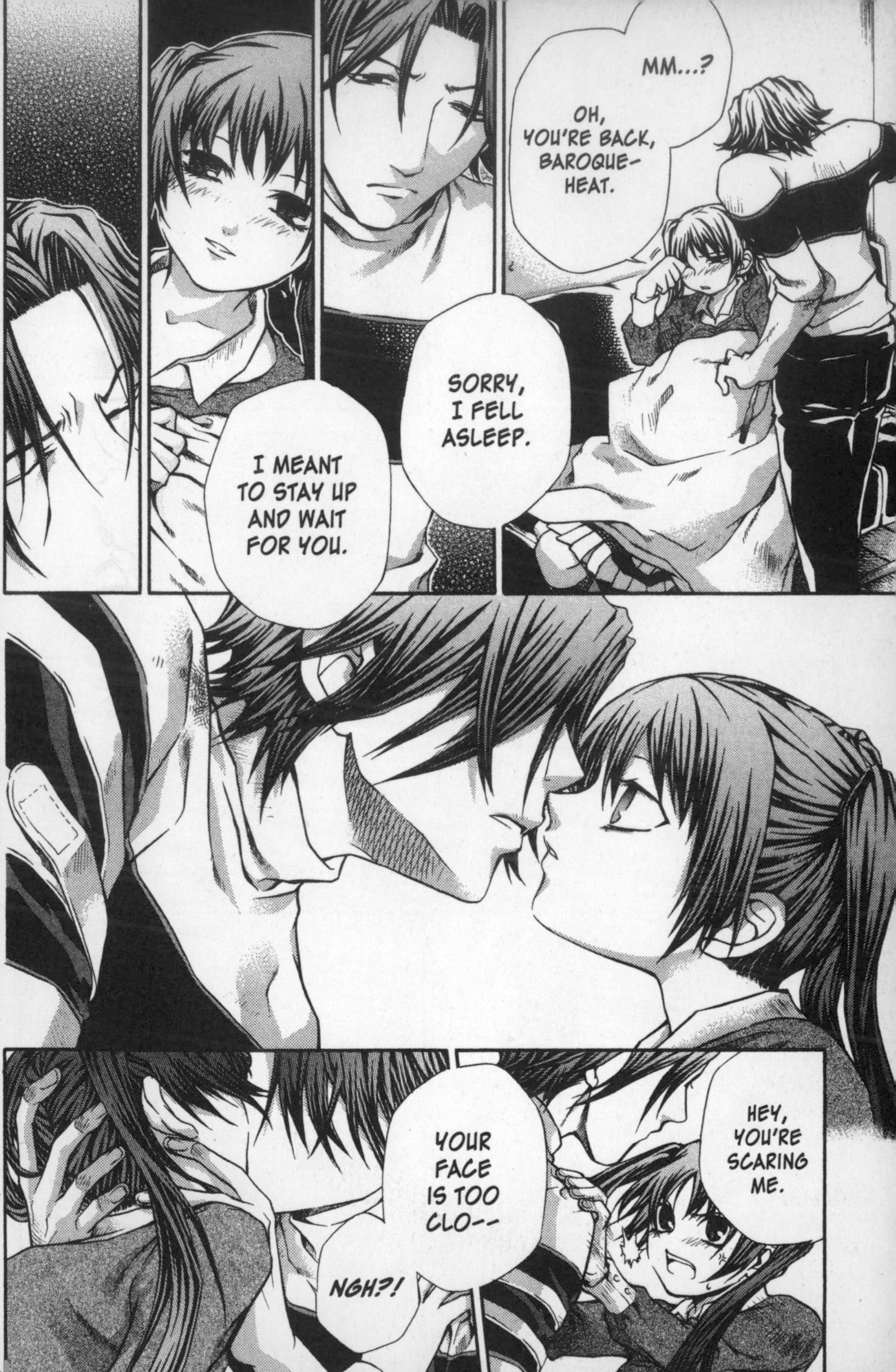
MM...?
OH, YOU'RE BACK, BAROQUE-HEAT.
SORRY, I FELL ASLEEP.
I MEANT TO STAY UP AND WAIT FOR YOU.
HEY, YOU'RE SCARING ME.
YOUR FACE IS TOO CLO--
NGH?!

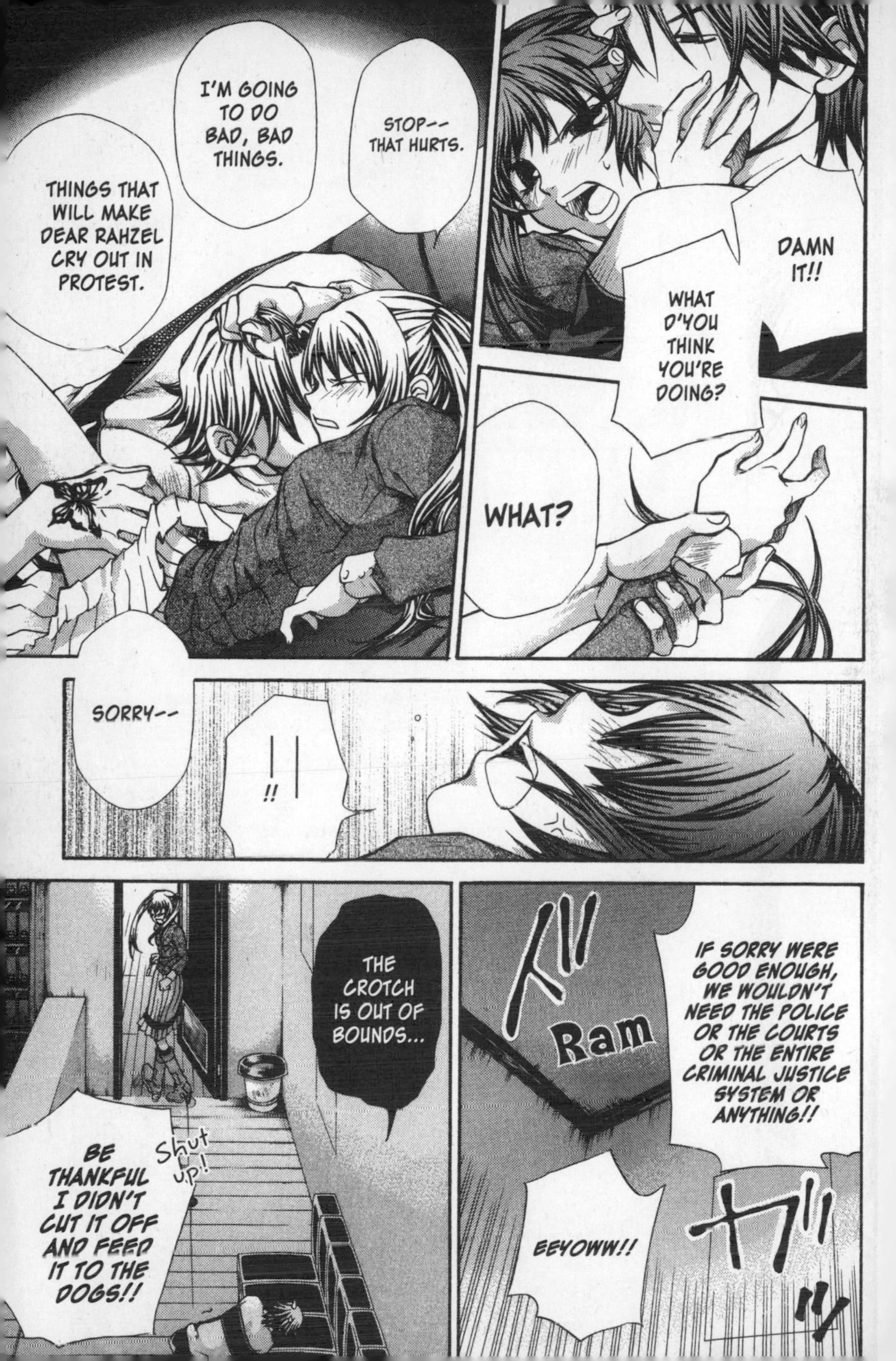
DAMN IT!!
WHAT D'YOU THINK YOU'RE DOING?
WHAT?
STOP-- THAT HURTS.
I'M GOING TO DO BAD, BAD THINGS.
THINGS THAT WILL MAKE DEAR RAHZEL CRY OUT IN PROTEST.
—!!
SORRY--
IF SORRY WERE GOOD ENOUGH, WE WOULDN'T NEED THE POLICE OR THE COURTS OR THE ENTIRE CRIMINAL JUSTICE SYSTEM OR ANYTHING!!
Ram
EEYOWW!!
THE CROTCH IS OUT OF BOUNDS...
Shut up!
BE THANKFUL I DIDN'T CUT IT OFF AND FEED IT TO THE DOGS!!

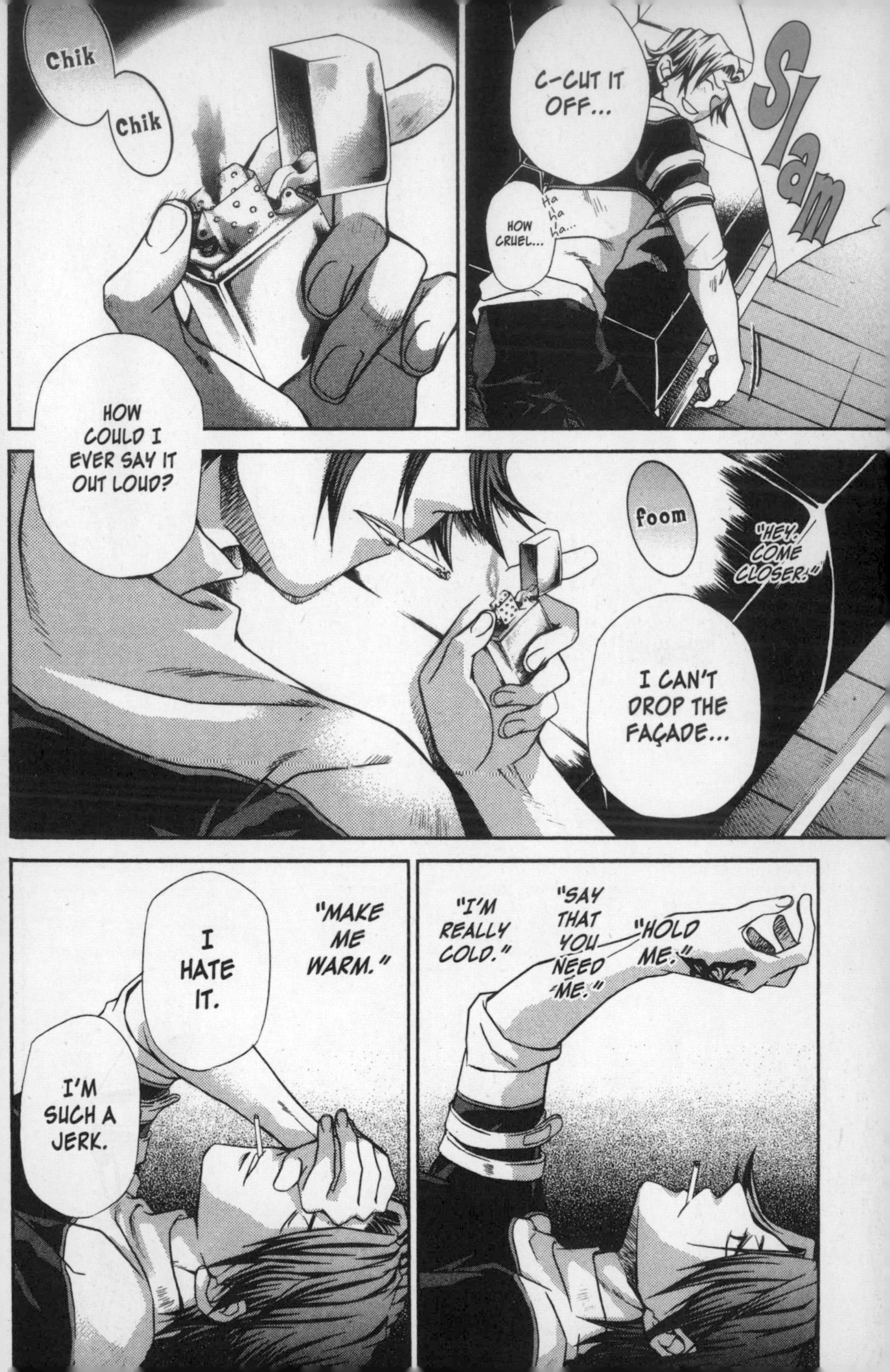

Slam
C-CUT IT OFF...
Ha ha ha...
HOW CRUEL...
Chik
Chik
HOW COULD I EVER SAY IT OUT LOUD?
"HEY, COME CLOSER."
foom
I CAN'T DROP THE FAÇADE...
"HOLD ME."
"SAY THAT YOU NEED ME."
"I'M REALLY COLD."
"MAKE ME WARM."
I HATE IT.
I'M SUCH A JERK.

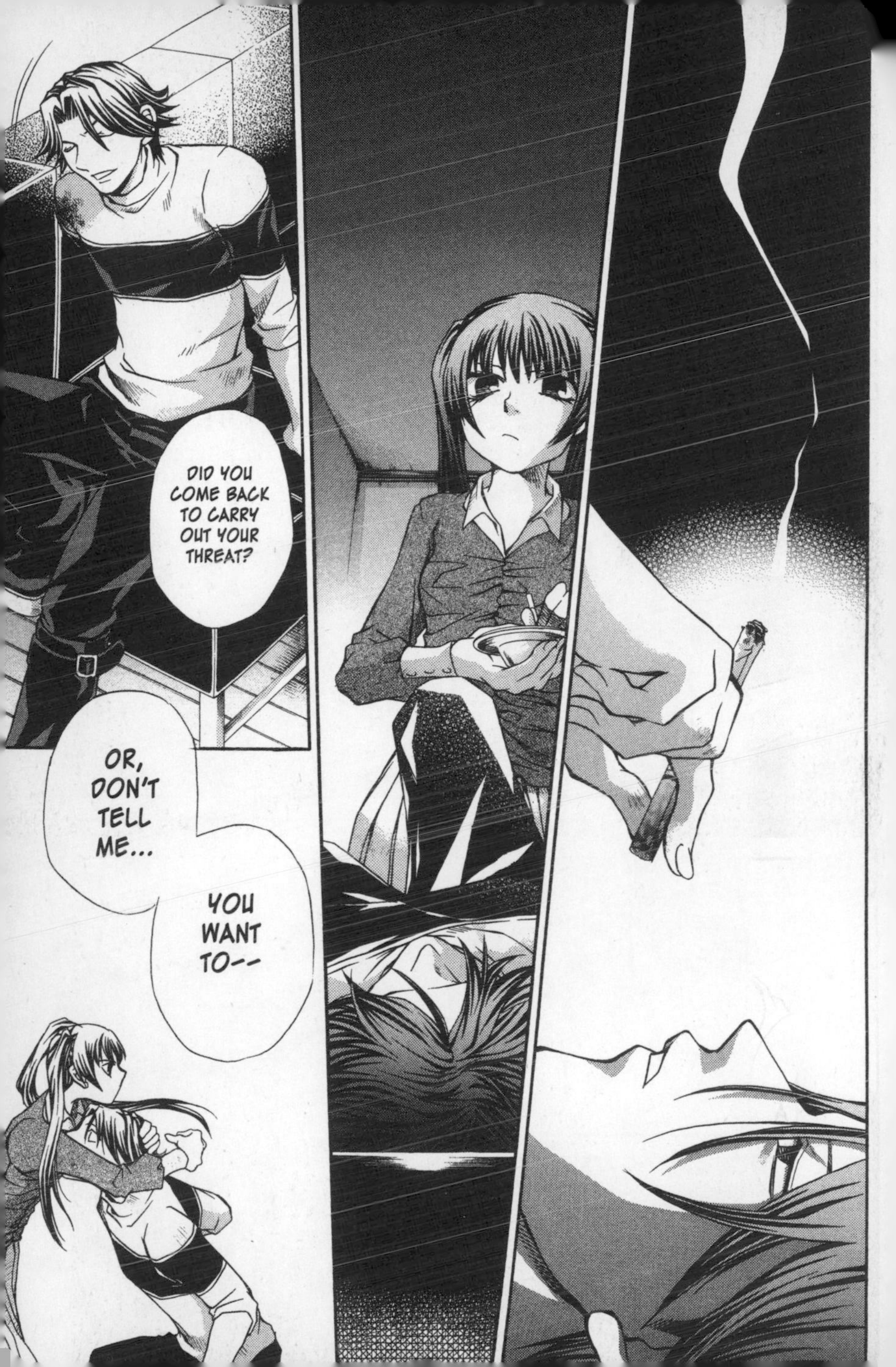
DID YOU COME BACK TO CARRY OUT YOUR THREAT?
OR, DON'T TELL ME...
YOU WANT TO--

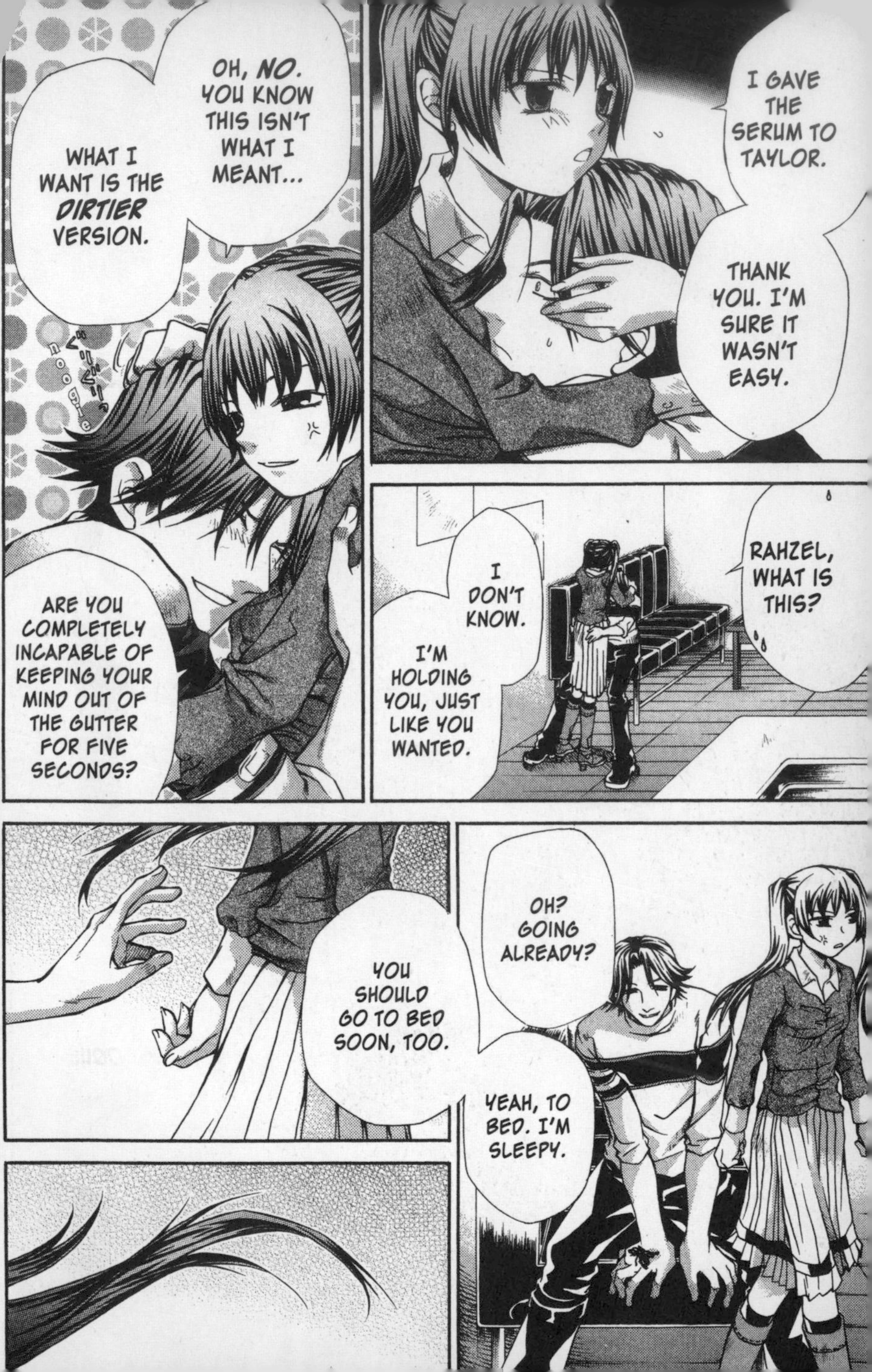
I GAVE THE SERUM TO TAYLOR.
THANK YOU. I'M SURE IT WASN'T EASY.
RAHZEL, WHAT IS THIS?
I DON'T KNOW.
I'M HOLDING YOU, JUST LIKE YOU WANTED.
OH, ***NO***. YOU KNOW THIS ISN'T WHAT I MEANT...
WHAT I WANT IS THE ***DIRTIER*** VERSION.
ARE YOU COMPLETELY INCAPABLE OF KEEPING YOUR MIND OUT OF THE GUTTER FOR FIVE SECONDS?
OH? GOING ALREADY?
YOU SHOULD GO TO BED SOON, TOO.
YEAH, TO BED. I'M SLEEPY.

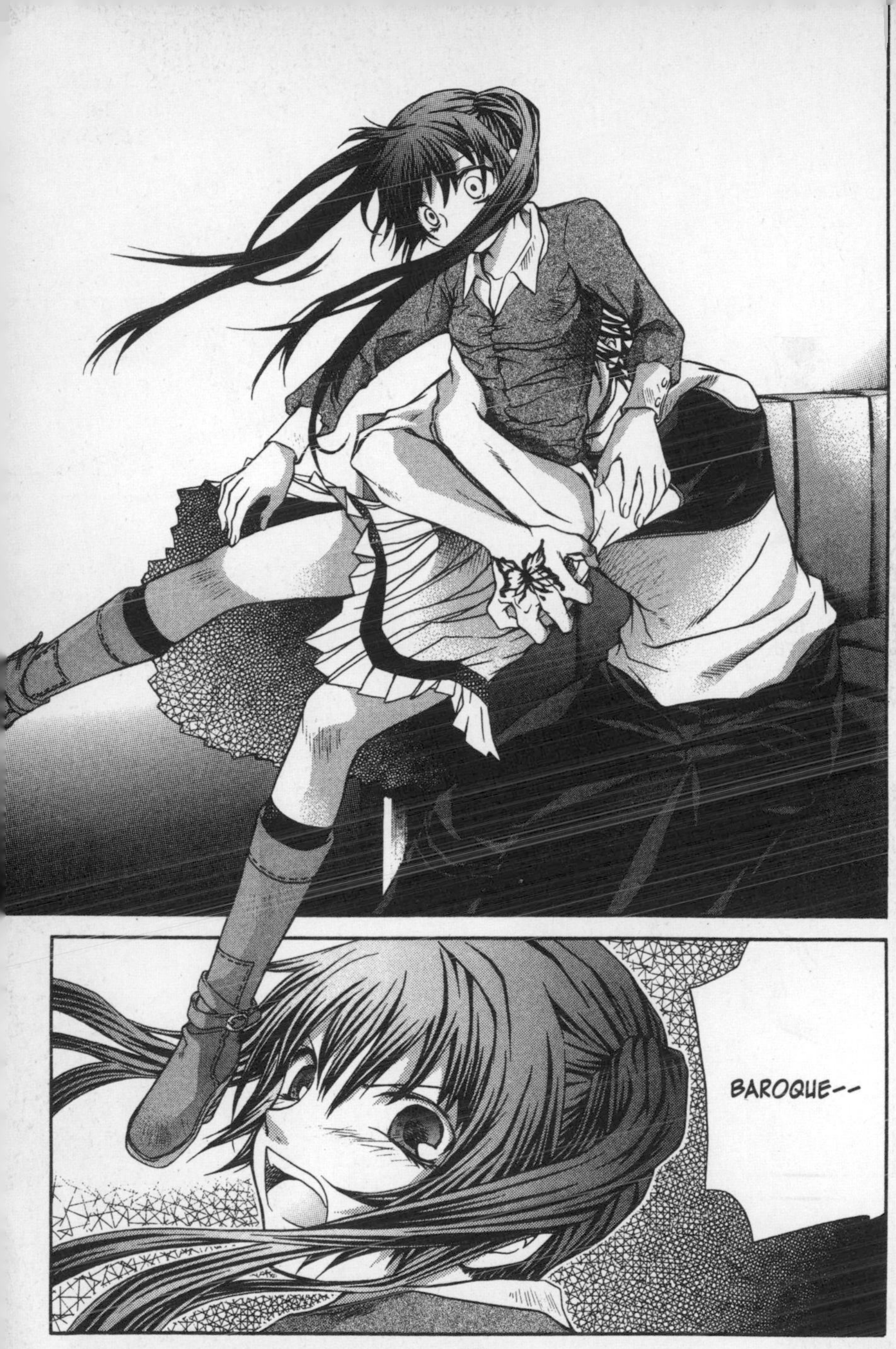
BAROQUE--

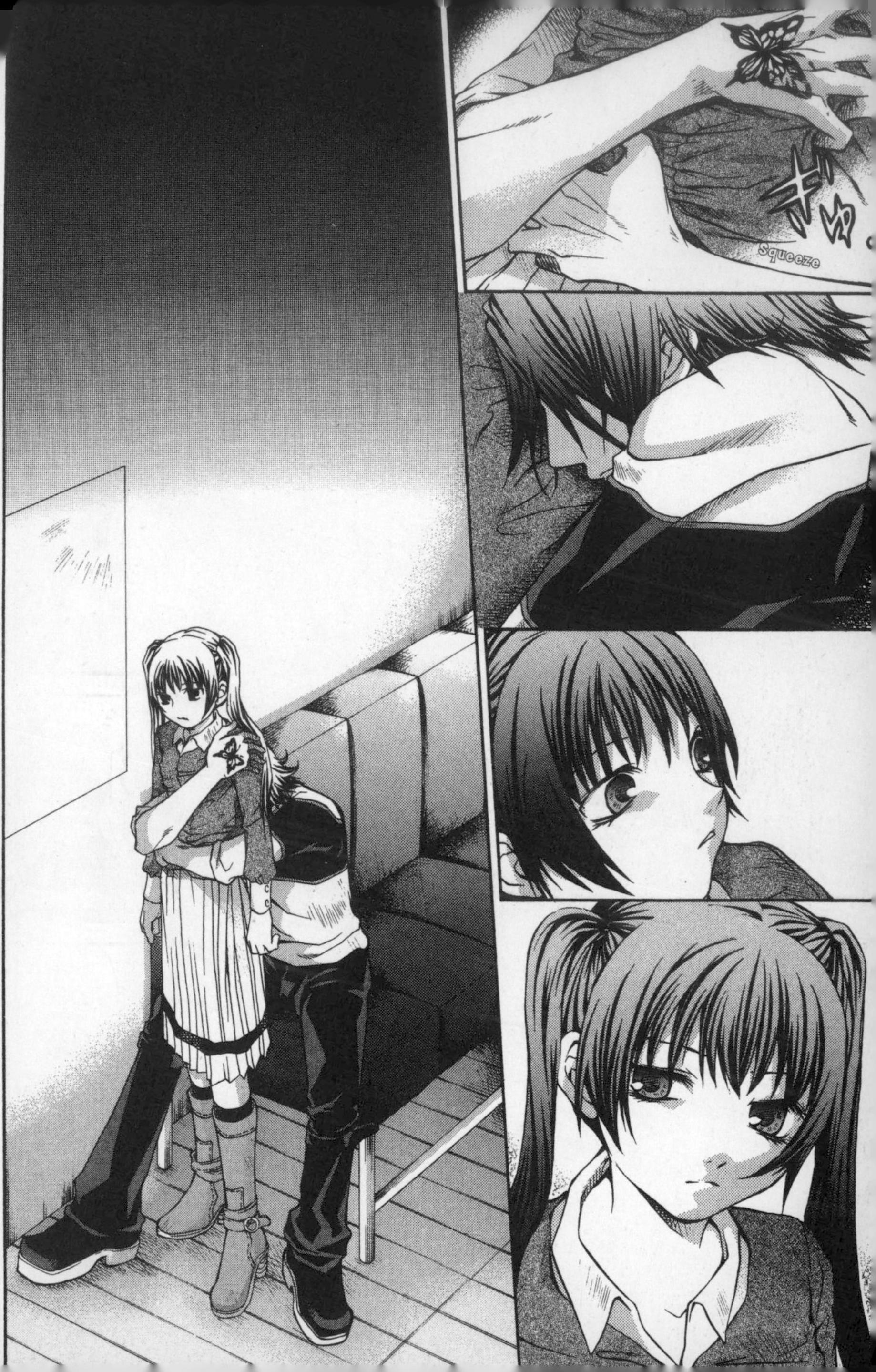
ギュ
squeeze

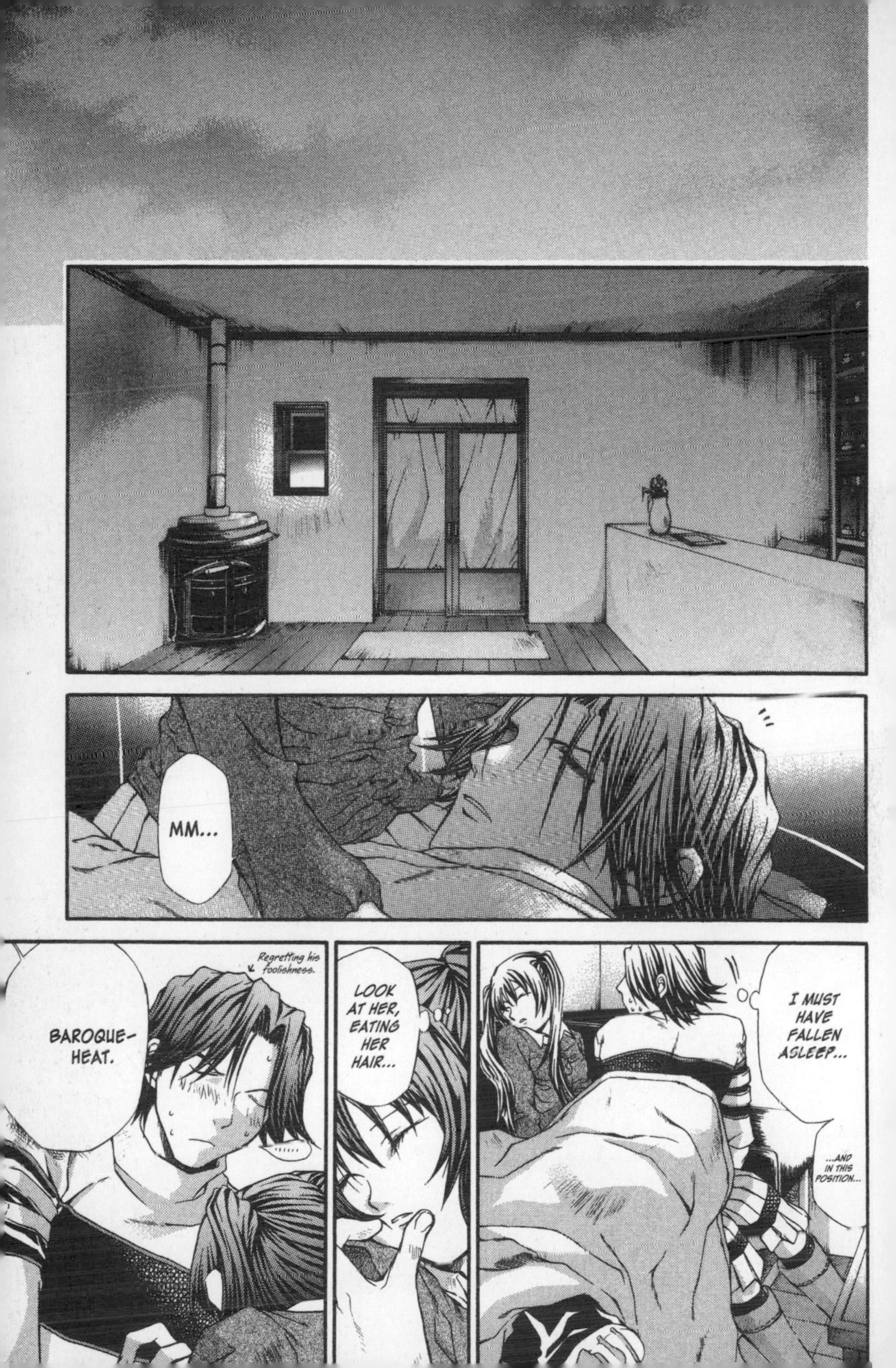
MM...
I MUST HAVE FALLEN ASLEEP...
...AND IN THIS POSITION...
LOOK AT HER, EATING HER HAIR...
Regretting his foolishness.
BAROQUE-HEAT.
......

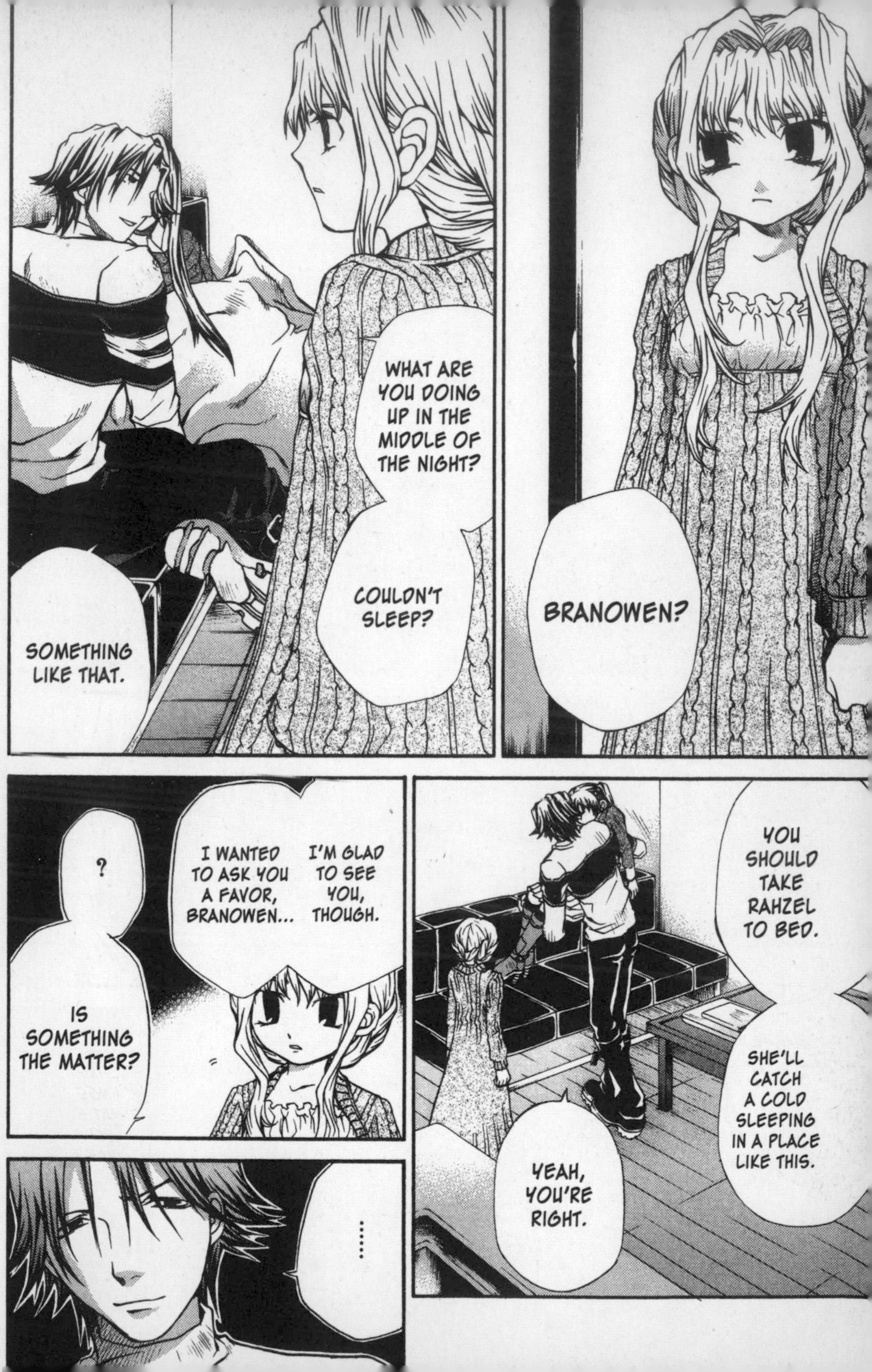
BRANOWEN?
WHAT ARE YOU DOING UP IN THE MIDDLE OF THE NIGHT?
COULDN'T SLEEP?
SOMETHING LIKE THAT.
YOU SHOULD TAKE RAHZEL TO BED.
SHE'LL CATCH A COLD SLEEPING IN A PLACE LIKE THIS.
YEAH, YOU'RE RIGHT.
I'M GLAD TO SEE YOU, THOUGH.
I WANTED TO ASK YOU A FAVOR, BRANOWEN...
?
IS SOMETHING THE MATTER?
......